REMEMBER THE RAMRODS

ALSO BY DAVID BELLAVIA

House to House (with John R. Bruning)

REMEMBER
— THE —
RAMRODS

AN ARMY BROTHERHOOD
IN WAR AND PEACE

DAVID BELLAVIA

MARINER BOOKS
New York   Boston

Map of Iraq by the United Nations Department of Field Support, Cartographic Section: Map No. 3835, Rev. 6 (July 2014).

HarperCollins books may be purchased for educational, business, or sales promotional use. For information, please email the Special Markets Department at SPsales@harpercollins.com.

A hardcover edition of this book was published in 2022 by Mariner Books.

FIRST MARINER BOOKS PAPERBACK EDITION PUBLISHED 2023.

Designed by Chloe Foster

Library of Congress Cataloging-in-Publication Data

Names: Bellavia, David, 1975– author.
Title: Remember the Ramrods : an Army brotherhood in war and peace / David Bellavia.
Description: First edition. | New York : Mariner Books, [2022]
Identifiers: LCCN 2022028384 (print) | LCCN 2022028385 (ebook) | ISBN 9780063048652 (hardcover) | ISBN 9780063048669 (trade paperback) | ISBN 9780063048676 (ebook)
Subjects: LCSH: Bellavia, David, 1975– | Iraq War, 2003–2011—Personal narratives, American. | United States. Army. Infantry Regiment, 2nd. Battalion, 2nd—Biography. | United States. Army. Non-commissioned officers—Biography. | Soldiers—United States—Biography. | Iraq War, 2003-2011—Campaigns. | Iraq War, 2003–2011—Regimental histories—United States.
Classification: LCC DS79.766.B45 A3 2022 (print) | LCC DS79.766.B45 (ebook) | DDC 956.7044/342092—dc23/eng/20220629
LC record available at https://lccn.loc.gov/2022028384
LC ebook record available at https://lccn.loc.gov/2022028385

ISBN 978-0-06-304866-9

23 24 25 26 27 LBC 5 4 3 2 1

To Marilyn B. Bellavia,
the toughest of all the Bellavias

In memory of
William D. Bellavia and James D. Hornfischer

CONTENTS

AUTHOR'S NOTE

THE RAMRODS

IN 2005, I RETURNED from war wanting only to go back to it. Preserving the peace found in American civilian life was the entire reason why we fought the War on Terror, but after I came home from Iraq, that peace felt unearned. I was safe in New York again, trying to get a job, provide for my family, and raise kids all while the people I loved the most were still carrying the battle to our enemies.

In this world of normalcy, the people who should have been in that innermost circle of my life—my children, my family—were almost strangers to me. I'd been a continent or more away for the majority of my son's young life. I barely had time to experience fatherhood before I deployed overseas. I had a family of my own, but I didn't know them. Rectifying that became the defining feature of my life for many years.

My *real* family was still overseas, scattered to different units and areas of operations. Fighting for us. Out there, with them, lay the meaning and purpose that defined my self-identity. I was a warrior. A Soldier. I was a kid from New York who learned about loyalty and love in a way the vast majority of Americans never do: in the heat of combat. In those horrific moments I saw the full power of the human spirit. I saw the strength of connection, the selflessness born from love so profound that giving your life so another might live was not exceptional. It was the unconscious reaction to seeing your own people in danger.

There was none of that at home in a civilian world where the vast majority of military-age males were not in uniform, despite the fact the nation had been attacked on September 11, 2001. The normalcy was disorienting enough—I mean, at times I wondered if my fellow Americans even realized a war was being fought on their behalf. That disorientation grew to a full divide when I saw young men bagging my groceries at the local supermarket. Healthy guys, the same age as the Soldiers in my squad, stuffing kale and cucumbers into sacks while making happy small talk with customers.

It was about then I developed what most veterans do: a sense of superiority over civilians.

That kid had never seen a friend die in combat. His tattoos weren't marred by bullet holes or shrapnel scars. He'd never tested the measure of himself or pushed others to do the same. He'd never bonded with men willing to die for him, and him for them. He had not sacrificed. He never willingly deprived himself of sleep or security, or of the arms of his beloved. He'd certainly never tried to keep warm by climbing into a body bag and spooning with his brothers-in-arms.

This was the conceit I brought into my civilian life. The Army tested me every day. It forced me to overcome challenges I thought insurmountable. I conquered them, but not alone. There is nothing more powerful than being respected by men you yourself hold in the highest regard. It fosters confidence and strength. It makes you strive to be better, always better. Those "insurmountable" challenges were overcome every time. Each one reshaped me a little bit more into the man I was when I returned home.

Civilians and warriors alike got it wrong. We combat veterans aren't better than anyone: we just think we are. That kid bagging groceries? I assumed he'd had a soft life, had never been in danger, and had never known privation. But those assumptions could have been way off the mark. Maybe he was working a third job to put himself through school. Maybe he quit school to take a shit job after his mother got sick. His sense of connection and loyalty to her trumped everything else in his life. Maybe he knew hunger, had lived on the streets as a child of homelessness, where constant danger was just a part of life. Who was I to assume he hadn't known sacrifice, hadn't shown devotion to someone or something he loved? Most of all, who was I to assume he'd never even tried to serve in the military and had been medically disqualified or medically retired?

My own assumptions, I learned, cleaved the divide even wider. The conceit I felt? It didn't affect him; it only isolated me more and made life at home that much more disorienting. And lonely.

There was another factor to that gulf between protector and protected that I had not understood until I returned home and tucked my uniforms away in my father's barn. The Army transformed me from boy to man by crushing adolescence. The boy is slayed through Basic Training. The man emerges on graduation day. Every branch of the military does this now with both men and women. The childishness within us, the immaturity to handle adversity, the dependence we had even in our teens on our parents and family—all that is destroyed and our warriors are rebuilt by the system to be capable, responsible, and dependable.

There is no similar process in civilian life. Our universities seem to breed perpetual adolescents.

Seventy-five years before, the Greatest Generation rallied together to defeat two of the greatest—and most evil—empires in history, the Third Reich and Imperial Japan. Fully a third of America's military-age males spent the War on Terror fighting it on their Xboxes in Mom's basement. No job. Not enrolled in classes. A generation living at home, letting Mom do their laundry as they played at clearing rooms with their cyber friends.

The first time I read those statistics, the divide between the warrior I was and the civilian world felt like a chasm. There was no redemptive arc in my own head on this one. There was no possible scenario, no backstory to match the ones for our grocery bagger that could ever justify in my head wasting the treasure of life on video games while not bothering to better yourself. I lived with tenacious ghosts riding my shoulder every day who reminded me of the enormous gift it was to be still breathing. I thought about them constantly, juxtaposing their lives against those squandering theirs here at home. It always made me angry. Unless we Americans accomplish with our time what they willingly gave up in theirs, the sacrifice of blood in Iraq and Afghanistan will have no meaning. I have tried to honor them by living for them, making something of value out of my existence here at home. I thought everyone felt that way. If you listen to Memorial Day speeches, we give lip service to that ideal. The reality? I kept returning to that statistic: one-third of a generation parked on Mom's couch. That reality left me trending toward bitter.

My greatest regret has always been leaving the service I so dearly loved. I tried to make it work at home, but the pull of the battlefield was too strong. Out there, I had meaning and purpose. You live on a ragged edge of danger that forces you to confront your own mortality. Every breath becomes euphoric. You exist in a different emotional framework. In rural western New York, life's color was drained away by a million little nicks. You stress over bills and taxes, a car that's become unreliable. The house needs siding, the floors in the kitchen need to be redone. All the logistical headaches of modern life take center stage and start to define your life.

Out there, on the battlefield, none of that shit matters. None of it. The complexities vanish, and everything boils down to this: *can you measure up?* When you do, you feel like a rock star. Nothing—no drug in the world—can compare to that moment of self-discovery. For me, self-discovery in combat convinced me the essence of life distills down to one thing: proving to yourself why you are needed in the fight.

I returned to combat in the summer of 2006 as a civilian war correspondent. I went again a few years later. I quickly discovered it was not the same. It wasn't the battlefield that gave me meaning, it was the men around me who did. Being there for them. I missed my tribe, not the combat I endured with them. That was the hole in my heart I felt open on the day I took off the uniform. It grew larger every year I was away from the Ramrods, the Soldiers I served with in Task Force 2-2 Infantry.

The Ramrods were part of the legendary 1st Infantry Division. Movies have been made on the Big Red One for its actions on D-Day and through Europe during World War II. The Fighting First fought in nearly every major American battle of World War I; it saw combat for five years in Vietnam before being forward deployed to Germany to face the Warsaw Pact/Soviet threat during the final decades of the Cold War. The Big Red One is the backbone of the American infantry. These days, it is sometimes overshadowed by the airborne divisions in the popular press. The 1st Infantry Division, with the Ramrods at the tip of the spear, has won every battle it has fought since 1918.

The truth is, combat is transformative, its effects largely permanent. It makes us manically aware of our own mortality. It makes us hyperconscious of our surroundings. Some dwell on actions they regret, others on actions they regret not taking. I fell into the latter category. It changed us in fundamental ways that we didn't even realize for years after the last bullet cracked overhead. We all tried not to let it change us. Some of us deluded ourselves into thinking we'd succeeded.

For almost fifteen years, I often felt like a foreigner in my own country. This book chronicles my true journey home, which took place long after I set foot in New York after the war was over. It is the story of how I found my tribe again at last, and how we all had struggled as to make sense of life here in the United States after the intensity of the relationships and experiences we shared in Iraq.

We said our goodbyes in 2005 after the hell of combat. The Army blew us across the world. Some, like me, came home. Others, like Colin Fitts, became eternal Soldiers, fighting in deployment after deployment until their bodies could take it no more. We went our separate ways and largely lost touch with each other. Life evolved. We married. We divorced. We had kids. We heard of friends who took their own lives and others who had dropped off the grid. The vast majority of us tried to carve out a version of the American dream. It all seemed hollow, incomplete. Anticlimactic. No matter how much we accomplished, we couldn't help but wonder if we peaked in our twenties. After all, nothing here at home compared to the connections and emotions we felt together back then. It was like living on the backside of a drug high.

Then, in June 2019, for the first time since those close-quarters firefights in the Middle East, forty of us reunited in Washington, D.C. The brotherhood we rekindled in those short days together helped all of us heal. This is the story of that bond, and how my tribe survived together through war and peace to ultimately save each other one more time.

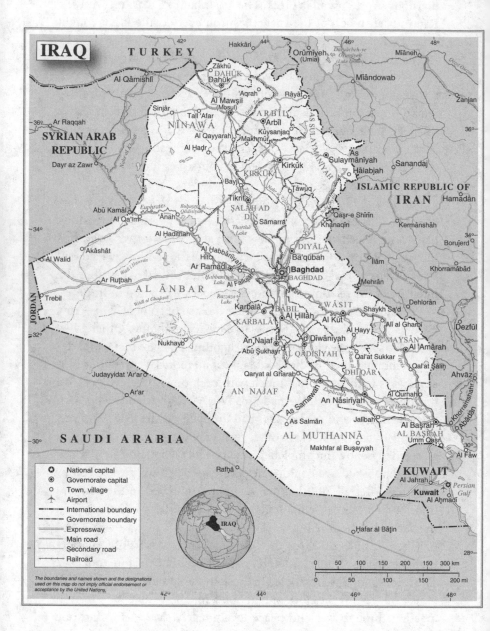

IRAQ

TURKEY

Hakkâri   Orūmîyeh
(Umia)   Daryācheh-ye
Orūmīyeh   Miāneh
(Lake Urmia)

Al Qāmishlī   Zākhū   'Aqrah   Rāyāt   Miāndowāb
DAHŪK   Dahūk   Zanjān
Sinjār   Al Mawşil   ARBĪL
(Mosul)   Küysanjaq   As Sulaymānīyah   Sanandaj
Tall 'Afar   NĪNAWÁ   Makhmūr   Hālabjah
Ar Raqqah   Al Qayyarah   Arbīl
SYRIAN ARAB   Al Ḩaḑr   KIRKŪK   'As
REPUBLIC   Kirkūk   Sulaymānīyah
Dayr az Zawr   Bayjī   Tāwūq   ISLAMIC REPUBLIC OF
Tikrīt   IRAN   Hamadān
Abū Kamāl   ŞALĀḨ AD   Qaşr-e Shīrīn
Al Qā'im   'Ānah   DĪN   Sāmarrā'   Khānaqīn   Kermānshāh
Euphrates   Bug̱ayrat al   34°
Qādisīyah
Akāshāt   Al Ḩadīthah   Tharthā   DIYĀLĀ   Borujerd
Lake   Ba'qūbah   Īlām   Khorramābād
Al Walid   Al Ḩabbānīyah   Mehrān
Hīt   Baghdad
Ar Ramādī   BAGHDAD
JORDAN   Al Fallūjah   Mehrān   Dehlorān   Dezfūl
Trebil   AL ĀNBAR   Razaza   WĀSIT   Shaykh Sa'd
Lake   Karbalā'   BĀBIL   Al Kūt   Alī al Gharbī   Ahvāz
Nukhayb   KARBALĀ'   Al Ḩillah   Al Hayy   MAYSĀN
An Najaf   Al 'Amārah
Judayyidat 'Ar'ar   Abū Shukhayr   Qal'at Sukkar   Qal'at Şāliḩ
AL QĀDISĪYAH   DHĪ QĀR
Ar'ar   Qaryat al Gharab   Euphrates   Al Qurnah
AN NAJAF   An Nāşirīyah   Abādān
As Samāwah   Hawr al Hammār
As Salmān   Jalībah   Al Başrah
SAUDI ARABIA   AL MUTHANNÁ   AL BAŞRAH
Makhfar al Buşayyah   Umm Qaşr
Al Fāw
Rafḩā   KUWAIT
Al Jahrah   Persian
Gulf
Kuwait
Airport
Al Ahmadī

National capital
Governorate capital
Town, village
Airport
International boundary
Governorate boundary
Expressway
Main road
Secondary road
Railroad

Ḩafar al Bāţin

IRAQ

0   50   100   150   200   150   300 km
0   50   100   150   200 mi

The boundaries and names shown and the designations
used on this map do not imply official endorsement or
acceptance by the United Nations.

FALLUJAH, 2004

WHEN THE UNITED STATES launched its invasion of Iraq in 2003, I was a twenty-seven-year-old noncommissioned officer serving with Alpha Company, 2nd Battalion, 2nd Infantry Regiment, or 2-2 as we were called. In November 2002, most of the battalion deployed to Kosovo on a peacekeeping mission that kept us out of the initial invasion of Iraq. As American forces drove on to Baghdad, we remained in the Balkans, a legacy force designed to protect the local population from further 1990s-style Serbian ethnic cleansing that had killed or displaced hundreds of thousands of Kosovars.

We were in the backwater, frustrated and afraid that we missed this next phase of the War on Terror, just as we had missed out on Afghanistan in 2001–02. When the fighting seemed to end after only a few weeks, it felt like we had not earned our keep. History had passed us by, and the chance to avenge the 9/11 attacks as a generation was something we thought would never be given to us.

By the time we returned to our home garrison in Vilseck, Germany, in June 2003, a growing insurgency against the American-led Coalition was taking shape. In the eastern districts of Baghdad and in the southern part of Iraq, Shia militias, each led by powerful, demagogic imams, formed right under the noses of the overstretched occupation authorities. Meanwhile, in the Sunni-dominated western region known as Anbar Province, Al Qaeda established a foothold among the tribes there. Foreign volunteers—religious extremists for the most part—trickled into Anbar to fight the Americans under the Al Qaeda banner.

The war hadn't ended with the fall of Baghdad after all.

Task Force 2-2 deployed into Iraq during a short lull in the growing insurgency in February 2004. The Army sent us to Diyala Province, a tumultuous region north of Baghdad along the Iranian border where both elements of the insurgency converged. Some of the Sunni in the area supported Al Qaeda in Iraq, while the Shia opposed to the Coalition found easy sources of supply across the Iranian border.*

About a month after we arrived, four Blackwater military contractors guarding a food convoy outside the Anbar Province city of Fallujah were ambushed, killed, and mutilated by insurgent forces. Local onlookers cheered their deaths and strung their bodies up on a bridge into the city. The incident foretold the start of two simultaneous uprisings that destabilized the Coalition's tenuous hold on Iraq.

The first occurred in Fallujah, which had become the nexus of Al Qaeda's operations in Anbar Province. The Marines and 82nd Airborne Division troops in the area had largely stayed out of the city (located about forty miles west of Baghdad), but after the Blackwater Bridge killings, they launched an offensive on April 5, 2004, to clear the insurgents from the area. In what was known as Operation Vigilant Resolve, the Marines and paratroops pushed into Fallujah and quickly found themselves in an urban hellscape where every doorway and window posed a threat. By now, some of the leading terrorist commanders in Iraq, like Abu Musab al-Zarqawi and Ahmad Hashim Abd al-Isawi (who had planned the Blackwater Bridge ambush), used Fallujah as their headquarters. Some thirty-five hundred terrorists rallied around them, outnumbering the two thousand American troops fighting block by block to clear the city.

Consideration for the civilian population, outrage at the offensive by the gestational new Iraqi government, and fierce resistance that inflicted heavy casualties on the Coalition forces all combined to

---

* The Coalition forces in Iraq primarily included the United States, the United Kingdom, the new Iraqi forces, and Australia. Thirty-nine other nations also participated in the Coalition.

bring Vigilant Resolve to an end in late April 2004. A cease-fire was arranged. The insurgents buried their dead at the soccer stadium, which became known as "Martyrs Cemetery," and the situation in Fallujah festered through the rest of the year.

At the same time, the Shia militias rose up against the Coalition in Baghdad, Diyala, and the southern provinces. Areas that had once been safe for American forces suddenly became ambush corridors. Fighting raged in Sadr City, an enormous Shia slum in eastern Baghdad, even after the cease-fire took effect in Fallujah. In Diyala, Task Force 2-2 fought pitched battles through the spring in and around the largest cities in the area until the militias finally went to ground in June and the fighting ebbed.

Shia militias, led by Muqtada al-Sadr's Mahdi Army, rose up against the Coalition a second time. Eastern Baghdad turned into a free-fire zone again, and hundreds of American troops were killed or wounded in ambushes and urban fighting. The holy southern city of Najaf became the focal point of the Shia insurgency that August, and a massive battle for the city unfolded. Alpha Company, Task Force 2-2 was sent to Najaf in April to take the fight to the Mahdi Army, led by Sadr. A cease-fire was concluded before hostilities broke out in the spring. That lull lasted until August 2004, when Marines and elements of the 1st Cavalry Division, supported by National Guard troops from Arkansas and Oregon, assaulted into Najaf, surrounding Muqtada al-Sadr's fighters, who were operating out of the Ali Imam Shrine, one of the most holy sites in the Middle East.

By then, we'd been in so many firefights in the cities in Diyala Province that Task Force 2-2 probably had more urban warfare experience than nearly any other unit in the U.S. Army at that time. When things spun out of control in Fallujah that fall, it was not surprising that the Coalition leadership selected 2-2 to be part of the offensive to clear the city.

Through the summer and fall, U.S. forces had largely left Fallujah alone, content to stay on the city's outskirts and not make any serious effort to patrol, police, or occupy it. This strategy kept American losses down, but the Iraqi Coalition efforts to regain control of the city without our help failed completely. What had been a hub for Al Qaeda grew into a lawless, fortified terrorist stronghold in the heart of the most important Iraqi province. From Fallujah, at least a dozen different terror groups launched attacks against Americans throughout Anbar. They laid roadside bombs and executed ambushes of our vehicle patrols. They mortared our bases in the area and mercilessly killed Iraqi police officers and security units trying to establish order.

The non-loss of the First Battle of Fallujah in the spring encouraged a new wave of foreign volunteers to make their way to the city and rally behind the jihad, or Islamic holy war. They went about fortifying this city of about three hundred thousand, all while Coalition forces largely stood on the sidelines, watching it happen. With the first free election in Iraq's history scheduled for January 2005, and the terrorist all-star team in Fallujah readying to stop it, the situation came to a boiling point that fall. American intelligence estimated there were some five thousand insurgents using the city as their fortified lair, preparing to unleash absolute chaos on election day in January.

The decision was made to clear Fallujah, setting the stage for the largest battle of the Global War on Terror.

The Coalition announced that all civilians needed to evacuate Fallujah. Checkpoints ringed the city to ensure that no other insurgents got in to join the coming battle. In the weeks before November, tens of thousands of civilians left their homes. Fallujah became a terrorist playground, and with the Coalition intending to enter and clear the city, finally addressing this problem once and for all, the insurgents redoubled their work to further fortify their positions. They studded every major road and highway into the city with thousands of improvised explosive devices (IEDs). They booby-trapped buildings with explosives and propane tanks. They dug tunnels between fighting positions established inside thick-walled structures, and cached ammunition, medical supplies, food, and water on nearly every block. To minimize the American advantages of firepower and close air support, they built fortified kill zones *inside* buildings, hidden from aerial surveillance. They had studied our tactics and knew that once we entered the city, we would send troops to clear every structure.

This was a uniquely American approach to fighting in a city, designed to minimize the damage to it. The Russians, when they fought their own urban battle in Grozny, Chechnya, in the 1990s, used firepower to crush that city's defenders. They flattened almost every building with artillery and air attacks before sending in tanks and armored infantry, which used direct-fire high explosives to add to the destruction. By the time the battle was over, Grozny had been ground to rubble.

America's kinder, gentler approach to urban warfare meant the onus of victory fell on the shoulders of the infantry, fighting dismounted from house to house. It meant we were willing to trade higher American casualties in return for minimizing the damage to the city. Ultimately, much of Fallujah was destroyed anyway.

The offensive to clear Fallujah began on November 7, 2004. Our company from Task Force 2-2 formed one of the spearheads that penetrated the city's perimeter defenses, secured breaching points, and pushed from north to south into the eastern end of Fallujah. The fighting was unlike anything we had ever experienced. We faced snipers, mortar fire, hidden bombs, and booby traps. The cityscape was already torn up from the first battle and subsequent barrages of Coalition artillery fire, and moving among the ruins left us cut up, bruised, and coated in concrete dust.

The deeper we pushed into the city, the wider a gap opened between us and our Marine colleagues, who had struggled at their breaching points because they lacked heavy armored support. Insurgents detected the gap and saw opportunity. They infiltrated behind us and launched counterattacks we repelled in furious rooftop firefights. For two days, we battled the enemy nonstop, day and night without respite or sleep. Then we had to turn around and advance north, doubling back over the hard-won ground we'd gained to clear our rear of those enemy infiltrators.

On the night of November 10, 2004, after an exhausting day of clearing building after building, destroying caches we'd found and enduring more enemy attacks, we came to a low-slung, fortified house in the Askari, or Soldier's, District. This was a neighborhood where Saddam Hussein's ruling elite built lavish homes. Each was like a mini-fortress, with stout outer walls, reinforced gates, and heavy front doors. The homes themselves were built of rebar and concrete, with rabbit warrens of hallways, rooms, and stairwells within them. They were perfect strongpoints for the terrorists.

It was my twenty-ninth birthday, making me one of the oldest members of my platoon. Instead of candles on a cake, the night was filled with red tracers and star shells lighting the city in a hellish glow. The acoustics in the city played havoc with our ears. Explosions and gunfire rattled around us, their sound waves bouncing off the buildings in such crazy ways we could never be exactly sure of their point of origin. Ultimately, it sounded like we were surrounded by dozens of firefights unfolding simultaneously as other platoons and companies ran into ambushes or were counterattacked by the enemy.

Dazed, weary, hungry, our mouths dry, our faces caked with grime, our platoon stacked up to clear this upscale house in the darkness of our third night in the city. We were all on edge, growling at each other, stressed, scared, full of rage at our predicament. This was the toughest moment of Soldiering any of us had endured to that point. It was a testament to the strength of our bonds with each other that we were still combat capable. We'd already lost our beloved battalion sergeant major during the first hours of the battle, and in the days to come we would lose even more of our leadership. Some units would have become combat ineffective after the seventy-two hours of fighting we'd gone through. Even though we were at the edge of our endurance, we still had fight left in us.

Our platoon swept into the house, clearing the entryway foyer, then moving into another room deeper inside. That's when the enemy sprang their ambush. Armed with AKs and a belt-fed machine gun, they opened fire at us from a makeshift bunker. Bullets poured through a doorway between most of the platoon and the only exit route available.

In such moments, I learned that it is instinctive to do whatever it takes to save the people you love. Our platoon was my family. I'd been lost, struggling to find my way before I joined the Army. When I landed in 2-2, I finally felt like I'd found my purpose and the people I was meant to be with, to serve with, and to protect.

What followed inside that room-to-room kill zone on November 10, 2004, would change all of our lives forever.

Staff Sergeant David G. Bellavia distinguished himself by acts of gallantry and intrepidity above and beyond the call of duty on November 10, 2004, while serving as a squad leader in support of Operation Phantom Fury in Fallujah, Iraq. While clearing a house, a squad from Staff Sergeant Bellavia's platoon became trapped within a room by intense enemy fire coming from a fortified position under the stairs leading to the second floor. Recognizing the immediate severity of the situation, and with disregard for his own safety, Staff Sergeant Bellavia retrieved an automatic weapon and entered the doorway of the house to engage the insurgents. With enemy rounds impacting around him, Staff Sergeant Bellavia fired at the enemy position at a cyclic rate, providing covering fire that allowed the squad to break contact and exit the house. A Bradley Fighting Vehicle was brought forward to suppress the enemy; however, due to high walls surrounding the house, it could not fire directly at the enemy position. Staff Sergeant Bellavia then re-entered the house and again came under intense enemy fire. He observed an enemy insurgent preparing to launch a rocket-propelled grenade at his platoon. Recognizing the grave danger the grenade posed to his fellow soldiers, Staff Sergeant Bellavia assaulted the enemy position, killing one insurgent and wounding another who ran to a different part of the house. Staff Sergeant Bellavia, realizing he had an un-cleared, darkened room to his back, moved to clear it. As he entered, an insurgent came down the stairs firing at him. Simultaneously, the previously wounded insurgent reemerged and engaged Staff Sergeant Bellavia. Staff Sergeant Bellavia, entering further into the darkened room, returned fire and eliminated both insurgents. Staff Sergeant Bellavia then received enemy fire from another insurgent emerging from a closet in the darkened room. Exchanging gunfire, Staff Sergeant Bellavia pursued the enemy up the stairs and eliminated him. Now on the second floor, Staff Sergeant Bellavia moved to a door that opened onto the roof. At this point, a fifth insurgent leapt from the third floor roof onto the second-floor roof. Staff Sergeant Bellavia engaged the insurgent through a window, wounding him in the back and legs, and caused him to fall off the roof. Acting on instinct to save the members of his platoon from an imminent threat, Staff Sergeant Bellavia ultimately cleared an entire enemy-filled house, destroyed four insurgents, and badly wounded a fifth. Staff Sergeant Bellavia's bravery, complete disregard for his own safety, and unselfish and courageous actions are in keeping with the finest traditions of military service and reflect great credit upon himself and the United States Army.

★

PART I

THE MAN IN WHITE

THE TOWN SEEMED EMPTY. Shuttered windows, closed shops, and no movement on its dirt streets gave it a creepy end-of-the-world sort of vibe.

Al Ali. A village with a wagon-wheel downtown. A large, open center public square. The rest of the population lived in the rural farmland spokes.

Foreign influence swayed the people of this region. They hated Americans. We started reciprocating the feeling in May 2004 after someone in an adjacent village sniped Staff Sergeant Joe Garyantes, one of our tank commanders, right out of his turret. That had happened just south of Al Ali, in a town called Dali Abas.

Losing an NCO as strong and steady as Garyantes was a blow we all took personally. He would have battled any enemy face-to-face if given the chance. Instead, he died from a bullet none of us had even seen fired. His death showed us the impersonal sterility of this peculiar battlefield. It also showed us the cowardice of the enemy—men who would supplicate to our faces, then snipe us from behind if given the opportunity. It made us alert, distrustful, and rage-filled. And for me, I grew to despise snipers. On our side or theirs.

A good sniper is nearly impossible to combat, especially in the terrain around Al Ali. There were a million places to build a hide among the civilians and their meager dwellings. The best Soldiers in the world cannot see everywhere at once, cannot maintain a hyper-alert posture for days on end while out on patrol. Even if we could, snipers are so well concealed and far away, spotting their hides requires binos—or pure luck.

Garyantes's death left us feeling powerless. We realized that at any moment, an enemy secure and far away could anonymously kill us. Thinking about it made us paranoid, especially around Al Ali, which in May 2004 was crawling with insurgents living among the populace. We'd done three patrols after Garyantes's death in support of our sister company from 1-63 Armor. Each time, unseen assailants ambushed us.

Today, in the brutal Diyala heat, our platoon patrolled into Al Ali after our Bradley Fighting Vehicles—basically armored infantry taxis with a turreted 25mm machine cannon—dropped us off about a kilometer outside of town. We walked up the main road out in the open, as if daring the enemy to oppose us. We moved past palm groves that once served as ambush hides for the insurgents, then broke out into open ground with an occasional farmer's hovel. Finally, we reached the town's little open core. Walled in a circle leading into shops and homes, Al Ali represented the very insecure Iraqi culture that lived in a perpetual state of paranoia under the Ba'athist regime. This town, like the Iraqi people, was ready at any time for an attack from their own government under Saddam Hussein. A few squalid houses, most made of concrete, were followed by its tiny commercial district built around the village square.

We stood in the middle of the square now, rifles in hand, fingers just outside the trigger guards, alert and scanning the rooftops and alleys. It wasn't a matter of *if* in this area of Diyala, but *when*. The thick vegetation made this more akin to South Vietnam than the open desert terrain of the Middle East. And in that vegetation, anything can hide. The enemy used this to their advantage.

For the last year, a strange mix of Shia militias, Sunnis allied with Al Qaeda in Iraq, Iranian Revolutionary Guards, and blue-eyed foreign fighters lurked in these palm groves, watched us from windows, and lay in ambush on rooftop redoubts.

Captain Doug Walter, our new company commander, gave exactly two shits about the enemy's affiliation or intent. He walked to the center of the town square, looked around at the dilapidated shops that lined this bit of communal space, then took a knee. He was here to meet the locals and let them know that the boys of Fallujah were back in town and itching for a fight, too.

Captain Walter dubbed this mission, plus a series of patrols in all the villages outside of Muqdadiyah proper, Operation Welcome Home. While the Ramrods were away, the insurgents came out to play. For two months, they launched crazy-brave assaults on the American and Iraqi National Guard units that covered for us while we took part in the Battle of Fallujah. When we came back to Diyala Province in December, the place had gone full Wild West. It was dispiriting—by the time we left in October, we'd beaten the enemy down. The place was actually getting quiet.

Not anymore. A few mornings after we returned from Anbar Province in December 2004, the enemy assaulted our forward operating base. I spent the firefight in a T-shirt and boxers, no boots, in a guard tower manning a machine gun as we poured lead at them. The Army National Guard unit that was occupying that tower didn't even complain about Fitts, Lawson, Brown, and myself just helping ourselves to their weapon systems and ammunition. The Soldiers stood back, with not even a question as to who we were or who gave us the authority to take over their mission. That is what came with our new Fallujah street credit.

Now, we were under time pressure to get the situation under control again. Iraq's first free election was only a couple of weeks away, and our command feared the enemy would attack polling centers and murder hundreds of civilians if we didn't handle business quickly.

Captain Walter studied the nearby shops, noting the bullet-scarred walls and blackened facades where rockets had impacted in previous fights. If those warning signs made an impression on him, he didn't show it. Not surprising; the man always seemed fearless.

Walter had once been a barrel-chested physical specimen. He played baseball at West Point, crushed Ranger School, and smoked men fifteen years his junior on company runs back in Germany. He could outrun, outgun, and out-endure every other man in the battalion. We worshipped him.*

That was Germany, a year and a lifetime ago. He looked frail now, his body wasted by an intestinal disease that robbed him of the strength we marveled at when he commanded our company back in Europe. He dropped to under 130 pounds before we left for Iraq almost a year before, which forced him to give up command of Alpha Company. His best friend, Captain Sean Sims, took his place.

In recent months, Walter had regained some of his lost weight, but he was far from healthy.

"Sir," I said quietly.

He wiped sweat off his brow and looked back at me, eyes squinting from the sun. "What you got, Sergeant Bellavia?"

"We came here on foot. And we're leaving here on foot. I am all about whatever you want. Just know this is gonna be a gunfight very soon."

Walter reached into a pocket and pulled out a map. As he unfolded it, he said, "We're not going anywhere, boys. Not moving."

I made eye contact with my best friend, Staff Sergeant Colin Fitts. Maybe five nine, he seemed ten feet tall and larger than life. Quick with a quip and quicker on the draw with the combat shotgun he hefted in every fight, Fitts was a man born without a filter. That made

---

* In Germany, our motor pool was atop a steep hill and our company area, Rose Barracks, sat at the foot of the hill in Vilseck. Most company runs were an adventure. Six miles became ten miles. The threat from Captain Walter of "Bring your IDs to PT tomorrow" meant one thing: we were leaving the gate on a run. Those runs could easily become twelve miles. And just as it was ending, the barracks in sight, he would swoop from the front of company formation, the poor bastard behind him with the guidon, and feign like we were done. Then he would pick up the pace and take the hill toward the motor pool. I wanted to run him over with the mil van on those days.

On those exceptionally cruel extended runs, the long formation of A Company would race up the hill and turn around at the top. The mass of infantrymen would predictably snake back. The leaders of the formation would run downhill as the platoons from the back were making it through the toughest part of the incline. At those moments, Doug Walter would turn back and run the hill again with the units that looked like they had quit in them.

Hatred became love again. His support became our strength.

him among the most honest humans I've ever met. It also got him in constant trouble. If somebody was screwing up, he'd tell them. Didn't matter the rank.

Fitts was also a brawler whose southern sense of honor was easily offended. It made him prone to throw the first punch. He also brooked no stupidity. Five months earlier, an Iraqi cop thought it would be funny to point his weapon at one of Fitts's soldiers and track him as he walked by. Fitts gave him exactly one warning with his shotgun at the ready. When the idiot didn't heed it, our Mississippian pulled off his Kevlar helmet and beat the Iraqi unconscious. When the cop's supervisor protested, he, too, received Fitts's sense of frontier southern justice.

Command frowned on the fact that this police supervisor had happened to be the deputy chief of police of Muqdadiyah. Those little subtextual points of contention meant nothing to Fittsy. Both cops were left in need of an endodontist when all was said and done. Somehow, Fitts avoided the wrath of our own chain of command.

For a change.

There in the middle of Al Ali, I watched Fitts approach me, the slight hitch in his walk a reminder that we almost lost him the previous spring. In April 2004, he'd been shot three times, by three different insurgents firing three different weapon systems. He could have stayed home and rehabbed his wounds. Instead, he returned to us in the summer, half healed.

"You ready for this shit, bro? I don't think standing around here is a good idea."

"It's Captain Walter," I said simply. Fitts stared at me for a beat, so I added, "Look, I am whatever he tells me to be. And today, it looks like we're gonna be infantrymen."

"I can do infantry today," Fitts drawled.

We both loved Walter. We'd served under him for two years before Iraq. We admired his attitude—hard-nosed and aggressive. Walter didn't want to pick a fight, but if one came to him he would smother the enemy with firepower. Today, though, he sure seemed like he was challenging the enemy to hit us.

You insurgent jerks have the stones for this? Bring it. I have no plans for three more months.

Two months after fighting the biggest battle of the War on Terror, the Ramrods of Alpha Company, Task Force 2-2 walked with swagger. We'd survived the worst the enemy could dish out and kicked their teeth out in return.

Not that they didn't get licks of their own in, too. We lost Captain Sean Sims during a point-blank gun duel fought in a kitchen of an abandoned house. We lost our executive officer Lieutenant Edward Iwan to a rocket-propelled grenade. We lost our battalion command sergeant major, Steven Faulkenburg, a father figure to all us sergeants in 2-2 Infantry. Staff Sergeant James "J.C." Matteson, a scout from our battalion task force, was also killed in Fallujah.

We never stopped fighting. We stowed our grief and flung ourselves at the enemy, killing with pent-up fury. They gave no quarter, and we asked for none. When we saw them, rushing us, bounding from building to building in the dead of night, we gunned them down. We dug them out of buildings, battled them room to room, captured and destroyed their arms caches and bomb factories.

Doug Walter returned to Alpha Company after Sims was killed. The same day he rejoined us, an Explosive Ordnance Disposal detachment filled a hole with captured mortars, mines, bullets, and artillery shells and detonated them outside the Industrial District in Fallujah. From five hundred meters away the blast crumbled walls. Vehicles were tossed across the street. The place looked like Armageddon. When the EOD Soldiers asked Doug Walter to escort them to do a post-blast analysis, Walter asked about "secondary explosions." He was told that the area was secure and that they did this all the time. Walter took four steps into the fifty-meter-wide crater when he vanished as a secondary explosion touched off.

We thought he'd been killed, but he staggered out of the swirling smoke and dust, deaf and dizzy, and laid out one of the EOD guys. Walter's dust-caked face cleared with snot, spit, and blood shooting from his ears and he tossed unknowing explosive ordnance Soldiers like they were rag dolls.

Walter was a force of nature when he was pissed. The loss of Sims, the pain his Soldiers were dealing with, and the continued unknown threat made that emotional journey travel at light speed.

He was our kind of leader. We rallied behind him, and the company survived the loss of our other leaders because of his example. When we returned to Diyala Province, we were cocky, confident that after what we'd been through, we could handle anything, defeat anyone. We were the victors of Fallujah, nationally famous now thanks to cover stories about us written up in *Time* magazine and *U.S. News & World Report*. We were on CNN, Fox; more stories appeared in *Stars and Stripes*.

By the time we left Fallujah, much of America knew of our unit and what we accomplished. New Army and Marine units coming into Iraq to relieve us saw us as rock stars. In the moment, Fallujah made us almost like Army royalty.

My men killed the enemy at extreme close quarters and proved American Soldiers did not need to rely on technology and firepower to defeat the enemy. We did it, in some cases, with our bare hands.

That grit and confidence forged in Fallujah was about to be tested here in the Wild West.

Staff Sergeant Scott Lawson, our weapons squad leader, jogged over to Fitts and me. He sensed the same danger we did and knew we'd need our M240 machine guns positioned to cover us.

He announced, "I'm going to get the guns up."

Lawson was a Michigan native, tough with a dose of unpredictable crazy that endeared him to me. Others found him a misfit head case, but we'd seen him in battle. He was a man we could count on, and we wanted him with us. Fittsy and I conspired to pull him into our platoon before the Battle of Fallujah, and he never let us down.

"I don't know where we're gonna be," I told him, looking around at the shops and homes abutting the square.

"Hey, if you're right about this place, we gotta have those guns up," Lawson answered.

"I understand that, Lawson," I said with frustration, "but you don't know where we're going and we don't know where the bad guys are."

Lawson thought it over. "How about I flex my machine guns at the front and the back of the formation?"

Fitts was losing his patience. "Hey, Lawson, just do what you gotta do, man. If I need your guns I am just gonna take your guns. No offense. That's just what's gonna happen."

Fitts probably didn't need to be so blunt. Lawson had a good idea.

It was hot. Everyone saw this town for what it was. Stress was in the air. We all saw trouble coming.

When Walter signaled to us to resume our patrol, Lawson put a gun team up with Fitts's squad as his men took point. His other gun stayed back with my squad. Walter and his security detail, led by Sergeant Travis Barreto, stayed in the middle of the formation.

We originally planned to stay no longer than forty-five minutes. Instead, Captain Walter knocked on doors and led us down alleys and side streets, meeting the few locals willing to show their faces. Captain Walter eloquently briefed Battalion that he intended to use these patrols to reassess the enemy situation in our area post-Fallujah in order to reestablish control in time for the upcoming election in late January 2005.

PowerPoint presentations to command aside, Walter was really just daring the enemy to attack us that day in Al Ali.

Two hours later, on the outskirts of town, we came to a house sitting atop a slight ridge. Down the slope behind it stretched a thicket of vegetation tangled along a five-foot-wide irrigation canal. On the other side of that was an open field, a road, plus a line of two- and three-story buildings.

Walter banged on the door. A sullen, dark-eyed man in a traditional white *thawb* answered it. We invited ourselves inside, looking for weapons or signs of bomb-making. Piles of foreign currency, spools of wire, boxes of cell phones and car batteries—these were the signatures of a roadside-bomb factory. We'd found dozens over the past year.

We discovered only two people in the house: the middle-aged man who answered the door and a teenage boy. They watched us search their home with pure hate stamped on their faces. They made no effort to conceal it. When I looked at the older guy in the white man-dress, he made eye contact with me. I stared back. He didn't flinch. As the search continued, his eyes never left mine.

We called this eye and body language "mad-dogging." We'd seen it many times before. As I held his gaze I sensed he would kill us the first chance he got.

His expression stoked my own. We fed off each other's quiet fury. I wanted him to make a move, to do something that would give me a reason to exact revenge for the men I'd lost. In that moment, I would have hunted him down through hell itself if he had made a move against us.

He didn't. Instead, he kept his eyes leveled on mine. He didn't move. Didn't say a word. Just stared on, as the emotional subtext played out between us.

Then the fear struck me, as it always did. Fury mingled with fear. A good Soldier knows how to harness it. Fear becomes power. It is a cycle that propels you forward, moves your body when part of it wants to be paralyzed in place.

The true lesson of Fallujah and its close-quarters battles was not that we were better trained, or better equipped. We didn't have any more fighting spirit than they did. As much as we depended on our skills and sense of professionalism, the chaos of war always has a say. In the end, luck, chance, the enemy's skill—all those things coalesce in an urban battlefield to ensure that we lost people we loved.

We did our best to deny chance for the enemy to play a role in our fates. But that was baloney I fed myself and my men to keep our fragile sense of sanity in balance. Once a Soldier realized there was no defense to luck, no way to conquer it, that fragile balance would be forever shattered.

As I stared at this belligerent old man, practically tasting his hate, I wondered if my luck had finally run out.

I touched my dusty backward American flag sewn on my right arm. Then I touched my bright red 1st Infantry patch above it. The old man broke eye contact long enough to watch my finger's path along my arm. Then his eyes returned to mine, shining with hate. Both of us were sweating in the heat, and beads of perspiration kept dripping into my eyes.

Staff Sergeant Fitts saw what was happening here. His head swiveled from me to the old man and back. Then he said, "Hey, Bell, this guy wants to kill you, man. Oh, he hates you. Look at him mad-dogging you."

Before I could reply, our Soldiers completed their search. Nothing. The house was clean. There wasn't even the single AK allowed for home defense anywhere inside. If the old man really wanted us dead, the weapons he would use lay concealed someplace else.

Our men filed out through the front door. I was among the last to leave. Before I did, I glanced back at the old man. No words had passed between us. Even if they had, we didn't speak the same language. But two men *know* the score when you're that close. Those eyes said everything. They transcended the differences in language.

Dare you. I will bend your ribs inside out, so help me God. I will take everything you have lived for away from you if you even contemplate hurting any one of these men. We will be the last thing you see on this planet. I will dominate you. I promise you it will hurt. You will suffer and wish you chose any other cause than to stand up to me, this unit, or my nation.

Outside, I gathered myself as we reassembled into patrol formation and set off down a road that descended the ridge.

"Hey, Bell, that old man get to you? You two wanna get a room or something?"

I was in no mood for Fitts's jabs.

"First squad on me. Let's let Sergeant Bell collect himself. He is having a rough day in Diyala."

We passed the vegetation, crossed the canal, and turned left to leave town on the road flanked by those few buildings on its right side.

Fitts led the way. His squad had been on point all morning, and he himself took the tip of the spear. That was how we did it. Neither he nor I ever asked our men to do anything we wouldn't do ourselves.

We patrolled up the road, eyes roaming in search of danger. To our right, the row of buildings looked deserted. To the left, we could see the house on the ridge we'd just visited silhouetted against the afternoon sky.

Sergeant First Class James Cantrell radioed me, "Hey Two, this is Seven."

"Go ahead, Seven."

"Get ready. You guys are about to get attacked. I got movement everywhere. We are on the way. Over."

"Roger that, Seven."

I turned to my A Team leader, Sergeant Chuck Knapp, and said, "Knappy, get ready."

He nodded and spun around to check on his guys, weapon at the high ready. Knapp was the first-round draft pick every platoon wanted in Alpha Company. A physical specimen, whip smart and courageous in a fight, he possessed the skills and judgment to do any job within our platoon. In many respects, I considered him my co-squad leader.

Right then, Fitts stopped abruptly. He raised his hand to signal the rest of the platoon. His men took a knee. I jogged forward, past Walter and Travis Barreto, who hovered beside our company commander. He'd been with Captain Sims that terrible day in Fallujah when Sims was killed in that house fight. Travis helped pull another wounded man to safety, which earned him a Bronze Star for Valor. Still, he'd lost his commander, and the survivor guilt he endured was slowly gutting him. No matter what happened, Barreto was locked to Walter's hip pocket. Any bullet that was fired his way was going through Travis before it hit the commander.

Fitts turned, saw me coming. A quick shake of his head, another hand signal, and everyone stood up and started to patrol forward again. I stopped, unsure what had spiked Fitts's Spidey sense. I saw no movement in the vegetation. The ridge behind it looked clear. The buildings on the other side of the road still seemed abandoned. I noticed a drainage ditch between us and those structures. At the bottom was a black slick of sewage.

This was exhausting. Adrenaline rush. Adrenaline drain. The heat. The stress. The constant state of alertness. These patrols had a cumulative effect on all of us. Now, in the waning weeks of our deployment, I walked back to my squad feeling strung out.

A machine gun shattered the silence. The gunner laid on the trigger and the weapon thundered over and over. The sound was like Morse code to us by then—a deeper, more metallic one than our weapons. And the undisciplined length of the burst telegraphed to all of us that no American stood behind that weapon.

Knapp reacted instantly to the threat. He pivoted, dropped to a knee, and opened fire with his M4, his rounds spearing into the vegetation to our left. I couldn't see whatever he was shooting at; others apparently did. A heartbeat later, one of our M249 SAW (Squad Automatic Weapon) light machine guns opened up. Then another. Within seconds, the platoon sent hundreds of rounds into the threat vector.

Suddenly the firefight ebbed. The enemy gunner went silent. Our platoon followed. For a few seconds, I heard our men calling out to each other, chattering over what had just happened.

That's when a second machine gun, even louder than the first, boomed to life. It belched a few short bursts, then the gunner went fully cyclic. The weapon was closer, but still concealed. I spun around searching for it and caught sight of the front of our platoon. The men had gone to ground, except for Fitts. He was still standing, bullets exploding the asphalt road all around his legs. Chunks of the stuff spun randomly as clouds of dirt plumed every impact. He dropped to his stomach.

"Holy shit! Fitts got hit again?" somebody shouted from behind me.

Fitts was a good two hundred meters from my squad. I could see his own men either firing while prone on the asphalt road or crawling into the sewage ditch.

Another long burst of automatic weapons fire raked around Fitts. He suddenly stood up, apparently unharmed. Ignoring the incoming, he charged at the enemy positions through the open field on our left. None of his men followed. Instead, they poured fire into the thicket beyond the open space, covering his movement.

Nearby, my men opened fire as well, unsure where the enemy was, but determined to suppress those automatic weapons. As they did, Travis Barreto tackled Captain Walter. The two went straight into the sewage ditch, where Barreto shielded his commander's body with his own. No way was he going to lose another commander on his watch.

In the distance, I saw a Bradley hauling down the road toward us. Then another. Cantrell was coming to our rescue.

Lawson grabbed his two gun crews at the back of our formation, jumped the sewage ditch, and broke into the tallest building on our right. The men flowed inside and rushed to the roof to get their weapons in the fight, showing a speed and sense of purpose rare among Soldiers lugging heavy machine guns.

I took my squad and did the same thing, entering a building next to Lawson's. We raced up the stairs and kicked open the door to the roof. My men quickly crouched into firing stances and hammered the brush line.

I ran to a corner of the roof and stopped cold. An AK-47 lay there behind the parapet, a stack of magazines beside it. I glanced at the other corners. Each contained an AK. The roof of the building next door did as well. The enemy had prepositioned weapons and ammunition on every rooftop along this road. Thank God nobody was up here to shoot at us. We'd have had a very bad day.

In the field, Fitts found what looked like a well flanked by a small stone wall. I saw him hunkered down behind it, still taking fire while the rest of the platoon hammered away at the invisible enemy from the sewage ditch and rooftops.

Two of my men barraged the vegetation with 40mm grenades. They arced over the field and detonated with muffled explosions deep in the brush. Lawson's gun teams joined the fight, strafing the vegetation. Leaves and branches were torn apart. Small trees were sawn in half. We still could not see the enemy. Whoever was in there was still shooting back.

Our tracked vehicles roared down the road. The sound of steel treads churning over sunbaked asphalt rose above the din of battle. They gouged grooves into the road as their tracks ate up ground to get to us the support we needed. Help was coming—those Brads carried 25mm semiautomatic cannons, high-explosive love that more than once had been our salvation.

They charged into the fight and their Bushmaster cannons boomed. High-explosive shells blew apart the underbrush as our gunners walked their fire along the irrigation canal.

In desperation—or stupidity—one of the enemy made the suicidal decision to shoot at the tracks from the house on the ridge with an automatic weapon. The bullets bounced harmlessly off our armored vehicles. The Brad crews spotted the threat. Shane Gossard swung his turret toward the house, the cannon's barrel shifted upward. A moment later a fusillade of high-explosive shells blew holes in the house's walls and roof.

These men in our Bradleys had saved us time and again in Fallujah. They were supremely aggressive and dominated every fight with the firepower they possessed.

The enemy machine gun went silent. Our men kept shooting, unsure if the insurgents had been killed or had just gone to ground.

I took advantage of the lull in incoming to run downstairs and get back onto the road. I headed over to Captain Walter to confer with him. He was halfway up the ditch now, radio handset to his ear, Travis Barreto kneeling right beside him. Both men were covered in black raw sewage. The smell was absolutely overwhelming. They were alert. No fear on their faces.

Something moved to my left. Instinctively, I stopped, spun, and set into a shooter's stance. A split second later, my brain caught up to my body. What was it? What is out there?

Doug Walter saw my reaction and called out, "Sergeant Bellavia, what's going on?"

"Shhhhhhhhh," I said, as if in a trance. Every synapse in my body seemed to be firing on full automatic. My stomach fluttered. I was outside my body. The enemy was near. And I was out in the open.

Twenty meters away, the bushes along the irrigation canal suddenly swayed. There was no wind, and nobody was shooting this close to the buildings. I brought my reflex sight to eye level.

A hand appeared through the thicket. Then another. They grasped some branches and pushed them aside, revealing a man in a white *thawb* with a black strap on one shoulder crossing his chest. A bandolier. Or maybe a weapon sling? I couldn't tell.

Christmas morning is exciting. Catching the enemy before they can kill you is an exhilaration that is impossible to comprehend. I had him cold and there was no way I would let him hurt any one of these beautiful American boys.

I slowed down, my brain focusing on one thing: eliminate the threat. *Don't overthink this. Don't panic. Breathe. And stay steady.*

I pulled the grip of my M4 into me tightly, settling the buttstock into my shoulder pit. That feeling was comfortable by then, natural. It was how we assured steady, smooth, and controlled pairs. Marksmanship on a range back home is one thing. In combat, with all the chaos, fear, and adrenaline, it is quite another.

I dropped to a low shooting stance and took aim.

Is this my buddy? Ol' Mad Dog Ali?

I couldn't see his face. My reflex sight's reticle settled center mass— right on his chest. Through my optics, I saw now what that strap was on his chest. He was carrying an RPK machine gun, complete with a metal drum magazine. The guy was heavily armed, but he was also very, very stupid. He stumbled around in all that vegetation in the middle of the firefight, looking for a decent firing position. Instead of finding it, he wandered right into my squad's position without any clue we were there.

This would be the easiest shot of my entire deployment. Point-blank range, enemy distracted by the tangle of branches slowing his headway and completely unaware of the M4 barrel pointed right at him. I couldn't miss.

I triggered my M4 carbine. One shot pair, followed by the *pop-pop* of the second controlled pair. Then a third. I paused, then fired again.

The man in white still stood, arms spread apart as he pushed his way through the last of the thicket's branches.

What the hell?

I fired again. This time, something sparked in front of him, and I wondered if I had hit his machine gun.

He froze in place. I pulled the trigger. *One . . . two . . . one . . . two . . . one, two.* He didn't move. How was I missing this guy? What was I doing wrong?

I drained the magazine, dropped it out, and shoved a fresh one into my weapon. It was a fluid action, something we could do in our sleep at this point in our deployment. It took less than two seconds.

I tightened my stance, sucked in my elbows even closer to my body. I was rock-stable, the pipper of the bright red reflex sight tacked to the man in white's chest. I flipped my selector switch to burst mode, something I rarely used. Three bullets spat out of the M4's barrel. Over and over I pulled the trigger until my bolt racked back and my mag went dry.

I dropped it out, swapped a full one in, and shot at him again.

How the hell am I missing this guy?

He stepped backward. The branches swung back in place and partially obscured him. I could still see enough of his white man-dress to know he was there, still on his feet.

I fired ten more rounds before he vanished altogether.

The firefight up the road had sputtered out. The men ceased firing and reloaded their weapons. In the lull, my M4's bark was the only sound. The entire platoon looked at me, standing in the road blazing away into the bushes sixty feet in front of me.

I heard Captain Walter's voice, as if from a dream: "Sergeant Bellavia, what's your report?"

Barreto echoed him, "Sergeant Bell, did you get him?"

I lowered my rifle, peering into the bushes.

"Lawdog, do you have eyes on him?"

Lawson took over a machine gun and stitched the area I was firing at.

Lawson replied from his rooftop, "Nothing's outside that tree line. Now. Guarantee that."

The Bradleys turned away from the house and made their way cautiously toward us.

"Mount up when they get here," Captain Walter ordered.

Staff Sergeant Cory Brown's Bradley reached our position first. He popped out of his turret and pointed at the road.

I gave him a thumbs-up. That's where we'd mount up. Time seemed to slow. The moment became surreal.

Did I hallucinate the man in white? Heatstroke?

"Sergeant Bellavia," Walter said again, "did you drop him?"

As if in a daze, I answered, "I don't . . . I don't think . . . no, sir. Negative."

The platoon was gathering in the road again, and when they heard my words, several men burst out laughing.

"Come on, Sergeant Bell. Of course you got him."

Fitts was still in the field several hundred meters away. He stood up and plunged into the vegetation. A moment later we heard two shotgun blasts just as the Brads arrived and dropped their ramps.

"I think I missed. I can't believe it," I said almost to myself. Captain Walter came over to me. I was still fixed in my shooter's stance, peering into the vegetation.

"That dude was twenty meters in front of me. I have no idea what happened."

Civilians started to dart in and out of buildings around us. Whether they were just curious or ready to cause more trouble wasn't clear. Either way, Captain Walter ordered us to fall back. If there was more fighting, the civilians in the open would be caught in the cross fire. Walter refused to risk their lives.

"We are falling back. Time to go. Civilians everywhere," Captain Walter said.

I barely heard the order. Instead, I said aloud, "I missed him."

"Sergeant Bellavia, let's mount up. We just started our day."

I turned and walked stiffly to our Bradley. My squad was already inside, staring at me strangely. I ignored them and sat down, head spinning, hands shaking.

I missed. I did everything right. I controlled my breathing. I didn't have sweat in my eyes. He was right in front of me, almost totally exposed.

That was him. The old man. I know it was him. All that rage. All that buildup. This will never, ever happen again. Dammit, you blew it, man.

The ramp closed behind me, and we were bathed in artificial light inside the Bradley's armored hull. Our driver moved out; the engine shifted gears. The Bradley lurched forward, taking us away from Al Ali. I noticed none of it. My head was still in the fight, replaying those fifty rounds I'd fired at the man in white over and over until my confidence was dismantled.

1

STIRRING DEMONS

THE HOUSE WAS EMPTY, smothered in darkness. Waking up to that black nothing, the same as the last moments of consciousness before sleep, always brought me comfort. In combat, we grabbed sleep where we could, and all too often we had to go from that blackness to action in seconds. Here at home, this transition that might have unsettled some proved a comfort to me. No threats loomed. No action was needed. I lay in the dark, eyes open now, listening to the sounds of the morning.

Today, the wind tore through the trees outside as rain lashed the roof and windows in sudden bursts. The branches swayed and rasped against the side of the house. Listening to the downpour distracted me from the storm clouds forming on my own horizon.

I dreamed of the Man in White again. For thirteen years, I'd seen him in nightmares. Sometimes, I could see his face, and I knew he was the old man from the house. I shoot at him and miss. I always miss him. He goes on to kill another American Soldier. He never shoots back at me in my dreams. I am in no danger, but I always feel the pressure that if I don't stop him, another American would die.

Who had died because I'd failed to do my job? Were there widows, children who would curse my name if they knew of my failure?

Parents? I would never know. The Man in White remained one of the dozens of loose ends every deployment creates.

Some vets have nightmares about the enemy they killed. I have them about the man I missed.

I had failed to do my job as a Soldier and protector to stop him. He lived to fight another day. Since then, I've carried the guilt of those he may have killed after I blew my opportunity. How many souls are on my conscience? I probably will never know for sure. I did know that each time the news reported an American Soldier had been killed around Diyala Province, I felt responsible. Those reports always triggered more visits from him.

Maybe this was transference. Maybe this was some expression of another underlying issue still festering from the deployment that I had not worked through. Still, the guilt was real. At times after I came home, it tormented me. At its worst, I would call Fitts and talk to him about that day. This had long consumed me as it lingered in our phone calls for years since we came home. He indulged it, listening as I recounted the same story over and over ad nauseam. He took the brunt of it. Those conversations were the outlet I needed, because elsewhere in my life, I had long since bottled everything up. There was nobody else in my life beyond Fitts who understood what the war was like. Trying to pull a civilian into those memories was like trying to explain a Rembrandt to a blind person. There's no frame of reference, no context for civilians who never served. This is especially true of Americans who've never been abroad or seen how the rest of the world functions.

So Fitts would listen patiently, saying just enough to let me know he was still on the line, ear in the handset. I knew it drove him crazy, hearing the same things over and over for years, but his patience was a reflection of the bond we shared. I loved him like a brother, and his actions proved he felt the same way, even if he couldn't share the words.

That fall of 2018, the Man in White returned again, triggered by the calls I'd received that something was going on at the Department of Defense, or DoD. According to several tipsters, the Pentagon had initiated an investigation into me and my life. News of this left me feeling as if a slow-moving freight train was coming straight at me, and my feet were cuffed to the tracks.

In the days that followed the first tip, I'd heard the investigators were going through my time in combat with a microscope. They were talking to people I had not spoken to in more than a decade. Stirring up the past was the last thing I wanted. I had tried to put it to rest, tried to focus on a forward-leaning future. I tried to live in the moment, enjoying the things in my life that gave me meaning and pleasure.

A combat veteran who thinks he can escape his past is kidding himself. It always comes back up. It is just a question of how, and why. During the opening stages of the War on Terror, America's veterans' facilities were flooded by Vietnam War veterans suffering from post-traumatic stress (PTS) again. They had laid their demons to rest for decades, but as their sons and daughters answered the call to service after 9/11, their memories of war returned. The demons stirred to assail them again.

Nobody had hit on a solution to this yet. It afflicted the World War I generation when their sons and daughters went to war after Pearl Harbor. The cycle continued when the parents of baby boomers who'd landed in Normandy, retaken the Philippines, or stormed the final defensive lines on Okinawa watched their kids head into the fires of Vietnam.

I wrote a book in 2006–07 as a way to honor the men and women I served with in combat. It evolved into a cathartic act that exorcised my own memories. In time, as interest in the war waned, I stopped talking about Iraq and suppressed those memories like almost every other veteran I knew.

Now, the phone calls from the people of that past were coming every day. Men I hadn't spoken to in decades "just happened" to call out of the blue to check in on me. It was all so strange.

Some of these callers were acquaintances. Others I knew from my political work in D.C. after I came home, but some of these guys were Ramrods, men I served with in Iraq.

"Hey, Bell? The Army keeps calling me. Do you know anything about what they are looking into?"

There would be an awkward silence on my end. What was I to say? I had no idea why they were digging into my past.

"Bell, I want you to know, we're still a family. We're looking out for you and everyone else."

Was this all related? Was it a mere coincidence?

Next came word that Pentagon investigators were scouring my personal history, overturning rocks I'd forgotten were even in my wake. This was getting uncomfortable.

What did the DoD want with me? I hadn't worn the uniform in a decade. I had stepped out of the political arena. I'd lost my family. My dad had recently died as well. Now I lived in a house that reflected my father's legacy. I just wanted to be left alone.

But the past never stays buried forever. Demons refuse to stay still. The memories swim to the surface of the here and now, triggered by a tectonic event, or sometimes by something as innocuous as a smell, a song, or the sight of something from those times.

The DoD's investigation caused a torrent of memories to boil out of long-closed doors. I dwelled on them in the daylight hours. I hated it, but I couldn't shut my mind off. I live a disciplined life—the Army ingrained that in me. The memories took that order away and sent me back to a place I didn't want to revisit.

In that place came the Man in White, like a parasite on my memories.

I got out of bed and wandered into the living room. Outside, the storm began to ebb. I sat in the predawn darkness, feeling utterly alone.

I'd grown up in this house. Every room contained memories of those years surrounded by a large and happy family. Now it was just me here on this farm. My parents had moved to Florida to enjoy retirement. That hard-earned reward for a life of work was cut so unfairly short when my dad passed. Fate robbed him of his golden years. It was a blow that leveled all of us Bellavias, and another reminder that time is not guaranteed.

My mom chose to remain in Florida after my dad's death. My siblings were scattered, with lives and families of their own. That left me at the farm. At times, I felt like a caretaker, a role I embraced as part of my postwar civilian life anyway. By writing the book, I inadvertently became the custodian of the Ramrods' legacy. After *House to House* hit the shelves, the media spots I did gave me an opportunity to share that legacy with a broad American audience. When I moved back to the farm, tending to it became the way I honored my dad's legacy.

He loved this place.

My family was still reeling from our patriarch's death. Terminal cancer is a diagnosis few beat. Yet we all had naïve hopes that his faith in God would somehow lead to a miracle moment, that he would defy the odds and recover his vitality.

It was not to be. Instead, we watched him fight a losing battle, inch by inch, with resolution and courage that made me proud I was his son. As his body slowly succumbed, he and I grew very close. Bearing witness to how my father faced death was enough to cement him as the superman he was to me when I was ten. He was at his best when confronted with narrowing options and battling for his life. I learned that how you combat such a diagnosis is the truest testament of a man.

In the nine months since his death, I've called the farm my home again. I settled into a quiet, solitary life and routine that didn't resemble what I envisioned for myself when the Ramrods emerged from Fallujah. Back then, I wanted nothing more than to wear the uniform and that flag on my shoulder. I wanted to go where the Army needed me, to protect the innocent and kill our enemies. A career in service of my country? I could think of nothing more sacred, or more meaningful.

That was not in my stars. In 2005, the arc of my life took a hard left turn. I lay down my M4 and hung up my uniform to become an everyday working Joe for my family. In those early days, I would do anything I could to pay the bills. I worked hard, menial jobs that left me as exhausted as I'd ever been. There were periods where I worked two full-time gigs, sleeping every other day, to ensure the best for my family. Those long hours were the way I expressed love for them. Back then, I didn't know how to show it any other way. I lived for that sacrifice. It took years to get anywhere, and every step up the ladder felt like summiting Everest.

These days, I hosted a regional radio talk show at a station in

Buffalo, five days a week during the afternoon drive. The weekends were spent trying to knock down the million things needing to be done around the farm while maintaining a small business. I kept largely to myself and rarely traveled anymore. Public appearances? Only for local veteran groups. I hadn't done anything outside of New York in years.

At first, the farm served as sort of a bolt-hole for me. I retreated into it like a refugee, returning to heal and contemplate how to move forward. My kids and their mother lived an hour away now. My kids commuted between parents. There was plenty of anguish to go around. Here at the farm, I could process and plan, could find ways forward, away from that pain for all of us.

I got up and walked across the wood floors into the kitchen. Those same hardwood planks were childhood favorites of mine. I'd wear socks and slide across their waxed and polished planks like I was surfing. My dad would watch me, and he looked ten feet tall to me back then. Infallible, larger than life, the hero of our family's journey. It was a rough transition for us both as I went from seeing him that way as a kid, to understanding the man he was when I became an adult.

In the kitchen, I brewed coffee, then lingered in the living room a few more minutes, listening to the wind die down outside. The first rays of dawn broke the horizon. I watched the new day from the window, sipping my coffee and waiting for one of my favorite guests to appear. In the broken early light, she emerged from the wood line down the hill from the house. A mother fox, soaking wet, escorted her young pup across the yard, ever watchful for threats.

I first saw her a few months back. Now her arrival was almost a daily ritual. Her fierce protectiveness of her young inspired me. That level of loyalty seemed all too rare among humans. At least, here at home anyway. In combat with the Ramrods? Loyalty defined us.

The mother fox and her pup padded past the gazebo as rain splashed off its red tile roof. A fresh squall crept over the sky, snuffing out the golden hour shine and bringing a downpour that soon drove my guests back into the woods. I watched them scamper away and finished my coffee while the storm's strength ebbed away again. I checked my watch. It was time to begin the day.

· · ·

Later that evening, I drove forty miles to an Applebee's restaurant in Batavia and found a booth with a view of the parking lot. I couldn't hide my excitement, and I anxiously watched the lot between sips of coffee as I waited for my boy to arrive.

Boy, hell. He's a young man now.

I didn't have to wait long before Evan's car pulled into the lot. A moment later, I saw my son walking for the front door. Tall and stocky, he had long since become an impressive-looking young man. What I wouldn't give to have had his frame at eighteen.

He entered the restaurant and I hugged him hard. He bear-hugged me back and nearly squeezed the air out of my lungs.

These meetings were few and far between these days. Whenever he could break away from college life, I'd meet him near his mother's house. This Applebee's became a common rendezvous point over the years.

We ordered food from a cheerful server and made small talk—chatting about B movies and their ridiculous special effects. He was in his second year of college, studying graphic art and film, so most times when we broke bread together, our conversations began with the latest movies we'd seen, or some arcane aspect of filmmaking that he'd just learned.

"Practical effects versus CGI. I mean, most people don't appreciate how it impacts the movie but also the filming experience. You get a better performance out of the actors. They see what they are actually doing. But it's super expensive."

He talked a technical depth that lost me much of the time, though in his mind I suspected he kept things pretty basic for his old man. I didn't care when he talked over my head. I missed this kid. Terribly. The film shop talk was our way of easing into a groove together. From there, our conversations would wander back to moments we shared together while he was growing up. We avoided the present. There were minefields in both our lives now. Rather than risk detonating one, we stayed on well-traveled paths, subjects we knew to be safe.

Evan was the first person I thought about when I got off the plane from Iraq. He was only five then, and I'd been gone so long I doubted he would recognize me. Soldiering and that reality go hand in hand. Still, he was the person I wanted to see more than anyone else. In

Iraq, I lived for that moment where I'd finally get to lift him up and hug him close to me. We'd get over the *Daddy is a stranger* phase, and I'd learn on the fly how to be a father again.

In every firefight, it was his face that popped up in my head. Memories of my boy morphed into the bugle call that triggered a stampede of rage or adrenaline during combat. I wasn't clawing at the eyes of my enemy out of the fear of never seeing him again; I was fighting for the path back to him. Every time a rifle would crack, or I turned a corner after an explosion in the chaos of urban warfare, I'd see Evan, small and slight, clad in my Soldier's uniforms.

I saw this as if it were real. At first I blamed dehydration, then sleep deprivation. Gradually, I grew to expect it. Like a medium who lives among the dead spirits around her, Evan's presence remained with me. He fueled me to push ever harder. Maybe his appearance was a tangible expression of how my brain calibrated in moments of crisis.

Step it up. Get to it. This is not going to be a bad day.

Or perhaps he was there to remind me that the Soldiers I fought beside were all an Evan to some mom and dad back home. They had people who loved them, as much as I loved my boy. That realization solidified my purpose in Iraq: keep them alive. Get them back to the States so they could have the reunion I so desperately wanted, too.

Evan's embrace would be the greatest reward for returning home—I knew that the first day we touched our boots to Iraqi soil. I tried to remember the smell of his hair. The warmth of his face. His toddler breath reeking of whatever snack he'd just eaten. Those memories of him? They drove me to conquer every fear and defeat any force in front of us because I knew the only way back to my son was through the enemy. Evan made me feel superhuman under fire.

I'd never told him this. I didn't know how, didn't know where to start. When you endure something as complex and interrelated as combat in an infantry platoon, and your audience is starting from zero context, finding the entry point to lay the foundations of understanding is always elusive. We hadn't found that entry point yet.

Thirteen years after I came home from Fallujah, my oldest son was already well launched into his own life. Sophomore year. Term papers. Dating hardships. Grades. Those were the guardrails in his world.

For years I'd hoped to see him wearing a uniform of his own, knowing the feeling of what it meant to be representing our country in it. And yes, following in my footsteps. It was not to be. His kidney issues kept him out of the Army, and that was probably for the best. He was much too kind and empathetic to be turned into a door-kicker.

Since he'd left for college, there were always so many things I wanted to tell him, so many words that needed to be shared. I missed every opportunity to do it—again I never seemed able to find an entry point. Just being with him, listening to him tell me about his classes and seeing how his mind worked always served to bring such happiness to me that I feared upsetting the dynamic with something that could lead us into that minefield around this safe path. So, I eased into the rhythm of our conversations, laughing at his quirky sense of humor while doing my best to keep things light.

The unspoken words, the conversations yet to be had, they lingered in the background like clouds on the horizon. Drama and divorce are very difficult journeys to navigate. Most of those topics had their wellspring in the war. It always went back to the war.

Consciously, we both avoided those subjects and often talked politics instead. Unlike many fathers and sons I know, the two of us saw eye to eye on this front. I'd ask him for his thoughts on the latest things unfolding in Washington, or Albany. Early in his teens, he became an astute observer of the swamp. As he matured and his knowledge grew, he developed a keen insight into politics.

Our meals came, and as Evan wolfed down french fries, he switched topics to the new movies I needed to see.

As we talked, I sensed he was circling the deeper issues he was facing at the moment, looking for an entry point of his own into something more important. He had recently lost one of his best friends to a car accident. That and the death of my father, I knew, weighed heavily on him. He was processing things at eighteen that most people face much later in their lives, and it was a struggle even for a tough kid like him.

I wanted to talk to him about those subjects, but figured it was best to let him broach the subject first.

Over the last year, with the wallop of losing his best friend and my father, death had been a topic we both danced around. Loss. The journey of life without people we love. We'd started and stopped this conversation for months. One time in a movie theater, he asked me from nowhere, "Dad, what do you do when your friends die?"

I knew exactly what I wanted to say, but I pretended I didn't.

Instead he got my famous, "I'm sorry, buddy."

Sitting across from him now, with no distraction to save me, I could see the pain coming into focus in his eyes again. He finished his last fry and looked at me in silence. He'd been dealing with far too much for a college sophomore.

I'd have done anything to shoulder his burden. I just didn't know how to do it here. Death and talking about its consequences is not a strong point of mine.

"Dad, when a person's gone. They're just cut out of life. Like your heart is heavy, and your body doesn't even want to move."

Here we go.

I had struggled with the same issue for years, making many mistakes in my own grieving. I didn't learn how to survive these wounds until I was a much older and mature man.

"Evan, people do many things to deal with this. And no one is right. I'll tell you, though, there is a lot of wrong out there. This is something we all have to deal with in life. We can't escape and no one has the answers to it, Evan. Some create a separate world in their mind where they are still with those they lost. Some seal them off in a pyramid, just forget they lived. Like they were never here, so they can move forward and keep living without guilt for still being alive."

Evan asked, "So what do you do, Dad?"

Like in the past, I dodged the question. Diversion is an ally of mine when conversations get too deep. "You know, the greatest works of art have come from the worst times in human history. The pain of the world is the fuel for the most beautiful displays of creativity."

I nodded at him and continued: "Evan, you have the one gift that can not only deliver you from your pain, but help other people ease their misery, too. Your films can send people to a place where you control the outcome. And you can help them heal and laugh. Use your own grief to fuel who you want to be and what you are here to do."

"You don't do that. You avoid it. You just work nonstop."

He was right, of course.

"Is that how you deal with it? Work nonstop?"

He was asking me about a major aspect of my life today that my Iraq experiences shaped. That was a topic full of mines for both of us. We were way off the path now, and he wouldn't back down.

"What did you do?"

I covered my discomfort with a sip of coffee. I wasn't ready to tell him how, when men I loved died around me, I pretended they'd just been transferred to another duty station. The Army was vast and its posts spread across the globe. It was easy to do, since friends came and went all the time. It worked for me until one day, years later, a Gold Star mom named Merrilee Carlson forced me to unburden my heart. I was breaking under the weight of that grief and didn't even know it. Afterward, I realized I'd nearly crippled myself with that denial. The catharsis she triggered ensured I would be able to move forward.

If I told him that, it could take us into a discussion about Captain Sims. Lieutenant Iwan. Command Sergeant Major Faulkenburg. Forty other men. I couldn't go there. Not on this evening. Not even for my boy.

So I shared another part of myself with him, one that I had never vocalized until that moment. "The truth is, Evan, part of me likes the suffering. It reminds me that I am strong enough to endure it, that I was born to carry what other people can't handle. It's my superpower. I can't be lonely. I don't hurt. And nothing can ever take me down. That's what I tell myself when I hear a noise in the dark."

I was dreading the next question, because it no doubt would go even deeper. We stared at each other for a long moment as Evan considered my words.

"Remember that night when you thought that racoon was a cat and you started to pet it?"

The non sequitur caught me totally off guard. Before I'd thought through it and realized he'd just let me off the hook, I answered, "Evan, that is the opposite of what I am talking about."

"That thing wanted to rip your face off. Didn't it?"

"Yeah," I replied, laughing with him now. "But that was years ago. You weren't even alive when that happened."

"That thing was pissed-off at you, Dad."

"I hate cats anyway."

"No you don't."

I finished off my coffee. The pain was still in his eyes, and I did want to help him, but we clung to the laughter.

At length, I went back to the point I had tried to make. "Look, Evan, what I'm getting at is this: we all need to be able to shoulder whatever burden the world throws at us, however and whatever it takes inside you. How you tell yourself how to do it, what you say to yourself and others. These things matter. It doesn't just affect you, though it is hard to see that in the moment. The more people who handle adversity without becoming the victim of it, or needing the attention of it, the better it is for all of us. We're failing as a culture on that front right now."

"That is very true, Dad."

"There's another aspect, too. Validation is a huge part of what an adult needs in their life, whether they realize it or not. The trick is to be your own validator. When you find the words for your own inner monologue that give you the strength to stand against adversity— that's where you'll know you're on the right path."

He thought about that in silence for a bit. I didn't get in the way, staying quiet and just watching him think. He would figure it out; I knew he would. I'd seen the validation seekers at every funeral. They are the ones whose grief is so huge nobody could have loved the departed as they did. The death of another became all about them and their need to show their wounds for sympathy's sake. They were the victims left behind by cruel fate. The need of that kind of external validation always struck me as the province of the weak characters. I didn't want Evan falling into that trap. Validate your own grief; don't show it off for others to comment on. Seek respect instead of sympathy. Those I admired the most always took this path during periods of grieving.

We switched back to safe topics. Movies again, then a revisit of New York politics. These moments were absolutely precious to me, and I wanted to draw them out as long as possible. On this evening, I also had something important to tell him. It was my turn to lead the conversation off the path. The Pentagon forced my hand on this one.

"Listen, Evan, I need to tell you something."

Evan's eyes shifted slightly. He recognized the tone change in my voice. He knew I was venturing off the safe path.

"There's something going on with the Army, and I don't want you to be caught flat-footed. Some stuff about Iraq might come out, and it could get pretty crazy. I really don't even know what."

I suspected I knew, but I wasn't going to get into that now. Long ago, there were people in my chain of command who threatened to open an investigation on me. I was caught in the fissures that the Iraq War opened in the Army over how a Cold War–era force designed to fight the Soviets in Western Europe could best defeat a counterinsurgency in the Middle East. There were many approaches to this problem, some of which conflicted with each other. That caused tension throughout the units deployed that year, and for years after as well.

"It could be nothing. It could be something. Either way, you are the only one I am going to tell. If it does get stupid, people will be talking about it around here. At least, for a few days."

He nodded and said, "Okay, thanks for the heads-up. You thinking this is good or bad?"

I didn't think what I was trying to tell him registered, but I had no idea how to dive deeper into it. We rarely discussed the war.

"I don't know. When it comes to that time in my life, it's never good."

"I am sorry this is happening, Dad."

His voice was filled with genuine concern.

"Thanks. I just need you to be prepared, okay?"

"Yeah. Sure."

The server cleared our plates and headed back to the kitchen. I waited for Evan to ask for details, unsure how I would respond. Show me the parenting guide that has a chapter on how to tell your son that the Department of Defense is investigating his father.

The wall around the Iraq War remained intact. Evan asked no questions. As a kid, he confronted me when I left to go back as a journalist in 2006 and again a few years later. He hated when I left, would grow angry at the sense of abandonment he felt. When I would return, there were tough moments between us. I promised him more than once that I would stay home. I broke those promises, as the pull of the battlefield always drew me back. Obligation and a sense of purpose are like an opiate to a combat veteran. We chase that dragon our entire life.

For Evan, Iraq became a lifelong sore point between us, a reminder that in his mind, the family came second to the war. He also suffered for his family, which inevitably became a casualty of the war. He told me that he read the book I wrote about Fallujah. I know he skimmed it. I doubt he read it cover to cover.

I understood. This is not easy for a kid. Later, he watched the documentaries on our platoon's experiences and his response was total shock. That was enough for him to understand there was a reason for the past to stay far away from our lives today.

My time in combat remained something he'd learned from others, as if it were a buffer. Perhaps learning about it from me was too painful after all that the war inflicted on him here at home. Now it was cropping up again, and it was sure to affect him yet again.

I mean, how would he react if the headlines du jour announced the DoD had charged his father for a series of unfortunate events dating to 2004 in Diyala Province?

Dad, you want to explain that one?

Not really. Let's just eat some more Spindip.

Never mind we'd caught this insurgent red-handed laying an IED. The political firestorm this caused between the Iraqis and our task force lingered for months and played a central role in damaging my relationship with our company commander, Captain Sims.

The papers would never report the nuances. They'd just do a drive-by number on me. Again. I'd had enough experience in the political arena to know how that worked. Truth didn't matter. Nuance didn't, either. The whiff of scandal was all that attracted the sharks in the press rooms. My family would endure hell for it.

On this evening, we ran out of time before that Iraq War barricade was breached with any follow-up questions. We left the table. I paid the bill, then stepped outside into the bitter autumn wind, walking shoulder to shoulder with Evan as we negotiated the puddles the storm left behind. We said our goodbyes beside his brown Mazda. Nothing emotive. Just, "I'll see you later. Maybe next week if you have time. We can see the new *Halloween* remake. Cool? Love you" and a quick hug.

In that brief embrace, I felt his head on my shoulder. It took me back to the days when he was an infant, when I always felt like I was carrying him away from some danger when I had him in my arms. He'd been so sick those first years. I fought for him while he was fighting for his own health. Being his dad back then made me feel more important than at any other time in my life. That little boy, now this large young man—he was the reason I was born to be on this earth. I just wished to God I could connect with him in a meaningful way for him to see that love. The cable of transmission was severed between us, cut off by our many minefields and my own sense of protectiveness. Nothing requires more trust than being vulnerable to your own son.

Still, it felt like we made a little progress today. Baby steps off the path.

I watched him drive away, and was suddenly stricken by a profound sense of sadness.

It was the same stab of loneliness that greeted me when I got off the plane from Iraq. Dead of night, another bitter wind blowing, with iced-over potholes to navigate around. That night's memory will never fade.

Someday, I'd find a way to tell Evan about it, and what he meant to me then. Maybe then, if he understood that, I could start talking about the rest of it. That could be our entry point. Someday.

2

IN THE
"WELCOME HOME" SHADOWS

VILSECK, GERMANY — FEBRUARY 2005

THE BUS GROUND TO a halt in a cloud of diesel exhaust, brakes squealing. I'd been dozing through the long drive from Ramstein Air Base to the Ramrods' home garrison post at Rose Barracks in Vilseck. The sudden stop woke me up—I opened my eyes and found my head against the cold window, streaks of icy water on its other side distorting the view in the darkness beyond. All I could see were a few lights in the distance.*

The driver killed the engine. The rumble of the big diesel machine died away, replaced by the sounds of the men stirring around me. Almost everyone had been asleep in their seats, trying to ride out the last hours of this transcontinental journey with a nap. Now we had

---

* All fifty states in the United States have at least one military base. Depending on your military occupational specialty and your active status, that number runs to around 134 places you can be stationed stateside in the U.S. Army. Infantrymen have fewer options. In 1996, as a part of the post–Cold War reorganization, the 1st Infantry Division was forward deployed and head-quartered in Germany until 2006. Coming home for us was Vilseck, Germany, where spouses, girlfriends, and children could live with soldiers just like they were stateside.

arrived right where we'd begun our Iraq odyssey a year and a month before. The exhaustion we all felt was shot through with a bolt of excitement, anticipation. A little fear. Beyond the bus, we could hear the hum and commotion of a crowd out there in the night, waiting for us.

For the men of Task Force 2-2, Germany was our home. Our families, our kids were here. The soil wasn't CONUS, but our people were out there, waiting for us. This was our homecoming.

Across from my seat, I saw Fitts stand up and stretch. He was clearly aching from the long journey from Iraq to Kuwait and now Germany. He moved like an old man. It was the price of returning to us before his three bullet wounds had properly healed. He flashed me a weary smile, then reached for his gear. Others were doing the same—John Ruiz, Charles Knapp, Scott Lawson were all in view, gathering their packs without any of the usual chatter between them.

I realized this was probably one of the last times my squad would be together. For over three years, they'd been my Army family. When we first came together here at Vilseck—a lifetime ago, it seemed—we were blank slates. Through nine months in Kosovo, followed by a full year of combat in Iraq, we learned practically everything there was to know about each other. Our pasts, our relationships, our goals inside the military, and our versions of the American dream trickled out of us in the many moments of boredom the Army breeds. In battle, we learned the measure of our characters, and the capacities of our hearts.

Our time as a platoon was coming to an end. This homecoming was the first step. We'd be given leave with our families, then we'd be sent on to different units wherever the Army needed us. I couldn't even imagine life without Ruiz on my left shoulder, Knapp on my right. Sucholas, Stuckert, Maxfield, these men were my everyday comfort. Out there in the darkness, however, the reality of service life awaited: our time together would always be transitory.

I checked my watch. It was well after midnight as the men of Alpha Company, Task Force 2-2 Infantry lined up and filed for the exit doors. Still groggy, I grabbed my pack and duffle, then stepped out into a sleet-soaked night. The Bavarian winter was milder than Buffalo, but in our desert gear the cold cut through our uniforms. Heaps of dirty snow lay in plowed piles on either side of the streets. The freezing rain had battered ice into slush, making for a sloppy, slick roadbed.

I'm not sure what kind of homecoming we expected. In retrospect, maybe we'd seen *Heartbreak Ridge* one too many times and figured there would be fluttering flags, red, white, and blue bunting, and a band playing Sousa tunes. That was probably unrealistic, but I don't think any of us imagined a return in the dead of a snowy German night, families waiting in the darkness between pools of light spilled by nearby streetlamps. Some held signs for their loved ones; others stamped their feet and rubbed their hands impatiently. As we dismounted from our buses, spontaneous cheers rang out. The crowd clapped wildly, and some shrieked with excitement.

A welcome home in the shadows.

Freezing weather and time of night may not have been optimal, but it did not stop my fellow Ramrods from rushing into the arms of their families. Wives, children, girlfriends. They collided in a chaos of kisses, smiles, and tears, their breath haloing around them in the chill air. Reunions played out everywhere around me. Our loved ones greeted us with such passion and love that it triggered an impromptu celebration in the slush beside the buses.

Fitts pitched into the middle of his three little ones, his then-wife holding their youngest in her arms. They mobbed him in a group hug, and the smile I saw on his face was unrivaled. Pure joy. Nearby, our company commander shared a similar reunion with his family. Knapp and Ruiz disappeared from view, swallowed by the swirling crowd.

My Army family had returned to our home garrison.

I stood for a moment beside the bus, watching the happiest moments I'd seen in this crotch-kick of a year. It was remarkable, as if the coiled spring that tamped our emotions down for the last twelve months had suddenly been released. The exhaustion of our long trip from Iraq vanished, replaced by a different adrenaline rush.

We had survived. And this moment was our reward for that achievement.

I moved toward the lower enlisted guys, the youngest of our men. I didn't want anyone from the platoon to see I was alone, take pity on me, and urge me to join them. This was their moment, and I would not intrude.

Our lower enlisted "Joes" had come to us as replacements late in the deployment. Most were still in their teens and had no chance to start an adult life before going to Iraq. I figured they wouldn't have people here.

I was wrong. Boy, was I wrong.

A wave of smiling, teary-eyed young women swarmed over our soldiers. Some jumped into their arms; others grabbed their necks and pulled them into deep, lingering kisses. I felt like the only solo guy at the prom.

I tried not to search for my people. I knew they weren't here, but some part of me hoped—ached—for them to surprise me. Maybe the suspense was building, like the end of a Hollywood rom-com, and just when I thought I'd be alone in the dark, surrounded by all this love and connection but not a part of it, a face I knew would appear in the crowd. I'd see Evan, waiting in the back of the mob, eyes searching for me. We'd have our own reunion then, the rift of time and distance healed in this moment of joy.

Heartache? Can't touch me. Loneliness? For the weak. I don't hurt. I don't feel pain. It is my superpower.

I was lying to myself as pure self-protection. I needed to see my son. Five years old now. Shortly after he was born, he developed a kidney ailment that left us terrified for his future. He required long-term, specialized care, including a pediatric nephrologist and lots of around-the-clock attention. Back then, my chain of command went to extraordinary lengths to ensure he received the best possible treatment. They hooked him up with a fantastic team of local doctors in New York who ultimately guided him through the worst of his illness.

But he couldn't travel. Not back then. So when I first received orders for Germany, Evan and his mother had to stay where his doctors were, at the Buffalo Children's Hospital.

I arrived in Germany alone and took up residence in the enlisted barracks with the single Soldiers at the 1st Infantry Division's base in Vilseck. Communal Army living in Europe taught me a lot about myself. It also taught me a lot about the Army and the men with whom I'd soon go to war. Included in those lessons was one major principle of combat arms Soldiers: we have the most physically fit alcoholics on the planet.

Problem: I didn't drink.

Mainly because of that choice, life in the barracks for me was never anything but a grind. Without any social life, I put my head down and focused on becoming the absolute best NCO possible. When others went onto the German bar scene, I stayed alone in my room, memorizing field manuals. I studied Vietnam, the maximum effective ranges of all our weapons and the ones our enemies used. I learned everything I could about Islam, the Iraq War, who was fighting against us, and what tactics they were using. It was a Spartan existence. I took it almost as a monastic calling devoted totally to the warrior profession. By keeping focused, I could keep the thoughts of Evan at bay. Or at least, that's what I told myself. The act of surviving that separation, missing him profoundly—that became my first superpower.

The weeks of focus blurred together, interrupted only when one of the Soldiers needed to be bailed out of jail on weekend nights. Being the only unattached NCO living in the barracks, I was the designated babysitter.

That was my experience in Germany before Iraq. No wild stories of nights in town. No torrid transnational love affairs. For me, it was all work and preparation for the crucible ahead.

Now, our crucible was over, and I had returned to the place that had distilled my life to that one fundamental purpose. My squad was everything to me. My sense of responsibility to them drove me forward every day, and in the back of my mind was the constant litmus test on every mission: *how can we get this done and get everyone home?*

That home moment had arrived. And now my job for them was done. They were with their families, untethered from me. I felt lost.

Some of the crowd began flowing down the street, away from the reunion point. As it moved, I caught a glimpse of Chuck Knapp. I stopped and watched him until his head and shoulders disappeared in the sea of humans around him. Liz, his beautiful wife, hung her arms around his neck. Without him, I was exposed. Vulnerable. My right-hand man no longer needed me; he was now safe with those he loved, carried back to Germany on the basis of our squad's strength and teamwork through the bloodiest battles America had fought since Vietnam. These emotions seemed disorienting and dissonant in the midst of so much happiness.

John Ruiz popped out from a huddle of Soldiers and family members. He was our wild one. Ruiz became my project to help unlock the Soldier I knew was lurking under the bad decisions and crazy antics that frequently sabotaged him. Once, while alone in the barracks for a weekend, I received a call explaining that one Specialist John Ruiz had been taken into custody by German authorities, who had delivered him to a mental asylum. He needed rescuing, and I was the only NCO around to help.

I drove through the night to find him in a padded room, tied to a bed. He was naked and had two IVs plugged into each arm. Shocked, I stood in the doorway staring at him until he saw me.

"Sergeant Bell, I swear I had my clothes on when they arrested me!"

I gave him my sternest NCO look.

"This talk that all the *polizei* speak English? It's bullshit, Sergeant Bell. Bullshit," he said indignantly.

Apparently, Ruiz refused to speak to the German cops who detained him. Whatever he'd been doing convinced the cops that Ruiz had to be insane, so they dumped him off at the mental institution. For my wild one, ending up tied to a bed instead of sleeping off the bender in a German jail came as a surprise. On the long ride back to Vilseck, I loudly educated him on my disappointment with his behavior.

How was I to know then that this kid possessed a lion's heart? It wasn't until Iraq that I witnessed it on full display, mission after mission.

Memo: The measure of the man was never found out on the German nightlife. Combat revealed it all—the good, the bad, and the truly loyal.

Being a force of discipline in their lives did not stop us from growing close. Our squad bonded in a way unique in my life. Never before, never since, did I share the kind of loyalty I did with these men. It became instinctive, an integrated part of who we had become through this experience of war.

The last Thanksgiving before we deployed to Iraq, I hung out with the guys who didn't have enough leave to get home. I took them to Popeyes Chicken at the base PX, where we feasted on Cajun fried turkey. Gossard, Contreras, Ruiz, Maxfield, Sucholas, Gross. The lost boys of our squad and me eating together at the PX that seemed to be open just for us. We didn't need anyone but ourselves. It was one of the best Thanksgivings of my life. We were totally at ease with each other, like a family should be though rarely is back in the States.

I'd never share that with them again. Our time together was over. Time and geography would tear apart the bonds we all depended on for our survival. I was starting to sense that this would be as difficult as grieving for the death of a family member.

I glimpsed my Soldiers one more time as a few of the family groups reached their vehicles. I wondered what would happen to us as we split apart. Would we find the loyalty that defined our squad somewhere again? Would our next units be this close and this fiercely protective of each other? I'd heard and seen plenty of stories that suggested what we had was not typical.

I doubt any of my men were thinking about such things right then. Their heads were with their families. None of the guys would remain on post. Hotel rooms had been reserved for them on the other side of the gate. Soft sheets. Room service. Running water. A mini-fridge stocked with booze and food. These were luxuries barely remembered after the 120-degree porta-johns, Army cots, and lousy chow we'd been used to in Iraq.

I slung my duffel bags and scanned the crowd again, telling myself I wasn't trying to find Evan. Yet my eyes kept searching, my brain resistant to reality, tenaciously clinging to hope.

I was a terrible liar to myself. I needed him more in that moment than I'd needed anything in my life.

Evan. Hey, buddy, where are you?

I knew the answer. I just didn't have it in me to accept it yet.

In December 2004, our pediatric care team in New York cleared Evan to move to Germany. In Iraq, we'd just returned to FOB Normandy after a month of brutal urban fighting in the Second Battle of Fallujah. As we settled back into our normal area of operations around Diyala Province, my chain of command moved heaven and earth to get my family's relocation pushed through channels and approved. They could come over and we could be a family, united in Germany after thirty-six months apart. It didn't happen; this wasn't my decision.

Now, on the night of my return, my mind and heart went to war with each other. I couldn't stand looking for them. I couldn't stand not to. Finally, the heart won. I stopped the self-denial and searched the night unrestrained.

More buses arrived and parked in orderly rows by ours. New families flowed into the area, waiting for their first glimpses of their Soldiers. There were hundreds, maybe thousands of Ramrods and their families now, surging around the buses, departing together down the street eager to make up for lost time. The ebb and flow of arrivals and reunions. It was an amazing scene, one in which I was an onlooker, not a participant.

Back in December, Lieutenant Colonel Peter Newell, our battalion commander, called me into his office at FOB Normandy. He had fought hard for me and my family, hacking through red tape, calling in favors and busting bureaucratic heads where necessary. He was proud and excited to tell me that the battalion had secured a house in Vilseck for my family. I wouldn't have to live in the barracks again after Iraq.

The house meant I could have a life while serving my country. It meant I could be a father again in our own space on post. They'd even found an excellent specialist in the area who could give Evan any further medical care he might need.

It was an enormous gift to me. Lieutenant Colonel Newell and Captain Doug Walter had gone to the mattresses on my behalf, something they didn't need to do. Part of what defined the Ramrods was the loyalty our officers showed to the enlisted ranks. We had no doubt they wanted what was best for us. This gesture epitomized that level of consideration.

Of course, the house and move of my family to Germany would come with a request to reenlist. I understood the game. Nothing in the Army is free. But having my family there would be enough to make this an easier decision. A career doing what I was born to do— hand me the paperwork. I had loved the idea of a life in the service of my country.

Excitedly, I emailed the news to Evan's mother. No response. I checked my inbox every day. Nothing from her at all. Eventually, I stopped even looking at my email.

I can't be lonely. I don't hurt. And nothing can ever take me down. Keep testing me: I can take it.

I knew that she had wanted to build a broadcasting career in New York. She had gotten a foot in the door with a local TV station, working as a weekend newscaster. Leaving her job would have been a big step. My head understood that. But it wounded me nonetheless. Everywhere I looked, wives were sacrificing for their husbands deployed at war. They came to Germany, and in the morning, they would be free to explore Europe together with the thirty-day leave the Army granted those returning from combat.

I was thinking about how much fun it would have been to explore Europe with Evan when the crowd suddenly came to a stop. Eyes swiveled to our company's senior NCO, First Sergeant Peter Smith. Seconds before, he'd been locked in a warm embrace with his wife. Now he was holding her with one arm, staring at a woman bundled in a winter coat who had appeared on the wet sidewalk behind our bus. The pain in our first sergeant's face was mirrored on the faces of every Soldier in view.

It was Tonya Faulkenburg, the widow of our beloved sergeant major, who was the first Ramrod to fall during the Second Battle of Fallujah. She turned out to greet us as an homage to her fallen husband, fulfilling this duty he could not. She stood stoically, her face obscured in shadow. Ninety days before, her husband had died instantly, killed by a sniper's bullet as he worked with our Iraqi allies to move into the breach we'd made in the city's defenses.

She took a step forward toward our first sergeant, and her face broke into a spill of artificial light. She was doing her best to be strong, but the same pain the crowd now felt was hers as well. She scanned the crowd, and for a moment we locked eyes. I couldn't hold her gaze.

She saw our reaction, and she retreated on the sidewalk, not wanting to interrupt or bring down the mood of the celebration. Her presence was not meant to be a reminder of who we had lost. This was not an attempt to bring down the festivities of the welcome back.

Rather, it was as if she was covering down for her husband, fulfilling the role he would be doing if he were here.

I looked at the ground, feeling guilty for the indulgent self-pity I'd been swimming in since I got off the bus. I would see Evan at some point. My heart would heal. That healing was a luxury the sniper would forever deny Tonya.

She moved toward her car. I think she felt like coming here to see the Ramrods return had been a mistake—for us, if not for herself.

The battalion would not let her slip away. A sudden rush of Soldiers streamed toward her, families in tow. They mobbed her, hugging her fiercely as one of their own.

"Welcome home, Ramrod," she whispered hoarsely as each one swept her into their arms. "Welcome home. He loved all of you . . . so much."

I turned away from Tonya Faulkenburg and decided to get out of the crowd as quickly as I could. I moved as fast as my gear and the slick footing allowed, heading away from that bittersweet reunion, my stomach in knots at the memories of our sergeant major.

I also had to face the truth: in the shadows of that Bavarian night, there was no rom-com ending for me. I wanted to be happy for our Soldiers, but all I felt were razor blades in my stomach. I wasn't going to be able to shake this off. It was a perfect, inescapable spiral of self-pity and shame, layered with guilt.

I will never forget that hike to the barracks. Like everyone else who was on the bus, I wore my DCU—Desert Combat Uniform. We'd been in the heat of the Middle East for a year. Now I shivered in the Bavarian winter. My tan boots, still encrusted with Iraqi dirt, looked ridiculously out of place juxtaposed against the snow and ice.

My imagination conjured Sergeant Major Faulkenburg.

"*You hurting, Sergeant Bell?*"

"*Yeah, Sergeant Major.*"

"*Good. Then you know you're alive.*"

An hour before dawn, I finally reached the barracks. Same room. Same sounds. My room had been sealed for over a year. It reeked of stale German cigarettes and mildew. After a year that transformed my life in so many fundamental ways, I had returned from combat to my exact starting point.

Nothing had changed. Except me.

I sat on the edge of the bed, untying my wet and muck-covered boots. Iraq dirt and German slush. Ramrod filth.

In the next few months, 2nd Battalion, 2nd Infantry would case its colors and be disbanded. Half the men would go home, their contracts complete. The others would be shuffled to a different battalion in another brigade, just in time for another Iraq deployment.

I'd be here until then, the unattached NCO who never left the barracks again. By default, I would again be the NCO babysitter of wayward enlisted infantrymen. I would be the guy available 24/7 to rescue drunk Soldiers from that German nightclub that featured roller-skating little people.

I shucked off my boots and slid them under the bed. The fatigue hit me like the weariness of an old man who's seen everything and wants nothing more from life.

The great awakening from combat doesn't occur on the battlefield. It occurs when you return and discover you've learned more about your home front than you ever wanted to know.

I thought that as Iraq transformed me, the rest of my world would change with me. That was either hubris or naïveté. Maybe both. The world had spun on in my absence.

I loved the Army. I loved my Soldiers. This job gave me purpose, it gave me meaning, but where I'd landed left me despising my situation. It was untenable, and I knew I couldn't go through it again. Not after Fallujah, and not after my long absence from Evan's life.

Just before the Ramrods left Iraq, Captain Walter came to talk to me. The house in Germany, the move allowance, the specialist on call for Evan had been rejected by his mother. The paperwork the Army sent to our home in New York was returned empty. No reason given. It was too late to do anything about it, as the deadline for all these things had passed.

As he broke the crushing news, Captain Walter showed considerable empathy toward me. He understood that I knew what a returned stack of blank paperwork meant to my life and future.

The last thing to die in an idealist's heart is hope. Sometimes it is sustaining. Sometimes it is torture. Sometimes it breeds denial.

I had been in denial, and I had tortured myself thinking they'd have come anyway to stand in the shadows between those streetlamp pools of light to celebrate my survival. Reality could not be denied in my head or heart any longer. That decision had been made before we even got on the plane back to Germany.

There were many rough nights under Iraqi stars. This one, although in the peace of our home base in Germany, may have been the toughest of my life.

Loneliness crept in like a winter wind, malign and bitter. I embraced it and made it my own. After all, it was my superpower.

3

THE SHADES OF THE PAST

OUTSIDE BUFFALO, NEW YORK — OCTOBER 2018

WHILE I WRESTLED WITH what to tell Evan about Iraq and how being away from him affected me, I received four phone calls from a number in Arlington, Virginia. Each time I saw the number, I put my phone down and didn't answer. Whoever was calling never left a message. It felt like something was closing in on me, and the normal life I'd lived until now was coming to an inexorable end.

How would I explain this to Evan? He was the most connected to my Iraq experience of our three children, since he was born before I left. He'd endured painful separations each time my conscience and heart drew me back in theater. I broke promises and left him behind to search for answers on the battlefields in 2004. He never understood why I did that.

I never told him how much not seeing him in Vilseck changed me. Those dotted-line moments in life are few and far between. When you look back on them, you can clearly see where your path branched. Sometimes you get to choose the branch, and sometimes the situation chooses it for you.

I had long since gotten over wondering what might have happened had we been united as a family in Germany. This was different now. I could sense a dotted-line moment coming, but I couldn't see what it would be, or how I could prepare my family. I just knew that this was probably one of those moments where the fork my life took would be chosen for me. Or maybe forced on me.

That week, I lay awake feeling a sense of helplessness. Whatever was coming was getting closer. Circling. The phone calls came more frequently. That number had even called my workplace. Next would be a visit to my front door. I had no doubt of that.

I needed to get out in front of this somehow.

Toward the end of that week, I woke up from fitful sleep determined to be proactive. If they were coming after me, I needed to prep the battlefield. Deep in thought, I went into the kitchen in a foul mood, breaking eggs and brewing coffee.

I hate this. I don't want to think about that night. I just want to be left alone to my life.

That wasn't possible now, not anymore. Pretending none of this was happening wasn't going to cut it, either. I would need to get a lawyer. And I would need to revisit that night and document everything I could.

As my eggs cooked, I grabbed my laptop and set it up at the kitchen table. Coffee poured, breakfast plated, I sat down to eat. And remember.

I would have to start with Captain Sims, and tension over the competing visions the Ramrods had over how to fight an insurgency that nobody saw coming but which threatened to destroy our entire post-9/11 strategy the year we arrived in Diyala Province.

When the Army deployed the Ramrods to Iraq in February 2004, we had a basic idea of where we were going inside the country. We ended up at FOB Normandy in Diyala Province, a section of Iraq between Baghdad and the Iranian border. Our area of operations (AO) included Muqdadiyah, a midsize city of about a hundred and fifty thousand. Fitts was wounded in an urban firefight in Muqdadiyah in April 2004, only a couple of months after we arrived in theater.

To the north of the city lay open, rugged terrain. When Americans think of the Iraq War, the images conjured are the street scenes in Baghdad, or the flat expanse of open desert in the western part of the country. But our AO north of Muqdadiyah looked more like Vietnam in 1968 than the desertscape of the Sunni Triangle. Thick palm groves grew in low spaces between gentle sloping hills. There were canals and rivers that the local farmers had harnessed to turn the land so bountiful that it had become known as the breadbasket of Iraq.

Among the heavy vegetation and irrigated fields, small communities straddled the roads leading out of Muqdadiyah. They were ramshackle, impoverished places, but seeded among them were wealthy Sunnis connected to Saddam Hussein's once-ascendant Ba'ath party. Below these elites, the vast majority of the population were Shia Muslims with strong ties to neighboring Iran.

After the American invasion in 2003, a kernel of resistance formed to the American occupation in one of these rural towns, called Sinsil. In the early stages of the insurgency, there were actually only a few locals involved, who forged ties within Iran to secure important weapons, explosives, and ammunition. The palm groves around Sinsil and its sister village, Khailaniya, became ideal places to cache those supplies.

When the Ramrods first arrived at Normandy, the 4th Infantry Division had been battling this growing threat. They had identified six men as key leaders in the nascent insurgency, known as the Sinsil Six. The 4th ID's intelligence guys had put their faces up on a wall map, then connected them to various known hideouts and accomplices with different colored yarn. The first time I saw their "bad guy map," it reminded me of a Hollywood stalker's lair, or maybe a 1920s-era FBI office that was hunting down Al Capone's cartel in Chicago.

With Sinsil being the nexus of the insurgency's leadership, it became one of the most important sectors in our AO. Captain Sims frequently took us out there to meet the locals, drink tea with their leaders, and discuss the needs of the community—classic counterinsurgency *win their hearts and minds* stuff that came straight from the Vietnam playbook.

Within thirty days of our arrival, the Sinsil Six had grown to the Sinsil Ten. We tracked down and killed two of the original members. When intel learned there were three brothers moving between Syria and Sinsil to arrange another flow of weapons to the area, they ended up on the yarn-crossed wall map, too. One of our special operations teams located, trapped, and killed one of the brothers. The other two escaped.

Each time we thought we'd dealt the Sinsil cell a crippling blow, they emerged stronger, with even more support from the local population. It was like fighting a contagious virus: for every patient we "treated," three more infections would crop up. The Sinsil Ten grew to the Sinsil Twenty, then Thirty. After that, we just lost track as a wave of recruits, organizers, and well-trained Iranian operatives flooded into the breadbasket.

That spring, the insurgency erupted all over the country. Between the first Shia uprising and the displaced Sunni ruling class's rebellion, nearly every Coalition unit was inundated with insurgents planting IEDs in their operational area, executing ambushes and launching attacks at key targets.

As the weeks wore on, our trips to Sinsil and Khailaniya turned into a kinetic version of *Groundhog Day*. We'd go out so Captain Sims could continue to try to develop relationships with the local Iraqi power base. While he was talking to them, drinking tea, the insurgents would be alerted to our presence and establish ambushes for us. One of their favorite places to initiate contact was a bridge between Sinsil and Khailaniya. The locals called it Shokorok Bridge. After a couple of ambushes, we started calling it "RPG Bridge."

In those first months, the company was hit seven times around Sinsil by these types of attacks. Bryan Lockwald, one of our engineers, was wounded when an IED exploded and splashed burning oil across his face and arms. On another mission out there, Staff Sergeant Joshua Franqui of First Platoon took three RPG rounds from the dense palm groves on the north side of Shokorok Bridge. They impacted against his Bradley Fighting Vehicle but failed to penetrate and kill or wound the crew. His return fire transformed the night into day, flaying the groves with the turret-mounted 25mm autocannon and coax machine gun.

While the Bradley spit tracers and high explosives, my platoon's weapons squad leader, Staff Sergeant Jamie McDaniel, broke from cover to make his way toward the bridge. McDaniel was an all-state defensive back out of high school in Florida. Discipline problems sank his Division 1 hopes, and he joined the 82nd Airborne. He still had the running gait of an NFL hopeful. That day at the Shokorok Bridge, I looked out and saw a rocket-propelled grenade streaking for him. Something was wrong with the rocket. It was spinning like a dying football pass, its engine sputtering. It twisted and writhed in midflight yet somehow still found its mark. The rocket struck the ground right at McDaniel's feet, ricocheted ninety degrees back into the air, missed our weapons squad leader completely, then petered out. It dropped to the ground again and failed to explode.

McDaniel was quick and agile. That night he was the luckiest man in Iraq.

Day after day, we went through the same stress, the same tension as we waited to get hit on these "hearts and minds" missions. Finally, we started to switch tactics and pushed out patrols into the palm groves. The enemy held many advantages here. Our orbital platforms could not spot them under the thick canopies that the trees and underbrush afforded. For some reason, the groves were always ten or twenty degrees hotter than the outside temperature. It made breathing a labor. Our eyes stung like we'd been pepper sprayed, and no matter how much we drank, we quickly grew dehydrated while moving through them.

Yet we learned the enemy was hot and dehydrated, too. Though they didn't carry nearly the load out we did in full battle rattle, they still had to contend with running through heavy vegetation in 140-degree heat. We learned to flush them out, maneuvering to force them to break out of their concealed positions, or fight a last stand.

We started killing the enemy, and that looked like progress to Fitts and me. Moreover, we were engaging the enemy away from the villages and towns.

Until we switched tactics, FOB Normandy routinely took incoming. Rockets. Mortars. Occasional sprays of small-arms fire. It was pure harassment, designed to keep us on edge, and for that reason it was truly annoying. After we started taking the fight to the enemy inside those palm groves, the attacks on our base tapered off. No doubt, the best defense is a good offense.

We began going out into the breadbasket to ambush our ambushers, lying in wait through long nights to find those insurgents who planted the roadside bombs we'd encountered. We got to them before they got to us.

We would come back from these missions to endless paperwork, writing "Serious Incident Reports" documenting what we'd done. We called them SIR reports, and the NCOs considered them one of the worst aspects of our job. We'd return from a firefight totally exhausted, only to face hours of this paperwork we knew would be scrutinized through the entire chain of command. After that, we'd have to debrief Captain Sims and often Command Sergeant Major Faulkenburg, our battalion's senior NCO.

More than once, Command Sergeant Major Faulkenburg would look at us in mock concern and ask, "Why is Alpha Company killing all the terrorists in Iraq? And Third Platoon every day, you are back with another blood count!" The truth was, he was busting with pride that his guys had found a groove that was both aggressive and effective. Then he'd ask for details, peppering us with questions. He'd ask for photos, study maps and diagrams we provided that detailed the firefights. When he finished, he would say to us, "Okay, good kill. Good kill."

Our successes resonated up from Battalion to Brigade and Division. They were bright spots in an increasingly grim situation. Our company, our platoon, was out making a difference. The fanfares and accolades rarely trickled down to those of us doing the actual fighting, but we heard and saw the pride that our small victories generated above us in the chain of command.

Except for Captain Sims. He never seemed satisfied with what we were doing. After every mission, he'd sharpshoot us, second-guess our decisions, force us to look at the event in different ways. His intellectual horsepower had few equals in the battalion. He was deliberate and insightful. He could see aspects to situations nobody else could.

He was also an enigma. He had taken over our company just before we deployed to Iraq, when Captain Walter fell seriously ill. He'd been the battalion's operations officer prior to the change. We rarely saw him before then, except when we were on ranges where he was acting as the observer controller (OC). On those days, he came across as easygoing, very chill and low-key.

In command of Alpha Company, he was detail-oriented and often focused on fighting a full-spectrum counterinsurgency. I wanted to kill bad guys. That was my path to victory. Every dead insurgent meant one less asshole shooting at my men. I was infantry. That was our job. We weren't cops. We weren't forensic investigators. We were infantry—the wrecking crew America deploys when shit needs breaking and enemies need killing. That spring, this was my mind-set and litmus test for victory. Sims had a different view. The path to victory, as he saw it, was to make friends of the local Iraqi power brokers. Bring them into the Coalition, and the attacks on us would cease. He was convinced of that. The truth was, there was growing foreign intervention within the insurgency that operated outside the local Iraqi social and political structures. Supported by Iran and by Al Qaeda, these networks were just taking root throughout Iraq. No amount of tea drinking with the local elders would have an effect on those nodes in the insurgency. At least, not in 2004.

As we removed insurgents from the enemy's ranks, Captain Sims didn't seem any more pleased with us. In fact, on many occasions, he rode me pretty hard for taking risks and being aggressive. We rarely received any praise from him, though we were getting it from elsewhere in our command. He was like a father who was never happy with his kid, no matter how many A's he got on his report card.

I wanted to support him. I wanted to execute his intent. I just couldn't figure him out.

In those early months, both Captain Sims and I developed stomach ailments. A lot of the men did, and some struggled with them for years after the deployments. Sims and I were pretty sick at times, and we ended up in adjacent porta-johns on many occasions after patrols.

Those plastic walls held no secrets. We could hear everything going on next to us. Such moments stripped us down to our barest, most elemental humanness. In a weird way, that created a vulnerability that opened a different level of communication between Sims and me that transcended the barriers of rank and place within the company.

Many times, we'd endure the punishment of our stomach problems and talk through the thin walls about things we would never have discussed in uniform face-to-face. It was almost like a confessional.

Erich Maria Remarque's timeless classic, *All Quiet on the Western Front*, touched on this phenomenon in a scene where the main characters sat side by side in the open, suffering from dysentery-born diarrhea together. It was a great equalizer, one that demolished all sense of modesty and propriety. A century later, in a different war in a different country, I learned that Remarque had been spot-on.

One night, I walked over to the company headquarters area in search of a less rancid porta-john. I had discovered that the A Company 2-2 Infantry headquarters held the most humane and clean porta-johns in our area, and would often head for them when I knew I was going to be trapped by my bowels inside one for any length of time. I was almost doubled over with stomach pain and needed relief, fast. I found one, plunged inside, and sat down just in time. A moment later, I heard the door to the shitter next door swing open, then bang close.

I could tell at once that it was Captain Sims. He recognized me right away, too.

"How you holding up?" he asked, his voice reverbing through the echo chamber of his porta-john.

My gut sounded like a trombone section. My face was squeezed in pain.

"Never better, sir."

We made small talk for a while. Nothing major. News from home. Sims had a son and wife waiting for him. He and his wife were deeply in love. He spoke of her often.

It had been a rough day. We'd been out in the AO, in the heat, our bodies locked away in our Bradleys, which were like ovens in the Iraqi sun. We'd grow nauseous from it, our heads would pound, and sometimes we'd get dizzy as we reached the edge of heat prostration. I was in a foul mood. Frustrated. Angry. Mad at the world. I didn't want to banter pleasantries. I wanted an answer.

"Sir, I need to ask you something."

"Go ahead, Sergeant Bell," he replied.

"You have me for a year. You point me anywhere and I'm going to do what you tell me to do. You are my commander. That's holy to me. I will never question anything you say or do. I just get the feeling you don't want me to do what I do best. We're killing bad guys. Everyone else loves what First and Third Platoon are doing. You don't. How do I make you happy and do my job? What do you want from me?"

Captain Sims didn't hesitate. "You're not here to make me happy. I don't care about being happy. We're here to win a war. And we can't kill our way to victory in this one. You don't understand what we're facing."

This really upset me. *Don't understand?* I saw it every day. I was getting shot at from palm groves, our guys were being hit by IEDs all over the province. I was a subject matter expert on combat in Iraq by then. What was he talking about?

"Wow. Okay, sir. I am just telling you, whatever you ask me to do, whatever your intent, I will make it happen and not ever take a step backwards."

"You create four terrorists for every one you kill and the locals witness."

"Sir? They're shooting at us. What would you have us do?"

"We're here to win the war, Sergeant. Not win the year."

I'm trying to get my men home. I can't do that and let assholes shoot at us when there are civilians watching.

Before I could respond, he said, "Sergeant Bellavia, I need to talk to you about something now."

"Go ahead, sir. I'm not going anywhere."

"What you do out there will affect the men under your command for the next ten or twenty years. Maybe forever. Are you thinking about that?"

"Of course, sir. I know my men more than their own families do."

"That's not what I'm saying."

"I'm doing everything I can to make sure they get home to their loved ones, sir. That's why I fight the way I do."

"Sergeant, do you acknowledge that this job is something that will have consequences down the road?"

I thought we were tougher than that. Combat changes you, yes. Consequences down the road? I was dealing with the people trying to kill my men now. What did ten years from now matter when in the next moment of the here and now we could be dead?

I was pissed now and disengaged. "Sir, do you have any wet wipes?"

I heard his door open, then smack shut.

"Left them out front for you. Good night, Sergeant Bellavia."

"Good night, sir."

4

THE GIANT OF KHAILANIYA

KHAILANIYA, IRAQ — MAY 2004

"BELLAVIA, ABSOLUTELY NO CONTACT tonight. Do you understand?"

Our platoon sergeant, James Cantrell, was in my face, eyes lasered on mine. I knew that look. It was the *I'm not messing around here, Bellavia* look I'd seen many times before.

So I messed with him.

"Sergeant Cantrell," I said, "*absolutely* is a strong word. I mean what if bin Laden shows up on a moped. Or I got Zawahiri in a black two-door Opal. I gotta do what I gotta do, Sarge."

To his credit, Cantrell kept his composure instead of flaming me to a rare crisp. Believe me, that had happened before. He rode us hard, worked us relentlessly in training, and demonstrated over and over in combat that he was a man who always had our backs. He was tough, sometimes brutal, but fair, and always put the well-being of his men ahead of everything else. A Soldier only messes with people they like or respect, and our platoon sergeant was often in our sights. One time, some nameless staff sergeant who looked a lot like me spiked his coffee with two tablets of a Viagra knockoff. It was called Miagara. As he spent six hours with an erection on patrol, his mood went from crusty to almost maniacally furious, stoked by noticing our side-eyed glances and barely concealed laughter. He never figured out what happened, or who had done the deed. It was like pulling one over on a revered older brother.

The truth was, we loved that man. We feared his disappointment more than anything an enemy bullet could do to us.

On this night, he needed me to take him seriously. "Bellavia, zero action. If fired upon, get down and radio me first. Understood? This is coming from command, and I am telling you straight. No contact."

A little late, I realized this was not the time for jokes. Battalion assigned us to a blocking position in Khailaniya, just off RPG Bridge, while other TF 2-2 elements gave an undersecretary of defense a tour of Sinsil. Another VIP dog and pony show. We were the outer cordon, supposedly to ensure that no bad guys flowed into Sinsil while our DoD bureaucrat got eyes on the world of counterinsurgency firsthand.

For whatever reason, command didn't want our guest to see any actual combat. That would not have put the right spin on what we were doing in Diyala.

"Yes, Sergeant Cantrell. I won't let you down." My voice conveyed the seriousness of that promise.

Cantrell was not fully convinced. "Repeat it."

I blinked. This was something I'd done to my lower enlisted soldiers, never to an NCO. I felt a little stung by the order. "If fired upon, I will radio you and tell you that I am getting shot up before I return fire."

Cantrell nodded, then added, "Look, we don't lose no one tonight, okay? Don't go out there looking for a fight, either. Get it done."

I knew Cantrell hated this order more than I did. He was born to mix it up with bad guys and had no regrets at the firefights we'd initiated. Dumping this restriction on me had to have been dumped on him by command.

We mounted up in our Bradleys and rolled out of FOB Normandy. Inside these armored ovens, sweating copiously in our full battle rattle, I sat side by side with members of my squad. They were tired, unhappy, and entirely fed up with the *Groundhog Day* life we'd been living through these past months. There would be more bad guys to shoot tomorrow after the task force's VIP climbed into his helicopter and headed back to Baghdad. He could fly back to D.C., tell the suits in the Pentagon that Sinsil had been pacified. Our strategy was working, since everyone knew that as Sinsil went, Muqdadiyah went as well. Then Baqubah after that, which meant the entire of Diyala Province. Right?

I really wanted to believe that. But a part of me I didn't want to acknowledge suspected that logic was predicated on flowcharts and graphs designed to reinforce the narrative, not understand the reality on the ground.

I explained Cantrell's order over the roar of the Bradley's engine. My squad stared at me as if this were a joke. To reassure them, I leaned forward a bit and shouted, "Guys, of course we're not going to not shoot back. The goal here is to avoid contact."

They didn't appear reassured. It is difficult enough to take incoming fire. Being told you can't shoot back without permission triggers plenty of worst-case scenarios where friends go down because you have to wait for an order that may or may not ever come. In the clutch, I wouldn't let that happen. I'd have rather taken the heat for violating an order than lose somebody that way. It would have devastated us.

We reached our blocking position and dismounted. The platoon's Bradleys fanned out around both sides of RPG Bridge. My squad took up positions just south of it on the Khailaniya side of the canal, finding a house we'd used in the past that had once been occupied by several known insurgents. From the windows, we watched the night, Knapp next to me with a wad of Copenhagen dip tucked under his bottom lip. As the first hour wore on, Knapp fell into a routine. He'd suck a little water from his CamelBak's mouthpiece, swish it around in his mouth for a few seconds, then spit it out with a slosh of dip juice. It was a ritual I'd grown accustomed to during the many nights we'd shared together like this one.

Around us in the house, other guys crunched sunflower seeds between their teeth. We gazed into the darkness with our night-vision goggles (called NVGs), seeing the world around us in shades of green.

Nothing. Not a soul on the streets. No movement around the bridge. Command was getting their wish for a quiet night.

Another hour passed. Finally, I radioed Sergeant Warren Misa, who had taken over Fitts's squad after Fitts had been wounded and sent back to Germany. Misa was seeing the same tranquil scene as we were from his position.

We decided to go link up with Misa's squad. I whispered the order to my guys to pack their gear. They made ready to move from the house. A second order whispered, and we filed out the front door into the night, where we instinctively established a patrol formation. We stepped off and headed for Misa, moving as silently as possible.

Something to my left caught my eye. I swung my head around and stopped, peering down a long road flanked by the occasional ramshackle building. There, in the middle of the street, stood a lone figure, perhaps two hundred and fifty meters away. A single street-light blazed between us.

He stood unsteadily in front of a dilapidated concrete house I knew well. Our intel shop had tracked several wanted insurgents to it earlier in the spring. Our platoon had been ordered out to go get them. We took the house down, only to find it empty. We waited fifteen hours for the bad guys to return as a firefight broke out on the far side of the bridge—the only one in the area my squad missed that spring.

It looked like the figure in the road had just exited that house. Middle of the night, known bad-guy lair. Dude alone in the street in the darkness. It looked suspicious as hell.

I watched him through my NVGs. He shouted something, then took a stumbling step farther into the road. He tripped, nearly fell, but caught himself. As he did, something flared out from his hip. Whatever it was, it looked attached to his belt.

A drunk Iraqi was not an uncommon sight, despite Islamic laws against alcohol. We'd also seen plenty of them high on drugs, likely opiates. Through the AO and Baghdad, Americans manning traffic control points had to make split-second decisions as cars raced at them at night: suicide bomber or stoned Iraqi driver out of his mind on heroin? Those were tough calls—the toughest.

This guy was on foot, so he was probably harmless. Just a guy trying to find his home in the dark.

Except, he'd come from that house we knew well. So I kept my eyes on him as the squad waited in the street around me, my instincts warning my brain.

He turned and lurched up the road toward us. We were cloaked in darkness, and he had no night vision, so we were out of his range of sight. As he moved, he suddenly flailed his arms skyward, as if punching an invisible enemy. A moment later, he let loose with a chilling primal scream.

Turn around, dude. Walk back into the night and leave us be.

Less than a hundred meters away now, he was growling. His movements grew jerky and spastic, and he was clearly unsteady on his feet.

Ten more meters and he passed through a wash of dim light from the streetlamp overhead. I saw his face, broad and thick-browed. He was an enormous man—the largest Iraqi I'd ever seen. Most of the locals were slight, under six feet tall. Teenagers here looked about the same size as eight-year-olds back in the States. They were undernourished, especially the populations out here in the rural part of Iraq.

This guy was a veritable giant. I guessed he was six foot eight at the minimum.

He stopped, drew himself up, and slowly turned his head until his eyes were locked on me. There in the edge of that wash of light down the road from me, I saw rage on his face. He'd seen us, nine heavily armed American Soldiers in his way ahead. Most civilians would have turned and left at that point. Not this giant.

He uttered a guttural sound—maybe words so slurred I couldn't understand. Then he reached to whatever was attached to his belt and dangling down his hip. It took me an instant to realize it was a scabbard.

Whatever happens, we're not shooting anyone tonight.

Still watching me, he held the scabbard in one hand. With the other, he drew forth a sword—thirty inches long with a concave, curved blade. I recognized it as a scimitar, a type of edged weapon that dated back centuries here in the Middle East.

It caught the light as he swung it up to a ready position.

I looked over at my men. "Do you see this shit?"

Knapp spat dip juice into the dirt. Ruiz shook his head in disbelief.

"Um, SSG Bell, this guy is looking pretty serious," Ruiz said, adjusting his posture.

"Hey, SSG Bell, what are we doing here?" Knapp asked.

"This guy's enormous and has a sword. Can we shoot him?" Ruiz asked.

A murmur went through the squad.

"We can't shoot him," I said, Cantrell's lecture in my ears. That didn't mean we wouldn't take precautions. I ordered my men to form a horseshoe around me, with each end pointing toward the drunk swordsman. They quickly complied, then took a knee.

"Keep your shooting lanes clear. Distance, men. Keep your lanes clear."

The men nodded. This all felt surreal.

The Iraqi was yelling again, still unintelligible. I started to wish we had our interpreter, Sammy, with us. Or Pat, our other 'terp, who later went with us to Fallujah. Both were with other elements of the task force that night. We were on our own to communicate with the Giant.

I started toward him, hands out to show I meant him no harm. My M4 carbine felt snug against my right side, where it dangled from its sling. On my left, I carried a slung Mossberg 500A shotgun, all chambered and ready to go.

In my best broken Arabic, I urged him to just go home. Everyone was good here.

He ignored my words and kept walking, swinging the scimitar. It raked the air in front of him, a long, thin tassel trailing off the handle. He was less than fifty yards away now.

After our arrival at Normandy, Sammy had taught me another Iraqi phrase. When the first warning was ignored, I used it.

"Aldhiyaab tuhajim alnisa'i. yurjaa aleawdat 'iilaa manazilikum litajanub altaearud lilhujumi."

Roughly translated, this meant, "There's a wolverine attacking women. Please go back inside your house."

The wolverine comment was something born from watching a bootleg copy of *Red Dawn* early in the deployment. Looking back, I'm not sure why it was funny to me back then. I had used it before, and people would hear my broken Arabic, then comply. I'd cleared more than one street in a moment of danger with that phrase.

Here on this night, with this massive Iraqi swinging a scimitar, probably loaded with Timothy Leary levels of narcotics, the phrase might have made things worse.

He stopped and listened to me. A moment later, he roared something like, "Ant alhayawan al'amriki 'ant hu alshaytan!"

Sammy had taught us a fair amount of Arabic. I'd listened closely to those lessons, and used the language often. I caught a little bit of what he'd said.

Something about American devils.

Oh shit.

He lurched forward, eyes focused only on me.

I said, half-aloud, "I think I just pissed off the Patrick Ewing of Diyala Province."

He swung the sword laterally in front of him again, cutting an arc through the air so viciously that I heard the swish of the blade. Had I been in its path, he would have decapitated me.

I called to Cantrell, "Blue Seven, this is Blue Two."

Our platoon sergeant's voice rang in my ear, "NO YOU CANNOT."

A pause. The sword-swinger started advancing on me again.

"Listen to me. Right now, Bellavia. I'm watching the entire thing. Go punch him, go detain him. I don't care, but do not engage the giant retard."*

I studied the approaching Iraqi. What I had taken to be the gait of a drunk could have been the staggering of a mentally disabled adult. Cantrell might be right.

Twenty-five meters away now. Still swinging the sword. I had a flashback to John Matuszak's legendary character, Sloth, from *The Goonies.*

No doubt about it now. A disabled man with a sword was advancing on me.

Does it matter if the man who lops your head off with a medieval

---

* The word *retard* has increased in offensiveness over the years, though it was stll plenty offensive in 2004. I hesitated to use it in this book and thought about excising it. But the truth is the truth, and we used rough words at times without care or consideration. It was part of living the life of an infantryman in a combat zone. Language that offends back home was used liberally in combat. Ultimately, I decided to leave it in to be accurate.

weapon has his full mental faculties? Dead is still dead, no matter the IQ of the person doing the killing.

"Bellavia. Do not shoot," Cantrell reiterated.

I was an infantry NCO. My job was to find, fix, and finish the enemy. We got the worst jobs and the toughest way of life, especially in wartime. We took pride in that and the whole "embrace the suck" phrase that became so cliché was part of our esprit de corps. We could take it, because we were tough, capable. Resourceful.

Nobody ever trained me on how to deal with this moment. I wasn't a social worker. I wasn't a cop. I had no less-than-lethal equipment on me, like mace or a Taser—hell, I was carrying a carbine and a shotgun on either shoulder just in case I needed a reminder of my role.

"You want me to punch this guy?" I asked, incredulous. I was five foot eleven and weighed a buck fifty after the brutal Iraq heat took twenty-five pounds off my frame. This guy was in his own size and weight class, way over mine. I figured he was at least three fifty.

I turned around quickly and saw Cantrell in the distance, his head and shoulders out of the commander's hatch of his Bradley.

"Sergeant Cantrell," I said, "I may have to shoot this dude."

Cantrell spat, "You will not shoot anyone. Aw dammit . . . you better. Aw no. Listen to me . . . . . . awwww hell! Bellavia, look, just hit him or something."

I glanced back down the street. The Iraqi giant was getting bigger by the second. We'd lost our window to evade him and slip off into the darkness. Plus he was screaming and yelling, making it clear we were in the area, which put us all at risk of being ambushed.

We would have to deal with him. I turned away from Cantrell and faced the Giant, trying to look as unmenacing as possible. As I did, Specialist Pedro Contreras appeared at my side. Back in Germany, he and I joined Alpha Company the same day. We became fast friends, and whenever I got promoted, I always pulled him into my squads. He was my age—twenty-eight—which made him a lot older and more worldly than the rest of the guys in the platoon. He'd grown up hard in Corpus Christi, Texas. Whatever he'd experienced there, it made him value loyalty.

"You're not doing this alone, Bell," he said quietly.

Contreras had been right there in the thick of it with me in all our firefights in Muqdadiyah and throughout Diyala. I trusted him implicitly.

We looked up the street together, then peered back. His eyes were set. Firm. He knew the stakes here. We were taking fists to a sword-fight.

Contreras glanced around at the guys. Knapp and Ruiz were closest to us, ready on a knee and waiting.

"We got your movement. On you, SSG Bell," Knapp reassured.

Still watching the Giant, I said, "Here we go again, Contreras."

"You good, Sarge?"

"As long as I got you. Come on, let's talk Mongo down."

"I'm on you," Pedro replied.

In that moment, after this show of loyalty, there was nobody I would rather die next to than Pedro Contreras. Without another word, we started walking up the road toward the oncoming giant.

5

THE FOLLOWING-ORDERS
BEATDOWN

KHAILANIYA, IRAQ — MAY 2004

THE SCIMITAR STILL GLINTED in the light of the streetlamp, now well behind the approaching giant.

With each step we took toward each other, the man's features resolved into sharper clarity. His arms bulged with muscles; a considerable gut hung over his pants. Snot flecked from his nose. Sweat streaked down his massive forehead. He clutched the sword in one hand, spitting as he screamed and growled.

I could feel my heart through my Interceptor Body Armor, or IBA. Jaws set, we matched his approach toward us, step by step, like some sort of crazy face-off between Wild West gunfighters. More like a Louis L'Amour novel remixed by Hunter S. Thompson.

Hands open and stretched out by my sides, I forced a smile. That seemed to make him more agitated. The sword cut the air. As we moved closer, the only sounds I heard were Contreras's breathing beside me and the swish of the blade as it slashed the air around the Giant.

As I watched the scimitar, I had a brief sense that we were walking straight toward a turbine engine. Something had to give here, and the house money was on Goliath.

And then, we met. A few feet separated us. The Giant stopped. There was a long pause as the three of us looked at each other. I saw the Giant's eyes, big yet unreadable. He'd gone quiet now. His sword was up in the ready position, but he'd stopped swinging it.

I tried to widen my smile as I made my voice as friendly as I could. "Ya sadiqi 'ant wa'ana linakun asdiqa."

Sammy had taught us that meant, "Hey, buddy, let's you and me be friends."

The man started screaming again, emitting a long, wailing cry.

I tried again, keeping my voice as calm and friendly as I could. The Giant was unmoved. The tip of his sword made little circles over his shoulder, as if he were summoning the resolve to swing it.

Contreras leaned toward me. "Hey, Sergeant Bell," he whispered from the side of his mouth, "whatever you just said, he wants none of it."

"Buddy . . . friends?" I tried again in broken Arabic. No response.

Hoping to distract him and break the tension, I broke character of the nice guy and shouted with venom, "Second squad! ON ME NOW!"

Behind me, I heard a gallop of bootsteps and gear clanking. A second later, my guys took a knee again in a horseshoe right behind us.

The sudden flurry of movement distracted the Giant for a moment. His eyes darted up and away from me as he watched the other Soldiers rush toward us.

Nice didn't work. Being as nonthreatening as possible didn't, either. The Giant's distracted gaze at the rest of the squad bought me a couple more seconds. The only thing left was to intimidate him into retreat.

His eyes shifted back to me. His sword arm locked back into the ready again, no longer distracted.

The sword's tip began to twitch again, like a cat's tail just before it pounced on a mouse. I saw the Giant's arm muscles tense. My fake smile evaporated.

He's going to swing. He's going to do it.

I either had to absorb the blow or strike first. No choice. I stepped into him as quickly as I could and jammed my open palm up into his jaw, hoping to knock him off balance or take the fight out of him. I struck him as hard as I could. This had worked in the past, stunning a person so you could get him on the ground and zip-cuff him safely.

My openhanded punch had no effect. It was like hitting a wall.

Cantrell's voice burst into my ear over our radios, "BELLAVIA, YOU ARE NOT . . ."

I thought about diving to the ground and letting the squad finish him. It was my worst-case scenario, and Cantrell's frantic voice bellowing at me made it clear we couldn't go there.

I had to try to subdue him myself.

I grabbed my M4 and swung the barrel into his right cheek.

The Giant roared with pain and rage. I heard the scimitar's blade clank against the ground as his arm dropped in surprise. Just then, my helmet shifted under the weight of my NVGs, mounted on its front lip. It fell forward, blocking my vision. I heard the swish as the Giant lifted the scimitar and swung.

I braced for the impact, throwing my head back to clear my view.

Contreras swore suddenly, and I wondered if he'd been hit. Before I could glance over at him, I was struck full in the face and helmet. My night-vision mount shattered, sending my goggles spinning away to be caught by their tie-down cord and left to dangle from my helmet.

The impact of the Giant's fist triggered a flash of light in my eyes. I lost all hearing, replaced with a steady ring.

I staggered and nearly fell. My situational awareness failed as my brain rebooted.

I opened an eye. I saw the road and part of the Giant's foot in front of me, and I realized that he'd knocked me to my knees. I was about to get the ass-beating of a lifetime, and I tried to brace myself for it.

I heard Contreras attack the Giant, striking him with the butt of his rifle. As he did, I tried to rise to my feet. One massive fist cannon-balled down onto my neck, pain reverberating through me.

The blow triggered an eruption of snot and blood out of my damaged nose. As my eyesight returned, the Giant grabbed the back of my gear and swung me, one-handed, laterally in front of him. It felt like I'd been caught by a crane's hook and was being flung around, helpless to stop it.

My feet dragged across the road. I bounced into Pedro just as he headbutted the Giant, driving his Kevlar helmet into the Giant's nose. The impact seemed to stagger him.

"Staff Sergeant Bell. . . . DO NOT SHOOT THIS MAN," came Cantrell's voice over my handset, still attached to my helmet's chin strap.

Pedro wheeled backward, clutching his face. "Bitch!" I heard him shout in alarm and pain.

I turned my head slightly, hoping to see what was wrong with Contreras.

Where is he hurt? Neck? Face?

Just then, I was hefted off my feet again. I felt like a toddler in a swing. One-handed, the Giant swung me left to right as if I were a rag doll. The entire squad watched their staff sergeant getting the shit kicked out of him.

Actually, it was worse than that. About then, Misa and our platoon leader, First Lieutenant Chris Walls, broke cover and ran to assist us, as they could see the situation was rapidly deteriorating.

As I was flung around, I caught a brief sight of the scimitar. The Giant had let go of the handle, but it dangled from his wrist and hand by the long tasseled cord.

He was still armed, and I was full out of audibles from my peace-keeping playbook. Yet I could hear Cantrell's voice narrating the brawl with his repeated warnings not to shoot our adversary.

Ruiz broke from the horseshoe and rushed to the rescue. He charged at the Giant and drove his rifle stock into his sword arm's elbow. Ruiz collided with me—or the Iraqi swung me into him. Nevertheless, the sudden strike paid dividends. I heard the scimitar clang to the ground, released from his grip.

I caught a glimpse of Ruiz's face—a fleeting one as I was thrown around by the Giant. It was enough to steady my own growing sense of panic. Ruiz's eyes were wide, brows low over them. It was his look of pure focus. When others would lose their heads, Ruiz remained in control, doing everything he could to save his squad leader. Those are life moments, burned forever into a Soldier's heart. It was the blood oath of loyalty.

I was dragged off my feet again. He was pulling me around from something on my left side.

My Mossberg. He's got a hold of my shotgun.

Holy shit. Ruiz wasn't just trying to get him to drop the sword. He was trying to get his other hand off my weapon.

The Giant twisted the shotgun upward. My head fell forward, and the shotgun's barrel came up toward my ear. I couldn't shake it free; it was slung across my vest.

The Mossberg didn't have a safety button like traditional shotguns, relying instead on a safety lever that sat on the receiver's bridge neck above the trigger well. That was designed for quick manipulation in a heated situation, but we'd learned that when it was slung, the lever would jostle against the rest of our gear and slip from *safe* to *fire*.

I always chambered a round when we left the wire.

A stab of horror. The absurdity of the moment drained away, replaced by the starkness of the danger I now faced.

The Giant yanked at the shotgun again. Ruiz tried to stop him, giving me an instant to propel myself to my feet. Ruiz bounced off me and lost purchase on the Iraqi's arm. The Giant pulled the shotgun, yanking me right to left this time.

I looked down to see his meaty hand gripping my weapon. A few more inches and he'd have an angle to shoot at my men. They wouldn't have a clear shot to return fire with Ruiz and me in the way. Pedro was nearby as well. This was a total mess.

He yanked again, and I stumbled, nearly falling. I lunged forward, forcing him to turn in order to maintain his grip on my shotgun. I couldn't run away. I could run around him, and that's exactly what I did. It seemed absurdly comedic, but it was the only thing I could think to do.

In close quarters, the decision to escalate to lethal force cannot be made by the most forward position in the engagement. That person doesn't have the full picture of what's going on and where the dangers lie. The biggest danger would usually be in a blue-on-blue accidental shooting. You've got to make sure that your Soldiers have clear lanes of fire and none of their bullets will hit a friendly. This took discipline and careful assessments of every situation we faced like this. It also took considerable trust in the men that they would know their roles, know their lanes, and keep their cool when everything was going to hell around them.

Cantrell was the farthest from the fight, but he didn't have the full scope of the danger we faced. I doubted he could see that the Giant had grabbed my shotgun. I had no time to convey that information, no way to even key my microphone, as both of my hands were locked in this life-and-death struggle.

I was slowing now, blood smeared across my face. My vision blurred, heart pounding. He was wearing me out, and I knew that even on my best day I didn't have the strength to deny him the shotgun. It was a huge mistake getting this close to him, giving him this chance.

I was out of moves. I played the last card I had. "Get a lane!" I shouted to my squad. "We have to shoot this guy!"

I heard the men ready their weapons. Buttstocks to shoulders. Everyone was staring down their barrels through their sights, waiting for the order.

Cantrell saw this, and I heard his voice bellow, "No! No! No! What the hell are you doing? Awwwww shiiiiiiit!"

I ignored him. In seconds, somebody would be dead or grievously wounded, and there was no way I was going to let this giant, mentally disabled or not, hurt one of my men with my shotgun. I'd rather have been collateral damage than let that happen.

The Giant set his weight on me, pulling me down as he wrenched the shotgun up. The Mossberg's sling ran through a loop on my shoulder. I was trapped now. Pinned in place, the barrel almost to my ear.

"Backblast! Backblast!" I shouted in desperation. It was an order normally given when using 84mm rockets to make sure nobody would be scorched by their launch if they were standing behind the tube. It was the only warning I could think of in the moment.

I got my right arm free just as he wrenched the shotgun another inch upward. My right hand found my M4 swinging on my hip. I grabbed it, my fingers sliding into the trigger well and flipping the selector switch to burst mode all in one motion.

My head was down. I was bent over at an awkward angle. I had no shot, and no way to break clear. He wrenched the shotgun out of my grip. Just as he did, I launched my left hand up and clutched his hair. He stopped, grunting in surprise. With all my weight and strength, I pulled him down by his hair, swinging my M4's barrel up next to my ear at the same time. The barrel touched his forehead, slid to his throat where I jammed it under his jawbone.

This was it. My last option.

I pulled the trigger.

6

THE RELICS OF WAR

KHAILANIYA, IRAQ — MAY 2004

THE CRACK OF MY M4 raced into the night. The Giant's hold on me went slack, and I fell to the ground. Before I could move, Contreras crouched and drove a knee into my back, pinning me down just as I was trying to get to my feet. I heard him trigger his own M4 right over my head. A split second later, Ruiz opened up, then Sucholas and the rest of the squad. M4s and SAW light machine guns raked the Giant until the bullets knocked him backward off his feet.

I saw him fall, blood pouring into the street around him as his body twitched in death's agony.

Contreras's knee eased up. Adrenaline still coursing through me, I tried to calm down and slow my breathing.

"Hey, you guys okay?" I heard Lieutenant Walls shout. Before we could answer, he turned and ordered, "Medic. Doc! Get up here and treat this guy."

A moment later, I saw Walls sprinting up to us.

I sat up, taking stock in the darkness. My ears rang. My vision was still blurred, and my nose ached from the Giant's blows. I looked around at my guys, weapons still pointed downrange.

Cantrell's voice came over the radio, angry and resigned at the same time. "Bellavia. Do you have any idea what's going to happen now?"

"Hey, Sarge," I said, choking out the words, "most importantly, we're all fine. Contreras looks like he got sliced, but it's minor."

"Goddammit," Cantrell stammered.

"Just want to point out that that escalated very quickly."

"Well, is he dead?" Cantrell asked.

I looked over at the Giant, whose sword was lying on the ground between us. Our medic, Doc Abernathy, crouched beside him, trying to assess which wounds needed treating first. There were too many of them to make this anything but an academic exercise. The squad didn't miss. He'd been hit probably eighty to a hundred times after I got free.

Doc would work on anyone, and in the midst of a fight never gave a thought to his own safety. He would charge into open ground as bullets crisscrossed around him to get to a wounded man. Or woman.

I once saw him working on a civilian woman who had been catastrophically injured after her car hit an American Bradley. He went through his checklist for burns, wounds, and fractures. He began running an IV into her. He started treating her wounds.

Frantically, he said to me, "I can't get a pulse. No breathing. I'm doing all I can."

"I know, Doc." Our medic was so focused that he didn't notice she didn't have a head.

On this night, he surveyed the damage our bullets had wrought on the Giant and shook his head. He looked back up at Lieutenant Walls, hovering just over his shoulder, and said softly, "He's not going to make it. Gone, sir."

I relayed this to Cantrell.

"Dammit."

We gathered ourselves. I got to my feet and the squad set security. Doc rummaged around and could not find a body bag big enough for the Giant.

We discussed what to do with him. We couldn't leave him in the street. Moving him would take half the platoon. There was no room for him inside our Bradleys—there was barely enough space for us.

There was only one option. Half dragging, half carrying him, the platoon got him back to Cantrell and Sergeant Chad Ellis's Bradley.

Ellis jumped out of the track and came to me, staring at the body. "Bell, I have never seen anything so totally insane as to what just went down. I saw the entire thing. And we will definitely be discussing it for perhaps the rest of my natural life. I thought you were killing yourself. Literally. Like you'd said, 'Screw it, I'm done here,' and you were trying to blow your own head off."

The adrenaline dump and parasympathetic backlash, combined with Cantrell's anger, left me in no mood. "Hey, we need to get him onto your track."

"I'm just saying it was nuts, dude."

"How are we going to get him up on the Brad?" I asked again.

Ellis thought about it. "Maybe call in a wrecker and crane up there?"

There was no time for that. In the end, the entire platoon converged on the Bradley, pulling, pushing, lifting the Giant until we were able to flop his corpse under the front of the turret. No matter what we did, part of his body sagged into the gunner's open hatch.

I looked over to Cantrell's track to see our platoon sergeant calmly smoking, only his head and shoulders out of his turret hatch. He had a small smile on his face, telegraphing his ongoing incredulity at all this.

He saw me glance his way, and he keyed his mic. "Bellavia, what am I going to do with you? That's the biggest Haj I've ever seen in my life. Corn-fed Sinsil boy."

The night had turned into a horror show. We were shaken, making dark jokes to deal with the situation. We laughed nervously, but I think all of us suspected this one would linger for a long time.

Ellis mounted back up into his Brad, only to discover the Giant's blood seeping through his hatch, spraying him as he prepared to move out.

I went back to the scene of the fight as everyone was getting ready to leave. The sword lay in the street, shiny but spattered in a few places with blood. I stared at it for a long moment. We never left weapons behind for the enemy to recover and exploit. This was the first sword we'd encountered.

Nobody will ever believe this.

I picked it up and studied it. Sharp. Well cared for. It was a family's treasure. I walked over to where my guys had stripped the scabbard off the Giant and gently slid the sword in place. I could see someone from Battalion would probably steal it, make it their own war trophy. Perhaps they'd put it on their Iraq-War-memories wall at their house after we got home, without any idea that the sword served as a reminder of this night's insanity, and the lessons to emerge from it.

I couldn't bear that thought, though we had to bring all captured weapons back to the FOB and document them for our report. After the report was filed, I thought maybe we could keep it in the NCO room as a reminder that when everything was going to hell, my squad had my back. That kind of loyalty you can never buy or borrow. It is earned with respect and trust. I can't think of that night without seeing Contreras pushing me back to the ground to ensure I was out of harm's way as the squad finished the job.

We mounted up and began a slow drive to the Joint Coordination Center, or JCC—basically a combined U.S. Army, Iraqi police station—in downtown Muqdadiyah.

Our tracks ground across the broken dirt road, jarring us and throwing our bodies against each other as we went. A full squad of Soldiers in full battle rattle barely fits in the back of these tracks. After what just happened, we were sweaty, filthy, smelling of body odor and the coppery tang of blood.

Suddenly Cantrell shouted over the radio, "OH MY GOD, ELLIS! HE'S ALIVE!"

Ellis nearly shot out of his hatch. Thoroughly freaked out, he twisted around to look above and behind him to see the Giant's unmoving corpse.

"Not funny, Sarge," he growled back. "Really not needed right now."

A moment later, Cantrell did it again. Ellis went ballistic. "This is funny to you, Sarge? I got a dude bleeding all over my shit here. He's eight feet tall and has two hundred holes in him. Thanks, Sergeant."

Cantrell eased off, puffing on his cigarette and randomly breaking out into fierce laughter. For a guy brought up in a U.S. Army cocked and ready to face a conventional threat like waves of Russian tanks churning for the Rhine River, the idea that his platoon would some-day square off with a giant wielding a medieval sword seemed to defy reality.

All our platoon sergeant could do was grab on and ride the whirl-wind. Iraq did that to all of us. Those who didn't adapt, who didn't find some intellectual and emotional flexibility, would ultimately be broken by these reality-defying moments.

It was a world turned upside down.

At the JCC, we pushed Goliath's corpse off the Brad. It fell into the street at the feet of the police chief, who stared at it in shock.

"What fuck is this shit?" he asked in broken English.

Cantrell replied, "Ali Baba. Big Ali Baba."

We returned to FOB Normandy to face the wrath of our chain of command. Both my eyes were shiners, bruised and blackened by the Giant's massive fist. My nose was still bleeding, though miraculously unbroken.

Word quickly spread through the company, then the task force. I couldn't get away from it. Jokes were being made. Incredulous spins on what had just gone down were told and retold among the men. I just wanted to write the reports I knew I had to write and get to bed.

Our company first sergeant, Peter Smith, sought me out and asked, "Bellavia, why did you shoot a retard?"

"Look, First Sergeant . . . he grabbed my shotgun. It was red direct. The safe on the Mossberg is on the receiver above the trigger well. I couldn't reach it. I had no choice."

"So this is Mossberg's fault?" Smith asked.

Exhausted, all I managed was, "No, First Sergeant. It was shitty is all I'm saying."

"Sounds like."

He reached out suddenly and grabbed my head like a father examining his son after a bruising schoolyard fight. His eyes grew stern as he studied me.

"He did this to your face?"

"Yes, First Sergeant."

The examination continued. I could see him getting angry. He hated seeing his men hurt outside the wire on patrols.

"Anything broken? You solid?"

I didn't answer directly. Instead words tumbled out: "I'm sorry, First Sergeant. I'm sorry. I shot this guy when you didn't want anything to happen in sector. I really didn't want to do it. I had no choice."

"This guy, he had a sword? He hit one of your boys with it?"

"I think Contreras got clipped. Or maybe punched, or the sword just missed him. I'm not sure."

Smith continued to stare at me. "Why did you tell him there was a wolf on the loose?"

"First Sergeant, I believe I said wolverine. But that isn't important. I was trying to get him to go back inside the house. I didn't want a confrontation."

"I am going to Battalion and your ass is coming with me to explain this to Ramrod Seven. You still got the sword?"

"Yes, First Sergeant."

"Let me have it."

I retrieved the sword from my gear and handed it to him. He looked it over and shook his head slowly. "Come on. Let's go."

I followed him to his Humvee and climbed inside. Ten minutes later, we stopped at the battalion HQ. When we walked in, Command Sergeant Major Faulkenburg was sitting drinking coffee around a pouch of Red Man tobacco tucked in his cheek. He didn't look happy to see me.

"What. The. Hell. Did you do out there tonight, Sergeant?" Faulkenburg demanded.

Before I could answer, First Sergeant Smith said, "Bellavia shot a giant retard. To be fair, the retard kicked his ass pretty good. Look at his face, Sergeant Major. He got him good."

"This true?" Faulkenburg asked me.

"Yes, Sergeant Major."

Smith added, "The whole goddamned squad shot him. Look, those are good boys, and Bellavia does a good job with them, Sergeant Major."

I started to get the feeling they had already heard from Cantrell, knew the details, and were busting my chops. I only hoped Captain Sims would be so inclined.

"I am sorry, Sergeant Major," I said.

"Don't be, Staff Sergeant Bellavia. You did well tonight. Good kill," Faulkenburg said.

Then Smith turned to me. "Look, Bellavia. Everyone. I mean everyone—this entire FOB—is laughing at you right now, homie. Half of them would've shit their pants in that position, I am sure. You always do good. Solid. But you're gonna get your balls busted. Don't let it bother you."

It has always bothered me.

Back in my kitchen, safe in time and place in New York, I swam up from that memory of violence into the tranquility of my childhood home. The words glowing on the laptop screen were a digital manifestation of those memories. The recollections had poured unrestrained out of me. And as I wrote, I'd gained steam as one memory triggered another, like lost bread crumbs leading me back to places I never wanted to revisit.

At the same time, I missed Iraq in that moment more profoundly than I had in years. Every time we left the wire, we faced something new. We lived on an edge long since blunted here at home by the peace we enjoy. That edge made us feel more alive than any life I'd found here in New York.

Yet, the memories of that night meant something different to me now as I'd matured and grown beyond the person I was at age twenty-eight. Back in 2004, I was harassed and teased over this event. The story morphed and grew into an urban legend, passed from Soldier to Soldier until there were links in a chain that stretched far beyond the horizon of those who were actually there that night.

I took the ribbing. I joked with them. But in 2004, what bothered me most was I'd lost the fight. It was humiliating. In front of my own squad, I resorted to scrambling around like a cartoon character to avoid being killed by that giant Iraqi.

I stared at the words on the screen. Could this be why the Army was investigating me now after all these years? Could somebody have reviewed the incident and decided I hadn't given the Giant enough warning? That we could have de-escalated the situation somehow? That this had gone from a tragic and insane moment to a war crime?

I didn't know. Stranger things had happened. What I did know was this: In 2004, our battalion investigated the incident thoroughly. Captain Sims, initially furious at what happened, backed off when the battalion report concluded the shooting was a clear case of self-defense, one that had been witnessed by more than twenty other Americans. Sims dropped the matter, but it damaged my relationship with him. It remained strained until our intra-theater deployment to Fallujah later that fall.

Sims was right about one thing, though. The shooting of the Giant directly damaged our efforts to win allies in the local population. In the days after the fight, we discovered the Giant was a local favorite of the townspeople in the area. He had been mentally disabled after all. They looked after him, and were rightfully outraged by his death. It fed into the growing hatred for our presence and destroyed much of the goodwill that Captain Sims had carefully tried to cultivate. The fallout had a whole ripple of unintended consequences that affected us for the next five months.

After I handed the sword over to First Sergeant Smith, I assumed I'd never see it again. One day later that summer, I returned from a mission to find it sitting on my bunk back at Normandy. I tucked it away and guarded it. It was a testament to how insane our war had become, as well as a reminder that I'd lost that fight. I needed to do better, be better, on every patrol.

In the years since, I have built a collection of military swords that I cherish. They are symbols to me of a time when the courage required to wield them in combat was far different than on today's battle-field. The American Army is lethal and effective, thanks to its fire-power and technology. But in the clutch, when the fighting is down to point-blank range, firepower and tech are irrelevant. It becomes man-to-man, just the kind of fight in the days for which my collected swords were built.

My first and only relic of the war came home with me. I had never taken anything from anyone we had killed. It seemed sadistic. I was drawn to this sword. Not because it was a prize, but because it represented my Road to Damascus moment. Holding it made me feel dirty. So I learned to protect it. Respect it. It reminded me of Contreras's knee pinning me to the ground, the sound of the M4's barking. A fight lost, and a man enraged, confused, without his full faculties, bleeding out in front of my men. A memory that time will never extinguish, no matter how many times we try to ignore those bread crumbs back to the X.

The Giant's sword never ended up on my wall. When I got home, I hid it away in the depths of our barn with my Iraq War locker boxes. As I thought about it that morning in the kitchen, words stretching across my laptop's screen, I felt defensive about the sword now. Protective. It is the last tangible item from a life claimed by the garbled reality of war. An enemy can be a good man to people who love him. An infantryman can be honorable for doing his job, even if it requires killing the same man. It is the dual tragedy of war: there were no winners that night. The Giant lost his life. I lost a part of me that I'll never reclaim. It took a decade and a half of distance to understand that part.

For all the teasing, for all the black jokes and dark humor that got us by in the moment back in 2004, I only feel respect for the man today. After all, the Giant faced down an armored infantry platoon with a sword, and crushed me in hand-to-hand combat. Disabled or not, that took enormous courage, and he never winced at the odds. The brutal circumstances, the words lost in translation due to dysfunctions in language and mind, led to a confrontation I never wanted but will always have to live with.

Because of that, no other person will touch the Giant's sword. The least I can do for him is guard his memory, protect it and ensure that the callous laughter that still echoes in my heart from 2004 never disrespects him again.

As I sat at the table that morning, I had another thought. No outsider would see the nuances. Nor would they see the emotional damage this caused to me and surely some of the other men there that night. Bad actors and media always looking for a story to undermine the military make for a toxic combination. I shuddered. Could this be the root of the Army's sudden interest in me? If so, this would be a terrible, dark, and difficult time ahead.

7

THE BREAK-GLASS-IN-CASE-
OF-WAR SERGEANT

WESTERN NEW YORK — OCTOBER 2018

I GOT HOME FROM THE office late that Saturday afternoon just as another storm started to roll in off Lake Ontario. The wind picked up; more chilled rain began to fall. The day turned dreary and gray again just in time for an abbreviated autumn sunset. I went in through the front door and bolted it behind me. Inside, all was still and the sounds of the storm grew muted.

On the farm, there was always work to be done. If I needed to get out of my head, the daily requirements of keeping the place going could always do that for me. I'd get lost in the work and escape the million things bouncing around inside my head.

Clearing trees on the bank of the river, an artery to Lake Ontario, was the current mission. The slope dictated respect. The wet ground made it necessary to create a Swiss seat, a simple harness made of rope that was attached to an anchor uphill. I spent hours hammering away at some eastern hemlock and a monstrous ash. Each stump marked my progress. If I got hurt—and anything could happen out there—the authorities wouldn't have known where to look, outside of a buzzard pattern.

As tough as this was, actually because of it, the work made me feel alive.

By dinnertime, the twelve-hour-plus day was starting to wear me out. I went into the kitchen and fixed something quick, eating at the family dinner table where my mom had taught us the basics of manners back when we were all kids.

When I'd finished and the dishes were done, I checked the time. It wasn't too late in Mississippi. I went into the living room, sat down, and scrolled recent calls for Sergeant First Class Colin Fitts's number.

If fate had given him a chance, Fitts would have been an eternal warrior. The type of NCO who just needed to be pointed to the sound of gunfire. A switch would flip, and he'd be at his best no matter his age or the mileage on his body. Wherever his country needed him, Fitts would be at the tip of the spear. It was his element, the place where he was at his best.

American history is filled with NCOs like Fitts. Those gems have held the Army together through its most rugged hours. Men like Command Sergeant Major Bennie Adkins, who served twenty-two years in uniform, volunteering for three Vietnam tours while with various special operations units. From 1963 to 1971, Bennie Adkins bore witness to all the phases of the Vietnam War, just as Fitts had in Iraq. He kept fighting, even after being wounded eighteen times during the Battle of A Shau in 1966, where he killed almost two hundred Viet Cong and North Vietnamese with every infantry weapon system in the U.S. inventory, as well as a few Soviet ones as well.*

I have no doubt Fitts would have stayed in, done far more than his twenty years. He loved being infantry. When things got rough, he

---

* During the height of the battle, after being wounded more than eighteen times, Bennie picked up a recoilless rifle and fired high-explosive shells directly into waves of assaulting Viet Cong. He used mortars, machine guns, handguns, and grenades. Adkins fought for thirty-eight hours in close-quarters combat, then evaded the enemy for another forty-eight hours after that. He crossed into countries the United States wasn't supposed to even be in. At one point, his only salvation came when a Bengal tiger attacked the enemy, forcing them to break contact. Bennie waited forty-eight years to receive the Medal of Honor, only to lose his life to COVID-19 in 2020.

rose to his best, embodying the culture, tradition, and ethos of the NCO corps. Being at the tip of the spear comes at a price, though, and Fitts's body footed that bill. Ultimately, his wounds cut short his career.

That career had been an unnecessarily rocky one. For all his courage on the battlefield, he had a habit of sabotaging himself with his abrasiveness. No bullshit, no filter. Fitts was the single most genuine person I've ever met. No matter what the truth was or how hard it would suck to hear it, Fitts always stayed faithful to it. Not many people appreciate that level of honesty, especially when they outrank you. I respected it. Admittedly, others found him to be just an asshole.

Life built Colin Fitts like this long before he and I crossed paths in Germany before our Iraq deployment. He grew up *hard* in a community full of down-to-earth, leather-tough, resourceful farmers. Fitts's county was also home to the largest Amish population in the South. Born in the tiny, unincorporated township of Randolph, Mississippi, he'd been raised by his father, who'd been an Army helicopter pilot. He later flew commercially after leaving the service.

His mom left the family when he was still a kid. Despite knowing Fitts better than any person in my life, I knew nothing about her or what happened there. Fitts almost never even mentioned his mom. That wound ran deep. I could see he had learned to endure pain in part because of her and her absence.

His lack of filter created many headaches for him as an adult. He said the things nobody else had the sense, or courage, to say. He ignored convention as easily as he ignored rank. If he felt slighted, or took offense to someone—which was often—he'd carry a grudge and retaliate whenever he had the chance. He was endlessly creative in how he got back at people who crossed him.

If he'd been a diplomat, he'd have triggered a nuclear war.

As it was, he was well placed as an infantry NCO. In battle, he was cool and calculating, singularly focused and willing to do just about anything—at first. Getting shot three times by three different weapons during an urban firefight in the spring of 2004 left him grievously wounded. When he insisted on returning to us, half healed and still hobbled with a limp, he had grown more cautious and deliberate. With him back, we became Alpha Company's wrecking crew again. His newfound caution tempered my more reckless instincts. We balanced each other well, and in Fallujah we kept our squads alive when men were being killed all around us.

He fought through three deployments, back-to-back, volunteering to return to Iraq to be with his men. From 2004 to 2008, Fitts had a front-row seat to the developments and changes in the campaign to defeat the insurgency. He saw every major phase of the war and fought in each evolution of its rules. From urban warfare to driving around in Humvees waiting to get blasted by IEDs, to the "heroic restraint" phase where shooting back at the enemy could result in an investigation, Fitts came to know Iraq as intimately as his Mississippi home.

After I left the service, more than anything else I missed being out there with Fitts. Almost immediately, I regretted my decision. Here at home, I felt out of place, far removed from Fitts and the battles that continued to rage. So I devised a way to get back there as a civilian. I went over as an embedded journalist and sought him out back in the Sandbox. It wasn't the same. He still slung an M4 and a shotgun. I had only a camera and voice recorder. It was like we were from different worlds. Instead of greeting me and welcoming me into the fold, he warned me to get out and go home. The war had changed while I was home in New York. During those brutal years, the troops were barely allowed to fight back. In my time, by contrast, we could be aggressive and take it to the insurgents. Killing an enemy who was trying to kill you was the best tonic for morale while in battle. Those subsequent deployments, with the increasingly restrictive rules of engagement and the insurgent's widespread use of cell phone–detonated IEDs, ensured the men couldn't dish out the kind of payback we did in 2004.

At the time, I was pissed at that sense of rejection. In time, I saw it as Fitts caring for me, trying to keep me safe. The two of us had long ago come to need each other in a way that other people who hadn't experienced shared trauma can't understand. More than once since Iraq, I knew I could endure anything, overcome anything, as long as Fitts was on the other side of a phone call. I know he felt the same way.

His first wife left him for one of his battle buddies in his unit. The divorce alienated his four children. As he fought a war to keep the homeland safe, his own home front crumbled. Like mine had. His just collapsed first.

By 2008, those four years of counterinsurgency, urban warfare, and rolling around the desert in armored, stiflingly hot Humvees had taken a savage toll on Fitts's body. On his final deployment he was dangerously close to a massive explosion that left him with a traumatic brain injury. The blast blew a chunk of his hand microphone into his skull and knocked him clean off his feet. Though he recovered, the explosion left him in constant physical pain.

Still, the heart was willing, if not the mind. The Army thought otherwise. In combat, Fitts shined, a *break glass in case of war* type of sergeant, whose true north always pointed toward the enemy. In garrison, he was every commander's nightmare: a bored, loose cannon who lost stripes almost as quickly as he earned them back.

The Army put its eternal warrior out to pasture. They medically retired him and, as a parting "gift," gave him a disability rating that ensured he'd never have to work again in the civilian world. Fitts had been in for fifteen years. He'd never really been an adult out of uniform. He stowed his gear, packed his boots in his locker box, and sent them—and himself—back home to Mississippi.

For the last few years, he'd been farming a plot of land outside of Pontotoc, Mississippi. Even though he didn't have to work, he never spent an idle day outside of uniform. He drove combines, grew everything from soybeans to corn. In between, he took the farmhouse he purchased and rebuilt it completely. During his downtime, he lovingly restored a 1971 Ford pickup. At times, he picked up construction gigs, building houses around his area. Somewhere along the way in Fitts's life, he acquired more knowledge on remodeling, construction, woodworking, and general handyman ability than anyone else I've known. At times, as I've tried to do work on my own place, I've called Fitts and had him walk me through each step over the phone.

As he transformed his physical world with his nonstop work ethic, he built out his personal life. He fell in love with a very good and faithful woman who returned his love in all the best ways. They married and he's raised her two daughters as his own. They gave him a second chance at fatherhood, and he's made the most of it.

Still, the war, and what he was in it, haunted him. Where I tamped the memories down and tried to forget, Fitts never figured out how to do that. He lived with the ghosts every day. For all he'd done for his new family, himself, and his home, nothing would ever be the measure of leading fine Soldiers into a fight.

That razor's edge where we lived in those moments made us feel more alive than we'd ever known. Back here, that vividness, the lushness of those days were replaced by the gray drudge of civilian life's infinite logistical battles.

Peace back home robs the warrior of his identity. Whatever we build in the aftermath of our time in battle will always be second best. It is just the reality we veterans face.

I stared at my phone, waiting for it to connect to Fitts's in Mississippi. He answered on the second ring.

"How you doin', Bell?" he asked in his deep southern drawl. His words were just on the edge of being slurred, which meant he wasn't too far into his nightly case of beer.

Without preamble, I dove right in. "Dude, I'm not sure what is going on. I think the Army might arrest me."

"Why the hell would they do that?"

"I don't know. The ghost of disgruntled Ramrods? The Army's coming back to destroy my life."

"That shit ain't happening."

He changed the subject to one of our favorites: the Amish. We both had Amish neighbors.

"Look, you gotta leave them AIM-EESH alone, Bell. Don't give us no trouble 'round here. They mind their own. They sweat a lot in their suits out in the field and shit. Why they got you worked up so much?"

Fitts knew that the only thing that remotely upset me and my quiet life those days was my Amish neighbors. Since moving into the area, they had tried to claim land my family owned. Their kids would sneak away and party in a grove of trees on my property. I'd find their empty beer cans lying around. One day, I'd been out working and discovered they'd even tried to move a posting fence so they could hunt on my land. I caught one of their teenagers using a thermal sight on his rifle. Amish. Using thermals. Hunting deer. On my property, no less.*

Of course, Fitts wanted to distract me. On most nights, this tactic would have worked. I'd have gone off on the Amish using my road as a drag strip during the summers. How many times had I come home to see them, carriages wheel to wheel, racing down the street—leaving chunks of horseshit in their wake?

This night, I wanted to stay on topic.

"Fitts, my issues right now are bigger than the Amish. I have done nothing wrong. The first incident was simple self-defense."

"What about the second? I don't reckon I was there for that one. Put the AIM-EESH on the phone. Let me talk to those guys for you."

"Fitts, it's not the Amish."

The second incident, the one that really triggered our company commander, Captain Sims, involved us severely wounding an insurgent who just happened to have a powerful uncle in the local Iraq power structure. That ugly reality of our war damaged our relationship with the locals and destroyed much of the progress Sims had made connecting us to that local power structure.

"Come on, Bell. The Army's got better things to do than stir around

---

* I fought them at every turn, and they detested me for it. To me, they were living in a reality TV show, *Let's Pretend It's 1849.* I refused to play along. They don't follow the rules everyone else abides by. If a person left a hot horse steamer on the road during one of our famous local Lyndonville, New York, Fourth of July parades, they would be fined by law enforcement. The Amish left James Bond–slicks of horse feces in their wake. If my kids rode their bikes without helmets, I would get a ticket as a parent. Amish kids wear straw hats and operate horse-drawn carriages on major roads by age eight.

One instance: I was getting roof work done and had a reputable contractor come and give me a quote. The next day, the Amish showed up trying to undercut the roofer. They actually said that they could save me money by having their children remove the shingles. I am sure my homeowner's policy would love the liability of having the Duggar family tumbling off my rain gutters. They also informed me they didn't have to dispose of the shingles according to the environmental standards of New York State. They're still playing by 1849 rules. Everyone else has moved on.

in all that shit. You know it. We all know it. Everyone there with you those two times'll set 'em straight. They all got yer back."

I didn't share Fitts's confidence. I sat there thinking about what happened after *House to House* was published. Instead of uniting us, the book fragmented some of us further. I wrote it for them, so this was a lasting wound. Two threatened to sue me. The rest of the crew loved it.

When Scott Lawson died, his family asked for the book to be buried with him. That touched my heart in a profound way.

Still, the Lawsons of the world are few and far between. The lesson learned from the book and talking with other vets who also wrote their memoirs is we have to deal with the law of fifty-fifty. Half the world will love you; the other half will try to destroy you. I learned the hard way to expect incoming, and to suspect people who would say anything to exact revenge on you for committing the crime of serving in a war and being someone whom people talk about.

So I didn't share Fitts's confidence. Maybe somebody in the company, outraged by *House to House*, would use the investigation as their mechanism for revenge. Or maybe that worst-case media scenario was playing out and the Army was just covering its ass.

We talked it over for a while, my concerns making no inroads in his confidence. There was nothing there. Sims and I had different views of how the war needed to be fought. Our internal conflict mirrored the greater one going on within the Army as it struggled to deal with the growing insurgency.

Nevertheless, Captain Sims considered disciplining me—until the Fallujah mission orders were cut. Then he stowed that talk because he knew he needed us. Me. Fitts. His door-kickers. This would not be Sims's kind of war. It would be ours, the NCOs of Alpha who understood the enemy was out there even if he did not wear a uniform. The enemy needed to be met in battle if this miserable war was ever going to end.

Fitts kept drinking through our conversation. I made no headway. He was not going to be concerned about whatever the Army was doing.

"What else ya got goin', Bell?"

I hesitated to bring it up. Fitts was the only one I'd ever talked to about the Man in White in Al Ali. He hated it whenever I did, but he always listened.

"I can't stop thinking about the Man in White, Fitts. I'm having those dreams again."

To my surprise, his good-natured humor vanished, replaced with an eruption of molten anger and exasperation. "If I have to hear this goddamned story one more time I'll kill myself. Keep on with your bitching. I can't take it. I did three years of combat. You are making me Lee Harvey unstable."

He listened anyway. He knew that was the moment I lost my confidence. I was like a kicker who missed the chip-shot field goal to win the Super Bowl, or the power forward who blows the shot at the buzzer. I replayed that moment over and over in the weeks afterward. Gradually, it ate away at me, like the tide sucking the sand from under my foundation. By the time we returned to Germany in 2005, I couldn't think of anything except Evan and that moment in Al Ali. I spiraled.

At first, Fitts teased me about it. When he realized how badly it affected me, he listened. That night, he listened again as I talked through every motion, every memory I retained from that moment.

I had missed the Man in White. How many Americans did he go on to kill? How many contact teams knocked on a wife's door to tell her she was a widow now?

I felt responsible for every one of those potential anguished moments here at home. He was right there, sixty feet from me. I could have hit him with a rock. But I couldn't hit him with an M4.

How many times have I prayed somebody else got him?

Fitts and I talked past midnight. That was our usual conversation. We were always incapable of short calls. A short call for us was two or three hours. We'd talk about anything and everything, the only constant being there was never any judgment and we both found wisdom in each other's insights.

"You know, Fitts, the Man in White's the reason I left the Army."

"Yeah, I know, man."

"I mean, him and Evan."

Fitts had descended into that place of most brutal honesty that is found in his tenth beer. He gets slow. Deliberate. Brutal. It was always the worst point of every call because whatever he had to say, I knew it would hurt. I also knew he'd be dead-on.

"My confidence was gone. My luck had run out, you know?"

"Bell, you wouldn't have been able to handle that second deployment."

"What do you mean? I wanted to be out there. With you."

"You were better off," he said again. His voice had that old NCO's authority tone. Meaning: *Case closed. Don't push.*

So I didn't.

I needed to get some sleep. Farm chores awaited before dawn, and then I'd have to be ready for my other job later in the morning.

"I gotta call it a night, Fittsy. I love you, man."

"Yeah, yeah, whatever." Emotion like that always made him feel uncomfortable. Tough shit. I was never going to miss an opportunity to tell him what he meant to me. Flaws and all. Fitts was family.

"Be good, Fitts."

"If I can't be good, I will be good at it, Bell."

We hung up, and I headed for bed, where once again, the Man in White inhabited my dreams.

8

THE LIE

OVER THE NEXT FORTY-EIGHT hours, whenever my phone rang I reacted viscerally. My heart rate spiked. I jumped like somebody had just scared me. I grew paranoid, and at times refused to even look at the phone. When I did, and I saw that Arlington, Virginia, area code, the sense of dread would surge back. I declined every call.

One evening late in the week, I was doing my radio talk show in Buffalo. My producer, Phil Kennedy, came over to me to hand me a note.

"Someone from the Pentagon called for you. Said they were from A1. And that they represented somebody in the Department of the Army named Karim Ernez."

The information made no sense, an actual game of military-to-civilian Telephone. I used to love it when civilians try to relay information from the Army. The only A1 the Army uses is on overdone steaks. Karim Ernez? Sounded like a new Dior cologne.

A touch of *Karim Ernez: When you need her heart to beat even faster . . .*

Certainly, this had to have been a hoax.

We cut to a commercial.

"What's this about?" I asked Phil.

"Dunno. They just said they needed to talk to you and it was urgent."

I thought it over. Was I supposed to believe that the United States government would attempt to call me at work?

No way. This was a hoax. A prank. It happened all the time at the station and this one was no different.

I ignored the message.

The next day, while we were discussing the important topic of accents and how long did a person have to live in a region before adopting it, our contest phone line lit up. At the station, we had several phone-in numbers. One set was for callers. Another was for guests we interviewed on the air. The last group was the contest lines. We would do the typical radio stuff: tenth caller gets tickets to Mannheim Steamroller. That type of thing.

That evening, we hadn't started any contests. Phil picked up the line anyway. A moment later, he called into the booth during a break.

"David, hey, this is the A1 calling about you. It seems legit, and this woman is pretty serious."

I took the number down and called it back after the show.

A gruff voice on the other end answered. Without prompt, she said, "Staff Sergeant Bellavia, there is a senior member of the Department of Defense that would like to set up a date to speak with you on the phone. This is something you have to take. I can't give you any more information about this other than to ask your availability. I can't even tell you why or whom you will be speaking with at the Department of Defense."

What. The. Hell?

I wasn't convinced. Not even attempting to hide my skepticism, I said, "Mmm, okay. How do I know you are real? What unit did I serve in and where?"

"Bellavia, David. 11B30. Syracuse, Recruiting Battalion. You had orders for Fort Hood. You then went to Fort Drum, but were sent back to Buffalo Main recruiting station. I would like to know more about that later, actually. Then you got orders cut for Vilseck, Germany. Thirty-six months all others tour of duty. You were in A Company 2-2 Infantry. Deploying to K4 Bravo in Kosovo, 2003. Primary Leadership Developmental Course, 2002. Operation Iraqi Freedom I and II, February 2004 to—"

"Okay, okay. You got it. I get it. You are legit."

"Be available tomorrow at noon. You will hear from us then."

The line went dead. Not even a goodbye, or even an "out here," something Army folks loved to do on the phone.

This was really serious.

I drove home wondering if I was about to be charged with something. Would there be MPs waiting for me? Would they recall me to active duty, putting me back in the uniform I loved only to be thrown into a military courtroom to face a trial for what happened at Khailaniya?

I couldn't sleep. The ghosts came again and haunted me all night.

I went out and hired an attorney. At noon, he and I sat in my car outside of a coffee shop in a parking lot near my home waiting for the call, cell phone in hand. Nothing happened. We sat for an hour. Then two, all the while my mind spinning scenario after scenario, gripped in every imaginable worst case.

Are these going to be billable hours?

Two days later, I received a call from the Pentagon asking to set up another time and date for whatever meeting was supposed to happen.

I agreed to another time. It came and went. No call. Somehow, the lack of communication had become even more stressful than the calls I'd ducked.

That night, I called Chuck Knapp, my old squad's A Team leader. He, Fitts, and Omarr Hardaway were the Ramrods still closest to me. I needed to get his insight into what was happening.

Long ago in combat, I learned to trust Knapp's judgment. Though only a corporal when we were in Iraq, he had the skills, coolness under fire, and split-second decision making to be an excellent squad leader in his own right. I could rely on him to always be there in a pinch.

That hadn't changed since he'd left the Army and raised a family. He'd gone from stalwart NCO to loving, exemplary father. In combat, I respected and trusted him. Now, as a civilian, I admired him. Tremendously.

"Hey, Knappy, why is the Army calling me out of the blue?"

"I don't know, man. I would be super nervous, too. What do you think they want?"

"I have no idea. This is freaking me out."

Knapp asked, "You think someone is talking shit out there? What could they possibly say we did wrong?"

We'd all heard the stories about other Soldiers accused of crimes in Iraq. Sometimes the Army threw them in prison for the crime of returning fire. It was an insane way to run a war, and one the enemy exploited all the time. They figured out our rules of engagement (ROE). In 2006, they learned we couldn't shoot back if we did not positively identify a weapon in their hands. So they would fire an RPG, or loose a burst from an AK, drop their weapon, and walk away from the fight knowing they were protected by our ROE.

Those weren't the rules of engagement during our deployment. But things had become so political and distorted when it came to the war, we'd come to expect the worst.

"Knapp, that's it. I'm thinking the same thing. Jail time. That's my biggest fear."

Knapp reassured me, "Bell, you are good. You have us. I am never going to let anything like that happen to you. We know what happened and we know who we are. Those things happen to other units that were doing stupid shit. This has to be something else."

Maybe Knapp was right. I'd gone through every firefight, every moment in combat, killing known threats without one ounce of guilt. I was a believer in American righteousness. We would have died for the civilians out there. We fought for them as hard as if they were our own. The only events that were controversial were because of politics—ours, and the local Iraqis'.

I exhaled a long breath, feeling some of the built-up tension drain away. "Thanks, Knappy. I appreciate you, man. Really appreciate you."

"Bell, I got you. No worries, okay?"

"Okay. Yeah."

"Hey, Santos and Swanson are coming out here to go rafting. You wanna come with us?"

"If I am not in Leavenworth by the summer. Count me in."

Knapp laughed. "That ain't happening, Bell. Never."

We said our goodbyes and hung up. I felt better. Knapp always had a way of keeping me balanced.

That good feeling lasted until my phone rang ten seconds later and I saw the Arlington number again.

I answered it and without preamble asked, "Look, ma'am, am I in trouble? What's going on here?"

"Staff Sergeant Bellavia, I can't tell you anything. I have my job and this is it. You are actually my responsibility. My name is Colonel Carrie Perez and you only speak to me. Trust me and everything will be crystal clear soon enough. There are protocols we have to follow. This is G1."

Okay, not A1, as Phil Kennedy detailed, but G1, which is Army personnel. I didn't really even know what G1 does at Army command level. Could there be some better news behind this? Like an award?

An award. That seemed a stretch. Fourteen years ago, there was talk of awarding me the Medal of Honor. Then there was talk of a Distinguished Service Cross. I was left out of Task Force 2-2's medal ceremony after returning from Iraq—the only member of my platoon not to receive an award during that event in Germany.

After I separated from the Army, I received a Silver Star and Bronze Star in the mail. The citation didn't match anything I'd actually done in Iraq. I was already dealing with the depression of leaving the Army. Reading the citation felt like being kicked while down. It felt like an afterthought—and a mistake.

Given that history, I had to go with the worst case here. Later that day, I called my attorney to have him run point with the Army from here on out. I didn't want to take the chance that something I said might be used against me.

I had seen that sort of thing during the war. It played out over the news, and through the NCO gossip network. Some disgruntled, disillusioned type would make an allegation. Somehow it would be leaked to the news. That triggered an investigation and sooner than later, the accused would find himself sitting at the defendant's table in a military courtroom without the same rules of evidence and procedure as a civilian court. That nightmare has played out too many times, and good Soldiers had to prove their innocence with little in the way of witnesses or evidence.

I was in full paranoia mode.

Two weeks passed before my attorney came back with a report.

"David, I have never dealt with something like this before. You are either going to be the next ambassador to France or you are going to jail for forty years. This is just a Jericho-size wall between us and what is happening. They won't give me any information, any indication of what's going on. I can't get anything. They just tell me over and over that no one has 'reason to believe' there is any trouble involving you. They will not confirm or deny any positive or negative disposition. They won't give me any other details."

Everyone I talked to in the military and government assured me that good news is never given this way. No one had a precedent. No one had experienced this before.

Yet, every one of these guys knew who Colonel Carrie Perez was at the Pentagon. The moment she was referenced, everyone stopped talking and got off the phone. Whoever this field grade officer was, she was important enough where no one wanted to be involved in her sphere of influence. It was wildly unnerving.

The last few weeks had been psychologically torturous. I went through the motions of my daily routine, my head back in 2004. Work was both increasingly difficult and a much needed distraction.

The following night after my lawyer checked in, Fitts called me back. His words were slightly slurred, so I knew he'd been drinking again. He greeted me with a note of seriousness that indicated he had something to tell me.

I started first, though.

"Hey, Fitts. I think something is up. I got the Army calling and they know everything about where I have been. They're asking questions that make me feel weird."

Fitts ignored that. "Bro, I gotta tell you something more important. You got me thinking."

"I just told you I think they are investigating something. I got an attorney and he isn't getting anywhere with—"

"Bell, I gotta tell you: you killed the Man in White."

"Huh?"

"The Man in White. Out there in Al Ali. You got him. The guy in the white man-dress in Al Ali."

"What?"

"You didn't miss him. You hit him like fifteen times."

I was speechless. My mind locked, trying to switch gears. A long, pregnant pause ensued. I could feel Fitts's tension through the phone as he waited for my response.

"What? What are you talking about?"

Slow, deliberate words, slurred but clear enough, came through my handset as I sat as still as a corpse in the living room.

"You shot him repeatedly. Sonny Corleone amount of times."

More silence on my end.

"Look, Bell, it wasn't all that impressive. You were practically six feet away."

Sixty-five feet away. I was about sixty-five feet away.

"I thought it was funny at first. And then you kept yammering on and on. And on—for weeks while we were in Germany. You wouldn't shut up about it. It was a joke. I didn't realize it broke your brain."

He let that hang out there for a moment. As crude as that was, he was not wrong.

"It was stupid. I am sorry. I made you think you missed him. And I should have quit giving you shit about it. Yeah, man, I got over there. He was done. If he hadn't been killed by your bullets, a few twenty-five-millimeter HE Gossard fired tore him into fun-size pieces. Lawson's 240s Z-patterned the area pretty good, too. I flipped what was left of him into a ditch. He was long done. I thought at the time you knew. I mean, you practically walked over him after the fight. You didn't see him, or you just weren't looking."

I tried to remember where I went after the firing died away. Mentally retracing my steps, I wondered how I never saw the remains of the Man in White.

Fitts continued: "You didn't miss him. Most of the guys know that. At least my squad did. I am sure Walter knew."

The more I thought about it, the more rattled I became. Maybe there was something more to it than the Man in White. Maybe that toxic memory became the focal point of all my heartache from the deployment. I felt it every day as my confidence and sense of self-worth ebbed.

What good is an infantry NCO who can't shoot? How does he lead men? How does he keep them safe in battle? How do you project utter infallibility to your men when you fumble the most basic task in a clutch moment?

I had shared all this with Fitts back then. I talked through what it meant to me. And I remembered the exact moment I realized that I was done. I had to go home and try to be a father. I'd known that if I went on another deployment, divorce would be the result. I wanted to save my family *and* serve my country. I realized I couldn't do both. I had a decision to make, the hardest of my life.

The Man in White tipped the scales for me.

Whatever had held me together through all those firefights—the aggressiveness, the decision making, and the fierceness I wanted my squad's response to be to any challenge—the wiring had short-circuited now. I realized that I wouldn't be the same leader I was in combat, not with the headspace I was in. Talking it through with Fitts, I saw the potential outcomes in combat if I were to reenlist. I'd second-guess myself in the moment, constantly. I wouldn't trust my own judgment, abilities. And I would be more focused on recovering my own self-esteem than the mission. There is no more obvious a recipe for getting good men hurt than putting yourself and your personal issues above the team.

Ultimately, the Man in White became my camel's straw. I shed the uniform and went home to Evan.

"Bell? You there?" I heard Fitts ask. His question pulled me back to the here and now.

"I left the Army because of this."

"You left the Army for a bunch of reasons. You wanted to be a father."

"Fitts, are you serious?"

"Yeah, Bell. It was a joke at first. You got him."

There was never anything to feel guilty about? Nothing on my conscience after all?

"Why would you do this to me?"

Silence.

A sudden rage swelled from the most wounded part of me. The man I trusted more than anyone else on the planet had lied to me. For years.

"Fittsy?"

"Yeah, Bell?"

"I am good. Leave me be for a while."

"I can do that, buddy. You super pissed, huh?"

"I mean a while, Fitts."

"Oh my gawd—"

I hung up the phone.

9

LIE AUTOPSY

I SPENT ANOTHER SLEEPLESS NIGHT lost. Ripping apart the catacombs of my mind and memory. I was physically ill trying to make sense of what Fitts had told me. He'd watched me free fall farther and farther downward in Germany until my self-esteem was gone. The award ceremony there in Germany steepened the spiral. In Iraq, I thought I was good at what the Army gave me to do. I thought we'd been making progress, hunting down bad guys and killing them. I returned and questioned everything I'd done. Maybe it hadn't been just the Man in White. I didn't need an award to validate who I was or what I did. If the Army gave me an Army Commendation Medal, or ARCOM, for Fallujah or a slap on the back, nothing could change the thought in my own head that I deluded myself into thinking I was something other than who I had actually become.

Fitts, why would you do something like that? What kind of human shit pile does this to anyone, let alone the one person who has always stood in the storm with you?

The months before the deployment, living in the barracks at Vilseck, I studied the NCO's craft with almost monastic devotion. No weekends out. No parties. No blowing off steam. I studied field manuals. I attended extra training exercises. I signed up for every school the Army had in Europe. I learned about explosives, the histories of counterinsurgency wars. I absorbed everything, from every subject matter expert in our division, and determined that by the time we deployed to combat I would have the skills, knowledge, and heart to keep my squad alive.

Al Ali made a mockery of all that effort.

Since then, I had wasted years of my life doing deep dives into my own psyche. Probing and imagining past actions, trapped in this feedback loop with no answers, and no resolution. I obsessed over those memories, that moment. With all the preparation, knowledge, and hard-fought experience, I thought I had failed. If I could fail with a royal flush in my hand, how was I going to measure up to anything in life, or any other clutch moment?

Years passed. I finally had to bury it all, my time in Iraq entombed in concrete in the deepest part of my heart. Between Fitts's revelation and the Army investigation, the lid had been pried off the sarcophagus. The memories poured out like angry spirits. *Remember us, asshole? Remember the guy in Al Ali? How about Khailaniya?*

They were out now, rampaging around my here and now doing all the damage they could.

It took me a long time to regain control over my emotions. Eventually, I calmed down and looked at the situation clinically. I put the Army's sudden reappearance in my life in the background for the moment and focused on Fitts.

Why would he do this? After all these years, why would he tell me now?

Maybe Fitts was trying to deflect my stress, being a good friend and just trying to make me feel better in a supremely stressful moment. Could that be it? That I did miss, and after all these years he just wanted me to finally put that demon to rest?

That pisses me off more. Like he thinks I'm weak and can't handle my business.

He is treating me like a scrub.

We did this all the time with stupid Soldiers.

Yeah, you hit that target. Good job, buddy.

Just get this shitbag off the range. Whatever it takes. I am done with this kid.

That actually made more sense than him letting me suffer for more than a decade.

In the morning, I decided to call him back. He'd be sober, and we could have it out, man-to-man, without the beer interfering.

He answered on the first ring. He sounded worried.

"Fitts. You have never lied to me before. Why did you keep this up for so long? It took a ton for you to maintain this story."

"It was funny at first," he answered.

"That's not good enough. Did the impact mean anything to you?"

"The more you talked about it in Germany, the more I realized you didn't want to do the Army thing anymore."

"That's not true! It was my life, Fitts! Our life. That is what *we* lived for."

His voice dropped an octave. "Hey, Bell, can I speak to you man-to-man here? Player-to-player? Pimp-to-pimp? Can I do that with you now?"

"Please."

A pause.

"Fitts?"

"That wasn't our life, bro. It was my life. You wouldn't have been able to handle those other deployments, dog. I mean the tours I did. The other guys did. No way. You would have taken three in the face. Or they would have tossed your ass in a prison cell. Everything changed, and the way you did business never would have lasted. Captain Sims's way of running the war won out to ours. That was the standard."

"You didn't know that in Germany!" I pushed back.

"Your heart wasn't in it, Bell. You needed to go home and be with your boy. That was where you belonged . . . and where you'd be . . . safe."

Safe? I didn't need a chaperone.

"I didn't want to see you go down like that. I helped you. We needed you home fighting for us in D.C. because nobody ever gives a shit about the Joes there. You couldn't do that dead. Now stop being a lil' bitch about it."

The words stung. I protested, "How am I being a bitch? I just wanted to know I wasn't cursed, that I could actually still do my job. I thought I missed a layup with time running out."

His response was like ice water thrown in my face. "Bell, if you couldn't deal with that, what makes you think you could have dealt with fifteen months of nothing but IED-related losses? We had units that never chambered or fired a round and still buried seventy kids. An entire deployment without firing one goddamned bullet."

His voice became strident, angry. The old frustrations were boiling up. "Can your brain even fathom that? No, it cannot. I will answer for you. No, it cannot. No one to shoot. Not one target. We'd wake up. Go out. Get hit. Pick up the pieces."

I heard him take in a deep breath. He was back there again. A bad place to be. "Pieces of our kids, Bell. Nothing to shoot back at. No revenge. Just get socked in the teeth and taste that sting all day. And then go out and get socked again, knowing we'd never get to hit back."

He was right. About all of it. That didn't make hearing it any easier.

"Shit changed, Bell. And you could never have conformed. You are far more bullheaded than I ever was. True that."

"You didn't know that in Germany!" I pressed. "I don't believe you. You would never do this to me. This is revisionist history."

Silence.

I held the phone, the wordless moment lingering as if it were a test of wills.

"Not you, Fitts. Fittsy, you would never do this to me."

"Bell," I heard him yell, "you were going to get yourself killed with all the risks you took. I know what it is like to go through that pipeline. I was the one who got shot, remember? You were still taking wild chances. I learned the cost of those. You never saw the reality of what happens when you push. It was a video game to you. You pressed our luck in Fallujah. Too far, more than once. Like in the house on November tenth, Bell. You got lucky. I got a list of names of boys who lost to the house in other situations."

He let that sink in knowing I hated hearing that.

"Well, let me tell you, Bell. You wouldn't have lasted fifteen minutes in 2006 on that second deployment. Not with your broken brain and the way we were ordered to fight. Or not to fight. Your luck was done, buddy. Fucking done."

"Are you saying you wanted me out of the Army? This was your way of manipulating me into quitting?"

"You had Evan waiting for you, Bell."

"You had four Evans at home, Fitts!"

"I never really cared for them, though. They are all horrible people. The worst ever."

"Horseshit. You did, too."

He laughed at his own sense of humor. "They love me more than I love them. Not sure these days."

Fitts had been a great father. This was him not dealing with the pain their exit from his life inflicted.

It felt like we were circling the truth, Fitts still deflecting. Why? The man with no filter, no diplomacy was keeping me from really getting to the bottom of this.

"You still hate me, Bell?"

"I want to shoot you in the face."

"Well, just know that if you tried to shoot me in the face, as of two days ago, you would have thought you had a fifty-fifty chance of missing. Now you know that when you shoot three magazines at the distance a basic remote control works at, you aren't a total failure."

He laughed. And I realized that I wasn't as mad at Fitts as much as I was embarrassed at how I saw myself. For years.

"That's funny to you?"

"That is hilarious to me. And to you. Come on, Bell. You're just being a stubborn child right now. You owe me a laugh when you pull your head out of your ass. I mean, look at the bright side. You can add another kill to your list. But you may be going to prison. That's a wash to me."

"Fitts, this isn't funny at all."

"You got self-esteem issues, Bell. Get over it. Everyone is Annie Oakley at fifty meters. It just takes a dude with balls enough to stand that close to take the shot. I am telling you, after our tour, no one got those shots anymore. And if you took one, you better have it on film. 'Cause they were tossing cats in prison left and right."

"I'm over it. Okay? I'm done with it," I said fiercely.

"Well a-okay, then. Happy day."

I said goodbye this time before hanging up the phone. I didn't think I'd be talking to Fitts again anytime soon. If ever. I felt betrayed. He had never lied to me. This cut to the bone.

I sat in the living room, staring outside at the sloping lawn beyond the windows. The little gazebos. It was the only thing I admired about the Amish. They could build a helluva gazebo. I wanted my children to love this place as much as I did. Wanted it to be their legacy, too, to be cared for with the same reverence I gave it now. I didn't see that ever happening. Not with all that had gone down since I came home.

That morning and through the following days, I gradually unpacked what Fitts was really getting at. I thought he'd been circling the truth. Gradually, I realized that our conversation went to the one place he was most uncomfortable: his own emotions. When I looked at what he had said from that context, everything started to make sense.

Your heart wasn't in it, Bell. You needed to go home and be with your boy. That was where you belonged . . . and where you'd be . . . safe . . .

Fitts had seen how Al Ali affected me and stopped teasing me about it. But he hadn't told me the truth because he wanted me to get out and go home. Al Ali was the crowbar he used to pry me out of the one life I had ever loved. He messed with my mind to get me to quit. And he did it because after everyone we'd lost in 2004 and the final, awful weeks we were in Iraq in 2005, he couldn't lose me, too. The bond between us was that strong, and if I had died, it would have broken him.

I remembered watching him get hit, over and over in Muqdadiyah. Limping, dragging himself to cover, still shooting as he moved. When he went down, I thought he was dying. It was like a tectonic shift seeing him like that. My world rocked. When Fitts was gone, back at a hospital somewhere safe, I'd never felt more alone. Even that awful night in Vilseck when we got home didn't compare to that.

No one gave us status reports on our wounded. Healthy-looking guys who got evacuated died. Men like Tyler Prewitt, a tanker medic whose foot was mangled by a rocket that struck his Humvee's door near Muqdadiyah. We raced to the scene, cleared the LZ for a dust-off. They loaded him onto the medevac. There was no sense of sudden urgency. He was a medic and treated his own wound. The morphine induced a smile and a "go kill that piece of shit" thumbs-up. He was fine. Prewitt's war was over. My squad found the plastic chair the insurgent used to ambush them. Two Humvees divided by an eight-foot canal about fifteen feet deep. Tankers never should have split their forces on both sides. They couldn't get to the insurgent fast enough and he disappeared into a palm grove. When I got there, I found the burn mark on the mud wall from where the insurgent fired at twenty-five meters across the canal road. The Iraqi National Guard who took over for the tankers, in their confusion, were spotting the wrong house. I took over. This is what I did. Knapp was a great tracker and I was tenacious circling bad guys on the run.

My squad went through hell to track this guy. Murder hornets, giant orange wasps native to that region, stung Joey Swanson more than eight times in the face as he was clearing out a cache this guy had on standby. We stayed well past nighttime in a dense palm grove, soaked to the bone, heads pounding from dehydration just to maintain the promise of shooting this guy for Prewitt. The vegetation was too thick. The trail dried up.

Two days later I was drinking a cup of coffee in the chow hall when his platoon sergeant told me that he died of a blood clot. This made no sense. I would have never given up for the night if I knew I was tracking Prewitt's killer. I would have lived out there for weeks. I was shocked and felt selfish for quitting.*

The lesson we learned that day was never far from our minds. Anyone who got hit could die. It didn't matter how they looked when we got them to the medevac bird. In the months that followed, we lost other guys we thought would make it. And guys we thought stood no chance pulled through. The uncertainty made it all worse for those of us left behind.

When Fitts got hit, I had to assume it was over for him. It was a shield against the crippling worry that uncertainty brought. I fo-

---

* Tyler's brother, Chad, played pro basketball in Europe and had a run with the Los Angeles Clippers. Tyler and I would always talk basketball. He was a very good baseball player and played in college in Arizona, where he was from. There is a great story about his old high school team: https://www.armytimes .com/news/your-army/2016/05/17/mom-says-home-run-at-high-school-game -was-sign-from-fallen-soldier/. Every insurgent we killed after that day in late September 2004, I imagined was the guy who got him.

cused on my job, lived minute by minute—and lived like he was dead. It was the only way I could cope.

I imagined his family finding out the news. How his squad was going to have to be babysat, too. All the work. All the lessons I learned from him. I was running all the guys out on patrol who were on the ground. All the while, burying the emotions his loss evoked. A squad leader can't show those things. I couldn't grieve. I couldn't process. I had to suppress. Shut down. So I locked that away, as I did with every other Soldier and officer we lost.

When Fitts returned to us, it was a Lazarus moment for me. I just assumed he would be the same as before he got hit. But that pipeline, those hospitals, and the physical debilitation . . . it always changes a person.

I couldn't understand what he was going through. I could see his physical pain. Also, he knew the sound a bullet made when it smacked into bone. Every round that cracked nearby reminded him of that possibility. He knew the agony of lead mushrooming into your muscle fiber. He blinked with every shot, expecting impact. Fitts was right. He'd seen that side of the war that I had missed. The combat support hospitals. The emergency surgeries as men bled out on the operating room tables. He'd woken up surrounded by burned, limbless men and women, clinging to life as the nurses and doctors struggled to patch them together. His war was different.

That was the root of his caution when he came back to us. It wasn't that he feared that for himself. He feared it for us.

Fitts feared it for me.

When we survived and got back to Germany, that fear evaporated. No more worrying that your best friend, the man who was more than a brother, would end up with his legs blown off, or his face burned beyond recognition. Blinded. Deafened. Wheelchair bound. A life faced with endless challenges as his new normal started with wondering if the building he had an appointment in was ADA certified.

Fitts saw my blown confidence. He saw my "broken brain." Maybe he did think I wouldn't have survived a second deployment. Really what it came down to was this: just as I knew I would have had an impossible time surviving our bond being broken by his death, he would have been destroyed by mine. That's how close we were.

That was where you belonged . . . and where you'd be . . . safe.

Fitts hadn't been circling the truth. He'd been the most honest he'd ever been, and I was too angry to see it in the moment. The betrayal of trust stemmed from the one thing that made him the most vulnerable and most uncomfortable. What started as a prank turned into his way of saving me, as sure as he did countless other times in combat.

He was giving me a chance at a life he knew he would never have.

It was manipulation. It was psychological warfare. It was an act of love. That realization made it hurt even more.

PART II

10

THE MOMENT I NEVER HAD

THE FIRST FEW DAYS after that last conversation with Fitts, I felt his absence in a hundred different ways. I was so used to just dialing his number at any given moment during a typical day, be it to ask a home improvement question or just make a remark on something that caught my eye in the news. Now, like psychological muscle memory, I would catch myself pulling out my phone to dial him, or check to see if he'd texted me since the last time I'd looked.

No texts. No voice messages. Since he was medically retired and went home to start a new life, we'd had a couple of times where we went weeks without talking, but that break in commo had been years ago. This time, he gave me the space I had demanded. Was that enlightened emotional understanding for a friend, or just stubborn Fitts? I wasn't sure, but it left me to replay the situation repeatedly in my head. Each morning I woke up without any clear answer on how to reconnect and make this right, or even if it was up to me to do that. So, I let it ride as the emotional dust settled.

As this break developed beyond a few weeks that fall, I grew closer to Knapp and Omarr Hardaway. We talked with more frequency than any other time since we'd left Vilseck. Knapp and I were never very close when we served together. I admired him—envied him at times—but our difference in rank and temperament ensured distance. Now, with our Army time in the rearview mirror, we discovered many common interests. He was an incredible father and husband, and we'd had countless conversations on that front over the years.

Omarr Hardaway and I never had much in common on the surface. The bond from our Ramrod days established the ground floor for what became a refuge sort of friendship for both of us. He came to our platoon in Kosovo. The guy was enormous, and his sweat was legendary. His eccrine glands were the size of contact lenses. The man changed T-shirts three times a day. He spent all his money on socks and European cologne. Every now and then, you find somebody who is a port in a storm. You don't even need to describe the storm. You don't even need to say you need a break from it. When you get together, the storm is forgotten amid the laughter. That was Omarr to me. Ten minutes on the phone, and my sides hurt. Omarr's sharp wit and insight spared no one, which made his humor truly egalitarian. Hardaway exudes wisdom and loyalty. He is a true blessing to have in my life.

Still, the gap in my life without Fitts made every day a grind. I had spent years trying to earn his respect, both in uniform and out of it. He was sort of a Yoda figure to me, the guy I'd go to for unvarnished and ruthless honesty. He would always tell it straight, no matter how much it hurt. In the Army, I discovered he was an excellent judge of character. I had come to rely on that skill as a civilian, vetting prospective business partners with him. Whenever I disagreed with his judgment, events would inevitably prove Fitts right.

One time, Fitts spent three days ripping one of those potential business partners to shreds, asking pointed questions, challenging assumptions or figures. He was blunt and utterly devoid of pretense. The target of his interrogation endured it all with remarkable grace. At the end of the three days, Fitts concluded, "Solid guy. He isn't a dick. I think we can trust him."

It was always "we"—no matter if he was involved in the deal or not. Fitts just assumed we were always going to be a team. I loved that about him.

The Army continued to call from time to time while Fitts and I weren't talking. Scheduled meetings would come and go again with no follow-up call. Each day when the appointed hour arrived, I would sit by my phone, waiting for it to ring so I could finally learn the truth of why the Army was suddenly interested in me again after all these years. The call never came, and that caused even more stress. Then, at the end of November, I stopped hearing from the Army entirely. No more elliptical conversations. No more friends tipping me that they'd been contacted. Everything went silent.

My first thought was relief. Then the crippling self-doubt wormed its way into my sleepless-night stress sessions and I'd wonder if this was just the calm before the storm. Some surprise was out there, lurking. And it would blindside me with all the force of a Lawrence Taylor tackle.

The truth was, I needed the Yoda-like perspective Fitts offered. He would have talked me off the wall. But I couldn't bring myself to call him. Our rhythm continued. Fitts did what Fitts always does—he was stubborn and ham-fisted. I followed my own well-traveled playbook, too. I dwelt on things I couldn't control. I fed the sense of powerlessness into a cocktail of self-loathing and invalidation.

Through these competing cycles of dysfunction, I did have the emotional intelligence to recognize that at its core, what Fitts did in lying about the Man in White was in his own way a beautiful gift. The engineering of it was a disaster, of course. Ultimately, I knew I would have to be the one to get over this, to reach for the phone and call him.

I can be stubborn, too. November slipped away with the comms between us silent. Christmas approached, and the weather turned ugly. Snow flurries lashed our corner of western New York and the temperature dropped down a well. In the absence of Fitts's Jedi skills, I devoted a little time every morning to writing through my Iraq memories, detailing everything I could remember in case they would be needed. I didn't trust the Army's silence.

Writing things down had long since been a Bellavia family strategy that not everyone understood or appreciated. Yet, there were complexities in our household that demanded it, and it became a life skill for me.

For example, back in 1995, I thought I had met a nice young woman. We had met in college. I'd built her up to my folks, probably in part because I was trying to convince myself she was pedestal-worthy. Naturally, they wanted to meet her. I put that off for as long as I could. Finally, an invitation was issued. We were set to go over to dinner later one week.

In preparation, I sat down with "Sarah" and said to her, "Listen. This is a big deal. I like you. I want my mother to like you."

She nodded as if this was self-evident. It was, of course, but things were nuanced in the Bellavia household.

"My mother takes her hospitality very, very seriously."

"Okay," Sarah said, smiling like this was a joke.

The smile made me instantly concerned.

"Please listen to me. Or better yet, write all this down."

No move. Just a laugh to underscore how much she thought I was overreacting.

I explained the situation: "My mother is going to be bouncing around like she's on crack. She will look completely flustered, like she can't manage this meal and it is just too much to handle. There will be six courses of food. We're Italian."

"I'm half Eye-talian. Relax, David. It'll be fine," Sarah interrupted. I also noticed she wasn't writing anything down. And she was German, Dutch, and Irish. No respectable Italian overpronounces the "I" like that. This was bad. This was real bad.

I continued: "There will be multiple pots on the stove boiling over. Some of them will just have water in them, nothing else. This is all for effect. The truth is, she prepared the meal hours before and it is tucked away all over the kitchen, expertly concealed."

None of this appeared to worry Sarah. But I was just warming up.

"Eat nothing for twenty-four hours. Saying 'I'm full' is not an option. You have to sample everything put on the table. Also, no matter what she says or does, you have to attempt to help her. You must *make* the attempt. Just say it. She will refuse it, of course, but the gesture is crucial. And you're not writing this down."

Sarah laughed and said, "David, you're overreacting! I got this."

"When she refuses your help, you need to stand there and talk with her. Never leave her sight, okay? That's very important. Be there in her presence while she runs around the kitchen. Just be sure not to get in her way. In fact, don't go in the kitchen; just stay right at the entrance. The zone of cooking is hers. Oh, and if something blows up or catches fire, don't move toward it. Just casually make her aware of it."

Sarah thought this was hilarious. I was as serious as the H1N1 flu. I sensed disaster.

"When the food is served, my mom's going to shit all over it. She was rushed. She ran out of seasoning. Her pans are no good. The mixer broke. The butter isn't salted. It is always something. She'll be panicked and apologetic. She may even suggest we just order a pizza because the food's probably so bad. This is all nonsense. The meal will be amazing. Incredible. And she knows it. We know it. She knows we know it. This is a ritual. Your role in this ritual is to eat the meal and compliment it. Tell her she's crazy, that this is the best dinner you've had. Ever. My mother will love you. If she loves you, my dad will love you. Are you getting this? Are you sure you don't want to write this down?"

Sarah didn't write it down.

Well, I had an unshakable sense of dread when the night arrived and I brought Sarah over to the house. My mom behaved exactly as advertised, flying around the kitchen like an Italian banshee, zinging between oven and range, grabbing pots, straining pasta, and chattering away the entire time.

When we sat down to eat, my mother seemed utterly despairing. "This is going to be horrible. The oven wasn't working right. The pasta sat too long. It looks soggy." On and on, she cut her own incredible effort to the quick. She was distracted by a phone call and something burned. The previous owner of the house was murdered in the kitchen, and the house is cursed. Therefore this meal is cursed, too.

We filled our plates and dug in, each Bellavia keeping up a steady patter of praise to set my mom's heart at ease. Sarah, though, was silent.

Gradually, eyes turned to her. Oblivious to the attention, she took a bite of the pasta and chewed with a look on her face that hardened the look on my mom's.

"You know what this needs?" she said cheerfully.

What. The. Hell. Are you doing?

My mother and father exchanged glances, then turned back to Sarah, staring as if she'd just taken our crucifix off the wall and dunked it upside down in a canister of urine.

"It needs more cheese," Sarah said, still laughing cluelessly under her breath. She giggled like a mental patient staring at a Ferris wheel.

She sprinkled some Romano onto her pasta, took a bite, and smiled broadly—like she'd just saved the meal. "See, don't worry, *now* it's perfect. Thank you, Mrs. Bellavia!"

My mother could not have been more shocked if Sarah had reached across the table and slapped her with a two-by-four. I had to rush her out of the house with my jacket over her head like a Secret Service agent moving the president after reports of shots fired. I tossed her into a moving SUV that sped her home, avoiding all traffic lights.

I never saw Sarah again. Within the family, the moment became known as "The Mistake of 1995." I got over that heartbreak unusually fast. She had hurt my mother, and that is unforgiveable in our family.

And this is why we always write things down. I wasn't going to be unprepared for the Army, even if they had stopped calling me.

This new routine continued until a week before Christmas. I was at the radio station one morning, prepping before the show, whose main topic for the first hour was "should single-use plastic bags be banned," when my cell phone rang.

Fittsy?

I pulled it out and glanced at the screen. Area code 202, Washington, D.C. Not Fitts, and now the Army was back in my life. I tensed and considered not answering it.

My radio partner was off that day but my friend Kate was visiting from New York City and had come down to the station with me. We met while she was an editor at an online journal. I was asked to write an article for my choice to head the Department of Veterans Affairs. She didn't know me from Adam. Had no idea that I served or had a book. She didn't even know why my opinion on such matters was relevant.

That made two of us, actually. I was long out of the national veteran political game.

My piece was dictated into my phone while I was driving. I didn't take it seriously. There was so much going on in my mind. I remember one of my supporting arguments was, "He would be good at fixing veteran-related issues. Especially since he is a veteran and there are a lot of veteran issues to fix."

Kate edited the entire piece. She rewrote it, actually. It was brilliant. She was kind. She was funny. From those first days, she started listening to my show. She was supportive and loyal at a time when I needed both. She traveled to Buffalo, caught a Sabres hockey game, and sometimes came to the station like that day to see how radio is made.

The phone continued to ring. The screen with the number was glowing in my hand, lighting up that sense of dread again.

"David, Colonel Perez here. The call is coming in two minutes. Stand by."

"Hey," I said to Kate, "that call from the Department of Defense is coming now. Can you film this? We may need this in case I pass out."

"Good or bad?" Kate asked.

Bad? We'd need it for my lawyer. Good? I wasn't even sure what the good could be. I didn't have time to think about that and just said, "Right."

That probably made no sense. My entire life was flashing before my screen protector on my phone. Kate intuited what I meant and trained her phone on me.

God, I hate this.

I took a breath, then answered the phone.

"Hello, David," an upbeat woman's voice said to me. "My name is Madeline, and I have President Trump on the line wishing to speak to you. Is now a good time?"

What. The. Hell?

I almost said that out loud. Fortunately, I caught myself. "Ahhh-FFhhh. Ah. Yeah. I mean. This is a good time."

Madeline put me on hold. My head was swimming, but I did have one thought come through crystal clear: *record this.* I motioned to Kate, who was completely losing her mind behind the camera on her phone, that it was President Trump.

She mouthed, "NO WAY!"

I shook my head in disbelief.

Oh my god. I am going to be the next ambassador to Libya!

My phone blinked. Suddenly I heard President Donald Trump's voice come through my phone's speaker.

"David, how are you? Do you know why I'm calling?"

"I'm a little nervous," I admitted.

"You should be nervous."

I should be nervous. Okay.

"Do you know what you have been recommended for?"

My mind shifted gears. All this waiting. All the dread and confusion. The concern that there would be a media circus surrounding some moment in Iraq that had been twisted out of recognition by time and ax-grinding. No way. Iraq. "Recommended."

This all made sense now.

He is talking awards for Iraq.

In that instant, I knew what was coming was far more life-changing than throwaway allegations. The war was over. I had moved on.

"Fourteen years ago, I was told I was nominated for the Medal of Honor, sir."

A lifetime ago.

Back then, the thought of being awarded America's highest valor medal was seemingly a dream come true, a validation of my skills and professionalism as a Soldier. It would erase the insecurities I wrestled with constantly, and be a tangible symbol of service to my father. After all these years, I could go home to him with something he could take pride in about his youngest son.

None of that happened.

"Well, David, you got it," Trump said.

I didn't know what to say.

Kate reacted in total shock. Eyes wide behind her cell phone, she kept filming, knowing that she was bearing witness to one of the most important moments of my life.

The president continued: "Boy, you are so lucky. You are brave. Brave comes before lucky. You're brave and lucky. But you are lucky, too."

I still couldn't find words. The president filled the void. "It's true. I am here with the vice president and a whole bunch of other people. We are going to bestow upon you the Congressional Medal of Honor. The highest honor of our country, for your great bravery."

"I don't know what to say, sir," I replied. "I am humbled, and I am speechless. Thank you, sir."

President Trump quipped, "You know I want one for myself, but they say I'm not brave enough, David."

I laughed and found myself firing back. "I dunno, Mr. President. That whole North Korea thing was pretty impressive."

What are you doing? Did you just bring up Kim Jong-un? Stop it. Just shut up and listen. Did you not learn anything from your awkward youth?

The president laughed at that, then gave me further details: "Sometime soon you will come to the White House. You and your family and friends. You will receive the Medal of Honor for your valor. They just told me the story, I mean, I knew the story, but they told me again . . . the highest award for our country, David."

We talked for a few more minutes, the news still not landing yet. It didn't feel real. The president said his goodbyes and the phone went dead. I sat in the conference room at the radio station, staring at the ceiling as I sank into a chair.

My mind was blank. Then, as if it were a beacon, a thought broke through the mental paralysis.

Dad. I wish you were still here for this.

What I wouldn't have given to be able to share the news with him. I could see myself coming to their home, finding him in the living room, my mom busy with dinner. I would sit down and, as casually as I could, tell him that the president called.

Oh yeah? What about?

My old man was never flustered. He would have taken that tidbit totally in stride, as if I had mentioned an old friend had rung me up after a decade of silence.

There in the conference room at work, I painted the picture in my mind. Earnest eyes. Warm smile. Waiting patiently for the punch line.

Dad, he told me I will receive the Medal of Honor.

He would have been over the moon. We always had a complicated relationship with the path I'd taken through life. He had wanted one of his sons to follow in his footsteps, to become a dentist and take over his practice when he retired. My brother Dan became a pastor. Rand went the academic route and was now a professor of library science. Timmy was also an accomplished educator. All my brothers had a stack of degrees that made the family proud. Me? I bailed out of civilian college and went to the University of Fort Benning, with infantry as my major.

When I joined the Army, my dad feigned pride. He was not a good actor, and while the effort was appreciated, his disappointment lingered below the surface. This was pre-9/11, and I think my dad considered the Army the last refuge of a young man who had failed at everything else.

The disconnect flowed both ways. Through Basic, I realized that I had always thought that my dad was soft. He was never a fighter, never brawled as a kid. When I started getting in fights, he had no idea how to handle that. I would come home after a complete beat-down, and he wouldn't say anything or offer any advice. He just watched and processed.

The thing was, I was getting my ass kicked at school by eighteen-year-olds while trying to defend my older brother Timmy. He was a frequent target of the local bully set, which my brother didn't seem to care about but which outraged me. Being loyal to him, I waded into every scrape.

I finally went to my dad and asked him to teach me self-defense moves. He taught me a couple of things he'd picked up from watching WWF bouts. I was twelve and didn't know. I just hero-worshipped my dad, and so I practiced the moves until one day I had a chance to employ them in a fight.

It went as expected. I came home after getting my head bounced off the locker room floor.

"Dad. Those moves you taught me are from the WWF Saturday night main event."

He looked like I'd just caught him in a lie, which I had. "I adjusted them for self-defense," he said weakly.

"Why would you do this to me?" I yelled.

He made up for the fraud by purchasing boxing gloves. Together we sparred after school every night. I learned to take a punch, but as for offensive fighting moves? My dad had as many as I did back then, which was zero.

When I went off to become a door-kicker, I think the whole idea of doing that for a living felt foreign to him. That his son was eager to do it made him uncomfortable, like he went wrong as a father somewhere. Achievement in the Bellavia house meant degrees, a professional career—not a blue cord and a pair of combat boots. As a dentist, he had dedicated his life to relieving pain in others. Now his son was dedicated to inflicting it. He couldn't wrap his head around that.

I suppose most of us go through a period to adulthood where we disappoint our dads. There's a time when future potential seemed limitless, only to be limited by whatever decisions we make. A good dad wants a better life for his sons. When we don't exceed and accelerate beyond the start we've been given, the disconnect can grow severe.

Combat changed that. I didn't realize how much Iraq had evolved our relationship until I called home about two weeks after Fallujah. I had no idea a *Time* magazine article had come out detailing our platoon's experience in the city. I hadn't even told my parents that my unit would be anywhere near that generational battle.

Right past the hellos, they told me about reporter Michael Ware's piece on us. We were in the national news. My dad excitedly said, "David, Aaron Brown on CNN said you did some incredible things that get big awards. Like the Medal of Honor. Is that even possible?"

I laughed. The Medal of Honor? For me? Get out of town. That's a unicorn award that didn't even merit thinking about to a mere E6. Look at who has worn it. Jimmy Doolittle for his suicidal Tokyo raid in 1942. Audie Murphy for saving his platoon and killing scores, if not hundreds, of Germans while atop a burning Sherman tank. Sergeant Alvin York. Thomas Hudner Jr. National heroes who have long since become icons and inspirations for countless young men and women.

Since 2001, almost all the recent awards had been posthumous, based on the self-sacrifice of the recipient while trying to save other Americans. What I'd done in Fallujah was nothing like that.

Throughout our history, we've fought more than a dozen wars. Somewhere north of forty million Americans have worn the uniform from the Revolutionary War generation to the Gen Xers I served with in Iraq. Since the Civil War and the establishment of the Medal of Honor by President Abraham Lincoln, only about 3,300 individuals have received the award. Of those, 40 percent were awarded during the Civil War, before the criteria became more structured.

In 2004, fewer than two hundred Medal of Honor recipients were still alive, most from the Greatest Generation, whose deeds were carried out in the maelstrom of World War II. Fewer than seventy today still are living.

So, the Medal of Honor for what I did in Fallujah seemed absurd to me that December in 2004.

"Dad, it's a chat room," I admonished. "That's not even a possibility. People have no idea what they're talking about."

I could sense disappointment in his understanding. I wondered about that for years after. As if the Medal of Honor would have somehow validated my path, showed him that I'd risen to something worthy of being his son, like the rest of my siblings had already done.

The president just made that my reality. With a start, I realized that this award would make me the only living Iraq War recipient of the Medal of Honor. My life would be changed forever by this. In the moment, I felt completely unworthy. I would have to earn the award every day with the life I lived and the choices I made.

"What are you thinking right now?" Kate said.

I ducked the question. That would have revealed too much of my own insecurities even to somebody as trustworthy as Kate. So I did what I always did and deflected. "I have to do a radio show. Can you send me that video?"

I sat staring out the window. Minutes rolled by. A knock on the conference door broke the spell of the past. Showtime. I got up and headed for the studio, trying to remember the most contentious points of the single-use-bag debate. Tim Wenger, my operations and program director, walked in. Kate told him that President Trump just called.

"What are you talking about? Did you ask him to do the show?" Wenger wasn't kidding.

"I didn't know what to say. I think I told him he did a good job with North Korea," I said in a daze, trying to remember everything.

"You did, actually, say that. And it was really weird. You were like, 'Good job with that whole North Korea thing.'" Kate laughed.

"David," Tim said, "seriously. There is no way you can do this show. I mean, do you want me to fill in for you? This is huge. When are they announcing it? Are you the only guy from Iraq? David, this is huge. I don't even know what to say. I am floored right now." In that moment Tim Wenger was saying aloud everything in my head.

I just took a deep breath and the next four hours flew by with me on autopilot. My mind was totally focused on my dad. I never loved him so much as I did on that cold afternoon in Buffalo.

Looking back, I can't remember a single call or commercial. I do remember summoning every detail of my father's face, conjured out of a tapestry of memories, to create a moment in my mind that we never got to share.

11

THE SCRUTINIZERS

WESTERN NEW YORK — WINTER 2019

ON A LATE WINTER morning, they came in a long convoy. Though I knew they were coming at some point that day, their arrival still caught me a little off guard. I was sipping coffee in the kitchen when I saw the first vehicle appear up the street, winding its way toward me. I put the mug down and went to the front door, where I watched the rest of the convoy snake up our country road to my driveway. I'd like to lie and say they rolled up my street in those black Chevy Suburbans with tinted windows you see government types driving in the Jack Ryan series. Not even close. The Pentagon rented what must have been every base-model Hyundai Sonata available at the Buffalo airport. They pulled into my driveway and parked, and for a minute I had an image of my Amish neighbors peering through their windows and wondering if I had just opened a dealership in my front yard.

The December phone call from President Trump triggered this odd convoy's arrival. Now the Defense Department was coming to comb through every bit of my life in preparation for the Medal of Honor ceremony at the White House.

I stepped out of the front door and into a biting wind coming off Lake Ontario. A *last gasp of winter* sort of storm had hit last night, the kind with such a bitter edge that it sucks the breath out of you.

People piled out of the Sonatas, some in uniform, some in civilian clothes, all shivering in the New York cold. They pulled cameras and lights and hard-shell cases out of the trunks while others rushed to introduce themselves.

Colonel Carrie Perez approached me first. She was a five-foot-two firebrand, totally in control, a natural leader. She'd been the one calling me in the fall. After President Trump broke the news to me, she went silent for several months. I actually began to wonder if this whole thing was a huge mistake.

Then Colonel Perez contacted me a few weeks ago and officially introduced herself as the Pentagon's Army public relations specialist assigned to Medal of Honor cases.

She told me, "David, pick a day. We're coming to see you. And we need to see everything."

I couldn't help but ask, "How bad is this going to get?"

"David, everything is about to be forever changed. You can detach. You can fight it, embrace it—whatever you want. But it is happening."

She didn't mince words. That was both a blessing and a curse. I think I was still in shock and maybe even denial that the award was actually going to happen. Now it was starting to sink in that my life here in New York was about to become public fodder.

It was hard not to respect Colonel Carrie Perez for her blunt honesty. At least now I had an inkling of what was coming. I think I had intuited some of it, thinking about what the award might mean as winter raged over New York these past months. But that phone call was the first time I heard my worst fears confirmed by somebody else.

Now she walked up the driveway to me, a warm smile on her face. As we shook hands, she offered a few words of advice, then turned back to direct the show. As she did, each member of the team approached to offer me congratulations and a few kind words. I tried to be polite, but already everything seemed to blur together. There had to be seven or eight people in my front yard.

An Air Force officer shook my hand and began telling me about my own life. "Hey, we just found your varsity baseball coach!"

Baseball coach? Why?

Before I could respond, Liz Chamberlain grabbed my hand and

introduced herself. She was another civilian media specialist working with the Army Medal of Honor task force. She was in charge of running press conferences and would be the point person for dealing with the media once the White House officially announced the Medal of Honor was to be awarded to me.

The Air Force officer cut in: "We talked to your Basic Training unit's drill sergeants, too. They went on the record. Really good guys."

"Basic Training?" I asked, still trying to wrap my head around them finding my baseball coach.

"Oh yeah. We've talked to a lot of people from your past, Sergeant," said Sergeant First Class Randy Pike, a public affairs NCO who once appeared on *Jeopardy!* It was something that I learned and have brought up since in every conversation with him. "Does that buzzer take time to get used to on *Jeopardy!*?"

"This is about you. But yes, they let you practice beforehand."

I realized they thought they knew everything about me. They had already dissected my past, followed chains of old friends and acquaintances, searching out anything they could find. Total strangers knew all this. My cloak of anonymity was stripped away in an instant. I felt profoundly exposed. Vulnerability like this generates DEFCON One levels of discomfort for me.

Colonel Perez came into view again behind the Air Force NCO and Liz. She was giving orders to everyone with quick, precise words, quietly spoken. The team in the front yard activated, and other members of the team burdened with armloads of gear flowed past me and into the house. I let them in, then followed them into the living room, where I introduced the team to my ninety-nine-year-old grandfather. I had picked him up the night before and brought him home to the house after taking him to eat at Olive Garden. He could eat his weight in free soup and salad and still ask for more. A massive, hulking man, though never obese, he had earned legendary status among family and friends for once eating twenty ears of corn at a sitting.

He had earned the gluttony back in his youth in Europe. He'd fought his way across France and Germany with Patton's Third Army during World War II, and his stories from those days were a childhood staple for me. Ultimately, his service became the inspiration for my own.

Colonel Perez and Liz began outlining what was going to happen in the coming months, and how it all would be handled. I listened, tried to take it all in, but the truth was I was totally distracted. My grandfather was already telling war stories, even though the camera crew was still setting up their equipment. Other members of the team seemed to be waiting, impatient for something else.

I knew what else. The *what else* was waiting in the garage.

The day before, I went down to our barn, shadows sharp across its concrete floor. In a dark corner, tucked away behind an interior door, rested a stack of locker boxes, some U.S. Army olive drab, others more like plastic bins. My name was stenciled on them. They were piled in the back of the room, behind a jumble of farm equipment, willfully forgotten for a decade and a half. A shaft of light from the main bay of the barn stabbed the darkness here, illuminating the stack between rows and piles of other stuff. They looked like my own personal Ark of the Covenant warehouse at the end of *Raiders of the Lost Ark*. Something vital within, but needing to be forgotten all the same.

I reached for the first one, wondering where I had left the Giant's sword. I couldn't remember. I didn't think it was in any of the locker boxes, but peering around this area of the barn, I couldn't find it.

Perez had told me they wanted to see everything. They would not see that. I refused to put that on display, or invite total strangers into the memories of that night.

For now, I set that thought aside and pulled the first locker box off the stack. It was heavy and covered in fourteen years of barn dust. Mice had nested around them, and I saw with embarrassment dried rodent crap on the top row of boxes. They smelled of ammonia and must.

I should have treated these better.

One by one, I carried them to the six-wheel Polaris Ranger I use to get around the farm and loaded them in back.

I drove them up to the house, opened the garage doors, and stepped into its empty bay. I'd already put down a couple of sheets, an old comforter, and a tarp on the garage floor in preparation for this transfer. Carefully, I placed each locker box on the center of each covering, ready for my guests. Like a viewing, I suppose. Or maybe an autopsy.

Now they were waiting to be opened, like personal time capsules, and I knew I was not ready for this.

So I was relieved that my grandfather busily regaled his audience with stories of the Glenn Miller era. His memories of Anzio, of Normandy and the drive across France. Battles into Germany. His memories tumbled out in a steady stream. He was unwittingly buying me time, but I could see the visitors getting antsy. They wanted the autopsy to begin.

At length, the Air Force officer turned to me and whispered, "David, we'd really like to look through those locker boxes now."

He explained they were looking for photos or other things related to my time in Fallujah that could accompany the stories they would write and produce once the Medal of Honor had been announced.

Deep breath.

"They're in the garage," I replied as neutrally as I could, then led them to the door. About half the team went inside, where the locker boxes stood ready for this inspection.

"You coming?" somebody asked.

"Nah. Nothing in there that's important."

My response surprised my guests. Liz sensed my discomfort. She made small talk with me in the doorway as the team circled those artifacts of my life like archaeologists in an unearthed tomb, reading the stenciling on the boxes. When they found the one marked FAL-LUJAH, my anxiety meter pegged.

All of us who fought and bled and lost friends in Iraq have handled the intervening years between our service and our civilian lives in different ways. At first, I talked about it all the time, especially when *House to House* was published. I wanted to write a *them*oir, not a memoir—something that told the story of what the Ramrods collectively accomplished. The public's view of the war seemed shaped by the political dogfight surrounding it. The war we Soldiers knew looked nothing like what people saw on the evening news.

When the Civil War veterans returned to their families after the surrender at Appomattox, they were shocked to realize that their war bore no resemblance to the narrative that had been crafted for the civilians. Their truth lay untold, deep within long nights tortured by memories of their most significant years.

I did not want our war to be subsumed by what the *New York Times* and ABC News told the folks back home. *House to House* was my attempt to capture the unvarnished truth about what we had seen and done. When the book came out, I thought I was done reliving the worst and best moments of my life. I boxed up all those memories and kept them deep within me, sealed and closed for what I hoped to be forever. I focused on family and career. I ran for Congress. I spent fourteen years searching for the meaning I felt when I carried a rifle and wore our flag on my shoulder.

Somewhere between Fallujah and home, we grew up—and grew old. Going back to Iraq now? Revisiting those memories? Hell, I'd rather be shot at again than open those locker boxes.

Now other people were doing that for me. I tried to focus on the small talk with Liz, but out of the corner of my eye, I saw the team opening the Fallujah locker. I felt a primal surge of territorial protectiveness.

Hey, be careful! Those are the counseling statements I wrote for my men.

Nothing important? Or everything inside the *most* important?

Unconsciously, I stepped into the garage, clamping my impulse to intervene.

Then I saw a yellowed, stained piece of paper boil up from the locker box as those hands dug deeper into it.

They ignored it, knowing nothing of its significance, or whose dried and long-browned blood was splattered on it.

Swiftly, I reached down and grabbed it. I felt its power in my hand, the memories it contained, like a sacred object revered by an ancient tribe.

My tribe. My platoon would know what this was, what it meant to us.

What it means now.

I held it, thinking I had tucked it away somewhere else years ago. To find it here, now . . . complete surprise.

I stepped back, the paper close against me. The others ignored me, heads bent, peering into the locker box. Somebody found the gloves I'd worn in Fallujah and pulled them out. "Wow, can you imagine what you can get for this stuff on eBay?"

There was laughter in my tomb, until another voice broke through it. "I saw a hat from an old Medal of Honor guy go for ten grand at auction once."

Ten grand? Selling memories and the treasures of one's life?

I backed away, holding the paper like a sacred object. The rest of the team still hadn't noticed, but Liz did. She watched me with razor-sharp intensity. She was on to me, no doubt about it. I slipped into the house and tucked the paper away out of sight. I returned just in time to see the Air Force NCO pulling out a long, skinny package wrapped in two garbage bags and secure with hundred-mile-an-hour tape. He picked at the packaging, tearing it off like a crow eating a corpse.

When the Hefty bags both hit the floor, I saw he was holding the Giant's sword. The tassels on its handle swayed as he moved to show the rest of the team, and for a moment I was back in Khailaniya, gripped in the Giant's headlock, watching those tassels flail as Ruiz and I fought our losing battle.

This was the worst nightmare.

The team oohed and aahed at the sight of the weapon. The Air Force NCO drew the blade out and the scimitar shined, its metal still bright after all these years hidden away.

"How cool is this thing?" the Air Force NCO exclaimed.

Please don't touch that.

Reflexively, I jerked toward him. Liz gave me a second sharp glance, but I barely noticed.

"How'd you get this thing?" he asked, half laughing, half in awe as he held the weapon up.

"Hey, dude?"

He stopped cold at my tone. Everyone else froze. They could hear the nerve hit in my voice.

"Hand that over to me. Seriously. Hand it over."

He stared at me, too surprised by my reaction to respond.

"I am not joking. This isn't cool."

"Sure thing, Sergeant. No problem."

Nobody moved.

"Hand it to ME."

The team recoiled at my tone. Vintage drill sergeant. A tone that dared anyone to disobey. Not a sound followed. The silence felt like a crucifixion.

One of the staff snicked the scimitar back into the scabbard and handed it to me. Confused and shaken, he offered a quiet "Sorry."

I took the Giant's sword, unsure how to fix the social catastrophe I had just created with my reflexive overreaction.

"Okay, everyone. Take five. Out of the garage," I heard Colonel Perez say. My eyes stayed on the sword as the team fled through the door to the main house. Dimly, I heard my grandfather open fire on them again with more of his World War II stories.

"Staff Sergeant?" Colonel Perez said sternly, walking to my side. I didn't look up. I could not take my eyes off the sword.

It clattered to the ground. With every revolution I ran around the Giant, I saw it lying in the dirt.

"Staff Sergeant Bellavia?" Her voice broke through the memory. My eyes tore away from the weapon and looked at her. Her face was set, tough. She was a rugged woman who had clearly seen moments like this.

"I get that this is super weird," she said when she had my attention. "I need you to trust me. I have done this before. You have not. I don't know what it will be like to be you to go through all this, but I can promise you one thing: without us, it is about to get a whole lot more crazy."

Worse. Than. This? If that's true, the rest of my life is about to become one long vulnerability hangover. Maybe that's why so many Medal of Honor recipients drank themselves to death.

"Do you understand? It is going to get a whole lot more crazy."

"Yes, ma'am."

"Our job is to be here for you. My job is to protect you."

She looked fierce in the moment, totally sincere. I felt my sense of panic abate, leaving a sting of embarrassment.

"We will honor what happened over there. I promise you that . . . the guys you didn't bring back."

I nodded, my eyes wanting to look anywhere but into hers.

"Most importantly," she added, "we are here to protect our Army."

I jerked fully into the moment at those words, as if they were cold water dashed on me through time and space.

She had my full attention now. There were only three things I loved in my life: my kids, my men—including our fallen—and the Army. Defending the Army, loving it even when it chewed us up and did not love us back, was the most selfless act of my life.

My face softened. Her eyes softened. She had landed the exact right words in the moment. The woman was very, very good.

"Listen closely. We need to know everything so that we can protect you and your friends. You may not understand this, but there are a lot of crazy people out there. Some are just stupid. Some are dangerous. Some of them are flat-out our enemies."

I needed no reminder of these facts, not after what happened when *House to House* hit the shelves. For every dozen or so who understood the book, understood its intent and meaning, there were a couple of hard-core haters. The larger the audience, the more stalkers, the more people sending death threats, calling us murderers and sadists, people who twisted my words and our experience to fit their political agendas. They squeezed my truth out of my words and infested the husks with their own commentary. It was gut-wrenching.

One of the worst moments came while watching a *60 Minutes* episode on a serial killer. A B-roll shot panned across the killer's room and bookshelf—and sitting there tucked among other war books was mine. I spent days dwelling on that, wondering if my shared memories somehow fueled his psychosis.

Colonel Perez was right. Once I was released into the public eye again, the knives would come out and the crazies would avalanche me.

"I can see you get that," Perez said, her tone sympathetic. "Remember. We here? The people under my command? We're not your enemies. You're safe with us, Sergeant. And I'm never going to allow anything or anyone to come at you."

Outside of my Iraq circle of friends, nobody had ever said anything like this to me. Colonel Perez wasn't just my guide navigating me through this process. She was putting herself willingly in my fox-hole. Stacking sandbags, digging it deeper. She would have my back when the first waves broke into view and surrounded me.

I felt ashamed for how I had behaved.

"Thank you, ma'am. I appreciate all of this. Let me apologize to everyone."

She shook her head. "No. No apologies, Sergeant. We're good. We got you. But you need to be prepared. This is the first and only Iraq War Medal of Honor that will go to a living veteran. That will make the media feeding frenzy unprecedented. Nothing like it. Some will want to roast you. Some will go after you personally. Politically. Some will use you and your story as a platform to dredge up the reasons we went to war, and whether it was necessary or not. You'll be used. By every side."

"Yes, ma'am."

"You will be the ambassador of that entire fight, its symbol," she added.

I don't want to be anyone's symbol.

"Everyone who served. Everyone who died. You are the living person who everyone will want to hear from. And you have points of vulnerability."

I looked away. She was right. I knew what she meant, but she told me anyway: "We have never had a Medal of Honor recipient with your profile before the award. You have your own radio show, for Christ's sake. You ran for Congress. You have political enemies. This is new terrain. Not just for you, but for us as well."

She paused and waited for a reaction. I mumbled, "It's all gonna change." It sounded halfhearted, like intellectually I understood, but this really had yet to sink in.

"No, David. It already changed. You just haven't realized it yet."

The words struck like a slap in a restaurant.

"Why is this happening? Why now?"

Perez was unrelenting. "President Obama is why this is happening for you at all. President Trump is why it is happening now. I've seen a lot of these awards. It's my job. But I've never seen an award with so many Post-it notes on the pages as yours."

I looked at her quizzically. "What do you mean?"

"Everyone had something to say. And not a single person voted against this award or the citation. Instead, they asked, 'Why did this take so long?'"

I thought about that award ceremony in Germany after we got home. The day I watched everyone I knew and loved have their service honored. I stood on the sidelines, feeling like I'd been exposed as a fraud, the NCO who went into Fallujah and whose service merited not even an Army Commendation Medal. It wasn't about the award. It was about the respect of my peers, and of my men. It was one more aching ass-kick in my final months in uniform.

Then the Silver Star arrived in the mail months later like an after-thought, delivered by a UPS driver. I opened it alone in my kitchen and read the citation, thinking, *Who was this actually meant for?*

"So, you need to know. The entire Army awards process, not one person in this Army is against you. Before the first call you received, we had been working this award. You are new to this, I get that. We've been on this for months, Sergeant. Over a year."

"Thank you, ma'am." Still, this revelation felt like I was being spied on. Stalked by my own government. Would they have still given me the award if they had found dirt? A whiff of scandal? What did any of that have to do with what happened in Fallujah in 2004?

"We need you to realize that we are here for you."

One last spasm, like a death clutch to my old life, boiled out of me. "I don't want this. But I know I can't say no. Wait. Why can't I just say no? I want to have my life that I have here."

"That is all gone. When this award is publicly announced, what-ever you do, wherever you go, the Medal of Honor will be the first thing that comes up. From now on, it will define you. You have to accept that."

"This is happening," I said, numb from the education.

"Yes."

"Okay. I am good then." I was anything but.

The lie was obvious and she tested me immediately. "What's the paper? And why's the sword so important?"

"I like paper. And I like swords," I said dumbly. Clearly, I wasn't up for show-and-tell yet.

The Ramrods. Fallujah, November 8, 2004. *Courtesy of the author*

Part of our wrecking crew in the ruins of Fallujah in November 2004. *Left to right:* Unknown EOD Soldier, myself, Staff Sergeant Colin Fitts, Sergeant Chuck Knapp, and Specialist John Ruiz. *Courtesy of CSM Darrin Bohn*

Command Sergeant Major Steven Faulkenburg (*center foreground*), with First Sergeant Peter Smith (*rear*) and Chaplain Ric Brown (*right*), just before the Second Battle of Fallujah in November 2004. CSM Faulkenburg was killed in action only a short time after this photo was taken.
Courtesy of CSM Darrin Bohn

Captain Doug Walter, our old company commander from Germany, returned to us after Captain Sean Sims was killed in action during the Second Battle of Fallujah. His presence lifted our spirits after we'd taken such heavy casualties. Photo taken on November 18, 2004, in the city.
Courtesy of CSM Darrin Bohn

Early on in the deployment we found this artillery-shell-turned-roadside-bomb near Muqdadiyah. We quickly learned that picking one up, as I did here, was extremely foolish. These old shells were very unstable and sometimes detonated on the insurgents, blowing them to pieces. *Courtesy of Christopher Walls*

When out on counter-IED missions, paying attention to suspicious signs on the ground beside the roads we used often meant the difference between life and death. This is one example: buried wires that ran to a hole the insurgents used to lay IEDs. The wire would be connected to the bomb, then detonated when the other end of the wires were connected to a battery. *Courtesy of the author*

Taken in the aftermath of a raid. Sergeant First Class James Cantrell and I discuss the mission, with a detainee on the ground next to us, back at FOB Normandy. The photo was taken in December 2004, just after we returned from Fallujah. *Courtesy of Peter Smith*

Riding a donkey to make the local kids laugh during a quiet patrol in Diyala Province in 2004. Years later, I learned that a 1st Infantry Division GI was photographed by a Signal Corps cameraman doing the exact same thing in Normandy in the summer of 1944. *Courtesy of Patrick Magner*

Staff Sergeant Omarr Hardaway, seen in the spring of 2004 in Iraq. Years after we came home, Omarr became a regular guest on my radio show and has been one of my most trusted friends since our days in combat together.
Courtesy of the author

Inside our NCO barracks at FOB Normandy, sharing stories from our latest mission in the spring of 2004. Seated (*left to right*): Sergeant Brad Unterseher, Staff Sergeant Wade Smith, and Staff Sergeant Cory Brown. I'm standing in front of the group, our battle maps behind me, recounting the last mission we'd undertaken. *Courtesy of the author*

Specialist John Ruiz grabs some late-night chow in the converted morgue that served as our dining facility at FOB Normandy.

Courtesy of the author

First Platoon, Alpha Company 2-2 secures the second story of a house in Fallujah on November 10, 2004. *Left to right:* Sergeant Wilson, Specialist Ofori, Specialist Howard.
U.S. Army

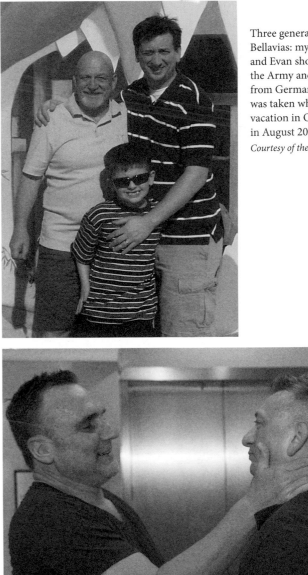

Three generations of Bellavias: my father, myself, and Evan shortly after I left the Army and came home from Germany. The photo was taken while we were on vacation in Orlando, Florida, in August 2005.
Courtesy of the author

On to D.C. Michael Ware greets me in the lobby of the hotel as we arrive for Medal of Honor week in June 2019. *Courtesy of U.S. Army SGT Kevin Roy*

In D.C., reunited for the first time since 2004 with Joey Seyford (*left*) and Travis Barreto (*right*), two exceptionally courageous Ramrods who engaged in the desperate point-blank firefight in a Fallujah house that claimed Captain Sims's life.

Courtesy of U.S. Army SGT Kevin Roy

After all these years . . . My mother finally meets my Ramrod friends she'd heard so much about, both in the letters I sent home from Iraq, and after I returned. She greeted each one as family. Here, she talks to Chad Ellis (*right*) and Peter Smith (*left*, in leather jacket). *Courtesy of U.S. Army SGT Kevin Roy*

Left to Right: Chuck Knapp, John Ruiz, and Gary Frey together at the Pentagon during Medal of Honor week. Knapp and Ruiz were two of the best Soldiers I served with in Iraq. *Courtesy of U.S. Army SGT Kevin Roy*

My children in D.C., dressed for the White House ceremony: Evan, Vivienne, and Aiden. *Courtesy of U.S. Army SGT Kevin Roy*

John Bruning and I wrote *House to House* together in 2006 and had been close friends ever since, but we had never met in person. This was the moment we changed that. At the sergeant major of the Army's reception, Medal of Honor week. *Courtesy of U.S. Army SGT Kevin Roy*

Reunited with the best senior NCOs a young infantryman could ever ask for: Darrin Bohn (*left*) and Peter Smith (*right*). *Courtesy of U.S. Army SGT Kevin Roy*

Media day at the Pentagon. Here we are under the lights, getting questions thrown at us. *Left to right:* Colonel Doug Walter, Lieutenant Colonel Joaquin Meno, myself, Colin Fitts, and Michael Ware. *Courtesy of U.S. Army SGT Kevin Roy*

Left to right: Chuck Knapp, Chad Ellis, Omarr Hardaway, and myself, together during Medal of Honor Week. It was the first time we'd all seen each other since our 2004–05 deployment. *Courtesy of U.S. Army SGT Kevin Roy*

The Ramrods of Alpha Company meet U.S. Army Chief of Staff General James McConville and Secretary of the Army Ryan McCarthy while at the Pentagon during Medal of Honor week. To my left is Ryan McCarthy; to my right is General McConville.
Courtesy of U.S. Army SGT Kevin Roy

Master Sergeant John Gregory, who'd been one of our team leaders in 2004, poses next to a photo of himself in Iraq that we randomly discovered at the Pentagon.
Courtesy of U.S. Army SGT Kevin Roy

Captain Sean Sims's son, Colin, with me in D.C. His arrival to meet the Ramrods became one of the most emotional moments of Medal of Honor week and led to the fulfillment of a fourteen-year oath we'd made with his father.
Courtesy of U.S. Army SGT Kevin Roy

The veterans of Alpha Company, Task Force 2-2 at the Pentagon's Hall of Heroes display honoring our unit. *Courtesy of U.S. Army SGT Kevin Roy*

President Trump reads the Medal of Honor citation to our national audience. The words took me right back to November 10, 2004, into that desperate room-to-room firefight we fought at the height of the Second Battle of Fallujah. *Courtesy of John R. Bruning*

President Trump awards me the Medal of Honor. Though the ceremony happened on his watch, and he signed the citation, the review that led to this moment started under President Obama's administration. The Medal of Honor is nonpolitical, and has served as a rallying point for national unity for generations. It stands as a symbol of America's long heritage of courage and resolve in the face of desperate odds.

Courtesy of U.S. Army SGT Kevin Roy

After the East Room ceremony, with two exceptionally special guests: Jennifer Connors and Tonya Faulkenburg, our fallen command sergeant major Faulkenburg's daughter and widow. *Courtesy of U.S. Army SGT Kevin Roy*

My mother, Marilyn Bellavia, and I share a moment at the White House after the Medal of Honor ceremony.
Courtesy of U.S. Army SGT Kevin Roy

Our company's interpreter, Sammy, stands to my right as all the Ramrods flood onto the East Room platform after I ask President Trump if they may be honored. Sammy was a trusted member of our team, carrying a weapon of his own and repeatedly engaging insurgents right alongside us. To my left is Victor Santos, one of our company's most dependable and capable Soldiers. *Courtesy of U.S. Army SGT Kevin Roy*

Our American prayer. The Ramrods on stage together with our president, before an audience of millions of our fellow Americans. A moment shared of peace, unity, and strength between those we fought with and those we fought for all those years ago. *Courtesy of John R. Bruning*

Before she could press, I turned away and walked back into the house to tuck the sword away where nobody would find it.

This house had been empty for so long. Now it was echoing with people again. It evoked memories of my brothers and me tearing around the place when we were kids. Then, as grown-ups, the family returning to pay homage to my father as he struggled against cancer. All of us gathered again, my mom fussing over us, feeding us her incredible meals as we held on to every moment we could.

This was my redoubt. My space. Here among the memories, I never felt totally alone. It helped me battle the solitude and the loneliness that defined my life. Now, as this band of strangers pored over my life's artifacts, that sense of safety was gone. Stripped away. Without it, I was exposed for what I was. A middle-aged, late-in-life introvert struggling to convince myself I wasn't lonely. I didn't want anyone to know that, and I certainly didn't want their sympathy, or pity. I'd rather die.

The radio career was my attempt to keep people away from my private life by hiding in the open. Nobody would care about the war if they listened to me talk about the traffic and weather. No one sees your face on the radio, either. I controlled the narrative on the airwaves, and I always steered it away from my Iraq experiences. I had no control over this now, and the narrative of my life would be redefined by complete strangers throughout the media.

I stood in the hallway for a moment, struggling to remember the echo of my dad's voice in here. I've heard it countless times, welling up from both memories of youth and my return from combat alike. I needed to hear it. Needed its comfort in that lost moment among those strangers who now had so much control over my life.

All I heard were their voices in the living room.

I sleepwalked back to the garage and told Colonel Perez I was okay. She called the team back in. Cheerfully, as if nothing had happened, they streamed back into the garage and took up station around the locker boxes. A moment later, somebody fished out my Fallujah boots, dog tags still tied to their laces. I walked back into the kitchen to hand the boots over to Liz Chamberlain as she studied her notes, her librarian glasses sitting mid-nose. Looking up from her paperwork, she tilted her head in confusion.

Then she realized what they were. "Oh my god. Are these the boots you wore in the house?" Liz asked. My silence confirmed their provenance. A million memories flooded through the vault door, behind which they'd been safe from mind and soul.

In 2004, those boots were covered in gore, muck and mud, treads worn and cut from all the miles of ruined city we'd patrolled through. They were mottled with the blood of my Soldiers, and the blood of my enemies. I had waded through slicks of human remains and open sewers. Those boots were like old friends bearing terrible images of the past. They had been through everything with me. They'd seen the worst sights of my life and never once let me down. As dumb as it sounds, every step of the way, they made me feel safe. When we got back to Germany, I pulled them off one final time, our relationship complete. They had done their job. I'd done mine. Now it was time to go home to a place I'd never need to wear them again. I stored them away in that locker box and forgot about them.

A wretched stench filled the garage, a mix of rotting human flesh, ammonia, and that coppery smell of blood that I will never forget. Like somebody pissed on a pile of pennies a decade ago.

The boots were dark and moldy, blotched with ancient filth. The person who had fished them out held them at arm's length, hands covered with rubber gloves like he'd just found a turd floating in a public pool.

A memory refused to be suppressed. Darkness. The sound of boots splashing in a flooded room. I squeezed it away.

I am not emotionally ready for this.

Horrified looks on their faces, the team took the boots to show Colonel Perez. She stifled a gasp and said, "Yeah, we won't be needing these."

Liz agreed. "We can't use them. They're caked with insurgent."

I felt a surge of embarrassment again. I didn't mean to make anyone uncomfortable. I had forgotten what lay inside these locker boxes. I cursed myself for not looking through them before the team arrived.

Somebody bagged the boots up, tied the top, and brought them back into the garage. Their stench lingered in the house for the rest of the day.

Photos were found and handed to me to identify and caption.

While the team in the garage dissected the contents of the locker boxes, several other people went through my yearbooks and family photo albums. I was going between photos of my friends who died in Iraq, to looking at pictures of my dad that I hadn't seen in decades.

My father had been gone just over a year. Now I was reliving the two great traumas of my life simultaneously. It was exhausting. The day disappeared into a haze, surreal and studded with memories and emotions.

When the photos were finally set aside in tidy piles, all copied and filmed by Colonel Perez and her team, Liz produced a notebook.

"David, I have some tough questions for you."

"More?" I asked.

She glanced at her notebook, then began. "Staff Sergeant Bellavia, did you ever joke around on the air that you thought President Obama was a homosexual?"

"Wait. What?"

"On your radio show."

Straight out of left field.

"Well . . ." I tried to think. Switching gears from Fallujah and my father, family, and the men I loved when I wore the uniform to some stupid throwaway comment I may have said on the air was not an instant transition for me.

Liz waited patiently. Staring at me like there was nothing funny about whatever I was going to say.

"I . . . don't think I ever said that. I have a cohost and we do four hours a day. I've been doing these shows for over seven years. I'm sure I've said many things that are dumb. That particular one doesn't make sense."

"You said it," Liz said, more a statement of fact than an accusation. "We have the audio of it. What did you mean by it?"

"Was it funny? Was it meant to be funny?" I asked.

She looked very uncomfortable. "No. I don't think it was. I know no one in the media will think it's funny. Were you serious when you said it?"

Thousands of hours on the radio, and this sliver of a moment, a sound bite in seven years, five days a week, has been brought to my attention. Was this what I was going to face when the news of the Medal of Honor broke? Thousands and thousands of internet trolls scouring every word I've ever said or written? And here Colonel Perez's team had already done that homework, had identified the cancel-culture fodder and brought it to me to explain.

"Liz, I don't remember. I don't really even know what you're talking about. If you have the audio, I said it. I can't imagine saying it in anything but jest. And no, I don't believe that President Obama is gay. Not that I have any issues if he, in fact, was."

Liz teed up on that. "Do you—"

"No. I don't have a problem with gay people," I said, cutting her off before she could ask.

"And I'm very offended that you don't find my radio show funny."

She looked at me, eyebrows set in an upward tilt. Attack position. I was annoying her. We were in the kitchen, sitting at the table, surrounded by the ghosts of happy family memories. This felt like an interrogation.

Who wants the Medal of Honor in their forties? Young people can run around with this thing. Impress people. Make a name for themselves. All I want is my safe little rut.

I had spent the better part of the decade completely removed from my military time. Friends I'd made over the past five years—some of them didn't even know I'd written a book, let alone that I served in Iraq.

I loved that. Took pride in it. What middle-aged man wants to be defined by an experience they had in their twenties?

Liz fired another salvo. "Staff Sergeant Bellavia, are there any women that could say . . . that you and they . . . could anyone . . . ?"

She looked miserably uncomfortable digging into this aspect of my life. I saved her the trouble. "Listen, Liz. There is one soon-to-be ex-wife. There are no men. No drugs. I don't drink."

She immediately went back to her questions as she scribbled notes on her legal pad.

My cell phone rang and I hid my anger and frustration by looking down as I pulled it from my pocket. I recognized the number and accepted the call.

"Hello?"

The kitchen was dead silent, and even though I did not have the phone on speaker, everyone nearby heard a bright, booming male voice announce, "Hey, honey! I miss your beautiful face!"

I turned bright red. Liz gazed at me with suspicious eyes. Her lips sagged into a hard frown.

I switched to speaker. "Hey, Knapp?"

"Yeah, Sugar Tits?"

"Please say you are joking around before I hang up. You're on speaker. The Army is here."

"Oh. Ohhhhhhhh. I'm really sorry."

"Knapp?"

"Hello, guys. Yeah, totally messing around. Sorry about that. Not gay."

The room around me looked unconvinced and quite stern.

Knapp hastened to add, "Not that we have any issues with people who are, in fact, gay. We're cool with all who serve."

Worst. Timing. Ever.

"Knappy?"

"Yeah, Bell?"

"I'm gonna hafta call you back."

A pause. Then, "Understood. Talk to you later. Not gay here."

The line went dead.

Liz kept her eyes steady on me. I felt like I was under cross-examination.

"Liz, look. I don't smoke cigarettes. There are no men. No scandal. I do a radio show. I have a small business. I work at a milk plant, for God's sake. And I have like twenty cats."

An eyebrow arched at that.

"Yes. I do. They're farm cats. Working cats. I'm not a crazy cat lady. I would really love it if they didn't get any media attention. I can't have anyone knowing that I have cats."

"I love cats," Liz said, thawing a bit.

"I don't. I hate everything about them. They are functionable. Barn cats. They hunt and chase mice. And none of this is for publication."

I sure as hell was not going to tell her they all have names.

"Okay. Okay," Liz relented. "Can you at least give me some more information about the man who just called?"

I sketched Knapp's biography. How he'd been one of the most outstanding junior NCOs in the entire division. Dedicated, brilliantly intelligent, and, in Iraq, one of the most reliable men who served under me.

They had clearly done their research; they already knew everything. This was like talking to insurance adjusters. They ask the same question six different ways to try to catch you in a different version. They knew who Knapp was, what we went through together. Hell, somebody in the group probably read the mountains of paperwork the Giant of Khailaniya spawned. Colonel Perez told me to trust her team, but the truth was I didn't trust anyone beyond a select few, most of whom had fought with me in Iraq. People always give you a reason not to trust them, and once they reveal it, I make haste to get away.

These people here? They may be Army people, but they aren't yours. And they aren't your friends.

Liz asked me another series of questions. She went deep, and I recoiled. I answered sullenly with as few words as possible. Then she probed around my family and my soon-to-be ex-wife. I dodged. She tenaciously refused to let up. Panic rising, I didn't want to face any of this, let alone talk to strangers about it.

"David—" Liz began, clearly winding up for another curveball.

I snapped, interrupted her, the words spilling uncontrolled out of me, "You are asking me questions and you all know the answers already? Right? What do you want me to say? I don't love this woman. I was raised with obligation. My family. My church. My Army. My unit. Duty first is our moto in the Big Red One. I was obligated to give my children a family with two parents. I worked my ass off to give them a great life. Eighteen-, twenty-hour days. Multiple jobs. No sleep. No weekends. I went to war. I did whatever I needed to do. And I failed, okay? I did all I could and it still failed. What more do you want from me on that? My men. My leaders. We all did what we had to do—both there and here. I am not asking for anything more than to not have my failures be rubbed in my face. I get enough of that every day."

My head dropped, I seethed inside. I wanted to run, clear off and never return, start over and forget everything. A perfect fifteen-year reset. Instead, I stayed rooted in my chair as I heard myself say, "I never wanted this. I don't want it. Go home. You are going to blow up everything I have worked my entire life to build. You are going to destroy it."

Liz stared at me, stunned. I fell silent, ashamed of the outburst.

At length, she said softly, "Yes, we are, David. I am sorry. We are going to blow up your entire life." For the first time I saw emotion in her eyes.

That put a crack in my wall. I added, "Liz, I have three children. The kids have been told everything through their mother's eyes. Maybe now . . . this award. Maybe it will help them see me for who I really am. They have to be there. They have to meet these Ramrods. Talk with them. It is all I have left. My last chance. I can have the attention the medal will draw be used to score divorce points on a global stage. Promise that you will protect my kids. And my Soldiers."

Automatically, Liz replied, "Yes. Of course."

A silence fell between us. The fire crackled in the lull, and I listened to it, trying to pretend I was alone, in my little cocoon of a life here in my father's home.

Liz changed the subject and gently started back up, "Okay then. We'll make that happen. Now, tell me about Basic Training."

I sketched my first few months in the Army's pipeline.

"There's a notebook in one of your locker boxes with a bunch of notes on somebody named Samuel Woodfill. We haven't seen him on a platoon or company roster. Who is he? Did you serve with him?"

"He was an insurance salesman."

"You have a notebook full of information on an insurance salesman?"

"Yeah."

Liz stared at me in total disbelief.

"Before that he served in the Philippine War and World War I. He was considered America's greatest Soldier of the Great War. Alvin York got all the press. Sam Woodfill got all the respect."

"Oh."

"General Pershing awarded him the Medal of Honor in 1919. He was considered the Audie Murphy of World War I—the most heavily decorated American who served."

Maybe they don't know everything after all. Certainly not about our history. Or the history of the Medal of Honor.

I added, "He sold insurance after the war."

"Oh."

She switched topics to cover the awkwardness. "Did you write an op-ed article called 'F Robert Fulghum'?"

"Yes."

"The author of the book *All I Really Need to Know I Learned in Kindergarten*?"

"Yeah. Is there a problem with that?"

"Why?"

"Iraq taught me I . . . strongly disagreed with his book's premise."

"Oh."

"Look, I need a break," I said, standing up before she could react. I swiftly exited the kitchen and found my way to the living room. My grandfather was still spinning stories, and for a moment, I felt the same pull to listen I'd felt when I was eight years old hearing them for the first time.

". . . that night it was so cold at Bastogne, I thought I was sleeping on a rock." My grandfather's voice lacked modulation since he'd lost his hearing. I was pretty sure the Amish could hear this story as well as everyone here in the house. "A rock. Ha! Some rock. When I woke up in the morning, I realized I'd been sleeping on a dead pig. Frozen solid. I'd slept on him all night."

His audience's reaction made him laugh. Soft, cushy twenty-first-century Americans have no frame of reference for such stories, and while some of my visitors looked at my grandfather with love and appreciation, others were shocked. They were sitting around the living room, listening to my grandfather while flipping through family photo albums and yearbooks. It was a complete invasion.

This is for my own good.

I fled, unable to watch further. As I walked down the hall, I encountered another member of the team. "Staff Sergeant, we have some more photos we need you to identify. We believe these are from your unit and your time in Iraq."

"Okay," I said wearily. "Give me a minute."

"Also," another one said, joining the first, "Sergeant, we have some questions about some of the paperwork we found in your locker boxes." This one was holding a sheaf of witness statements, after-action reports, and evaluations.

"Give me a minute, please," I said again, then escaped through the back door into the yard. I took a deep breath of bitter-cold Lake Ontario air.

This is all for my own good.

These people are from the government. And they're here to help.

I don't want any of this. Yeah, maybe in 2005. Maybe after the humiliation of that award ceremony in Vilseck. Something to show that when shit went south, I stayed in the game. I did my job, and I did it well. That's all I wanted. Not this.

This felt like a life colonoscopy. All my failures. All my successes. The deepest wounds and the worst moments turned over and examined by people now to prevent or counter others from doing it publicly after the award was announced.

Wait, does that mean I'll have to go through this all over again?

What's worse than a life colonoscopy? A life colonoscopy conducted by the modern American media-political complex. How many things would be twisted out of context? How many tweets from ten years ago would be dredged up and offered as red meat to the cancel culture? Every word, every action scrutinized by hostile eyes.

I am doomed.

Suddenly, Liz seemed like the better deal.

Colonel Perez was right. They needed to know everything and be prepared for whatever firestorm the press could manufacture from it. No wonder why America's political class had become so utterly mediocre and bloated with fringe types these past thirty years. What normal, intelligent, and balanced individual would willingly subject themselves to this treatment? We all would fail the test of media scrutiny—and that includes the scrutinizers. That was its very purpose.

America's highest honor is a sacred award, but it comes at a cost as steep as service, and the scrutinizers in my house confirmed my life would never recover. I turned back for the door, steeling myself for umpteen hours more of questions, photographs, and artifacts from my life that had been long put to bed in the shadows of my heart.

12

MAIL CALL

LATE THAT AFTERNOON, THE team packed up and headed off to shoot B-roll footage around my hometown. They wanted to capture a sunset, then a sunrise in the morning. I wished them the best. They left, and I took my grandfather home.

When I returned to the house, the locker boxes were still open in the garage, their contents scattered around the floor. Useful items had been photographed or filmed. Stacks of photos lay piled beside where they'd been copied.

I looked over the scene. My memories had been ripped out and put on full display. Meaning little to anyone but me. My uniform lay draped over one lid. I walked over and regarded it.

The clothing I went to war in.

The desert-tan camouflage pattern—dubbed DCUs—looked old-fashioned now. Back in the day, they were comforting. Wearing this uniform gave me a feeling of strength and partnership, a sense of belonging I've never experienced since.

I took it into the house and tried it on, wondering if it would still fit. I needed to feel its comfort once again and prepare for the trial ahead. My life would be under increasing scrutiny from here on out. I'd have to soldier up to handle that.

Today's visit gave me an insight into what was to come. My life here in western New York was over. I was on the radio. No one knew what I looked like. I wrote a book in 2007 that was no longer connected to my identity. This was all going to change. That was clear, though I was still processing that reality. In a few months, the Pentagon would introduce me to the country. For the rest of my life, my time in Iraq would be with me every day, out in the open and on display like those open locker boxes. The things I tried to forget would be the things audiences would want to hear about, again and again. For years to come.

I needed to get back into the infantry mind-set. Tough and relentless, unfazed by anything.

Hardship? Bring it. Heartache? Can't touch me. It is my superpower.

In Iraq, whatever happened next, I knew I could handle it because I was with my tribe.

In the years since, I had noticed the differences between my father and me. He was emotional and expressive. I had my feelings on full lockdown 24/7. He would weep unashamedly at family events. Graduations and Christmases, all the usual Hallmark moments— we'd always see him tearing up. It was the currency of his love for us.

I started to understand. I was changing. I was different. In Iraq, my squad had a look. Buckled up, dead eyes, stoic. A look of toughness. Endurance. Come what may, it would never faze us. We were alpha males. We didn't cry.

My dad and life taught me a crucial lesson. You can only deny your essential humanity for so long before the dam bursts. Once it breaks, there's no rebuilding it; the torrent will always be too strong.

I walked back into the garage. There was a pile of things I needed to revisit. As the team had gone through it all, I had set certain items aside just for me. The team ignored them, as they did the bloodstained paper.

Among those things I had collected was a small box of letters. After the *Time* article came out in 2004, I started receiving mail. While I was out on missions, somebody put this box next to my bunk. On each mail call, the stack inside grew a little bit taller.

I had never read any of them. I'd never even looked through them to see who had written. I'm not sure why. Maybe the whole thing seemed so unreal. Fan mail from home? I was just a Soldier.

I picked up the box, took it into the house, and found the blood-stained piece of paper. By now it was long dark. The house was quiet. The storm outside had abated.

I was alone.

I had spent most of the last decade consciously not remembering November 10, 2004. My twenty-ninth birthday. We'd been fighting in Fallujah, building to building, for days. Then we ended up in a house filled with insurgents who had built a machine gun nest under a stairwell designed to kill anyone entering the place. I got my men out, then went back in with Scott Lawson, our heavy weapons squad leader. Lawson got hit and withdrew to get help.

Then it was just me, alone in the dark in a partially flooded house with insurgents in nearly every room.

I wouldn't be able to outrun that day anymore. The Medal of Honor would see to that. How many times does the past well up to redefine a man's future? This was what I had to look forward to now.

When my dad first started practicing dentistry out here in rural New York, he and my uncle built an emergency exam room onto the house. Long after my dad moved into a medical complex, that space remained unchanged. Over the years, it became a sort of *I Love Me* room for him, a place to mount his many awards and degrees. As the years passed, the walls in the old office grew covered with photographs and plaques.

After he died, I left the room untouched, like a time warp to my childhood. It became my homage to my dad, the place where I could connect with him and our memories together.

I put my phone on the kitchen table. No service in the old office. My uncle had lined the walls with lead to prevent X-rays from leaking into the rest of the house. That shielding is still there, and it blocks all electronic signals. It is like my own personal SCIF. Sometimes getting away from the digital era is exactly what I needed.

In the middle of the old office stood my dad's first dental chair. Pale, pea-green leather, cracked and aged now. Beside it was a spit sink and all the old equipment he used. Even the X-ray machine sat ready to be used on a swinging arm over the chair.

I sat down in it, and put the box of letters beside me on the instrument tray.

I would have been able to get through this with my dad to support me. He always was there, pushing, guiding, educating. You never really know how much you need that advice and constant support until you lose it. He was brutally honest, a great listener. We had many heart-to-heart conversations in here. At times, he'd deliver shotgun blasts of truth that would take a second dad session just to unpack. But he was always willing, always ready to guide and lend his insight.

I dug into my pocket and withdrew a can of dip. I hadn't used chewing tobacco in years. I'd quit after coming home and stuffing my uniform away. Since the president's call, I had picked the habit up again, another sign that I'd backslid into a 2004 wormhole. I tucked some into my lower lip, feeling the rush as I closed my eyes. Unconsciously, one hand went to the spit sink's handle and turned it on. Water swirled in its little bowl. I leaned forward and spat chew in it. Just like back in the day when I lived in the barracks in Germany. While the rest of the platoon was out on the town, I'd be in my bunk, reading and spitting chew into an empty Gatorade bottle.

I was on my own now. No late-night talks with my dad, or anyone, in this room anymore. No dadvice. Maybe it was for the best, honestly. Though he was well acquainted with blood and stress, his generation's war in Vietnam left him with deep scars from friends lost and family forever changed. When I went over to Iraq, I learned quickly to give him the page thirteen view of the war. Any more details, and he just couldn't handle it. He worried himself almost to death thinking about me out there in all that violence and barbarity.

When I first came home, I filtered my war for his consumption. We sat in this room, one of us in the dental chair—usually me—the other atop the wheeled stool sitting nearby, talking through all hours of the night in what became a PG-13, *Reader's Digest* coverage of my Iraq memories. I think he knew I was censoring them, but he never wanted to delve deeper.

That changed when the book came out. He read *House to House* over and over, gleaning every detail of my life in combat, wanting to know everything now that I was safe here in New York.

Still, the book was a safe barrier. When it was just the two of us, I couldn't tell him those things detailed in the book. That wall remained.

I missed him right then with elemental force. Like part of me had been cut away when cancer finally claimed him.

Dad. I need you now. We would've figured all this out. Together.

A moment passed, my eyes on the ceiling, head back against the padded rest of the dental chair. Then I ran my hands over my face and tried to turn a mental page. No good thinking like that.

I looked over at the instrument tray and the box resting there. Why did total strangers write to me back then? What was it that was so important they would take the time to pen a letter in the age of email and Instant Messenger?

I felt like a dick for never having looked.

I picked up the box and peered inside. Letters with postmarks from all over the country lay in there. I riffled through, and halfway down the stack, I saw familiar handwriting. I pulled it out and looked it over. Sure enough, it was from a high school girlfriend. I tore the envelope open and started to read.

"Dear David . . . I saw the *Time* magazine article and wanted to write. I'm not even sure you'll be alive to read this. . . ."

Words of concern and care echoed through the past as I read for the first time. I finished and peered back up at the ceiling. Sweet girl. Beautiful note. I wish I'd read it in Iraq; it would have been a comfort.

I reached back into the box of unopened letters to see if anyone else I knew had written me. My fingers froze on one.

My dad's handwriting.

I held it up, the envelope yellowed and aged, but the flap unbroken. For a minute, I didn't know what to do. I held it to my heart, eyes circling the room at all his certificates and postgraduate work. A lifetime of investment into his craft. He never stopped learning. Had I mentioned how much I respected that? I don't think I ever did.

I wanted to open the letter. My fingers trembled. I stayed in place, thinking about how he so vehemently objected to me joining the Army. After 9/11, he became my biggest fan, like an out-of-control Little League dad.

I don't think I treated him well back then. Part of it was because by the time we got to Iraq, I was a father figure to the young studs in my squad. Somewhere along the line, I had assumed that to be a father figure meant closing off your own dad. Look down and support, not up and for advice. What a load of horseshit. I was young and dumb, and I know my distance caused my dad pain. I tried to explain it after I got home, but unless you've been through it, there's no way to understand.

Yet, as always, he forgave me.

My eyes played across the walls. They stopped on his Golden Pen Award from 1987. He was an artful writer and would send op-eds to the local papers. He always had a direct way of getting words down, just like his double-barreled truth blasts in our face-to-face moments.

I pulled the letter from my heart and studied the envelope. It was postmarked in mid-November, before the *Time* magazine article came out. How had I missed this one?

I flipped it over and gently pried open the flap. Inside was a single folded piece of stationery. The date at the top read: November 10, 2004.

The night I was fighting for my life in that Fallujah house, my dad wrote me a letter I had never even seen until today.

Dear Son,

I couldn't sleep tonight. Had a weird feeling that something was wrong and you're struggling. I just wanted to write you, tell you how much I love you. How proud of you I am.

I couldn't read any further.

Suddenly I was back in the Fallujah house, slowly climbing the stairs, knowing I was probably going to die up there on the second floor. My luck was done. My heart was numb. The insurgent I had been chasing was moving around, panting, making noises. How many more were up there? It didn't matter. With less than a mag of ammo left for my M4, I couldn't walk away. This had to be finished.

I looked down at my boots. Dog tags on my laces. Once desert tan, now coated in muck and gore.

Another step. Rifle at the ready, head behind the sight as the second floor came slowly into view.

Back home, in that exact moment, my dad sat here on a restless

November night, penning these words at the desk beside his now-antique dental chair, driven to do so because in some cosmic way we are connected to those we love so completely. Distance, geography—that doesn't matter. There is a *feeling* sent across those miles in times of deep turbulence. Others in uniform have experienced it, too. Sometimes we used to talk about it in quiet tones, among those most trusted.

Somehow, my dad knew.

I held the letter, seeing the war from his perspective for the first time. Bound by these walls and this bastion of peace back home. Hoping to see glimpses of the Ramrods on the evening news, but dreading what those scenes might look like if he did. The helplessness. For a man of great strength, used to having power over the province of his life, I was in a dreadful exile he could not control. This letter was the best he could do, and I knew it reflected that sense of helplessness.

All he could offer me were words of comfort in the dead of a sleepless night that had tormented him with worst-case scenarios.

I had never known, never thanked him. Never read those words until long after we shared our last moments together. I felt a stab of guilt.

In order to be surrogate father, you've got to abandon your own.

How had I actually believed that?

He had his war. I had mine. I was so fixated years ago in trying to explain my war, I'd forgotten to listen to his. Now I saw it, and I understood the toll it took on him.

I finished the letter and placed it reverently on the instrument tray, beside the bloodstained piece of paper. Unconsciously, I picked that up, and like a sudden shift of gears, my mind went straight back to January 2005, to that moment in a muddy street in Hembis, Iraq.

I stood in the street in the aftermath of a firefight, watching a scene of complete chaos unfold as people rushed to treat the wounded civilians the enemy had deliberately targeted.

A woman, shot through the neck and jaw, screamed. I thought she was screaming for help. Blood poured from her wound, pooling around her as she continued to cry out. Members of the platoon ran toward her.

That's when I realized she wasn't calling for help. She was scream-ing, "Paper! Paper!" Over and over, like a clarion call, she uttered that word. Then we saw her reach out, clutching at something only she seemed to see.

"Paper! Paper!" she wailed.

Our medic began working on her as an Iraqi ambulance arrived nearby. The crew dismounted and came to join the effort to save her life.

Around us, civilians stood beside a bullet-riddled schoolhouse, qui-etly watching this tragedy play out in the street in front of them. They were dressed in their best clothes—including the kids whose wide eyes remained locked on the wounded woman, who still cried out, even as she grew weak from blood loss.

An elderly Iraqi woman stepped out of the schoolhouse. Under one arm she carried a sheaf of papers. She walked to the wounded woman. With trembling hands she reached down and gave her one sheet of paper.

The woman clutched the paper and drew it to herself as if it were a talisman. She'd lost so much blood. Our medic did what he could, but her cries turned to wordless gurgles as the ambulance crew lifted her onto a stretcher.

The paper. She wanted it more than anything else, and she gave her last breaths to a desperate plea for it. She held on to it even as she was loaded into the ambulance and carried away.

The old woman, traumatized by what she'd just seen, dropped the sheaf of papers. They fluttered into the street, blown by the breeze into water-filled potholes and into the pool of the stricken woman's blood.

I hurried over and scooped them up, chasing them as the wind played them across the muddy street. Several were dripping wet with blood or filthy water.

Ballots. They were ballots from Iraq's first-ever truly free election. The insurgent attack had hit this polling place, established in the town's school, to try and stop the voting process through sheer terror. Shoot civilians as they stood in line to vote, and they figured others would flee or never queue up.

The civilians weren't having any of it. The line remained. Nobody ran away. The dying woman set the example for the others. She wanted only to have her chance to vote before her life gave out.

I gave all the ballots back but one. It was stained with the young woman's blood and beyond being usable. So I kept it as a reminder that what we take for granted back home was worth dying for to others here in Iraq.

I folded it reverently and slipped it into my DCUs, aching at the sight of what had just gone down.

I jerked out of the memory through searing tears, sitting rigidly in my dad's dental chair. For a moment, every detail, every cry and sound and smell had returned as if I were actually there in Hembis on election day 2005.

There was profound meaning in that moment for us at the time. It felt like everything we'd gone through in our deployment was vindicated by that day. Free elections. Democracy.

It all went to shit after. So that memory became a high-water mark for me. One I worked really hard to forget.

I looked down at the bloodstained piece of paper. Iraq's first ballot. That dying woman's blood faded and brown now. I kept this one out of all those I picked up on the road that day as a reminder of what we had fought to achieve, and what the people of Iraq risked to have their voices heard for the first time.

I couldn't read any of it. It was in Arabic. We had no idea who the candidates were or what they stood for back then. That was Iraq's business, not ours. All that mattered at the time was that this process had happened.

Colonel Perez had told me what to expect. Interviews. Speeches. The ceremony at the White House. The Medal of Honor is a national symbol, one of unity and pride. Wearing it would ensure I will never escape these memories. The locker boxes were opened. There was no closing them now.

In that moment, I knew what I had to do.

I stood up, put the ballot next to my father's letter. Fifteen years ago, I went through hell with my blood brothers of 2-2 at my side. I needed them now, and that included Fitts.

If you've got to go through hell again, go through with the people you've already been there with. The problem was, we all had issues with each other. There were reasons we didn't stay in touch. Deep wounds, made worse by the stress and trauma of war.

Maybe, just maybe, after all these years, we'd find we needed each other again.

I returned to the kitchen to retrieve my cell phone. I had a lot of calls to make.

13

A SACRED PROMISE

ASK ANY VETERAN WHO served in the enlisted ranks, and they'll tell you that the majority of officers they bumped into during their time in service were forgettable. Box checkers and straitjacket conformists trying to divine how to be leaders from the pages of field manuals. Careerists and ring knockers who see their rung on the ladder only as a stepping point to the next one. We respect the rank, but all too often, the men or women who wear it we judge to be tools.

The chasm between officers and enlisted has always been a wide one, so this is nothing new. But get us talking about the ones who found a way to bridge that divide and you'll find the Army's true leaders.

They are rare. They change lives and careers. They hold units and organizations together when everything else goes to hell. We followed them not because of their rank, but because we trusted them. They led by example, shared our hardships, never used their rank as a privilege, but as an asset to help those under their command. Leaders like those? We never forget them. And they make the tools all too easy to forget.

One person embodied all the intangibles a great leader needed. He had all those boxes checked: leather-toughness, resolve, dedication, intelligence, creative thinking, aggressiveness. He was a warrior down to the last cell in his body, a man who was totally defined by his commitment to the profession—calling—of combat arms.

He loved his men, genuinely, not because he had to but because taking care of subordinates was always the right thing to do. He fought with us on the battlefield, and he fought for us in countless administrative skirmishes. He demanded the best of us: the best of himself, and the best for the men under his command. He built our company from the ground up, trained us for two years to be as relentless in the fight as he was in life. Though only a few years older than I was, he became a mentor, a role model, a father figure to all of us. Following him into flying bullets and exploding IEDs took no leap of faith. We trusted him that much to get us through, and get us home.

Doug Walter was that man, our original company commander who stood before us just before we deployed to Iraq and told us he could not go with us. We could see the anguish written on his face, the sense that he had let us down by not leading us directly from the Vilseck training ranges to the battlescapes we faced in Iraq.

He hadn't let us down, of course. His body had failed him. For months, we'd all noticed his weight loss. He had been five ten, 190 pounds as he trained us. That February, as he spoke to us, he was a skeleton at 130. He looked haggard and bone-weary, heartsick as well, fighting some traumatic medical battle he refused to burden his men with. It wasn't for years that I learned the nature of his enemy: ulcerative colitis. The medication the doctors gave him was as bad as the ailment, and he could not sustain the treatment for extended periods. So he roller-coastered between being sick while on the meds, or sicker off them.

By that day in February 2004 when he told us he could not lead us into battle, his doctors had recommended he have his colon removed. He faced life-changing surgery and a medical discharge from the Army—and the life he loved as much as I did.

In his place, Captain Walter's best friend took the company. That was Sean Sims. The two were thick as thieves. Their friendship was the closest I'd ever seen among officers. They were like brothers. Walter, a bit more aggressive and fiery. Sims, a bit more cerebral and contemplative. Brothers, nonetheless.

Walter defied the odds. He found a dietary regimen that saved him from surgery and restored his health enough that he rejoined his beloved Ramrods in Iraq. While Sims led Alpha Company, Walter played a supporting role on the battalion's staff until the fighting in Fallujah took his best friend's life. That's when he came back to us and led the company through the rest of our deployment.

I'd last seen Doug Walter in 2015. He was a battalion commander, stationed at Joint Base Lewis-McChord in Washington State. Amazingly, our old Ramrod first sergeant, Peter Smith, was Walter's brigade command sergeant major. It was a mini TF 2-2 reunion on the other side of the country, and the far side of the world from our battlefields.

That year, Lieutenant Colonel Walter invited me to his battalion's annual ball. It was a formal event, part of a long tradition every U.S. Army unit has enjoyed since George Washington led us to victory in the American Revolution. There was no way I could refuse such an invite. I hopped the first thing smoking and went to see them both.

When I arrived, Lieutenant Colonel Walter called his entire battalion to attention. Everyone was in their dress blues—their best, most meticulously tailored uniforms—and they looked sharp. I was humbled by the greeting. As I stood there, in a civilian suit, Walter called another officer forward, who declared, "Attention to orders!"

My old company commander called me forward, and I passed the ranks of his new battalion as they stood rigidly at attention. Doug Walter proceeded to read my Silver Star citation aloud, then stepped up to pin the award to my suit jacket.

Here, ten years removed from that day in Vilseck when the Ramrods celebrated the symbols of their service at the awards ceremony, Doug Walter took the time to balm an old wound in one of the countless NCOs who had served under him. That night, he made sure I received the award properly, the Ramrod way. If I'd had an internal microphone hooked into my brain, it would have come in broken and distorted. A gift like this comes along once in a lifetime. I couldn't believe anyone was looking out for me all these years later.

That was Doug Walter. He loved us, and long after we went our separate ways, he continued to look out for us. That's the kind of man we all should aspire to be.

That night, after he pinned the award to my suit coat, his was the first hand I shook. The second was Command Sergeant Major Peter Smith's. It would have been exactly the same in 2005 in Germany.

At the end of the surprise ceremony, Walter addressed his men: "This Soldier was one of mine. And he still is. One day, this man will be wearing the Medal of Honor. I won't retire until that gets done."

Lieutenant Colonel Walter didn't need to do that. Any of it. I always felt I owed him an unrepayable debt. His leadership. His kindness to me expressed countless ways in Europe and Iraq—they ensured that letting him down was a fate far worse than anything the enemy could dish out to me. Both Smith and Walter—they shaped me into the Soldier I became with their tough love and mentorship.

That moment in 2015 was one of the best nights of my life.

Four years later, Doug Walter had been promoted to full colonel and was the deputy commander of Fort Jackson in South Carolina. I called him several times to tell him about the Medal of Honor and the White House ceremony, but he was always out and about in the thick of things. I wouldn't have expected anything less. We played phone tag for a bit until, finally, we connected.

"Hey, sir!" I said as I put him on speakerphone at my house.

"Staff Sergeant Bellavia, how are you? How you doing?" Colonel Walter's voice sounded weary. Normally he was upbeat and relentlessly optimistic, even in the worst of moments in Vilseck during his illness, then later in Iraq. Now, with just these few words I could tell something was wrong.

"Sir. You first."

Is he sick again?

There was a silence that was very unlike him. I stepped into it: "I just want to say, I miss you so much. And I am really grateful to have you in my life."

No words followed. At first, I thought our call had broken up, but then I heard him breathing. He was still there, and I sensed he was struggling with what to say.

"Sir?"

"It's been tough, Staff Sergeant Bell. Really tough."

"What's going on, sir?"

Another long pause. Then his voice, choked with emotion, came through my cell phone: "I'm going through a rough divorce. Really rough . . . My kids . . . It's just ripping me to pieces."

Colonel Walter had no idea I was traveling the exact same path. His pain, his worry? As I listened to him it was like hearing a testimonial to my own 0300 inner monologue.

"Why do people get so angry?" I asked him. "So bitter? Why would anyone use their children as a cudgel to punish the person they once loved?"

"Sergeant Bell, there's a formula they use against guys like us. We're painted as the crazy, unstable war veteran. We will kill our own, because we killed the enemy in battle. There's no distinction. Like we're just killers."

This was so true. I'd heard of it happening over and over within our Ramrod community over the years. There's little understanding in the court system, which doesn't see we fought in Iraq *because* of our people back home. To defend them with our lives. Coming back and inflicting violence on our own? Yes, it happens. The media reports every case with breathless excitement, heaping them onto the antiwar, anti-administration plates and politicizing interfamily issues for their own narrow bias confirmation.

According to one study, a third of combat veterans suffering from post-traumatic stress reportedly were involved in domestic violence situations in the past year. Somewhere between 8 and 35 percent of American combat veterans suffer from PTS at some point in their postdeployment lives. Those committing violence against their loved ones are a third of a third of our community. Yet their actions have been weaponized against the vast majority of us who love our families and would never do them harm.

Colonel Walter was right.

"It is so cruel, Bell. So cruel."

"Yes it is, sir."

"We fought to get back to our kids, not to lose them because of the things we had to do to survive."

Every firefight. Every battle. I saw Evan. Felt his presence. Knew I had to return to him at all costs. In the darkness of a Fallujah house, surrounded by enemies, I uttered a Soldier's prayer, asking God to give me the strength to get home to my boy.

It was all that mattered to me.

"Sir, this is the exact same discussion I've had with my attorney."

"I'm really, really sorry to hear that, Sergeant."

His voice nearly broke, and the emotion in it took me right back to the last time I'd heard him speak this way. Valentine's Day, 2004. We should have been celebrating love back home with our wives and girlfriends. Instead we stood beside a column of buses, surrounded by our bags and gear as then-captain Walter stepped up to address us.

He was a mess. A scarecrow of who he once had been four months ago, when we served in Kosovo under him. Nobody knew what was wrong with him, but everybody saw the effects. His face was gaunt, eyes hollow. He stood in front of us, no bags, no gear at his feet. Nearby, Captain Sean Sims, the battalion operations officer and Walter's best friend, waited for Walter to speak beside my platoon. Sims's arms were folded, his face devoid of expression.

"Men, nothing more . . ." Captain Walter began, but his emotions overwhelmed him. He fought for control, and restarted. "Nothing more I want to do than lead this company at war as I have while we've trained these past eighteen months for that fight. We have prepared for this throughout our entire careers in the Army. This is all I want."

We had never heard him talk like this. It was so personal that I felt like he was speaking these words directly to me, just the two of us instead of the hundred and twenty gathered in formation in front of him.

"I cannot do it," he managed to say. "My body won't let me."

The company looked visibly stricken. Nobody said a word, but I saw the faces around me. They mirrored my own shock. Walter was bulletproof. The larger-than-life leader who defied every obstacle, every roadblock. We counted on him to be infallible.

"Captain Sims . . . he's going to lead you. He is my best friend. He will fight. He will do everything I can't do physically. And I'll be watching, chiming in when I can. And I know you will not let me down."

"Sergeant Bell?" Colonel Walter's voice brought me back from that memory.

"Here, sir."

"I don't mean to bum you out. I am . . . just going through a lot. Tell me about you. How are you?"

It was my turn to lay my own burden on the table. I told him about my own family's dissolution. The sacrifices I'd been making. The solitary life on the hill. It became a core dump, and the words flushed out of me in a torrent like they never had before.

"Oh, Bell. I am so sorry you're going through this, too. What a load of BS."

"Thank you, sir. And you as well."

"I worked so hard to get your family to Germany. Your son. His medical needs . . ." Walter's voice trailed off, frustrated and angry at the decades-old effort.

I stood in that cold Vilseck night, studying the crowd for Evan. Telling myself not to, that he wasn't coming. But hope dies so hard.

"I'll always be grateful for the effort, sir. It is indicative of how much you loved us. You have always been our rock."

What followed was a three-hour conversation that lasted well into that night. The more we talked, the more I admired my old company commander for his strength and wisdom. A man of such character as this in my life? What a blessing.

By the time we signed off for the night, both of us were smiling. We'd gone from bearing our scars to cracking jokes. Our conversation flowed effortlessly from the serious and heartfelt to the light and laughter.

I was back with my family again. My people. My Army tribe. And Colonel Walter was our village elder.

I glanced back down at the phone. The call ended, and I burst out laughing. After three hours, I had forgotten to even tell him why I had called in the first place.

Quickly, I dialed him back.

"Sergeant Bell?" he answered.

"Hey, sir? I totally forgot to tell you. The president called me. They're giving us the Medal of Honor for Fallujah."

"Wait. What? You talked to who?"

"The president."

"You waited three hours to tell me this?"

"Yeah, sorry about that, sir."

"The president. Of the United States."

"Yes, sir. The Medal of Honor."

Dead silence on the phone again. Then I heard Colonel Walter breathing again. It sounded like the news had just deviated his septum.

"Sir, listen to this."

I put him on speakerphone and played the recording I'd made of the phone conversation with President Trump. When it ended, I took him off speaker and put the phone to my ear.

Colonel Walter chose that moment to let out the longest war cry I've ever heard. He screamed and cheered like our team had just won the Super Bowl. This is how he raised us, *we, not me*. Us. We won. This was our award, and we both were sharing in its moment. Hearing him, 180 degrees and a thousand miles from where I found him emotionally three hours before, was a wonderful feeling—and the first insight into what good the award might do for my Ramrod family.

"Sergeant Bell, I don't even know what to say. I am . . . I really, really needed this. I needed to hear it."

"Sir?"

"Oh my god. We worked so hard for it. I told every general I ever met for the last fifteen years about this. About you. About this award. And I thought it had been shot down in 2014. Dead and buried at the Decorations Board."

I hadn't known that.

"Fifteen years," he said again.

"There will be a ceremony at the White House, sir. With the president. And our guys. I want to bring everyone back. I'm going to ask them all to come. I don't care what it costs. I'll get a third job if I have to. I'll take care of it all. And we need you there, sir. With us."

"Of course I'll be there, Sergeant Bell. Thank you. I would not miss it."

"Sir, I need one more thing from you."

"Name it."

"I need Captain Sims's wife and his son to be there, too."

"Absolutely. I'll send you her contact information."

"That'd be great, sir. Thank you."

A long silence followed. Not uncomfortable, as it would be with somebody else. It let me know he was winding up to tell me something.

"You should talk to First Sergeant Smith. He spoke to Sims the day after all this happened. You know what Sims said, right? What he told Battalion?"

"No, sir. I do not."

About a month before we left for Fallujah in October 2004, Doug Walter arrived at FOB Normandy, healthy enough to join us. He had avoided colon surgery by radically changing his diet. It took steel discipline, but he cut out all sugar, complex carbohydrates, and a laundry list of the best food life has to offer. He had regained some of his lost weight and was eager to get into the fight with us. Battalion left Captain Sims in charge of our company and had Walter training Iraqi police and national guardsmen. Between his training duties, he would come back to his beloved company and work with Sims to plan and brief missions. They made an incredible team, Sims in charge, Walter doing everything to assist him. They prepared and planned for Fallujah together, and I know Walter took it very hard when TF 2-2 moved out for that coming battle without him. He stayed at Normandy, training our allies.

Walter had been bunking in Sims's room, right next to First Sergeant Peter Smith's billet at our FOB. He was there when a headquarters Soldier came to tell him that Sean Sims had been killed in action in Fallujah. He had sat silently, processing the fact that his best friend was dead. Then he stood up, walked into the night, and threw his helmet into the air out of sheer grief and fury. The headquarters Soldier later told me he flung it so high and far that he lost sight of it, and only the distant sound of it thudding to the ground was evidence that he'd thrown it in the first place.

Our chain of command had been decimated in Fallujah. We had lost our company commander, his executive officer Lieutenant Iwan, and our battalion sergeant major. Alpha needed steady leadership. Our new command sergeant major, Darrin Bohn, and First Sergeant Smith called 1st Infantry Division headquarters and asked for Captain Walter. Major General John Batiste personally allocated a Black Hawk helicopter to bring Walter to us. He arrived less than twenty-four hours after his best friend's death.

I'll never forget the look on his face when he arrived: jaw set, eyes burning with fury and focus. He was going to get back what the insurgents took from all of us. Our morale, which was circling the drain, was instantly revived by his presence, like we'd found an energy pod in a video game and were good to go again.

"Sergeant Bell. According to First Sergeant Smith, Captain Sims wrote everything down that happened in Fallujah. When I got there, I got the brief. After November tenth, everyone said that Sims had mentioned 'Bellavia—Audie Murphy.'"

"Okay?"

"After that everyone started talking about that story. And it became clear that there was something here that wasn't typical. That's when I first started speaking about the Medal of Honor with our leadership. It wasn't laughed at. It was something the more I spoke about with Battalion or Brigade, the more people agreed with me."

"Sir? What?" I was stunned.

"This award. This was for all of us. For Sims. Everyone. When we got back, I went and interviewed everyone who was there that night to find out what had really happened. To find out what went down and what you did."

I knew none of this. I nearly dropped the phone.

"I worked with LTC Newell to get this pushed up. Nobody at Division had ever written up a Medal of Honor before. We didn't know how to do it. There's no book on it. So we wrote the book. We busted our ass. I made it my personal mission, because I knew Sean Sims wanted this, and it was my way of honoring his wishes."

A sacred oath, shared between best friends and brothers.

I had no words.

"David. Sean would have been so happy."

"Sir," I began.

How do you even respond to this?

"Thank you, sir. For doing so much. For always being there for us. For your fidelity and leadership. You were always there when we needed you. Always. What you've done for me personally? Well, sir, I do not know a better man in my life."

"Sean Sims. He's looking down on us. He made this happen."

Shell-shocked, we said an emotional goodbye and signed off. The silence in my living room was deafening. I don't do emotional well. Never have. My dad? He could do it. I've tried to live in his footsteps there, to open spaces in my heart to it. But my natural inclination is to deflect, distract. Be a smart-ass. And so, part of me wanted to call Colonel Walter back a third time and say something like, "Sir, I forgot to tell you the big news. I've transitioned to a woman. And I'm pregnant."

Maybe that would have been too politically incorrect. "Sir, I got signed as a free agent by the Buffalo Bills and I'm starting at free safety this fall."

I felt foolish for thinking these things as soon as they came across my brain. I desperately wanted to break up this feeling with laughter. Make a joke. Laugh it off. The best way to handle what I was currently feeling. I shoved the impulse aside and tried to get a handle on the moment. I had thirty-eight more calls to make, and if even a couple more ended up with some sort of revelation like this, my entire understanding—perception—of my own past was going to be radically redrawn. From the Man in White to the discovery that the officer I thought wanted my hide actually wanted this award for me—I didn't even recognize my own past now anymore.

I closed my eyes and let the memories flow unfettered.

14

THEY SHALL FEAR OUR FEROCITY

DIYALA PROVINCE, IRAQ — SEPTEMBER 2004

"Whaddyou wanna do?" I asked Fitts as we stood before our map board in our barracks NCO room. Lieutenant Joaquin Meno stood nearby, posted up by our "seat of privilege"—a chair in the middle of our space reserved for those who had engaged and killed the enemy. Only then could you sit in it and tell stories to the other NCOs.

The map board hung on otherwise jailhouse-bare walls, right beside my cot and the homemade crucifix that held my helmet and body armor. No photos of home near my space, just that board with three maps of our area of operations: one depicting the road net, one depicting the political demographics, and one topographic. Surrounding them were the latest satellite and overhead images that Lieutenant Colonel Newell's intel shop had pushed down to us.

"Hackworth says we need to out-Muj the Muj."

"What the hell does that mean?"

"Work harder. Stay out longer. Be ferocious. Never let them out-work us. Dig in sometimes. Take the high ground when possible. Grab rooftops without turning lights on in a house. Never do the same thing twice."

"I wish I'd never given you that damned book."

Lieutenant Colonel David H. Hackworth had been a staff guy in Vietnam, writing counterinsurgency manuals in the Pentagon, when he was ordered to put his theories into practice. He was sent to Southeast Asia and given command of the worst battalion in theater. He transformed it into a Viet Cong–threshing machine known as the Hardcore Recondos. They damaged the enemy every time they left the wire.

Fitts had given me Hackworth's memoir, *Steel My Soldiers' Hearts*, before we left Vilseck. I read it and absorbed its lessons. Then one day at Normandy, I sent him a random fanboy email through his publisher and his agent.

He responded. He was in Mexico, dying of bladder cancer. Without violating operational security, I sketched our situation and asked what he would do. He offered excellent advice, like a tactical Dear Abby. We corresponded often.

"I'm telling you, Fittsy, he's an almanac of information."

Never let them outwork you and you will never be ambushed again. Your men will bitch. They will hate you. But in twenty years when you are all older, they will realize how much they appreciated the attention you paid to the details of war. Work harder. Do your best to leave your enemy where you killed him. If your command makes you police the dead, make him bleed enough for his buddies to know what happened there. Send the message. "Mess with us and get wrecked. They shall fear our ferocity."

"Call me in thirty years and I will sound pretty smart, too. Everyone knows everything from ten thousand miles away on a beach. Come out here and actually do it in person. Screw Hackworth. You pen pals with Oliver North, too? Or anyone else I need to know?"

"Jesse Ventura thinks you're a pussy."

The bay erupted in laughter and broke the tension. When order was restored, we all turned back to the map board and got back to the detail planning of our next mission.

Our men were out there, dying every day. Americans killed by a weapon we'd never really encountered before: the roadside bomb. We rolled into Iraq in 2003 more a motorized army than an armored one. For every Bradley Fighting Vehicle and M1 Abrams tank, there were thirty unarmored Humvees conducting vehicular patrols without any crew protection whatsoever.

The first bombs encountered were small and not particularly

threatening. In Vilseck, we were told to watch out for booby-trapped soda cans, or explosives concealed in dead dogs thrown like roadkill alongside highways.

If that had been the norm in 2003, it most certainly was not by the time TF 2-2 arrived in early 2004. The pop-can bombs had been replaced by mortar rounds wired by homeschooled terrorist bomb makers and emplaced in piles of trash, under culverts, and in freshly dug holes on dirt roadbeds.

The threat only grew from there. The improvised explosive device, or IED, became the insurgency's most effective killing weapon against our troops. From mortar rounds and Russian plastic explosives, they moved on to artillery shells pilfered from the countless ammunition stocks left behind by the Hussein regime.

Sometimes these would-be bomb layers would expose shocking levels of stupidity. One night, Sergeant First Class Cantrell's B Section was watching a suspected bomb maker while A Section and my squad were at the JCC on standby. Cantrell and his Brad were quietly watching our suspect from long range, using the track's thermal optics. The plan was to follow him after he completed his work and see where he went, whom he talked to, or where he laid the bomb.

Captain Sims had drilled into us that not all kills were good kills, in the sense that their deaths did not further our mission. We needed guys alive whom we could interrogate and get a better understanding of the threat we faced. When we did bring in detainees, our battalion intel shop was doing amazing work with our local special forces detachments and CIA interrogators by their side. They would get actionable information out of our prisoners before they were handed over to the Iraqi police—who almost always immediately let them go.

We understood that sometimes we needed intelligence more than we needed body bags filled. But capturing the same guy planting another IED over and over felt more like we were part of the Chicago Police Department than the infantry. Nevertheless, we needed information. So we'd lie in wait, see whom the welder interacted with, then wrap him up and bring him back to Normandy for questioning.

That night, the plan went awry, though not through any fault of our own.

I heard Cantrell call over the radio, "Hey Six, this is Seven."

First Lieutenant Meno radioed back to Sergeant First Class Cantrell. "Seven, this is Six."

"This idiot is trying to weld two . . . no three . . . holy hell, three one-five-five shells together. This is gonna be bad. I'm getting out of here."

Three minutes later, an enormous blast and apocalyptic mushroom cloud rocked the entire city of Muqdadiyah. Cantrell had it right. Our would-be bomb maker obviously never took that online class on *The Anarchist Cookbook*. He certainly had no clue what trying to weld three high-explosive heavy artillery shells could do to him. Heat, plus pressure, plus stupid equals boom. He took care of himself, his home, and the entire IED factory he had built.

It wasn't often the insurgents did our work for us, but we appreciated when they did.

Spectacular stupidity aside, stopping the IED attacks was an unglamorous, gut-grinding game of cat and mouse. The insurgents were compartmentalized, cagey, watchful. We learned they had eyes everywhere, and comms with all their pals.

We began working against the IED layers like any other line unit. We quickly discovered we had to get creative, had to listen to Lieutenant Colonel Hackworth's advice if we were to have any hope of stemming these deadly attacks.

The wake-up call was hard-earned. For me, it started with a night where we dismounted from our Bradley at nearly the same place we had the night before. We piled out of the back of the Bradley under a star-filled sheet above us. As soon as our boots hit the ground, we saw it: fifty meters away and on the other side of the road, beside the tracks in the sand that our Brad had left the previous night, was freshly disturbed soil. A hole. When we investigated—carefully—we discovered a hastily buried 155mm shell wired to a cell phone.

Insurgents had been watching us, learning our patterns, planting bombs where they expected our return. Our track commander, Staff Sergeant Cory Brown, chose to dismount us in a slightly different place, and that probably saved all of us.

Routine. Pattern. Units would get complacent and fall into a rut and do the same thing patrol after patrol because it was easy. That got people killed. So, before every mission, we would gather to go over the night's plan. Fitts, Meno, Lawson, Cantrell. We stood before that map board for hours, building calculated chaos into every trip beyond the wire. We planned three fake dismounts from our Bradleys for every one that produced infantrymen. Our Bradley commanders would scream, "Drop ramp!" then drive off, with our men still inside. Sometimes we waited until the last time. Sometimes the first or second. We even stayed in our Bradleys entire nights at times. This way, we kept the watchers off guard.

When we did dismount, we always selected different remount points. We would link up with our track several kilometers from our drop-offs and never got exfilled from the same entry point at the start of our patrols.

This allowed us to be more creative and lie in wait for bad guys who thought they were lying in wait for us. Ambush the ambusher. Counter-ambush operations became counter-IED missions. These became my entire reason for living.

This was the daily grind of war in the gray spaces of Iraq. We faced an elusive enemy that flowed around us—an enemy who never wore a uniform and swam in the civilian stream, trying to look like any other fish. There were no set-piece battles, no sweeping charges. No massive effort that captured the martial imagination of our nation.

Instead, the nuts and bolts of this war boiled down to trying to stop Iraqis from planting bombs in the roadbeds. Doing that successfully and consistently took discipline, long, miserable hours, and relentless planning based on good intelligence. It required a delicate and careful balance between the kinetic and the investigative approaches that so conflicted the Army that year. At our level, our platoon represented the kinetic approach—we wanted to kill everyone planting these infernal bombs. Captain Sims? He represented the investigative approach. In our map board discussions, we tried to integrate both.

It started with every blast and every bomb in our area of operations. We put a pin on our map for each one. Each time another attack occurred, a new pin went up on our board as if we were detectives tracking a serial killer. Fitts, a month back from Walter Reed National Military Medical Center in Maryland and still in considerable pain, would go over the satellite imagery of the area. Our Bradley guys would cover the terrain maps, studying the ground around each attack site. I would harass our 82nd Engineers to teach me about crater analysis, to find out what kind of explosive was used, how it was detonated, and if there was a particular bomb maker's signature found within the blast seat.

Our team leaders would run back to Battalion to see what vehicles were on the BOLO (be on the lookout) lists. Wade Smith and Omarr Hardaway would handle Bradley movement on the maps. Brown and Cantrell would decide the off roads to take to lie in wait. Fitts and I were in charge of splitting our forces up and marching to areas where no one would expect to see us. Our platoon leaders approved each plan. We would lie in wait. Use the Brads to bait someone to either attack or emplace an IED. And with luck, we would kill them in the act.

We pulled all this information together during our map board skull sessions, then built our own operations order before we rolled out on the night patrol.

Through the summer, our battalion intel shop (S2) started to divine patterns in the seeming randomness of the attacks. Few of the grunts understood the work these officers and NCOs were doing behind the scenes. They assembled the puzzle, though many pieces remained to be found, which was the key reason Captain Sims wanted bad guys detained—arrested—not killed. Using them to walk back their chains would yield more puzzle pieces and give us a more complete picture of what we faced that fall.

Yet for all our efforts, we had a few key knowledge gaps. We couldn't figure out who was the mastermind behind the bomb cells. The coordinator of all the components. Somebody was orchestrating all this. Insurgencies are naturally decentralized, but we sensed somebody was in charge despite all the compartmentalization. Penetrating the leadership chain proved to be an exceptionally difficult challenge.

We didn't know who was paying the bomb cells, either. Money would just show up, get passed around to those in the game. We often found some of it during raids or searches. A random guy in Diyala with wadded-up hundred-dollar bills stuffed in his underwear. A dirt-poor family with thousands of dollars tucked away under the floorboards of a shop full of wiring and disassembled cell phones.

The clue bat hit us hard in such moments. Those people we detained and fed into the Iraq War version of the urban American *catch-and-release* cycle.

We soon learned that the rank-and-file bomb teams were largely composed of out-of-work Iraqis involved only for the paycheck. They needed to feed their families, and Al Qaeda, or the Iranians—or whoever—paid them to kill Americans. These were not ideologues, or patriots. Just guys who needed money. Sims did not consider them combatants. We did, because, out-of-work average Iraqi Joes or not, they were still murdering our friends.

These hired hands worked in tiers. The lowest tier were the guys who dug the holes at preselected spots. Then another tier of component guys would drive up in search of that hole. Once found, they would throw some wiring and a cell phone or a car battery into the pit and drive off as if nothing had happened.

Next would come the ordnance guy. He would plant the bomb. Another tier would arrive to wire it up and bury it. At the top of this org chart would be the actual Muj who clacked off the bomb or marked the area for a cell phone call.

Most of the time, none of the tiers communicated. None knew each other. It was a double-blind operation to ensure we could not catch one guy and take the entire network down. To get any real intel and divine the minds behind the attack, we needed to find the insurgents who coordinated the tiers. Somebody was telling these devilish worker bees where to go and when. They were supplying the bombs, the wiring, the detonators, and the cell phones. They were the ones spreading the money around. But they had built in layers of buffers between themselves and the civilians-for-hire doing the actual legwork to ensure their kids got their next meal.

Lieutenant Colonel Peter Newell and Captain Sims wanted one of those guys, badly.

To catch them, we began setting our own traps. We dug our own holes along routes known to be targeted by the Muj. We filled two-liter pop bottles with sand and spray-painted them so they looked like mortar rounds. Then we emplaced them at the bottom of the holes we dug, covering them with sandbags and leaving wires coming out of them. It was enough of an Acme trap to snare a few Iraqi

Wile E. Coyote types of terrorists-for-hire. When it came to facing off against the Ramrods, curiosity most certainly killed the cat.

After the insurgents began using rigged propane tanks concealed in elevated positions around Muqdadiyah to incinerate our M1 Abrams tank commanders as they stood at chest defilade in their hatches, counter-IED missions became my only purpose in life. We threw everything we had at them. One night, my squad made a production of loading back up into a Bradley. We spoke loudly and used white light, as if we were an undisciplined bunch of newbies. The next night, Fitts and his squad dismounted six kilometers from that scene and crept up on two IED layers emplacing a bomb right where my squad had been the night before. Our B Section's Bradley blew them to pieces with Shane Gossard's 25mm chain gun.

"Look," I said as we stared at the map board that night, "Hackworth is right. I know what we're doing is laborious. It is exhausting. It pisses the men off. We're out there in forty-degree weather freezing our asses off, lying in the sand for hours without smokes. The insurgents are used to lazy units doing the same thing over and over. They don't know what to make of us. We're confusing them, and it is working."

Fitts conceded the point: "That it is, Bell. Maybe there's a way to separate the guys who kill for profit from the idealogues."

"That's what Captain Sims wants to do," Cantrell said.

The Sims way of thinking, then applying the knowledge his way produced, was yielding dividends despite the ongoing friction between us. We were an infantry battalion. We were infantry NCOs. We were not trained to be cops. This wasn't a criminal enterprise to us; it was war. The truth was, Sims saw it as both, a hybrid that demanded a nuanced approach. We were slowly leaning into his way of thinking, but it was a mind-set change for us that did not happen overnight.

We finished up our planning and headed out to the Brads. On this night, we intended to set another Wile E. Coyote trap along a route the insurgents often studded with IEDs. There were so many half-filled-in blast craters that the insurgents were getting lazy and just reusing them. Also, it made it harder for them to pinpoint the location their controllers wanted to use. We intended to exploit that.

Sometime before midnight, we dismounted and quickly dug a

hole, heaping the fresh dirt nearby to signal for any of the second-tier guys that this was their assigned spot. Then we retreated into the darkness and established an overwatch position.

Hours passed. We shivered in the miserable weather, cold and hungry. When we had to urinate, we couldn't simply get up and walk to a nearby tree or bush. Any watchers out there would spot that, and our trap would be compromised. Instead, we rolled to one side, relieved ourselves, then rolled back onto our bellies to continue the stakeout. It was extremely hard to keep the squad focused, clear-headed, and poised to react for those long, freezing hours. We grew stiff. Our joints ached. We jonesed for smokes or dip. Our heads swam. We waited, and waited, and waited.

Five hours into this, a car came into view. Traffic had been virtually nonexistent all night—there was a curfew in place, and the locals knew that moving around at night in a battlescape was a bad idea anyway. So the fact that a vehicle approached was our first red flag.

The car pulled up and stopped beside our freshly dug hole. Two men got out. One stepped away from the car and acted like he was taking a piss. The other loitered near the hole. For ten minutes, the guy stood there, pretending to pee while he peered around in all directions, searching for any signs of a trap. He was clearly the lookout.

The second guy reached into the car, came back to our pre-dug IED honeytrap hole, and threw a bundle of stuff into it.

These were the wire and detonator guys, for sure.

Suddenly the lookout pulled out a cell phone, and that instantly made me nervous. Cell phones were the detonators of choice for the 2004 Iraqi bomb set. Had we been made? Were the ambushers about to be ambushed? Could we have hunkered down by an IED we never expected?

The man began to dial.

Split-second decision time. This was the hardest part of any counter-IED mission, but particularly so on this night. When do you spring the trap? Sometimes after waiting so long in a hide, your instinct was to immediately take down your target. Sometimes you waited to see how the situation developed, though that always produced second-guessing. Worst of all, sometimes we would overthink and never end up pulling the trigger or attempting to detain the targets. Statistically, anyone out at night was probably a bad guy. But that wasn't good enough for Battalion, or for Captain Sims. We had to have 100 percent certainty they were insurgents. Sometimes we waited too long to get that 100 percent.

I looked over at Knapp, lying nearby. I could see he was ready. Ruiz, his AT4 rocket launcher beside him, stared expectantly over at me. The rest of the squad followed their leads. Victor Santos was near with his 40mm ready to thump. Alex Stuckert was breathing steam to calm his nerves as he practiced sweeping his SAW over the targets. Tristan Maxfield steadily looked at me, stretching his fingers back into life like he was working a puppet. Piotr Sucholas lased his section targets with his infrared laser, assuring each Soldier had his enemies picked out. All eyes on me for the moment, waiting for me to give the order.

I looked back at our target area. The lookout still had the phone in front of him, looking around nervously. He finished dialing and brought the phone to his ear. Another few seconds, the call would connect. To a person who could be part of this cell? Or to a bomb somewhere in the ground around us or our hidden Bradleys?

I couldn't risk that phone call connecting. I gave the signal to engage. Ruiz sprang to his knees, shouldered his AT4, and fired the rocket. Without any night sight to guide the 84mm rocket, this was going to be an educated guess. Ruiz had fired more AT4 rockets than anyone in the task force, maybe division. This was our bugle call to battle. It sizzled through the night like a flaming arrow and exploded against the side of the car. After five hours of near-total silence, the sudden swell of sound from the blast seemed enormously outsize, like a Fat Man going off in the parking lot of a yoga meditation session.

This was my squad's invitation to the counter-IED party. Everyone did their jobs like a perfectly rehearsed brass section. Santos got off two 40mm's in succession. Knapp was already into his second magazine when I noticed the flames and smoke engulfing the car; rounds pinged off the asphalt, punctured the car's hide, smashed the helpless windows. I sat with my cold rifle slung as the lookout dropped the cell phone and bolted like a terrified deer. He sprinted up the road, his buddy hard on his heels. How they avoided getting hit by fire or any shrapnel resulting from the AT4 impact or 40mm grenade is anyone's guess. Both guys were running flat-out.

Headlights suddenly bloomed in the distance. There had been another car hidden in the night, watching the wiring team. It sped toward them, even as my men hesitated. The shock of the blast, the noise, and the appearance of the car threw all of us off. But the squad recovered quickly to send downrange a fusillade of bullets. Knapp and Specialist Tristan Maxwell both wounded the lookout, who spun from the impacts, recovered, and kept running. The car reached him, and arms shot out from one window. They pulled him inside even as the driver swung the car in a U-turn and stomped the accelerator to the floorboard. Ruiz, who had started this salvo, tossed his spent AT4 rocket shell. Rifle at the ready, he was quick to follow up. His staccato blasts hit the running lookout as he was being pulled in. Knapp and Maxfield shadowed the tracer rounds. Lookout guy, who was being pulled into the vehicle, was no longer doing so under his own power. Like a sand-filled rag doll they heaved him in as his arms splayed lifelessly.

We put a few rounds into the back of the fleeing car, then disastrous luck befell us. Right at that moment, another vehicle showed up farther down the road. After a quiet night, all the traffic seemed jarring. We had to cease fire, lest we risked hitting the new rig, which may or may not have been involved in this.

Our targets had gotten away. I was furious at myself and thoroughly upset that we missed the backup car. It dawned on me that the second vehicle probably was watching the drop team to make sure they carried out their job before getting paid. It was a new piece of the puzzle that we could exploit on future missions. Target the backup car, try to detain whoever was inside, and we might just gain an entry point into the leadership structure of these cells.

In the moment, though, all I cared about was trying to stay on these guys and catch them. At least one of them was wounded, maybe both. Would they be dumb enough to make for the local hospital?

Maybe.

I radioed Cantrell and told him what happened. He took Fitts's squad and went over to the hospital about an hour later. Both NCOs went inside and asked if anyone had been admitted for bullet or shrapnel wounds.

The hospital staff dimed the insurgent out. They told our guys that one man had been brought in with what looked like a critical, possibly mortal head wound. He gave a fake name when he was admitted.

"How do you know the name wasn't his real one?" Cantrell asked the hospital staff.

An administrator answered, "Because we know him and his family."

Cantrell and Fitts exchanged glances. This was the first sign that we'd gotten into something bad. A dude so well known in Muqdadiyah that the staff at the hospital knew who he was? That only meant one thing: the guy was from a connected local family.

Fitts followed the hospital administrator to the insurgent's room. There they found the window open, blood on the bed and the walls, and the sheets knotted together to form a makeshift rope.

He had gotten out of the hospital just ahead of our guys arriving in his room. Given the blood, Cantrell and Fitts figured he couldn't have gotten far, but he was nowhere to be seen. Somebody must have come back for him and picked him up to effect his escape. A quick few words to the staff, and they confirmed a couple of armed men had shown up and taken him out. He was badly wounded, and the nurses and docs said he probably had only a fifty-fifty chance at the hospital. No chance without care. He'd been hit by our bullets in the chest, neck, face, and head. It was actually a miracle he had made it to the hospital alive.

Not taking their word for it, Cantrell got the administrator to give him the insurgent's address. The squad loaded up and rolled for it. When they got to the house, they found they had just missed him again. The place looked like it had been tossed. Drawers open, stuff thrown around. He and his buddies had returned, grabbed some essentials, and bolted, our B mounted section hot on their heels.

While all that was going on, we had our hands full at the ambush site. A mass of Iraqi police vehicles sped down the road to our location and soon swarmed the area. We had no opportunity to grab the cell phone or exploit any other potential intelligence. The Iraqi cops were nervous and apologetic. They asked us repeatedly to stay and talk with their senior officer. In the interests of inter-allied cooperation, we backed away from the kill zone and waited.

A few minutes later, an Iraqi police SUV screamed down the road, lights flashing. It skidded to a stop on the far side of the cops already on the ground, away from us. A door flung open and a senior Iraqi police commander leapt out, screaming in white-hot fury.

Several others dismounted and tried to hold him back. He shoved them off and stormed toward us, eyes flaring, screaming incoherently.

I stepped forward, signaling I was in charge.

The enraged commander swung toward me, words pouring out of him. Our interpreter, Sammy, was with Cantrell and Fitts. We'd have to do this with my broken and more than slightly twisted take on Arabic.

I waited. The man remained out of control, waving both arms, a clipboard in one hand with some papers attached.

When it became clear he wasn't going to calm down on his own, I carefully said, "Calm down. Or I will beat you with your own clipboard."

The commander looked stunned, but fell silent.

Another cop who spoke a little English joined us.

"Good guy! Good guy!" he said on repeat.

"He is a good guy?" I asked, dubious.

"Yes, mistah. Mistah, Ameriki shot good guy. No Ali Baba."

"How do you know?"

"The rocket. Boomdilah. Rocket. Missile. You shot good man. Not Ali Baba."

Our attack was less than ninety minutes old by now, so this kind of detail sent another warning flag up.

"How do you know we shot a boomdilah? Who told you we fired a missile?"

The commander, still screaming at me, paused as the cop who spoke English translated that for him. In a heartbeat, he went from red-faced and livid to looking like he'd just been exposed as a fraud.

He turned to leave.

Something's not right.

"Knapp, Ruiz. Do not let this man go," I said.

They moved on him.

"Oh no, sir, I need to take you with me," I told him in English. He froze, turned around, and stared at me, fear in his eyes now.

I added, "You seem to have real-time information on a person we can't seem to track down."

"I have work to do," he said in English.

I had already heard over the radio that Fitts had already left the hospital and was at the insurgent's house. So I tested this guy.

"We need you to raid your hospital. We need your police to go immediately to the hospital to get Ali Baba."

"No," the commander said flatly. "He is not even there. We will not search the hospital."

"How do you know that? This is really interesting to me. I am sure my officers need to speak with you on this."

"No. I will not go."

There was defiance in his eyes now. This guy was dirty. That was the only explanation. The question was, how deep were the Iraqi police involved in all this? Were they coordinating the bomb cells?

I decided to push. "Abu Ghraib. Clothing optional."

The prison at Abu Ghraib inspired absolute terror in most detainees. They'd heard the stories the media broke about prisoner abuse by Americans, but also the Iraqis in charge there could be brutal and ruthless.

"No. No Abu Ghraib! I will not."

The commander went to push through Knapp and Ruiz. Knapp lowered his shoulder into him. The Iraqi police started to get excited.

I told them all in my best broken Arabic, "A wolverine is loose. All women go back into your homes for your safety."

This was my go-to phrase I learned after Sammy taught me some basic Arabic and watched *Red Dawn* with us.

Everyone stopped and looked at me as if I'd just gone mad. The police commander started to swing his clipboard in frustration.

One of my Soldiers quickly took the clipboard from him and handed it to me. There on the clipboard was a photocopy of an Iraqi police officer's identification and information.

This was the lookout? The man we'd shot in the head?

"This is official Iraqi police work," the commander said lamely.

He reached for the clipboard, intending to snatch it out of my hands. That crystallized the situation in my head.

We may have just uncovered that the bomb network included Iraqi cops.

The commander put his hand on my shoulder and grabbed my IBA as I pulled the clipboard away from him. His hand on me touched a nerve somewhere deep within me. It was a sign of extreme disrespect.

I slammed the clipboard down on his head, breaking the board in two.

I cuffed him three consecutive times with an open hand like Butt-head slapped Beavis on the MTV classic cartoon of my generation.

Everyone froze.

I got right in the commander's grill. "DO NOT TOUCH ME."

He stared back, eyes cold now.

"YOU UNDERSTAND ME? NEVER TOUCH ME."

A glimpse of fear now.

"Do that again, you will get to the bottom of this Muhammad/Jesus debate once and for all. You got me, sir?"

That was it. I'd had enough of this guy. We needed to have a long talk with him, and probably a number of other cops at Normandy.

"You're coming with me. Hands up."

Within seconds my guys took his Glock pistol, spun him, and flex-cuffed him while the rest of the squad kept an eye on the other cops. They all seemed remarkably pro-American all of a sudden. Especially when Ruiz searched the commander and found a large roll of crisp, sticky hundred-dollar bills. All new. They looked uncirculated.

First Lieutenant Meno arrived a few minutes later and took over the scene. I explained everything, and he concurred with my assessment. We shoved the police commander into the back of our Bradley, put a hood on his head, and took him back to FOB Normandy, convinced we'd just found the biggest piece of the puzzle yet.

The victory lap for this coup never happened.

It turned out we tripped into something that altered the political balance between the American Army and the Iraqi power structure in our sector. The lookout we'd shot turned out to be the nephew of the Muqdadiyah chief of police. The nephew was also a cop. The Iraqi police commander we hauled to our FOB railed to our chain of command that all of this was a huge misunderstanding. He claimed the nephew had been doing the same thing as us: hunting Ali Baba. This later became a go-to excuse whenever we caught wind of dirty cops or local politicians, or dirty Iraqi national guardsmen. The truth became very evident after this incident that the insurgency, which we thought was contained to the Sinsil cell, had grown significantly. And there were plenty of insurgents and insurgent sympathizers within the ranks of our erstwhile "allies."

We later recovered detonation wire and some Russian PE4 plastic explosives from the hole, which the driver of the car had tossed in. This slammed the door shut on the "all a misunderstanding" line the police commander gave our chain of command.

What should have been a significant revelation in our counter-insurgency efforts turned into a major incident with cascading second- and third-order effects. Captain Sims had been on excellent terms with the chief of police. After this night, that relationship was permanently hobbled. It increased the hostility against us, and the cops swung toward working on their own, sans American reliability. This seemed to only benefit the insurgency.

Sims was furious that I gave the order to engage the car. Without my knowledge, he went to each member of my squad and ordered them to give him a sworn statement describing in detail what had happened that night. When my guys told me this, I was stunned. Going behind my back like that signaled to me that Captain Sims was going to initiate an investigation against me for my order to open fire.

I went to see him about this, feeling both disbelief and outrage.

He was calm to my agitation, and told me bluntly, "I've told you several times, Staff Sergeant Bellavia, this is not how we do things. You could have detained them. You chose to engage them. These actions don't help us down the road. They kill our synergy."

He loved that word *synergy*.

He added, "And beating the police commander over the head . . . that's not how we do things, either."

"I used an open hand. And a clipboard, sir."

"Doesn't matter. He will not forget that humiliation in front of his men."

The evidence was overwhelmingly on my side. These were dirty cops. The guy's face on the clipboard turned out to be the guy who threw the det cord and explosives into the hole. We'd caught them red-handed and revealed that the rot within the local department went all the way to the top.

By discovering this and killing a relative of the chief of police, the political equation had changed. Looking back, there was no other way that could have gone, given the extent of the police involvement in the insurgency. It only got worse from there in the years ahead.

That AT4 had blown a hole through Captain Sims's relationship-building effort. There would be no more hearts and minds to win for him.

Still, I argued that what we had done was the right thing to do. The cell phone had been found by one of my guys and passed to Battalion. It yielded considerable information that a special forces team acted on. Other nodes in the bomb-laying network went down as a result.

Sims saw this as a criminal case, not a kinetic combat one. He wanted to build an ironclad legal assault on these terrorists, detain them, and hand them over to the Iraqi courts. The problem with that strategy was abundantly clear to those of us in the fight that September: the courts were sieves and those cases, so carefully constructed, rarely resulted in anything but the release of the insurgents who had killed our men.

Were we fighting a war, or a criminal conspiracy? The entire Army struggled with that question for years following the initial invasion and President George W. Bush's declaration of victory. So my conflict with Captain Sims was nothing exceptional. The schism was happening everywhere, in every unit and every level of command.

Before I left Captain Sims that night when we talked this over, things got pretty heated. At one point he said, "Bellavia, this is over for now, but only because that wounded man fled the hospital when Coalition forces showed up."

"He went out a second-story window, sir. That seems ironclad," I said. Sims did not reply, but I could see how angry he was. Our executive officer, Lieutenant Iwan, backed me in this dispute as well. So had the rest of the chain of command, including First Sergeant Smith and Lieutenant Meno, leaving him isolated and frustrated. I thought he was trying to fight a war that only existed in his mind. The reality on the ground just didn't match up.

"What am I missing, sir? Do you not believe me?" I said, then added, "Or my squad?"

He shook his head, frustrated that I still didn't get his point. "It's not about what I believe. Or that I want to see anything happen to you."

"Sir? Then what is it?"

"I have many, many locals who need to know we did everything we could to determine that this is what happened. The good Iraqi police need to know that we trust them. The bad Iraqi police need to know they still have a chance to be good. This is very delicate."

Chance to be good? Was there a reform school for dirty cops? To me, this was binary. If you were dirty, if you were working for the insurgency, you needed to die, or at least be captured and interrogated. Captain Sims looked at a larger picture. He concluded that all the killing would just produce more terrorists with a grudge against U.S. forces.

"What if SSG Fitts and SFC Cantrell didn't go to the hospital?" I asked, wanting to know if he really would have initiated an escalated investigation against me.

"You should be very glad that they did, SSG Bellavia."

"What does that even mean, sir?"

"Synergy. We are building synergy."

"I don't understand, sir."

"It's over, SSG Bell."

I never quite believed that this was entirely over. Our relationship was never quite the same.

A month later, a few nights before we left for Fallujah, Captain Sims came over to a range Fitts and I were guarding. Training for Fallujah required a twenty-four-hour security detachment to keep economically starved marauding locals from stealing our pop-up targets and sandbags.

He started with some awkward small talk. But as we chatted, I realized he was trying to bury the hatchet. He needed his kinetic, door-kicking, wrecking-ball platoon in the coming fight. It would be our kind of battle, not his. No hearts and minds to win in Fallujah, only stone-cold religious fanatics willing to die in place. He needed us, at least for now, when there would be no delicate balances to worry about or political equations beyond the ten-meter targets Fitts and I saw night after night.

The gesture meant a lot to me. I think Fitts saw it as transparent. Afterward, I wondered if he was just kicking the investigative can down the road, and once through the set-piece Second Battle of Fallujah, he would revisit September and go after my stripes.

Less than a month later, he was dead. Killed in a house a few blocks from where my squad had bunked down a week into the Fallujah meat grinder.

For years after, I wondered if the Army would revisit that September incident. It felt like unfinished business, one of those countless loose ends that trail behind every combat deployment. Some paper pusher somewhere would find something Captain Sims left behind and initiate an investigation.

A decade and a half later, I discovered Sims had said I'd done something Medal of Honor–worthy. Captain Walter read it the night he took over Alpha Company after his friend had died, and it became the catalyst for his effort to secure my nomination for the award.

In Fallujah, Sims displayed the kind of intellectual flexibility that took me years to understand, or develop on my own. The Medal of Honor represented that. He'd fought the hearts and minds battle, both within his own command and out in the streets of Diyala Province. In Fallujah, he came to our side and fought the stand-up fight right alongside us.

Less than a week before Fallujah, Captain Sims was walking from the Battalion Operations Center as I was heading back from a late-night meal after mission. He had just pitched an idea where we would enter and clear the entire city of Muqdadiyah alongside the Iraqi National Guard and Iraqi police force. It would be a real-time run-through to prepare us for Fallujah. Even I thought this was radical, but I loved him for even suggesting such a ballsy idea. He moved with defeat. Obviously, this *Shark Tank*–esque pitch had just failed at winning over Lieutenant Colonel Peter Newell's approval.

"Hey, sir."

"They didn't take it. Thought it was too heavy-handed."

"Synergy, sir."

He forced a smile to match mine. "Synergy, SSG Bell."

Sims kept moving and I stopped him by shouting to his back.

"Sir, anything you ask me to do, I am here. You know that."

Sims stopped, slowly pivoting on the peastone. He walked back to me.

"I know that, SSG Bell. I have never once questioned that in you."

"Sir?"

I took a moment. It was a cool night. The silence of this area of open nothingness was now invaded by giant generators humming, blasting lights brighter than a Texas high school football stadium. An area that was essentially a path that required night vision two weeks ago was now amassed with Army heavy equipment, trucks, cranes, and Conex trailers of worker-bee contractors and Soldiers, endlessly moving equipment twenty-four hours a day for the big intra-theater move to Fallujah.

"What'ya got, Sergeant?"

"I am more worried about losing people now than losing people in ten years. And I don't mean to disrespect where you were coming from. I just can't think that way."

"We are going to lose people. We will lose some of these men."

The reality of what he just said seemed to impact him in real time, as if he was unaware of what was coming out of his own mouth. He paused.

"Sergeant, I don't know that I am prepared for that, either."

We both looked away from each other. All I wanted was the Fallujah fight. I dreamed for this test. I was so excited about the prospects of actually impacting this war. Now, with Captain Sims, the reality of it seemed to hit me at once.

He looked at me. Bags under his eyes. Stress. Worry. His wet eyes seemed red from long hours and late nights.

"No way around this. I need you. This is going to be really rough."

"We need you, sir. You got us here and you will get us home."

"Let's get as many back home as we can."

"Yes, sir."

We walked in two opposite directions that night. Captain Sims toward the glowing lights. Me into the pitch blackness of the barracks.

When I think of Sean Sims, I see him in his DCUs, bright in that night's glow of light. With only a helmet on his head and a sidearm on his leg, walking into the light.

That night in 2019, after I spoke to Colonel Walter, I got to thinking about that divide between Sims and me. He moved to us. We never swung toward him and his view of how to win the war. In hindsight, he had been correct. Giving the Iraqis the opening to switch sides was exactly what the Anbar Awakening was all about a few years later. The Sunnis in western Iraq, once the loyal allies of Al Qaeda, were persuaded to switch sides, join the Coalition, and drive the terrorists and their foreign fighter volunteers out of their communities. It was a bloody, painful path, and many Sunni leaders died horribly for that about-face. But it worked.

It took me fifteen years and plenty of introspection to see what he saw in the moment back in 2004. Captain Sims had been right all along.

15

GETTING THE BAND
BACK TOGETHER

IN THOSE FINAL WINTER weeks, I went to work searching for my long-lost Ramrod family. The truth was, aside from Fitts, Omarr Hardaway, and Knapp, I had lost touch with most of my Alpha Company Soldiers. Fitts and I still had not patched things up; that would be a difficult call. I decided to start with Knapp and Hardaway.

"Docta, how are you doing today and all my friends in western New York?" Omarr asked as soon as he answered the phone. He'd been one of the Alpha Section Bradley commanders during our time in Iraq. The two of us had been very close, both during the Kosovo deployment and during Iraq. Somehow, where I'd lost contact with most everyone else, Hardaway and I had remained in frequent contact.

Over the years, he's been a regular guest on my radio show, which generated a kinship in him with the callers he's talked to from our area, even though he lives in Chicago, where he works as a train conductor. Honorary western New Yorker.

"What's up, Big Smooth? How you holding up?"

Big Smooth and Docta. Nicknames that dated back to our pre-Iraq deployment to Kosovo, where we were roommates at Camp Monteith. My dad would send a fifteen-page letter every week, which normally included a carefully typed play-by-play review of the week's Buffalo Bills game. At the end of each letter, he'd sign off as "Dad," then include all his degrees and professional associations below. He had almost a thousand postgraduate hours and had spent his life earning more degrees to hone his craft.

Omarr would peer over at my letters, look down at my dad's signature, and ask, "Why is your dad a FAG, D?"

It is true that the Army gets a lot of flak for its overuse of acronyms, and its insistence on using them all the time. None of them are nearly as cringy as being a Fellow in the Academy of General Dentistry (FAGD). To be fair, my dad urged the academy to drop the "G" for "General" for years, to no avail. Nevertheless, the acronym became the entry point into Omarr's interest in my dad. I spent countless hours telling him stories about my father. Ultimately, he started calling me "Docta" for it.

We called Omarr Big Smooth for his size and mannerisms. Raised on Chicago's South Side, he was a giant of a man at six four, 260 pounds.

"Worried about you, brotha. Army still calling you? What da hell does the Army want with us after all these years, man?"

Omarr always made everything about "us." If I had a problem, we had a problem. It was impossible not to love such devotion.

"Dunno. Said it was something about me hanging out with Black people who voted for Hillary."

A rolling wave of laughter flowed across the miles and filled my living room. We disagree on everything. We came from different worlds. But we are bonded by two things: our time together and the loyalty it created between us, and the fact that we loved to laugh at everything and everyone. There were no sacred cows.

"They say that? Sure they did! And your boy Trump's over there actin' like a fool, Sarge. He don't know how to be right."

Given what I was about to tell him, I couldn't stop smiling.

"Why you playin', Docta? This is for real, Sarge. Just know, I got you. You need anything, I'm right here."

"They are giving me the Medal of Honor."

"And I'm gettin' a Daytime Emmy, Sarge. Why you playin' with my emotions?"

Hardaway waited for my report of laughter. It stalled.

"Hey, Bell, one day, I have no doubt you gettin' that thing."

"They are giving it to us. Now. Bro, President Trump called me. And you better start showing your commander in chief some respect, 'cause you are coming. And you're a giant Black man. And there is no way anyone is missing that photo opportunity."

"Oh my . . . are you serious? Bro. Are you? Is this for real?"

"Absolutely, man. I don't know what to say."

"You want me to go?"

"I demand it. Everyone is going. The whole crew is coming back together for this. When we are done, we are heading to the motor pool and we are taking out the Ayatollah in Iran."

Omarr started laughing. "Why you so stupid, Sarge? I can't be seen with that man, Trump. They won't let me come home. Please, I love you. I will be there. But I can't be seen in any photo with President Trump. I live in Chicago, bruh."

"Not only do you have to come. You have to endorse him. Live. On C-SPAN. And the president himself asked me to round up every Black Soldier and have them swear an oath of loyalty to him as president."

"I won't be doing that, Sarge. But man . . . I am so proud of you. My family is proud of you. I love you so much, Docta."

"Love you, Smooth."

I hung up the phone and called Knapp.

"Knappy, how's Izzy doing?" I said when he picked up.

Knapp's oldest daughter has cystic fibrosis. This young lady had been in the hospital more times by age ten than most adults are in their lifetime, yet she is strong as steel, thanks to the peerless support of her parents. What Knapp did in uniform was the stuff people write books about. And what Knapp has done as a father for his three girls? They are the things nobody back home notices outside his immediate circle. The love, care, and devotion he has shown his little girls has never wavered. The world needs more dads like him, and more than once I listened and closely followed his parenting advice to me.

"Bell, she had a hard time getting her PICC line out. Her O_2 levels are back to normal, though. Two weeks in the hospital. I guess that is what vacation is for."

"Work didn't give you the time off?"

"No. I have to take vacation time. Sucks."

My own parenting challenges pale compared to Knapp's. Every day was a battle for his girl. Before I could say anything in response, he asked, "Hey, we're more concerned about you. Any more from the Army?"

I deflected. "Keep doing what you're doing, Knappy. I can't tell you what it means to me to see you set such an incredible example for your daughters. You're juggling a lot of balls right now."

Instant regret. Ramrods are quick. Ramrods are lethal. And the Ramrods will take any phrase and find some homoerotic punch line to fire back at you at the speed of light.

"When you gonna juggle my balls for me, Bell?"

"That wouldn't be a good look."

"Army still hounding you, Bell?"

"That's why I'm calling."

"Oh?"

"It was an investigation. They decided to give us the Medal of Honor for November tenth in Fallujah. The house fight."

"What? The Medal of Honor? The Blue Max?"

"Listen to this."

I played the recording of President Trump.

"Holy shit. That's Trump, man. This ain't somebody messing with us? That's the man I voted for. Holy shit. What are you gonna do?"

"I don't wanna do it. I am old. And this is nothing but trouble."

"Stop it. You can't say no. You literally can't say no. It was a board question."

Knapp was not only one of the best Soldiers in our battalion; he was Soldier of the month and quarter multiple times. He would sit in on boards where they asked the most absurd questions about regulations, customs, and unit history. Knapp was our *Ramrod Jeopardy!* champion.

"I want you there. I want everyone there. Also, I want to write up every single guy who didn't get what they earned. I am not going to sit here with this and not take care of the rest of you turds."

"That's my sarge. That's what I am talking about. Bell, you got me. Proud of you, man."

"I gotta run, brother," I told him.

"Me, too. I love you, Bell."

"Thank you, Knappy. Give those little ones a squeeze for me."

Oh no. I see it coming . . .

"Will do, but when you give your little ones a squeeze, think of Kosovo and me bending you over like the human greater-than sign."

I had walked right into that one. Knapp burst out laughing, and I joined him. For a second, the laughter stripped time away, and we were back in the barracks in Kosovo again.

"Be safe, brother."

We hung up, and I went back to work, trying to track down our Ramrods. I must have called and left voice mails and Facebook, Instagram, and Twitter messages to more than fifty people, looking to find the numbers for some of our people I hadn't spoken to in fifteen years. As I worked the phones and net, it began to dawn on me that some of the Ramrods had vanished deliberately, and nobody more so than our platoon sergeant, Sergeant First Class James Cantrell. After a divorce, he simply disappeared. Nobody knew where he was or how to find him. Others didn't want to be found. They had put the past to rest and wanted to leave it there.

Unlike the generations that came before us, we never organized a reunion association. There were no beer-fueled, annual weekends at a hotel, sitting around telling war stories and making fun of each other's potbellies and gray hair. We had just gone on our way and left each other behind for the most part. As I called, I found that most of us had kept in touch with at least one Ramrod buddy. In combat, we all grew close to a small number of people. A trio here. A pair there. Time had not taken those friendships out, but it shook loose everyone else on the periphery.

As I continued to make calls and issue my invites to D.C., the responses from my old crew varied. All were excited for this award. All saw it as validation of our efforts and our fight. There were some who deeply appreciated the offer to share the moment, since by rights it was all of ours to share. Others were leery. Iraq was the crater in their hearts, and revisiting it in any way was something that would take an emotional toll. I hadn't expected that. I thought everyone would be delighted to get my call that we were getting the band back together—in the White House.

Gradually, talking to everyone, I realized that most of us had buried the war, not healed from it. We tried to fit into civilian life, and some of us did better than others. Ruiz, our AT4 rocket gunner, became a "rocket scientist" working on America's space program with lasers and lenses. The kid always had a gifted mind. His path through the civilian world became a shining example of what a combat infantryman can achieve elsewhere in life.

Some hadn't done well. Several were deep into addictions. I never have judged those guys. I know who they are inside. They can never disappoint me. They will always be warriors. But warriors need people in their lives who get the nuances of their hearts, the wounds, the scars, the memories. Without somebody to nurture them, to help carry that load, some of us turn to substitutes for that kind of love.

Talking to them on the phone again after so many years, their blunt honesty about their own perceived failings left me touched. To share that vulnerability showed that the bond hadn't been broken by time and distance; it had only gone dormant. I told each one that they had shown what kind of fighter they were, and I knew they'd regain their lives. I would be there for any of them.

In the end, I found that, by and large, the Ramrods came home and tried their best to become average Americans again.

Back in 2004, we may very well have fought and died in Fallujah in complete anonymity, just like we had in Diyala for most of the deployment had it not been for Michael Ware's presence. "Mick," as we called him, was an Australian-born combat correspondent working for CNN and *Time* magazine. He'd made plenty of enemies with his bluntly honest, sometimes horrifying reporting from the middle of firefights in the worst places of Iraq over the past year. He'd been in Afghanistan before that and had experienced more combat than anyone in our battalion by the time he embedded with us.

Mick's reporting headlined newspapers, captivated CNN audiences, and catapulted the Ramrods into the national spotlight with a feature piece on us that came out in *Time* magazine later that month. No longer did we toil in anonymity like so many other Army and Marine Corps units. Mick Ware made us rock stars.

For the remainder of my life, I will state that the Medal of Honor would not have been possible without Mick's documentation. His imagery, the audio his camera captured, and his own statements buttressed the facts the platoon's members later reported.

Mick meant far more to me than what transpired between us in the November 10 house fight in Fallujah. Over the years, as I missed the Army and its sense of purpose, I reinvented myself as a combat journalist. I went over to Iraq twice and embedded, doing my best to emulate Mick's sense of professionalism and exceptional courage. I was a reporter with an infantryman's heart, and so was Mick. Yet, the more time I spent in the field, the more I admired Mick for all he did. Reporting honestly and accurately from a war zone is among the most difficult things I've ever attempted. Mick made it seem effortless.

He had to be in D.C. with us. He was a key part of the Ramrod family for all he did in Fallujah. Yet, his was a very difficult call, and I was not sure how he'd react to me after all these years.

In 2014, a documentary crew contacted me for a feature piece on Mick for *60 Minutes Australia*. They flew a camera crew to my house, where the show's host interviewed me remotely. Too easy. I just told funny stories of Mick's time with us. I shared what I felt he did for us and all the times I saw this guy risk his life for a story. There was no need to exaggerate when you are telling the truth about Michael Ware. At no time did anyone tell me the theme of this documentary or the tone it was trying to convey to the audience.

Little did I know, the final cut of the documentary focused on Mick's trauma from Iraq and how he was struggling to deal with it. My anecdotes were totally out of place, and in the tone and context of the documentary, I felt like what I'd said diminished how Iraq had affected him.

The first time I sat down to watch it, I saw Mick's face on the screen and the look in his eyes. I'd seen the same expressions on the faces of my men, even today. Right then, I realized that Michael Ware was carrying a ton of weight on his shoulders. I wanted to reach out to him. Be there for him. His face was my face. Mick just had the courage to expose it for everyone to see. Mick was a veteran just like us. The only difference was he didn't wear the uniform, and he didn't come home to a VA home loan and reintegration support. He was literally on his own to find a way forward after Fallujah once he returned from the war.

I never made that call. I'm still not sure why.

Five years later, I had no choice but to deal with this lost, loose end of a friendship. We could not be in D.C. without him. I dialed his number, and it didn't take more than a few seconds for Mick to allay my fears that I'd done him wrong in that documentary. He greeted me as his usual, over-the-top self.

I played him the tape of Donald Trump's call, and when it finished, he said simply, "About time they did the right thing, mate. Count me in."

In the years since the war, Mick had quietly advocated for the award whenever he had the chance. I didn't know that, but on the phone that winter evening I called and reconnected, he listed all the people in D.C. he had trapped in elevators and offices and asked them over and over to look at the MOH for David Bellavia. Michael Ware was the first journalist to be asked to write a supporting deposition for a Medal of Honor award packet.

We laughed and joked and found ourselves in the same zone we'd been in together years ago. Yet, in his exuberant acceptance of my invitation to join us at the White House, I sensed a little fear. Just a glimpse, something that broke through the cover of the happy-go-lucky, effortless facade he'd always so studiously worn.

Mick had nothing to fear from the Ramrods. We loved the man. I thought about it a lot after the call. Perhaps that glimmer boiled up from the rejection and hostility with which the U.S. chain of command treated his stories during the worst years of the Iraq War. There were plenty of times, from the Pentagon's standpoint, that Mick's truth contradicted the information being fed to the home front. Perhaps that was what I'd sensed: Mick realizing that he'd be around some of those senior officers and officials who'd once considered him an enemy of the effort, not a guardian of unvarnished truth.

This attempt to bring the Ramrods together in D.C. had been an emotional one for all of us. What had happened to us through the past fifteen years ran the gamut. The Ramrods mirrored our generational experience in microcosm. Now, it was time to invite our Gold Star families. I knew this was going to take me to a rough place I still hadn't made complete peace with yet.

One of the last things Captain Sims said to us before he died in

Fallujah still haunted me. We were talking about Lieutenant Iwan's death, which had hit him as hard as it hit us all. We were all reeling. Sims knew we had to be at our best to survive the ordeal ahead. So he said to us, "We'll deal with this later. Right now, we need to stay focused."

I begged him to let us clear these other buildings. We had just had contact with the enemy in this area only a few hours before. But he insisted.

"No, you guys have been through enough. Rest up. I got this."

Later never came for me. Long after we were home, that grief lay inside me, wrapped in an armor of denial. Afraid to let it out, I clung to my wartime self-psyops campaign that kept me functional in battle. Iwan and Sims and Faulkenburg. They weren't dead, just transferred to a new duty station. The Army was vast. People come and go through units all the time. Friends get posted on the far side of the planet, and you gradually lose contact as the commonalities in your lives fall away and you both go your separate ways.

It was surprisingly easy to convince myself that they were not gone forever. That was the heart of how I managed their deaths for years, and the truth I'd avoided telling my son Evan every time he brought the subject up.

There was one person who saw right through my defenses. Merrilee Carlson, Michael "Shrek" Carlson's mom, made it her mission to make sure I learned to grieve and let the pain out. It took her years, and much patience. Along the way, she became my Sherpa guide into facing the things I didn't want to face.

Shrek was a Ramrod beloved by everyone, a towering kid from Minnesota who carried a heavy machine gun like most of us hefted a carbine. He loved his cigars. His smile was bigger than a Cheshire cat's. He was absolutely loyal and always right with us in the thick of a fight. He was in Second Platoon, Alpha Company, and he was a beast of a guy. Six foot, 250 pounds, I once saw him jump onto a Smart car's roof in Germany and crush it flat. That earned him the moniker Shrek, a nickname he loved.

He was killed right at the end of our deployment. Merrilee turned her grief outward, forming a nonprofit that supported Gold Star families.

For a while I was in fear of meeting Mrs. Carlson. I didn't know how she was going to treat us, the guys who served with her boy. Was she going to be angry? Was she going to ask us why we lived and her son died? There was nothing I could say, no way to fill the void left when Shrek died. So I dodged meeting Merrilee like I dodged facing the trauma of his death.

For all the psyops I waged on myself, I couldn't change the truth. I couldn't change Shrek's fate, and the denial I lived in for the first years after I came home slowly ate me alive from the inside out. Shrek wasn't at another duty station. He drowned in five feet of water while trapped in an overturned Bradley. At night, in bad weather, his Bradley flipped over when part of a dirt road gave way under its weight. The big armored vehicle rolled down an embankment and came to rest upside down in a muck- and sewage-filled canal.*

After building a friendship with Merrilee based initially on our work with our nonprofit advocacy groups, we met one rainy afternoon in Texas during a bus tour to raise awareness for veterans'

---

* Shrek and our friends Staff Sergeant Joe Stevens, Sergeant Javier Marin, and Specialist Viktar Yolkin drowned in the back of the Brad. The driver, Private First Class Jesus Leon-Perez, was killed on impact. There was a true hero that night who did everything humanly possible to save our friends. Sergeant Kyle Sherwood made numerous attempts to keep his men alive, braving fuel and hypothermic water conditions, the unbelievable stress of the moment. His actions that night are those of legend, risking his life to pull out our men. He was unable to open the back ramp or crew door, both of which were jammed in the mud. A heavy equipment crane couldn't do that, let alone a Soldier in those conditions. This did not stop Sherwood. He was relentless, and he was able to save Specialist Jeremy Kane's life.

The event gutted all of us. It happened after Fallujah, and their Bradley had been tail-end Charlie for an engineer convoy. Somehow, nobody noticed their absence until it was far too late to help the men trapped inside. We were mere weeks from going home, and that road had been traveled countless times by Ramrods and other units alike. Yet, in the cruelest twist of fate, it was that night the weight of the Brad finally caused the road to collapse. In the dark, our friends died. Our devastation turned to rage—not at the universe for such a weird fluke, but at the engineers Shrek's Brad was escorting for not seeing the accident happen and responding right away. This has been a very difficult issue for the men of TF 2-2, perhaps the most bitter pill to swallow of the entire deployment.

causes. She convinced me to meet her at a national cemetery, where she and her Gold Star families were going to be for the day. It took supreme effort to even show up. I wasn't sure I could handle being around families so recently devastated. I avoided veteran cemeteries. Soldier funerals. I couldn't stand to listen to Taps, either.

In Iraq, after those men died, we couldn't even make it to their memorial service, which was held at FOB Warhorse instead of Normandy. We were on patrol that day. I never got to say goodbye. All those guys from Second Platoon were hurt so badly by that loss. Secretly, I was relieved. They'd remain on duty elsewhere in the Army. There'd be no finality, no moment of acceptance.

Despite my long history of avoidance, something in me said to trust Merrilee. When we finally met, instead of a bitter and angry mom willing to vent on Shrek's Army buddies, I found one of the most loving and accepting humans I'd ever encountered. She of all people had plenty of valid reasons to rail at the world, savage the Army and the Iraq War effort. She didn't do that. Instead, she used her experience with pain to set out and try to heal others.

She possessed the ideal temperament for that mission. She was kind and gentle, with a soft insistence and quiet sort of authority that demands attention. She wasn't going to give up. If I didn't show at her event, I knew she would keep trying. In the moment back then, I didn't quite understand why she wanted me there. Only later did I realize she was trying to save me from myself and my caustic denial.

Two years after Fallujah, I took a trip to Houston National Veterans Cemetery in the summer of 2006 that changed everything.

We walked together to the rows of names carved in stone, surrounded by other Gold Star families here to visit their loved ones' final resting places. Merrilee introduced me to some of them. Moms who've lived the nightmare I'd avoided. They hugged me close, as if I was one of their own. I felt them, reed-thin, their bodies worn by their own battle with grief. Each one said to me, "Come, come and meet my boy."

I stood with them while they told me stories, the families around us spread out now, each sitting beside their Soldier's grave.

The iron door within me fractured that day. I heard Captain Sims's words echo in my heart. "We'll deal with it later." Today was the later. Merrilee stayed close, her arm in mine, not saying much, her presence a comfort.

You're going to be okay. Let it out.

The headstones made it real. The names with the dates I remembered all too well. They made death real. I'd hoped to go through the rest of my military career and life as a civilian without ever exploring that dungeon.

Just leave it be, our friends aren't dead. They just were redeployed elsewhere.

The cemetery in Texas destroyed that illusion forever.

That day was my first step toward learning how to grieve, and to find meaning in the process. Years later, the lessons Merrilee gently imparted helped me when my father passed. Without her showing me the right path, I'm not sure I would have known how to survive his death.

For years after that moment in Texas, every time I saw Merrilee, she would wrap her arms around me and say, "Come on, let's go see Michael." It was the final test, the final moment of full acceptance. He'd been laid to rest at Arlington, a warrior among generations of warriors. And he would forever lay with his brethren, bound by shared service and sacrifice.

It took years before I was ready. Merrilee waited patiently until I could acknowledge my friends were gone. I knew that if I saw his headstone, I wouldn't ever be able to lie to myself again about his fate. Every email she sent would finish with two words, "Someday, Arlington."

So one day, in that late winter of 2019 after weeks of calls, some warm and receptive, others painful and wrenching, I dialed that all-too-familiar number in Wisconsin. She answered quickly, her voice welcoming, excited to hear from me. As we talked, the anxiety eased. I felt a comfort and peace that few people can bring to me. Merrilee can, and she does it naturally with just the tone of her voice.

I explained what was happening, and I asked her to come to D.C. with us. She will always be a Ramrod, and bore our service and survival from it as her personal mission. This was her moment, too.

"David, Michael would be there in a heartbeat. Thank you for always reminding people that my son lived and what he died for."

"Ma'am. If the roles were reversed. He would be talking to my mother. Telling her about me."

"He absolutely would have done that. Thank you." Merrilee accepted the invitation to the White House ceremony. As we were about to say goodbye on the phone, she added, "Let's visit Shrek while we're there."

I hung up feeling calmed by Merrilee's voice. I was almost done now, and I felt the strength to finish this.

Heidi Sims answered on the first ring.

She sounded guarded, curious, a little confused. Over the years, though we never talked, others would tell me how she was doing. Her boy was born just before her husband died. She never remarried. Some love is so deep, so connective, that once lost there seems no point to try again. Who would want to play second to that? And after the love of your life is gone, what can that realm of life even offer? She devoted herself to raising our commander's son with all she had, even as the grieving never eased. The level of strength and courage that required? Most people will never see it, never know it. It is not celebrated or honored. There is no Gold Star Widow day, no memorial for their own journeys and battles. They fight in the shadows of the war, ignored in books and newspapers all too often because our country as a whole is very grief-averse. Yet the kind of courage and love, grit and determination Heidi Sims possessed is transformational for those who do feel it, and see it. That much I knew.

I started nervously, "Ma'am, thank you for taking time to speak to me. It's been a long time. I just wanted you to know how much I admired and appreciated what Captain Sims meant to me and our unit. I am so sorry we weren't able to bring him back. I am haunted by it. There is this unbelievable guilt that we all carry that you have this hole in your life. That your boy . . . Colin, has to endure. He deserves to know how much his father impacted our lives. What his dad meant to us. Those men would have done anything to change what happened."

"I know. I know that, David. Thank you. And that's why we are at peace. Sean loved you all so much. And he was so proud of you guys."

"I'm so sorry," I repeated.

"You don't have to be sorry. He was your commander. He saved you. It is what he wanted to do. David, it is so odd you've reached out now. The timing. I mean, Colin's been wanting to know more about Sean, and he's never asked before. He's been reading our old letters, too. This literally just started happening."

Colin, their son, was now seventeen. He'd been gradually moving toward his father and his memory recently. This was a new development. He asked Heidi for his father's Bible, the one he carried to Iraq. He asked for his dog tags.

As I listened to Heidi explain her son's interest in his father, I realized this would be a unique opportunity for all of us, even more important than meeting the president.

"Ma'am, they are giving me the Medal of Honor for actions that occurred during the Battle of Fallujah. And I know this is going to be one of the most difficult things a person could ask you to do, but I really want to honor Captain Sims. If you and Colin could attend, meet the guys, hear the stories of what your husband meant to us, it would mean the world to me. To all of us."

"This is going to be tough," she said softly, after a long pause.

"I completely understand. I just want you to be a part of whatever you feel comfortable being a part of. No obligation. We will cover all your expenses. I don't want this to be a burden at all. I just—we just—want to tell your boy what his father meant to us. And how we are alive, because of what he did for all of us."

"There is just so much I want him to endure. He is only seventeen."

"Ma'am, you are in total control. Whatever you feel comfortable with. I want this to be healing. I am not interested in anything other than introducing our legacy, our memory to the son of the man who gave his life for us. We need him to know. We need to meet him. Can you let us meet him?"

"We will be there. We are proud of you. Congratulations. This is going to be very difficult. I wouldn't miss it for the world. Thank you for reaching out," she said, her voice filled with emotion.

"Thank you, ma'am. Thank you."

A silence filled the space between us again. Almost thinking aloud, she added, "I think Colin will love this."

When we said goodbye, I knew the final pieces had fit into place.

Part of our oath to each other in combat was a promise to make sure our sons and daughters know what we did, how we lived, why we fought. The measure of their fathers lay in the memories of every Ramrod. When we realized not all of us would make it through Fallujah, we talked it through and knew it was our duty to share our stories with those whose fathers were taken by the war. In our quest to come home and forget the war and get on with life, we hadn't done that. We'd neglected a promise as the years rolled by and those kids grew from infants to teenagers. We stayed in our lanes and just tried to get by.

Maybe D.C., this award, would be the first step to finally seeing those stories shared and that oath fulfilled. For the first time, I started to look forward to what was about to come.

Now the toughest call remained: Colin Fitts.

Through the worst moments in my life, Colin Fitts remained my most loyal friend. Still, our relationship had been damaged by his confession that he had hidden the truth about the Man in White from me all these years. I didn't want it to impact us; I just wanted to forget about it and move on. But I couldn't do that. The revelation, even all these weeks later, was still raw.

We had to move past this, and it was up to me to make the first step. I knew that, and I knew that eventually I'd come to a place where I would know there was nothing to forgive. He either did it for the motives he'd mentioned, or he had just been busting my chops and it got out of hand. The longer he said nothing, the more damage it did and he just wasn't sure what to do.

Either way, the onus was on me. I shouldn't have responded the way I did. I shouldn't have dwelled on it all these years and let it damage my self-confidence.

Besides, I had always felt a strong measure of guilt for not being out with Fitts for his other deployments. His two other tours to the Sandbox were nightmares filled with unimaginable chaos. He lost rank again. He absorbed the blast of an IED that sent a piece of a radio hand mic into his skull. He lost Soldiers. Killed more of the enemy. He was gone for two more years. In the middle of it, he went through a hellish divorce.

I wasn't there for him. I was working my tail off. Starting businesses, trying to establish myself as anything other than a professional veteran. I just wanted to be respected in any other field than to be known for shooting insurgents in the face.

I found his name on my phone and hit send, feeling a mix of shame for letting this go on so long and nervousness at his reaction.

He was relieved to hear from me, as it meant our friendship was still alive. Fitts and I have had ups and downs over the years. Maybe this wasn't anything major after all.

I played him the audio of President Trump. He sat in total silence for perhaps a minute or two after.

Finally, he said, "About time. About damn time. This is right. And this is what you deserve."

"I want you to be there in D.C. with us, Fitts. We went through this together; we'll be together now."

"I gotta go," he said abruptly. He hung up the phone and didn't call me back. It was really odd.

Later that night he called me back and said, "I love you, man. But I gotta tell you something. I am agoraphobic. You know what that means? I hardly leave the house anymore. I drink all day. I know what you are gonna ask me to do. And, brother, I just can't do it for you. For me. For anyone. So before you talk me into something that I don't want to do, I am gonna let you go. But listen, your old man is proud of you. All the guys are proud of you. But no one is more proud of you than I am."

I gave him the night. I could tell he was a few beers in and he wasn't really thinking this through carefully. Early the next morning, I called him back.

Sober Fitts still did not want to go. "I want to be there for you, bro, but it's a bad idea. The guys think I'm an asshole. And no one likes me like you do. We are tight. I don't do these things well. And I don't want you to be embarrassed of me."

"Fitts, I have always been embarrassed of you. That is something I have long gotten over."

"This is different. This is the White House. D.C. I drink all the time, brother."

I made another joke. Fitts found no humor in my attempt.

Slowly, with words tinged with regret and pain, he said, "You are

asking all of us to go back there, man. This isn't just D.C. The memories. The fighting. Iraq, man. We all have demons. This isn't easy. Not
for you. Not for me. It might be a bad idea for all of us. My demons
are kicking my ass enough already."

I answered, "You never left my side. Not ever. You took bullets for
me and for those guys. That's what matters."

Silence.

I kept going. "Let's just all do it together. I am going to stand next
to the president of the United States, and you have to be standing
next to me. I can't think of anyone else who I'd want there. I need
you, Fitts."

More silence. I couldn't tell if I was gaining traction or not. So I
pressed on.

"I know this is tough. I know it's surreal and incredibly selfish of
me. I am asking you, please, don't let me do this by myself. I want the
entire platoon. Everyone we loved, hated, and don't even remember.
I want them all there. Fitts, this is all of ours. We can make this about
everyone."

Our unit was a family. And just like any family that's been through
major trauma, we all had old conflicts that were never addressed.
There were many loose ends, words that shouldn't have been spoken,
or words that needed to be that never were. There were the cheap
shots and the rivalries. The modulations of courage and commitment. The way we came home and some of us thrived while others
fought their demons every damn day, year after year.

That Band of Brothers thing is a product of selective memories
and marketing. Our platoon? We fought each other sometimes almost as hard as we fought the enemy. Fitts wasn't being overdra-
matic. He wasn't anyone's friend. They revered him. They listened
and respected the rank, but the fact was, plenty of the men truly
despised him for his lack of filter and sheer bluntness. He alienated
many of the Ramrods with his abrasive behavior back in 2004. I
think that as he looked back on his time in service, this was a major
regret for him.

With all this happening now, the reality of being side by side with
those men was unnerving him. He couldn't bear the thought of being
rejected by our old tribe now because of what he did back then, when

trying to keep his men alive. They meant too much to him, and given his slow slide, he knew he would not be able to cope with that.

"Fittsy, you're my family. Those guys from Alpha Company are our family. We love them. They love us. This is a gift. We can all be back in each other's lives together again. I can't do this without you. Cory Brown. Omarr Hardaway. Gossard. First Sergeant Smith. Meno. Knapp. Hall. Misa. Ohle. Gary Frey. We will invite the Faulkenburgs, the Iwans. Sims's wife and son."

"No way, man. Not Heidi Sims. I can't deal with that. They hate me, man. Not after all that shit from Fallujah."

I hadn't thought about that.

In a rush, the last moments with Captain Sims came back to me. We were covered in dirt, grime, blood, and sweat. Fitts and I were exhausted, our men totally smoked. We had been fighting for days in the streets and buildings of Fallujah. We were beat up, wounded and aching with pain.

November 12, 2004. Two nights after the house fight that earned this Medal of Honor.

We had just learned the news that Lieutenant Iwan had been killed. We struggled to hold ourselves together. He was revered, like Command Sergeant Major Faulkenburg. Captain Sims came over to check on us, and when he saw the condition of our platoon, he ordered us to stand down for a few hours, to get some food and rest. There was a house down the block that needed clearing, and we told Captain Sims we would do it. He shook his head and said he'd take care of it. We needed the break. We protested. He made it an order, and we fell in line. Both of us were unsettled, though. This was our job, not his.

I watched him go, linking up with some of his command element and followed by a television news crew that wanted to see some of the effects of the war from inside one of the many half-ruined buildings in this neighborhood.

Sims entered the house and died in a point-blank fight. We heard the gunfire, and the platoon quickly pulled boots on and rushed off to help. It was too late. When we realized what had happened—that we'd lost our third leader in as many days—the reality shattered us. Lieutenant Meno, Fitts, and I all knew we had major fighting ahead—maybe worse than anything we had experienced to date. The task force was about to plunge into the heart of the Al Qaeda stronghold in the city, and we needed our men mentally in the game.

In the moment, I covered the pain with fury and hate. We pulled the platoon together and had an NCO talk with everyone. My off-the-cuff words to the men were designed to fire them up. I knew they were hurting—so was I. I was running on adrenaline and rage. We all were.

"This is who we are and what we do. There is nothing on the other side of the street we won't rip to shreds. And we're going to avenge that man. Captain Sims. We're going to do it for him."

We had a new reporter join us that afternoon. Michael Ware had left us earlier that day. We'd been sorry to see him go. He'd become close to all of us. The new reporter had not established himself with us, but he sensed a story here. He moved close and started taking notes.

"Whatever's left in my tank is ready to go. I know it is with all of you, too," I continued. Then I went to wake them up with a warning about lowering our security posture. "You know this now, after who we've lost and what we've seen. This isn't a game. You let your guard down one time, and you're dead. That building Captain Sims was in when they killed him? We'd literally been sleeping next to it. We cleared it five hours before they went in there. Any building you are not standing in currently—it is dangerous and uncleared. Understood? We're not going to lose anyone else like this."

Fitts stepped in as my rasping voice started to give out. He delivered a solid blow meant to be a wake-up call. "The CO's dead," he said bluntly. "And I'll tell you why—they were just a gaggle walking into some house. They weren't properly clearing it. We've been doing that, and that's why we are alive. DO NOT let your guard down, or you'll be the next one dead."

Words in the moment spilled across the front page of the London *Telegraph* on November 15. Out of context, the Sims family took them as an insult to their warrior's final moments, and Fitts's words felt like a knife in the gut after the contact team delivered the worst blow of their lives.

That was never patched up. Fitts was asked to apologize, which was like asking a Hatfield to say, "My bad, brother!" to a McCoy. Fitts was a gentleman who never went out of his way to offend anyone. But his inability to modulate truth and hard realities did enormous damage.

"Bell, it has been fifteen years. I want to talk to the Sims family like I want another paid vacation in Anbar Province."

"Fittsy, I promise you. This is all about honoring our fallen. Come to D.C., show the world who we are and what we did. We need this. All of us. And I need you."

"Do you realize what you're asking of me?"

"Fitts, in the history of these Medal of Honor ceremonies, there will never be one like this. I want to make this about the Ramrods. All of us. I am telling you, these kids never got attention. They never got the awards for what they did. Let's remind the Army who the Ramrods were and what we were asked to do. I promise you it won't be weird."

In that Fallujah house fight that the Medal of Honor was based on, there was one moment that stands out to me after all these years. One moment that I still see almost every time I hear Colin Fitts's voice. I was on the ground on one side of a room, almost the entire platoon doing the same on the other. Covering my head. Waiting for bullets to impact me. My rifle wasn't shooting. Damaged from incoming rounds. Glass. Tracers. Bricks. The hiss and screeching sounds of hot lead flying at 2,970 feet per second.

Fitts?

He was leaning back, looking up to the ceiling. The wall around him was ripping apart with each burst of incoming and outgoing fire. Bullets were streaking through the wall over his head, coming at us through the door. Our machine gunners firing back had us all trapped between the enemy's machine guns and our own. He was contemplating the end. This was going to be over for all of us, unless something happened.

He looked over to me and said, "Brother, I need you, man. I need you in a bad way."

I can never forget that. I will never forget that.

The only reason I moved from my position was that look. That man. Those words.

Brother, I need you, man. I need you in a bad way.

Something he has never asked me before and something he has never uttered since.

We never discussed it one time in our lives.

"Fitts. I need you, brother. I need you in a bad way."

"Don't even go there Bell," he said, recognizing immediately the reference. It was part of our inner language that nobody else understood. Half-indignantly, he spat, "That's some bullshit. You bringing up the past like that."

"I can't do this without you. I am here because you told me you needed me. You know it. This award doesn't happen without you. No way. You never once let me down. Not once. I need you. In a bad way."

"Stop it. You sound ridiculous right now."

"I will do it with your accent next. Even put some dip in my mouth for effect."

Fitts would be loyal to his last breath. He surrendered to that truth. A long exhale, a moment of silence, then at last I heard the words I needed to hear.

"Okay, brother. You win. I won't let you down. I can't say no to you. I'm in. Let's do this."

PART III

16

THE LAW OF UNINTENDED CONSEQUENCES

OUTSIDE BUFFALO, NEW YORK — JUNE 2019

I DROVE THROUGH MY OLD neighborhood, wearing a golf shirt and slacks, feeling unsettled. My mother sat beside me, relaxed and calm. I needed some of that. Today was the beginning of our trip to D.C., and the last few weeks had been a flurry of crazy logistical issues and preparation to ensure that all the Ramrods would be there. Now everything was in motion.

I turned a corner and drove to the old house I purchased for my family years ago. I parked in the driveway, almost even with the three-point line Aiden's mother had painted lovingly on the concrete for his personal basketball court. He was so proud of it. It was a beautiful hybrid of NBA specs and street ball, complete with a key and a glass backboard mounted at regulation height. The post was even padded.

I paid for everything having to do with that basketball court, but I didn't do any of the work. In years past, I would have done it. But this? It was the first time that the kids understood that their parents weren't ever going to be a couple again.

I cut the engine but didn't move for a moment. Neither did my mother. She knew that what had once been home was uncomfortable at best for both of us.

The last time I'd been at the house was when I told the family about the Medal of Honor news.

I found Evan that late afternoon in the kitchen of this house. As the oldest, he was entitled to the news first. Besides, without him guiding me home, I never would have been here to receive it.

"Evan. You know the Medal of Honor? The award?"

He stopped and stared at me. "Yeah, Dad. Is this happening?"

"I think so," I said.

"Is it?"

"I know so. Yeah. It is. I'm really shook over it."

"Oh my god," he said at last. "Dad! This is incredible. Finally happening!"

I grabbed his neck and pulled him into me. The hug I'd needed for fifteen years.

"I love you, Dad."

"Love you, too, son."

I kissed the top of his head and saw tears in his eyes. For the first time, I wondered if my son understood now. At the very least, it resonated with him. I could see that on his face, and his expression meant the world to me. It felt like this was the first real step toward that long-pushed-off discussion about the war.

"What's going to happen next, Dad?" he asked.

"We're going to D.C. You're going to meet all the guys from the unit. And President Trump. You're going to do everything I do, be everywhere I need to be."

"What about Aiden and Vivienne?" he asked, concern in his voice for his younger brother and sister.

"Screw them. They voted for Hillary."

The two of us broke out laughing. A long-established Bellavia tradition: when things feel serious, or emotional, or weird, over-the-top jokes return the balance.

"That could be awkward at the White House," Evan conceded, a wide grin on his face.

I hugged him again, and I wondered how different everything would have been had that night in Vilseck included him.

In the car, I fumbled to adjust my shirt, tucking it into my pants, mentally trying to get ready for what was about to unfold. A deep breath, and I was as ready as I'd ever be. The Army taught me never to sit on a decision. Make it. Be decisive. Get it over with.

I stepped out of the car and onto Aiden's basketball court in the driveway. The glass backboard shined in the sun. The paint they used for the key and three-point line was still holding up.

Aiden had been shooting hoops out here when I told him the news. I'd gone from the kitchen out the front door and watched him sink a trey. He was growing like a weed, tall and lanky. He was twelve, with all his hormones teed up to deluge him in the months and years to come. He dreamed of playing for the Lakers, a Buffalo-born Italian kid sinking outside shots for the storied LA franchise.

I walked out to the driveway court and he slung the ball my way as a greeting. I took a shot. He grabbed the rebound, spun, and drained it.

"Hey, big man, how you doing?"

"Doing good, Dad," he said and hooked the ball to me.

I dribbled the ball a bit, then shot again. "Hey, got something to tell you."

"Yeah?" He rebounded the ball, turned, and held it as he saw my face.

"I'm getting the Medal of Honor."

He looked blankly at me.

"Do you know what that is?" I asked.

"No. Is it a big deal?" He tried to deadpan it, but a wry smile broke across his face. He had an inkling.

"Big deal? Not really. I mean if you're a communist it isn't. If you love America, it's the biggest of deals."

"My bad, Dad. That's really cool!" he said, the wry smile turning to a big grin.

"We can't tell anyone right now. It's super secret. But soon everyone will know."

"How will they know?" he asked.

"'Cause the White House will announce it," I said, then added, "You know what else that means, right?"

"No."

"You get into West Point automatically."

"I do?"

I stole the ball from him, pivoted, and tried to take a shot. He blocked it.

"Yeah. Not a bad deal, eh? World-class education. Free tuition. And you can play for the basketball team. NCAA Division 1 basketball. And all you have to do is a couple of tours in Syria, but that won't be nearly as bad in a few years as it is now."

"I don't wanna go to war, Dad. I'm not like you," Aiden said softly.

"That's what Teddy Roosevelt's son used to say. You know what? His dad earned the MOH in the Spanish-American War. Then Teddy Jr. earned one, too, on D-Day. He was the only general in the first wave to land. First off the boat. His son landed at Omaha Beach that day, too."

Aiden sidestepped me and sank a basket. I turned and snared the ball. Dribbling out toward the three-point line, I added, "Course. Not a good comparison, actually. Sorry."

"Why's that?" my son asked.

"Teddy Jr. died of a heart attack a few weeks after D-Day. In Normandy. His brother Quentin died in France in 1918. He was a pilot. But you know? Teddy Jr. was a stud. Fought in two wars, Legion of Honor in both. Medal of Honor. Made his country—and family— proud."

We took turns shooting baskets; the talk turning silly. The two of us laughed together like we used to when I had lived here four years before. Aiden was only eight then, but we used to have so much fun together. Now? Everything was complicated now. I wanted to hang on to this moment, suspend it above our timeline and let the world march on while I shot baskets with my son.

"Hey, Dad, does West Point have a good team? Has anyone ever made it to the NBA?"

"Ever heard of David Robinson? Played for the Spurs?"

"He was awesome!" Aiden said, lighting up. "Dream Team. Hall of Famer. He went to West Point?"

"Well, no. He went to Annapolis. Navy. Wasn't brave enough or smart enough for the Army. But it's basically the same thing."

Aiden shook his head. "No, it isn't. Is the Army even any good at basketball?"

I fessed up. "Not really."

He looked at me hard.

"Well," I said, "we could wipe out any Dream Team in a firefight. I mean, what's really important in life? Shooting a javelin at a speeding suicide truck bomber is better than dunking with two hands."

"Dad. You can't even dunk with one," Aiden said, laughing again.

"I used to be a lot taller, Aiden. Serving in the Army compacted my vertebrae. I shrunk many inches."

He tossed the ball at me and I took a final shot. I saw him grinning as he dashed over to field the ball. Seeing him smile again? That was one of the great moments I've had. He's such a beautiful and kind young man.

The memory froze me in place until I remembered my mother, sitting in the car behind me. I shook it off, walked around the key of the court, and opened the door for her. She eased out and I helped her to the front door.

This was the house I'd bought my family after I came home from Iraq. I had remodeled so much of it. My sweat and love went into it to give the people I cared so deeply for a home they could be proud of. Brazilian cherry hardwood floors. Every piece of drywall. I learned skills on the job. I went from falling into formation early morning for Army PT to mustering in a Home Depot parking lot as it opened. That house was my obsession.

The door opened and the kids greeted us on the front lawn with hugs and hellos.

Two large maple trees once adorned the front lawn. My father helped me cut those down when their roots grew into a water pipe. That project took days. My dad was impressed at how deep and far I could shovel. The little things in life that make your father proud of you, we hold on to years later.

Vivienne was the last to hug me. My girl, whip smart, funny. She was only nine but could bust my chops at a twelfth-grade level. Billy Bigelow, a character in Rodgers and Hammerstein's classic *Carousel*, famously quips, "You can be a dad to a son, but you have to be a father to a girl." Truer words were never written, or spoken. Vivi's arrival changed my life, just as I know she's going to change the world someday. All heart, all passion. A Bellavia to her core.

I lifted her up and hugged her, just as I did a few months before when I showed up to tell the family the news. That day, I had found her right after talking to Aiden, and ran to her and lifted her into the air, saying, "Listen to me, sweetie. Can you keep a secret?"

She looked me dead in the eyes and said, "I'm nine. No. And put me down please."

I hugged her to me and she flung her arms around my neck. "You know how much you love President Trump?"

"Ugh. No, Dad. I hate President Trump," she giggled. "I supported Governor Clinton."

"You're not allowed to vote in any state but Illinois. Also, Hillary was a senator and secretary of state, not a governor. But that isn't important. She lost. And Trump is our president. And you are going to meet him."

She fake-pouted, putting on a frown that was completely endearing. "I don't wanna meet him, Dad. He's angry and mean. And Cheeto-colored."

"You are angry and mean. And also Cheeto-colored."

"Not as bad as he is!"

I put her down and grew serious for a moment. "Vivienne, you are going to meet the president. He is the most powerful man in the world. The Army is giving me a thing. It is going to be on television and millions of people will see you. All your friends. It'll blow up your TikTok account. Get you some followers."

"Really?" she asked, eyes wide now.

"You shouldn't even have a TikTok account. China runs that."

"That's what Trump says, Dad. It isn't true."

"Vivienne, this is a big deal. We're going to be going to the White House."

She considered this and hedged. "I will think about this, Dad. Definitely a maybe."

The kids, my mother, and I assembled near the mouth of the driveway. Their mother was still in the house.

We waited outside in an awkward silence, broken only by a few comments from the kids. Their mother had insisted she come along to D.C., despite our impending divorce. If I hadn't agreed, the kids would not be allowed to come with me, so I had no real choice on this. The discomfort of two estranged people looking at a weekend together in Washington, D.C., under a microscope of media attention, was something the DoD tried to prepare me for, but until I was living it in the moment, I don't think either of us understood what this would mean.

I suppose this should have been obvious from the outset. I should have clued in the day the news broke in the national media. It was early June. I was on my way to the radio studio when I got the phone call from Colonel Perez.

"Stand by. The White House is announcing as soon as POTUS wraps up the D-Day speech."

"Today?"

"Yep, it's happening. This is going down ASAP."

President Trump was in France to commemorate the seventy-fifth anniversary of the Normandy landings, a battle that has long been celebrated by my own 1st Infantry Division, which suffered heavy losses taking Omaha Beach.

That the announcement of the Medal of Honor would come on the heels of honoring this seminal moment in American—and world—history left me humbled.

We waited all day for it to happen. Then we were told it would be announced the next morning on Friday, June 7. It didn't happen that morning, either.

In the studio that afternoon, we went on the air with a discussion on the generational impact of school traffic zone cameras. Behind the scenes, my stomach knotted up. I started thinking of what the president might say, what the press would report. My attention drifted from our callers. I realized I had not prepared my family for this at all. I should have been more proactive, talked to them about the award, what it meant and why I was getting it. If they saw the news, they would learn more about me than I had revealed to them.

No word from Colonel Perez. As the hour marched on, I sat in the studio waiting for the press release to drop, staring at a digital clock with all the anxiety of a NASA flight director waiting on Apollo 13 to reenter the stratosphere.

What do I do if this happens while I am on the air? Has this ever happened ever? Do I talk about it? Did Bud Day ever have a radio talk show? I wonder what Alvin York would have done if he hosted a podcast?

Texts flooded into my phone. If vibrate was on, it would have sounded like road construction. The time kept changing.

"1600, definitely."

"NLT 1645."

"1700, now. Sorry."

"Hasn't landed yet. Maybe 5:10 p.m. at the latest."

"Five thirty p.m. Eastern time, definitely."

I couldn't focus. I couldn't swallow. I was marble-mouthed and sweating.

An update came over the news radio station's banner.

"*ARMY TIMES* REPORT: TRUMP TO GIVE MEDAL OF HONOR TO FIRST LIVING IRAQ WAR VETERAN."

Oh shit. The media reported it before the White House.

My phone blew up. In the swamp of messages I received one from Paula Smith, the army's senior media guru.

"Not happening today. Monday morning."

WHAT?

One of my White House invited guests also works at the Veterans of Foreign Wars. This guy embargoed a story on the VFW blog to go live the moment the story broke from the White House. His contacts at the Pentagon assured him that the release would come at 5:30 p.m. His blog went up, automatically scheduled by time. The *Army Times*, already embargoing the story, read it, used it as confirmation, and were the first to report it.

Not the White House. One of my guests, on his blog. What was a secret for six months was now public and the White House had not said a thing.

And I was live on the air in Buffalo, New York, talking about traffic lights.

We cut to a commercial break and I excused myself from the radio studio and frantically called Paula Smith.

"What do I do, ma'am?"

"First off, breathe. Count to three. Exhale. Do it again."

I followed orders. Something I am good at.

"Now, you may not believe this but not only are you the first living recipient from the Iraq War. You are the only recipient in the history of the United States to have a live afternoon drive-time talk show to receive the Medal of Honor. So let's do this . . ."

"Please, just tell me what to do."

"Go back on your show. Confirm the story. Tell people that this isn't the way it normally happens. But yes, it is true. Monday morning, June tenth, the president will confirm this story."

June 10 was my father's birthday. He would have busted with pride to be here for this moment. I felt a sudden swell of calm.

"You got this, Staff Sergeant. I am proud of you. And you are now ready for what is going to be asked of you. I have seen the change in you. You are ready to serve again. Now more than ever before."

"Thank you, ma'am."

Back from commercial, everything had changed. From that point to now, outside the house with my kids, life went from a sedate forty-five mph to Mach 1. There was a press conference in my hometown. The International Peace Bridge, one of the connections between Canada and the United States, was lit up with the colors of the Medal of Honor. Both local international airports in Buffalo and Rochester did the same. The mayors of those cities sent their congratulations. Senator Chuck Schumer and the lieutenant governor of New York said they were proud of me. Former bitter political opponents suddenly sang my praises. In the days after the news broke, it was an exceptional thing to see how much this award meant to our community in western New York. Love was everywhere, and patriotism proliferated all around my little sphere.

I looked across to the eaves of the house I once loved. The memory of how slippery and dangerous it was cleaning those things every fall. Halloween with the kids. Mowing that lawn. Just then, the kids' mom came out of the garage and closed the door, saying nothing, but clearly as uncomfortable as I was. The kids sensed it. My mother sensed it. The mood was so tense I began to second-guess the decisions that led to this moment.

Evan. Aiden. Vivienne. I looked quietly at each in turn. That night in Vilseck returned. An empty, cold night that left me so bitterly lonely, fighting a war within myself. All I wanted out of life was to be a father. To do right by everyone. I couldn't handle the thought of another dotted-line moment in my life without the kids. I could not leave them behind and stand in the White House alone.

So here we were.

The silence, broken by a few nervous words. A laugh from Viv, whose broad and beautiful grin eased the tension a bit every time she flashed it. Hair pulled back, she is the only girl from four Bellavia sons. She looked and acted beyond her years. I couldn't help but think again what a formidable presence she would be when she launched into her adult life in the years to come.

Outside, a police-escorted limousine pulled up to the house. I opened the front door in time to see Sergeant First Class Blake Gibson emerge from the back of the limo. Sizing up Sergeant First Class Gibson made me instantly jealous. Strapping, fit, his uniform meticulous and perfect. He walked with the swagger of a combat veteran, self-possessed with an air of authority. I could see he was around the same age as I was. He was central casting's stereotypical honor guard Soldier. I was looking at what I could have been, should have been, had I made the choice to stay in.

Gibson was a veteran of not only combat, but also the Old Guard: the 3rd Infantry Regiment, the Army's elite drill and ceremony unit. The Old Guard is the oldest active-duty unit in the Army. Since 1784, they have provided direct security for Washington, D.C., and all official ceremonies, and functioned as the official escorts of the president of the United States. They can polish anything. Iron George Burns's face. There is nothing these guys can't class up.

I found out later that before he ended up on my family's doorstep, Gibson had spent three days rehearsing for President Jimmy Carter's funeral. That struck me as odd, since President Carter was still very much alive that June.

"No, we rehearse everyone's funeral. Everything is meticulous. Feet in the right direction. Flag. We take the casket out and put it back in. This is a battle drill for us. We are ready. Hell, give us a few weeks and we will be planning your untimely demise. That's what we do."

We shook hands as he introduced himself. My mother, standing beside me, thanked him for his service.

"Hey, big sarge, honor to meet you," he said as we stood in the doorway. "I am here for you this entire week. I will be stuck on you. For everything. Where you go, I go. Thanks for what you have done. This is going to be a crazy time. My job is to make it less crazy."

"Thank you, SFC Gibson. Appreciate you."

Then, with a giant friendly smile, Sergeant First Class Gibson helped my mother into the limo. "Ma'am, anything you need, I am here for you. I am here to protect you. To keep you safe. Answer any questions. Anything. You are my priority."

Then he turned to the children.

"Evan, Aiden, and . . . yeah, that should do it. No one else is on my list," he deadpanned.

My boys exchanged glances, Vivienne between them. She looked miffed.

"Oh wait, you are Vivienne!" Gibson exclaimed. "Oh! You are my VIP, Ms. Vivienne; come on in. I got food and snacks. Whatever you need."

The children's mother stepped outside and stood apart from us at the top of the driveway. She looked scared, uneasy and sad. Maybe I had to be more patient and understanding. This would be tough on her as well.

For our generation of warriors, more than the World War II guys, the complexities of a broken marriage and a byzantine, contentious divorce became part of the consequence of our service long ago. Most of the Ramrods have gone through it, emerging with deep battle scars that challenged their ability to ever trust again. To be clear, there is no clear right or wrong in these situations. It takes two to make a marriage fail. Right or wrong isn't the point. The dynamic has been repeated throughout the combat arms, the Marine Corps, the Navy. The lists of reasons are as long as the lists of failed marriages. There are some commonalities, though, including distance—the physical separation was always the most difficult. When the Ramrods first went to Iraq, the deployments lasted a year, but training up for them took six months. So, really, especially with the stateside units and National Guard, going to combat meant being away from family for eighteen months.

For those who weathered that first long separation, there was the next deployment on the horizon. Just like Fitts experienced. Good marriages could survive a deployment and eighteen months, but it took an extraordinary one to survive a second, or a third, or a fourth. By year eighteen of the War on Terror, some men and women had deployed upward of seven or eight times.

Marriages just couldn't thrive in that kind of cycle. During World War II, the separations were longer in continuous duration—usually less than three years—but during the War on Terror, our troops were away from home much longer in shorter spurts. That was the product of the all-volunteer force, and the fact that the burden of the war fell on such a small percentage of the American population.

Trauma always creates dysfunction, and so many of us came home with demons that we never could shed. Alcoholism, addiction, physical injuries, and debilitating wounds with all their second- and third-order effects caused havoc on families. More than thirty thousand of us were wounded in action. Thousands more were injured on the job, in accidents or noncombat mishaps. One study concluded that on the high end, just under 10 percent of the troops deployed to Iraq suffered from some form of PTS before going into combat, usually related to childhood trauma. After coming home from Iraq, the number jumped another 10 percent on the high side.

The challenges we faced beyond our demons included a sense of alienation from the country we served to defend. It was one of the roughest, and least understood, aspects of the war, especially when the Ramrods came home during its early years. In retrospect, coming home from war to reintegrate into a society thinking and behaving as if it was at peace should have raised alarm bells earlier than it did. This was not an easy transition for anyone to make, but most made it eventually. A lot of marriages didn't survive the transition.

When a spouse is deployed, the remaining parent wears both hats. Theirs is a service, often a burden, that is rarely celebrated with fanfare, in comparison to the Soldier off at war. A strange dynamic may occur during that time. After the war, the spouse who plays both mom and dad sometimes never gives up that role. That has become their new identity and power. It is their validation. As difficult as it was to pick up the slack in the absence of a partner, the war is something that doesn't deserve to be revisited. That time may represent loneliness, pain, or poor choices that bear guilt. The spouse has their war at home just like the veteran who fights. To the Soldier at war, most times forgetting the war is exactly what they prefer as well. Inevitably the war doesn't go away, just like the feelings of abandonment or the accountability of actions never leave us. Life always seems to make us accountable. Accordingly, we are forced to address the war. The time that reminded us of separation and guilt now can become a cudgel of more difficult times that lay ahead.

War doesn't cause divorce. War magnifies and weaponizes all the other problems around a relationship that make a marriage unsustainable. It forced us to deal with decisions we made in our lives when we didn't have a guaranteed tomorrow. In the security of peacetime, we have to live up to the commitments we made. Tragic as it may be, everyone changes. Sometimes the spouse doesn't want their warrior to come home to be a partner; rather they are looking for some type of transactional back pay for what they did in the veteran's absence.

The generational damage the war inflicted on our families will not be fully understood for years. Our kids, caught in the middle of all these challenging things, on top of the usual worst aspects of a romantic relationship gone off the rails, are the ones who will carry that burden. We saw this play out anecdotally with the Greatest Generation and their kids after Vietnam. World War II, Korea, Southeast Asia—the effects rippled through the children of our warriors who never saw an enemy Soldier or enemy plane, yet endured as much because their fathers had. It affected every aspect of their lives, from their socioeconomic status to their own views on marriage and relationships.

I hated the fact that my own kids were facing this as well. Now we were left with a big mess, the effects of which were obvious on the faces of my children.

The limo began to move. We rode in the same awkward, tense silence we had settled into at the house.

I looked over at the kids. They were sitting together, perhaps a bit awed at the limo ride and the attention the family was getting. Vivienne's bright and earnest eyes met mine, and I could see in them confusion.

They were the most innocent victims of the war, part of a generation of children afflicted by the unintended consequences, the second- and third-order effects that reframed our home fronts and their young lives.

They didn't even know why. I never told them much about Iraq. They knew some of the story, bits and pieces that came out over the years. Evan, I think, read pieces of *House to House*. Even after that, though, he and I never talked about the war like I had with my father. That was a clear failing. My failing.

Just before we went into Fallujah, Fitts and I sat on the ramp of a Bradley, watching a sunset together. Captain Sean Sims joined us to make peace.

Sims buried the hatchet with us in a way that was so incredibly bold and kind. We talked about our kids. I grew sentimental. Sims got emotional. You could see that the love he had for his wife and toddler son was his foundation. That evening, he spoke of the bond he shared with them. It changed my perspective. I saw him as a family man, not an officer, for the first, and only, time.

"When you get home, sir, sit your little boy down. You tell him about us, okay? Our war. The way we fought."

We promised each other we would do this. The Ramrods would not be forgotten, at least not within our own families. We would tell the stories to our kids, of Fitts and Knapp and Iwan. The kind of men they were, and how in the worst moments of our lives, they were pure clutch.

Sims never got the chance to tell his son Colin about us.

As I sat in the limo, looking at my kids, I realized I had never told them about Captain Sims.

What would I have said? My captain was a good man. He saw the world and wanted to make it better. I saw the world and wanted to make it better by killing those who threatened it. He was right. I was wrong. You can't kill your way to understanding. I would have died for him so that he could get home to his own wife and son. Instead, he died for me, and was my life worthy of that sacrifice?

If I saw Captain Sean Sims today, could I tell him that I took the gift he gave us and I made him proud?

That was a tough one.

It was time to honor that moment on the ramp. Colin Sims was ready to listen. It would be our duty to tell him about his dad. He deserved to know what his father did for all of us.

I knew I could do that for Colin.

I wasn't sure I could do that for Evan, Aiden, and Vivienne, though. Plus, despite all that had unfolded since the president's call, I wasn't sure they were ready to listen.

17

ON TO D.C.

JUNE 23, 2019

THE LIMO ROLLED ON toward Buffalo Niagara International Airport, picking up an escort of Patriot Guard motorcyclists along the way. We rode in silence, flanked by four police cruisers and the long line of black-vest-clad vets riding Harleys, American flags fluttering just over their shoulders.

The kids watched out the windows and one of them exclaimed and pointed. Outside, along the sidewalk, we saw knots of people who had lined our route of travel to wish us well. Some held signs. Others waved little flags. Veterans saluted as we passed.

The outpouring of support and pride caught all of us by surprise. The knots of people grew into a steady line of cheering, smiling, happy Americans. Businessmen and -women in suits, skirts, and blazers, soccer moms in yoga pants holding their kids' hands, young and old, people of every color. We drove through them, looking out the tinted windows at the scene on both sides of the road. They couldn't see into the limousine; the windows were too dark for that. Yet all those New Yorkers took time out of their days to show us this kind of love. It was awe-inspiring and humbling.

Our nation had been battered for twenty years. Dot-com bubbles bursting, the Great Recession, endless wars large and small, draining our generations of vitality and potential even as they drained our

Treasury. We had become increasingly a house divided—at least according to the news media—neighbors and families turned against each other by politics and a raging culture war inside our borders.

But this? This sight. They weren't there for me. These people were there on those sidewalks to demonstrate that America still mattered to them. Their love of country was on full display, and that meant more to me than anything else. As long as the bedrock of this country holds, this reservoir of love for all we are and the values we embody, America will flourish and survive any challenge, no matter how great.

We reached the airport only to find our flight delayed. Twenty minutes passed, then an hour. We sat at the gate with hundreds of other travelers, all growing increasingly anxious.

Out of nowhere, an American Airlines employee ran up to us with a cell phone in her hand.

"Sergeant Bellavia, there is a representative from American Airlines on the phone for you."

"Hey, Sarge, Randy Stillinger with American. I'm the manager of Veterans Services and Initiatives for the airline. Your flight has been canceled."

"Are you serious?"

"Yeah, but check this out. We consider this an honor to have you flying with us, so we are actually bringing in a plane just for you and your family. We made it happen. I am sure all the other passengers who just got canceled will also be appreciative that we are doing this. You will be a hero two times to them. Just to let you know, American loves our veterans. We salute your service. And you are going to D.C. ASAP."

They brought my family a plane?

I relayed this to my mom and the kids. Sergeant First Class Gibson grinned. The kids looked poker-faced, like all of this was unreal and not actually unfolding with them in the middle of it.

A few minutes later, the new aircraft rolled up to the gate and the otherwise stranded passengers began to line up.

When I stepped into the cabin from the Jetway, I was focused on getting the kids and my mother to their seats, taking their carry-on bags and getting them packed away. I noticed something on the seats in the cabin, but I didn't think anything of them until I saw my mom's expression. I stopped, looking at her quizzically, half in a daze from the already overwhelming reception.

Vivienne and Aiden were holding something in their hands. Evan was looking at his seat. Aiden showed me what he had found. I did a double take. It was a poster with my service photo and the Medal of Honor citation. My mom nudged me and pointed. American Airlines had decorated every seat on the plane with one of these posters. I think I went a little numb at that point. All this attention, and I was just a western New Yorker. I served like countless others. This felt wildly awkward and humbling. Undeserved. Now my face adorned every seat. I couldn't even process this kind of gesture.

I sat down, staring straight ahead, feeling every minute of my age. Around us, people stuffed their luggage in the overhead bins and settled in. The sounds of the cabin filled my ears. The clicks of safety belts. A baby crying. The dulled murmur of people talking in low voices.

We hadn't yet pushed away from the gate when the pilot's voice came over the intercom. Quiet, calm, unflappable—a typical airline pilot's voice reassuring the passengers with his tone that he was in charge and had everything in hand. I was barely listening to the standard preflight welcome, words I'd heard a million times. Then he veered off script.

"Ladies and gentlemen, we have the honor of taking a special guest to Washington. He is getting ready to receive the Medal of Honor from our president in a few days. On board today is our special guest, Staff Sergeant David Bellavia, and his family."

I looked at my mom. She was over the moon with pride, and the look on her face became one of the unforgettable moments of my life. I thought of my dad right then. How much he would have loved this. If only . . .

To my astonishment, the pilot began to read the Medal of Honor citation to the entire plane. "While clearing a house, a squad from Staff Sergeant Bellavia's platoon became trapped within a room by intense enemy fire coming from a fortified position under the stairs leading to the second floor. . . ."

Hearing the words brought the moment back. The aircraft drained

away, replaced by that shoddy brick wall inside the house. Bullets ric-
ocheting around us. Fitts's face swam in front of me, smoke-stained,
covered in grime and concrete powder.

Bro. I need you.

I wanted to answer. Instead, I sat looking straight ahead, fighting
the images.

The pilot kept reading. The citation is a long one, and as he continued, his voice cracked. I had never heard that from an aviator
before. He paused, composed himself, and picked up. Then he got
choked up and stopped again. The aircraft was dead silent.

I wondered if he was a veteran, too. What his war was like. Air
Force? Reservist? What would have been the odds if he'd been the
C-17 pilot who flew us back to Germany? Or into Iraq? The war made
for a very, very small world as the tiny percentage of our population
carried arms to the enemy.

Whatever the case, by the end of this gesture, there was no doubt
how affected he was by the words he had just read to his passengers.
For a long second, there was silence. Then the *tink* of lap belts being
unbuckled.

Movement around me. I looked away from the past and saw average Americans, just like me, rising to their feet in every row and
aisle. I barely heard the applause that swelled in the wake of those
words.

Nothing I had learned in the months since Colonel Perez first
contacted me had prepared me for this moment. How do you say
thank you to a planeload of people who've just given you the gold-
bar standard of welcome-homes fourteen years after the fact?

I never told Aiden or Vivienne much about the war or Iraq. They
knew some of the story. They didn't know the details. They didn't
know about the house in Fallujah and what happened inside the
night of my twenty-ninth birthday.

Now they had heard an American Airlines captain read the official
narrative of that terrible night. Both were looking at me, eyes wide.

Dad. You did what?

For the first time my children looked at me like I had looked at
my own father. I could sense a mélange of shock, love, and pride.
There was no time to talk about it, or savor their looks. Passengers

approached, leaned toward me, and shook my hands. They took selfies with me. They shook my mother's hands. Said kind words to my children. My mom beamed, tears filling her eyes at the kindness of total strangers who were nevertheless part of our American family.

Our flight attendant came over and asked me to sign a poster for her. As I did, she told me that her brother served in Iraq and had been wounded in action. It was a moment of unity between us, a connecting bond shared in a brief discussion that transcended whatever differences we had and never knew. We knew this: the war connected us. She felt it. I felt it. I sensed there was something more happening here that wasn't about me or the award. This was becoming a moment to share those bonds, talk about them, and bring the experience to light again after so much discord and division drove them underground. I wondered if this event might spark a catharsis far beyond the Ramrods and our small circle. At least for other veterans who served. If so, it was long needed.

We pulled away from the gate and the plane began to taxi for the runway. As we did, the Buffalo Niagara Airport Fire Department flanked us with their trucks. As we approached, they sent two enormous plumes of water arching over the aircraft as a salute of honor and respect.

"Dad, why are they washing the plane?" Vivienne asked in astonishment.

"This is something they do to be nice to people. It's a real kind gesture."

A guy from outside my beloved western New York nearby said loudly, "Even in June in Buffalo they are deicing the planes. This place sucks."

I broke into a grin. The reality check pulled me back into the moment, far from visions of some grandiose national healing experience. This passenger's little bubble, his world. That was the real one, not the one my family found ourselves in at the moment. Tomorrow there would be no posters on the seats, no water salutes.

None of this is real. Stay in your lane. Stay grounded. The world will go back to normal soon enough.

. . .

We landed in Washington, D.C., at Reagan National Airport a few hours later, where we were met by Colonel Carrie Perez and the members of the Department of Defense's Medal of Honor team. They led my family to a bus and helped us aboard. Once again, we received a police escort—motorcycle cops, this time. We sped through D.C. traffic to the hotel, cars pulling out of our lane to let us pass. It reminded me of Iraq. We owned the roads when on patrol back then.

To be honest, threading through the Sunday evening beltway traffic like that was probably the single coolest experience of my life. Those cops were amazing. They treated us all like we were the most important people in the world.

Wouldn't it be something if every veteran received this kind of appreciation at least once in their lifetimes? To have strangers show Soldiers this much love and respect couldn't help but be healing and reconnective. What a welcome home that would be.

When we reached the hotel, the motorcycle escort dismounted and stood at attention as we exited the bus. I thanked them, talked to one who'd held off on his retirement just so he could pull this duty. Escorting a Medal of Honor family was the last thing on his professional to-do list after decades of service in our nation's capital.

I would have stayed out there talking to those guys all afternoon, but out of the corner of my eye, I could see through the hotel's glass front doors that the lobby was full of people. *My people.* The Ramrods.

My family from another life were waiting. We had never had a reunion. The wounds were raw. The contentions within the platoon still ran deep. Yet we were always going to be bound to each other, no matter how many years rolled over those memories.

I broke away from the motorcycle officers and bolted through the lobby doors. As I entered, a general I didn't recognize approached me, three stars on his shoulder board. I braced to say hello as he stretched out his hand. I shook it, half hearing his kind words and introduction. A cameraman stepped forward and snapped pictures of us. All I wanted to do was see the Ramrods.

The room devolved into blurs of colors. Joe Montana, the legendary Super Bowl–winning quarterback, once said that on the field, as soon as he took the snap, the world turned into motions of color to him. He didn't see faces. He didn't see numbers. He just saw color.

The same thing happened in that lobby. People moved into me, hugging me, taking selfies. Some I knew. Others I did not. I was anxious, disoriented, the anticipation of seeing the Ramrods splitting me open.

Suddenly John Ruiz was in front of me. Ruiz, our AT4 guy. Where Ruiz went, the rest of the squad went. Time after time, this man proved himself in the clutch to be courageous and calm. I depended on him, and more than once he repaid that trust by saving my life.

Seeing him in front of me, in the flesh again, was like being Rip Van Winkle. I had woken from a decades-long sleep to find the people I loved right there with me again. It was the same John Ruiz, only different. Trending toward middle age now, gray flecking his hair, eyes a little wiser, a little less full of the exuberance that I had to ride herd on over in Germany.

Ruiz was almost the perfect Soldier. He'd been a wild one in Germany, but in Iraq, a switch flipped inside him and greatness shined through. No matter what we endured, I never saw him fatigued. His energy seemed boundless. He never complained—something that is a Soldier's God-given right. I also never saw him make the same mistake twice.

In Iraq we never emoted with one another. After rough moments, we'd sometimes touch helmets. Face-to-face, we would tap our helmets together. That was the extent of the emotion we displayed. Well, rage and anger—we displayed that. It was part of our tackling fuel in the fury of a fight. Bro hugs and "I love you, man" was not part of our culture. We tamped that stuff down, didn't do well with it. I didn't do well with it.

In middle age, my dad started to show emotion at graduations and other events. He was unashamed of his tears. As a kid, I was embarrassed by the displays. Honestly, part of me sometimes felt contempt. This wasn't how I wanted to be perceived. Seeing a grown man cry was like seeing an elderly person fall.

In that lobby, I understood my father's powerlessness. He didn't want to cry at my brother's graduation, it just happened. He felt tears well up and did his best to keep it in. At some point, the feelings won out and he wore them with pride instead of shame.

There were no helmets to touch this time. Instead, we bear-hugged each other like the lost friends we were. I hugged him so tight, I thought I broke his ribs. God, I love that guy.

I held on to him long enough for the hug to be considered a vertical cuddle.

"Hey, Bell?" he asked, still trapped in my grip.

"Yeah, bro?"

"Remember how I told you over the phone a few weeks ago that this was all gonna die down and get back to normal?"

"I remember."

"I was wrong. It'll never be normal again. You're screwed."

"You mean *we're* screwed."

"Yeah. That."

How right he proved to be.

The lobby surged with people, Ramrods and their families. Pentagon VIPs and Sergeant First Class Gibson standing watch over everyone and everything. In action movies, I always loved how our hero would fight a group of twenty villains. Each bad guy waits patiently for our protagonist to dispatch them one by one. In real life, we all storm in. No one waits. That moment in the lobby of the Sheraton at Pentagon City, everyone waited for me. A hug and greeting, I was spun toward another awaiting hug and hello. I was twirled. Kissed. Shaken. Squeezed. I had no idea what was happening. Like Joe Montana, all I saw were colors.

Gradually we tried to make our way to the elevator so I could get my family settled into our rooms. That's when Michael "Mick" Ware appeared, dressed in jeans and a black V-neck T-shirt. He looked Hollywood, like an Australian Simon Cowell. All smiles, larger than life, he electrified everyone in the lobby. I man-hugged him hard, as I had Ruiz. After we broke the embrace, he put his right hand on my neck and jaw and said, "You and I, mate. We are forever linked. You are my blood. And I couldn't be more proud to be there for that moment. I love you, Digger."

When I looked over at my family, they were smiling widely—the first genuine smiles since we left the house. They stood and watched the two of us pick right up where we left off a decade ago, our national political divide forgotten in the joy of seeing each other once again.

. . .

That evening, after my family got settled, Mick and I met up again inside the hotel. It was just us, and the jovial life-of-the-party Mick we'd seen in the lobby soon gave way to the man I saw in his documentary. Serious. Hurting. Wondering how the Ramrods would receive him.

That was an easy one to straighten out. "Mick, everyone loves you," I said. "I mean, look at how people responded to you in the lobby today."

A dark expression crossed his face. I said it again, reassuringly: "Everyone loves you."

"Except the ones who think I got Lieutenant Iwan killed," he replied.

I stared at him. He couldn't make eye contact with me.

"What?"

He sat, miserable, looking at the hotel carpet.

"Mick, what are you talking about?"

"Bell, we live with ghosts. Every day. There they are. Everywhere we turn. You need to acknowledge it."

He had switched the subject. Or at least I thought he had. Deflecting. All of us were adept at that. It is our first line of defense.

"This isn't about me, Mick. I don't understand."

"You know exactly what I am talking about. You need to admit how screwed-up you are. Stop acting like this is all normal. You know how far from normal all this is."

"I manage to deal with it," I said defensively.

He looked up and said softly, "You are a horrible liar, David. I know you better than you know yourself. Because I see you every day in my own mirror."

"Mick?"

"You've carried the guilt for Captain Sims's death. I've carried the guilt for Edward Iwan's."

"I guess I don't know the whole story," I finally said.

"No. You don't."

His eyes dropped to the floor again, and he began to talk.

18

THE FATAL GOODBYE

WAR AND COMBAT HAVE the unique ability to bond strangers into lifelong friends in a matter of days, or even hours. Michael Ware joined our platoon just before we launched our assault into the fortified city of Fallujah on November 7, 2004. He came to us a stranger, a foreigner, and a representative of a profession almost all Soldiers detest. You'd think with those three strikes against him, he would have been an outcast among the Ramrods, an Aussie in an American combat arms unit reporting for news agencies that had been overtly hostile to the Iraq War effort and the U.S. military. It didn't help that when he embedded with us, a crusty, hard-bitten Russian photographer named Yuri Kozyrev came with him.

A Russian.

I didn't trust him at all. Mick Ware had a growing reputation as a Western mouthpiece for the Islamo-fascist insurgents who were trying to kill us. He'd been known to embed with enemy cells as well as Coalition units. I saw him through very cautious and skeptical eyes.

At first, the platoon ignored this unlikely pair, universally feeling the same way I did. How do you trust a foreigner whom the enemy takes with them on their own missions against us? Our own command hated him for the way he reported the war. Gradually, I came to understand that Mick was probably the purest journalist left in the business. He had no ax to grind, no politics he wanted to buttress with his reporting. Nor did he have any allegiance to anything but the truth as he witnessed it. Before we attacked into Fallujah, it became clear he didn't care whom the truth pissed off.

A scribe like that was tough to hate.

The first crack in our wall around Mick and Yuri came from, of all places, our company executive officer. This was the unlikeliest of sources, given Iwan's history. He grew up in small-town Nebraska, a town called Albion with a population of less than seventeen hundred people. A small downtown composed of turn-of-the-last-century buildings full of small businesses. Oceans of corn surrounded their little town. Iwan's family was Catholic, and he was baptized at St. Michael's, the hundred-year-old brick and stained-glass church whose arched bell tower and steeple dominated the little town. He grew up in FFA (Future Farmers of America), was a leader in school and was elected to the student council.

Out of high school, he joined the Army and served in the first post–Cold War years of the 1990s. He returned home, went to college via the ROTC program, and got a degree in criminal justice. After 9/11, he went regular Army after spending time in the Nebraska National Guard.

A small-town kid from the middle of flyover country would be the last person I would suspect of bonding with a leathery foreign journalist, but that is exactly what happened in the days before the Battle of Fallujah. Instead of going home during his mid-tour leave, Iwan's sense of adventure took him to Australia. That became the entry point for a friendship with Mick that quickly flourished. The two would sit and talk about golden beaches, beautiful Australian women, the bars and pub crawls in Sydney, and all the little things that made those twenty days of freedom from Iraq a beautiful memory. Ware had spent his second consecutive year living in the Iraqi war zone, and these conversations reminded him of a life that seemed long forgotten.

As they talked, Iwan drew Mick out, and through their conversations we'd learned that our journalist was from Queensland and started out as a professional rugby player before going corporate and becoming a lawyer. He soon found that gig way too boring for his blood. He made his way to Iraq and became the Western journalist the insurgents would give beheading videos to, of all things. Before Fallujah, he'd had enough of that and refused to accept any of them. Still, between those little revelations and his tactical knowledge of how the insurgents fought against us, I started to listen to Mick. He was definitely not your average journalist.

On the night of November 7, 2004, when we assaulted into the city as the main effort's left flank, Mick spent the entire attack smashed together with the men inside the claustrophobic confines of Fitts's Bradley Fighting Vehicle. He experienced the fear, the maddening prolonged wait before we got the "go" order and started rolling for the fortified city. The hours we spent inside that armored can showed me that Mick had balls. He showed all of us that. The truth was, he and Yuri had seen more combat than we had. It was Mick's second year in Iraq. Yuri had been photographing man's inhumanity to man since Chechnya in the late 1990s.

In the brutal days that followed, as we fought our way deeper and deeper into this shattered city, Mick Ware was always in the middle of the action. He appeared fearless, devoted solely to documenting our story by experiencing everything we did. He never lingered in the rear, and bullets, danger, and threats seemed to have little effect on him.

As the fighting wore on, every time Lieutenant Iwan came to check on our platoon, he would see Mick and light up. "Digger. How are you, mate!" he'd call out to Mick in his best Aussie accent.

Through the brutal building-by-building searches, the firefights, and the deadly events on my birthday, Mick Ware proved himself as an infantryman with a camera. Few men were ever as rugged. Initially an outcast, he earned respect. And from respect, he became one of us—the writer who knew our truth because he lived it right alongside us.

November 12, 2004, was our worst day in Fallujah. We'd been fighting nonstop for five days. At one point, we had to backtrack and clear ground we'd already cleared because the Marines on our flank got bogged down in heavy fighting. Lacking heavy armor and Bradleys, their line companies took heavy losses. We'd advanced too far, and the enemy flowed through the gap between us and the Marines, getting into our rear to cause havoc.

We about-faced and dealt with the threat, then pushed on southward again. Ware, however, had to file his story about the November 10 house fight that would eventually become the cover article in *Time* that made the Ramrods Army famous. He'd been in Iwan's Bradley when the time came to get back to the rear and get that story in. He dismounted, and Iwan handed him his gear from the Brad's turret.

"G'day, mate!" Iwan said cheerfully. Mick smiled, shouldered his load, and started to walk away.

"Hey!" he heard Iwan shout over the din of the Brad's engine and the not-so-distant sounds of gunfire echoing through the blocks of devastated buildings in Fallujah's dying heart.

Mick turned to see Iwan lifting his right arm in a last wave goodbye. Two friends, bound by the experience of combat, probably never to see each other again, but their brief friendship in theater the sort that would always be stamped on their hearts, shared a final moment. Mick raised his hand to wave back. Iwan grinned broadly, standing in his Bradley's turret hatch.

A rocket sizzled out of nowhere and struck Ed Iwan in the ribs. Mick's happy grin turned to screams of "Medic! Medic!" as Iwan collapsed, half in, half out of the turret, the RPG embedded in his body.

The rocket didn't explode, which made the suffering all the more cruel for Iwan and his gunner, Sergeant Tyler Colley. Colley's job was to gun, secure the area, and provide aid for Iwan at the same time. Not many young NCOs have been put in a similar situation as Colley. He handled it like he handled everything else with 2-2. He was a rock.

"It burns . . ." was all Iwan could manage.

"MEDIC! MEDIC!" Mick screamed on, his words swamped by an eruption of gunfire. Our Brads opened up in return, firing their 25mm auto-cannons furiously as more RPG volleys lanced past our tracks while enemy machine guns sent our dismounts diving for cover.

"MEDIC!"

If only the rocket had hit Iwan in the chest. Or the back. Or if his arm had been down it might have deflected the rocket just enough to give Iwan a fighting chance.

In that sinister moment, the million little things required to destroy our XO's life *snicked* into place. The RPG team went undetected. They'd maneuvered into range, or lay in wait for what they saw as a perfect moment. The RPG gunner's aim was true. And the rocket? Ordnance degrades over time, and cached in holes or underground, moisture inevitably affected RPGs. Earlier in the day, a poorly stored one hit our radioman in the back and failed to detonate. The rocket fired at Iwan was probably stored better, in a drier place, handled with more care. A slightly bent or dinged fin created errant flights and ensured misses. The rocket hitting Iwan flew straight and true.

All of these things had to align perfectly with Iwan's exact position in the turret. Fired a few seconds earlier, he would have been in a different position and the rocket would have sizzled overhead harmlessly.

Mick had spent fourteen years driving himself crazy, blaming himself for Iwan's death. He was convinced the final pieces of this terrible puzzle fell into place simply because he waved back at Iwan after our XO called down to him a final time.*

Until that night Mick Ware told me the story, I'd never known he'd carried such guilt. It clarified why Mick's own postwar journey turned so dark that he didn't even speak of this episode in his documentary.

If carrying the guilt wasn't enough, Mick had been around enough units to know what happens when a beloved member dies. Rarely does the enemy get blamed. That would have empowered the insurgents. Instead, we turn inward to deny that they have any say in a fight. Our casualties are always the result of somebody messing up. It is our caustic, soul-destroying talisman that keeps us in the fight, but eats us alive afterward. No enemy could touch us. Only Americans

---

* Staff Sergeant James "J.C." Matteson, a Ramrod scout and western New York native, died hours before Iwan, not more than four hundred meters away. Atop a Humvee with a 40mm auto-cannon, he fired on the enemy who took his life. The kid never thought to get out of the turret and run from the rocket that exploded his own ammunition. Instead, he stayed on his weapon and remained in the fight to his last breath. He was awarded a posthumous Silver Star for his actions.

can defeat Americans. So we find a scapegoat who becomes reviled and exiled.

Mick had assumed some of the Ramrods blamed him, and that fed his own guilt and sense of responsibility. The years passed and he never made peace with the moment.

Mick was still smiling as the rocket pierced Iwan's body. The last thing his friend from Nebraska saw was Mick's happy, grime-stained face wishing him farewell.

He played that image over and over in his mind like I did with the Man in White. His guilt over Iwan was the same as any Soldier's who'd watched a friend die. Mick was right. I never even suspected I was looking at him when I looked in my own mirror.

Back in the hotel, after he related the full story, I wanted to reach into him and pull this toxicity out of his heart. There's no way another person can do that, though. The journey we're all on is ultimately a lonely, solo one. You either purge the broken pieces, or you live with them. Nobody can do it for you.

"Mick, you can't blame yourself for Iwan's death. The guy who fired the RPG killed him. You don't own any of this. You know that."

He shook his head, "I can't . . ."

"I know. I feel that, too. Your head and logic may get it, but your heart never does."

"No, it doesn't."

"Mick?"

"Yeah, mate?"

"Nobody blames you. I've never heard anyone say that. The man who killed Iwan was the shithead with the RPG. And First Sergeant Smith took care of him."

Ware looked unconvinced.

"You know why this hurts you so bad?" I asked Mick.

Ware just stared at me.

"The moment you saw that happen, you realized you were in the wrong line of work. You were made to avenge. You were born to control the chaos. Mick Ware is here to defeat evil."

He stared on, but I saw in his eyes I spoke the truth.

"You're right. We are the same, you and me. You're an infantryman at heart. You were just trapped behind a camera."

A half grin started to form.

"You are a part of us until you die. You are a part of my family. You have no choice. All those men down there feel the same way."

"I love you, too, Digger. Proud of you, brother," he said quietly.

Ware's eyes filled with tears, and he wrenched my neck into his chest, kissing me on the head. We sat back down and stared out the window at our view of Arlington Cemetery at night. Shrek, Merrilee Carlson's son, was down there, laid to rest among the rows of American heroes from every war since 1861. Our legacy could be found in all corners of the country, but Arlington would always be its heart.

At length, Mick asked, "Is Iwan's family here?"

I shook my head. "I've tried to reach out. I went to Nebraska a few years ago. They didn't want to talk."

Mick nodded. Iwan's family had been through more nightmares than anyone could imagine. His older brother was killed at eighteen in 1989. The family lost both their sons.

He pointed at Arlington, "Is Ed there?"

"No."

His family laid both brothers to rest in the same small-town cemetery, each with a short inscription that defined what they meant to the family.

Our XO sleeps under the following words:

Ed lived every moment
He stood in the rain
Heard the Thunder
Danced to the lightning
And believed in rainbows.

His older brother's matched what we knew of Edward Iwan, too:

All hearts grow
Warmer in the
Presence of one
Who gave freely
For the love
Of giving.

Edward Iwan carried his brother Matthew's heart and spirit with him to Iraq. We saw it every day. He was the heart of our company, and when the insurgents tore it from us, our lives were never the same.

"He had no kids. No legacy," Ware said, his voice a harsh whisper.

"He has us, Mick."

And my son. Aiden Edward Bellavia.*

---

* Edward Iwan was named after his maternal uncle, Edward Dugan, who was killed in action in June 1970 while serving with the 17th Cavalry, 1st Aviation Brigade in Vietnam. My son Aiden carries the name of two of America's sons killed in wars a generation apart.

19

THE FATE MACHINE

THE NEXT MORNING STARTED way too early for most of the guys, who were beginning to realize that their ability to metabolize alcohol was not the same as it was fifteen years back. Gibson gave me updates on the goings-on downstairs periodically as the previous night wore on. Apparently, my Ramrods drank the hotel bar dry in one evening together.

Fortunately, the main event of today required only Lieutenant Meno, Fitts, Ware, and Colonel Walter. Today was media day, and even after all the preparations the Army's team had put me through, I was still dreading facing reporters.

I showered and dressed quickly in a custom-made gray suit, white shirt, and yellow tie. I put on my thick-rimmed glasses and looked myself over before heading out of the suite. I looked like a world-weary actuary. Or maybe a tax attorney in April. Dressed well, yes, but bags under my eyes and a face a good decade removed from when I last recognized it.

Ready or not, it was showtime.

I went down the hall from my room to the conference room Gibson had selected as our rally point.

The first thing I saw as I walked in was my mother, bouncing around the room, eyes wet with tears, a joyful expression on her face. She had never met any of the Ramrods, yet I'd sent her photos of us with letters home, and later showed her many more when I returned and left the Army.

Without noticing that I had arrived, she rushed up to Lieutenant Meno, my old platoon leader whom I'd not seen in fifteen years, and got first crack at him.

"Is it 'Wakeen' or 'Jo-aquin'? Lieutenant Meno? You're exactly like your pictures."

Now a lieutenant colonel, Meno smiled warmly at my mom and said, "'Wakeen,' ma'am."

She lit up. "Honey, my son loves you so much. You have no idea how much he's told us about you. Can I hug you?"

Meno, engaged with a loving Italian mom for the first time in his life, laughed and said, "Yes, ma'am, of course you can. And Mrs. Bellavia, it is so nice to meet you."

My mom almost squeezed my former PL in half.

As Meno was trapped in an Italian mom hug, Colonel Doug Walter walked into the room. With his dress blues absolutely immaculate, tall and broad-shouldered, his head was shaved bald like the old days, eyebrows almost gone, too. He looked like he'd been through hell since 2015, the last time I'd seen him.

I started to make my way to him, but my mother, moving at the speed of light, broke away from Meno and bolted to him, cutting me off. I stopped and just shook my head, laughing at the level of happiness on her face. This was a woman who had heard stories of the men, but little of the combat we'd experienced. I'd spoken often of what they meant to me, the silly stories from Germany and Kosovo. The good moments in Iraq.

Meno followed my mom over to Walter. "Hello, sir."

Before he could answer, my mother said, "Captain Walter? From A Company? Right?"

"Yes, ma'am. Doug Walter. Are you David's mother, Marilyn?"

Her answer was swift and decisive. She grabbed his face with both hands, pulled him down to her, and kissed his cheek. Then she Italian mom–hugged him.

"My son . . . loves you so much . . ." she said as tears streaked her cheek.

Meno and Walter stood together, this firebrand woman they'd never met showing megatons of love and warmth to them. Few greetings would ever match this one. Walter's eyes filled with tears as he caught my line of sight, still hugging my mother. It was as if my mother was working as a surrogate for the love I never got to show these fine men in my life while we served.

There was no role for me in this, so I hung back and soaked in how quickly my mom won them both over. They were touched, instantly loyal to her.

Fitts walked in a moment later, dressed in a navy blue business suit and lavender cross-hatch tie. His salt-and-pepper beard was neatly trimmed, and his dark hair was recently cut. He looked like a businessman.

He was also holding a beer. A breakfast beer.

My mom turned and saw him. "Staff Sergeant Fitts!"

"Yes, ma'am. You are Momma Bellavia?"

"I am!" she cried.

"Momma, come give me a hug. I love you, too!"

She rushed to him and engulfed him. This was becoming a Ramrod rite of passage. Fitts hugged her close, his beer against her back.

And then, she put her head against his chest, and I saw her crying now without restraint.

"My husband always said, 'We have David because of Staff Sergeant Fitts.' Because of you. He said that many times."

Fitts clenched his jaw. Tried to toughen up. But nobody can resist my mother. I could see that in his eyes.

"You are so special to me," she said.

"Well, ma'am, your son is awful special to me, too. Let me give this ugly guy a hug right quick."

I walked up to them and said, "Hardaway? Why are you playing with my mother? She thinks you're Fitts."

The room erupted in laughter.

My mom regarded me with faux indignation. "I know Omarr. Knapp. Brown. Chad Ellis. Walls. Ruiz. All of them, David. This is

Colin Fitts. I have seen his face too many times . . . I know these men. . . ."

"Mom. Mom," I said gently, "I know. I'm joking. Look at this guy. Fitts. Come here, dude."

I gave Fitts a big hug. He hugged me back fiercely.

My mom watched us and addressed the room: "Thank you for all that you did for us. You are all a part of my family. Every one of you."

I realized I hadn't seen Fitts in person since 2009. He and his family came to New York to visit relatives in Niagara Falls. We met up and had pizza.

A moment later, Gibson entered the room and underscored the rigid timeline. We needed to load up and head out.

Media day was about to begin, and I was incredibly grateful I wouldn't have to fight this battle alone. Walter, Meno, Fitts, and Ware would all be with me through the many interviews and events. Having them in this foxhole again was an enormous comfort.

The entire Ramrod family had been invited to the Pentagon for a private tour. We all assembled at one of the buses and climbed aboard, the police escort joining us for the short run over to the hub of America's military.

Of course, Fitts raised some eyebrows almost the minute our buses pulled up to the broad stairs of the Pentagon's main entrance. We piled out and lined up to go through a sophisticated and elaborate security screening. Just to even get there, the Ramrods had to pass an extensive background check—which eliminated two of our guys long before anyone got to D.C. Now we took turns going through metal detectors and all the other force protection measures in effect.

Just before we were ready to move on into the Pentagon, an alarm went off. I turned to see Fitts covered by two uniformed NCOs.

"Excuse me, sir?" one of them said to Fitts, a little incredulously.

"Whatcha got, Master Sergeant?"

"Is that a beer in your hand?"

"Why yes it is, Master Sergeant."

"That is completely against regulations. You must empty that immediately. You can't bring that in here."

"Give me two seconds and I will do just that. This way we're both happy."

Fitts chugged the beer. The two NCOs exchanged glances, unsure what to do.

The Ramrods stood dumbfounded, whispering to each other, "Did Fitts just bring a beer into the Pentagon?"

I understood how difficult all this was for him. The man hadn't left Mississippi in years. This was his coping mechanism.

Fitts drained the beer and handed the empty to the master sergeant, who stared at it, then flicked his attention back to my best friend.

"Is that all of them?" he asked sternly.

"Well, what do you think? Who brings one beer into the Pentagon?"

"Sir, I need them all or you will be barred from entering."

Colonel Carrie Perez scowled at me like this was somehow my fault. I just shrugged. Fitts will always be nothing but Fitts, no matter where he is or whom he is with.

She walked up to him and did not call him sir, or address him like a civilian, like the Pentagon NCOs were doing.

"Sergeant First Class Fitts," she said sharply. That got his attention.

"Yes, ma'am," he replied automatically.

She leaned forward and spoke quietly into his ear.

He nodded, pulled out two cans of Bud Light from his suit, and dumped them in the trash. Then he walked *around* the metal detector.

We all knew there was another Bud Light in his pocket. Fitts was still a master of the art of survival. That first beer was but a decoy.

The Ramrods made their way into the Pentagon with a sort of Dorothy in Oz vibe among the group. We had known nothing but the tip of the spear through our careers. We were warfighters. Door-kickers. Now we found ourselves in the military's cerebellum, the nerve center that fired off the signals that sent us into Kosovo, then Iraq, and finally into Fallujah. So much of our lives had been shaped by the orders flowing from these offices. It was like tumbling onto the place that created Fate.

The military's Emerald City was absolutely enormous and filled with so many people—like a busy pre-COVID day on a Manhattan street. Elevators, escalators, maps, bathrooms everywhere, all inter-connected with the most polished white floors in North America. As we followed our hosts, we passed steady streams of officers from all branches of the service. I had never seen so many full-bird colonels in my life. Colonels at the Pentagon are as thick as privates at Fort Benning. I wondered if somewhere in this place, there were colonels taking out the trash.

Every ten or so minutes, a group of civilians interrupted us as another tour moved down the hallway. Gaggle after gaggle flowed down each ring like clockwork. Each tour group was led by one backward-walking uniformed guide. I noticed there were actually markings on the floor to assist these guides and show them when to turn and when to stop. They could literally walk backward in perpetuity, guided by the floor.

As we walked along together, one of our guys, Sergeant First Class John Gregory, stopped suddenly at a giant poster-size photograph framed on the hallway wall.

"Check out that handsome stud!" he exclaimed. "Get a photo of me looking at me. Then get one of Bell looking at me looking at me."

Gregory came to us from the 101st Airborne, fresh off an Afghanistan combat deployment and an Operation Iraqi Freedom I tour. In 2004, a two-combat-deployment veteran was almost unheard-of in the Army, especially in the 1st Infantry Division. Gregory became my A Team leader. A broad, muscular NCO, he was whip smart, super funny, a straight-leg infantryman in a mechanized infantry world with a consummate handle on dismounted tactics, but a lot to learn with Bradley operations. The best part of John Gregory? He had already seen considerable combat in two theaters, giving us an invaluable knowledge resource as we prepared to go into the fight.

Then our brigade came out with new guidance on deployments, and Gregory would not be able to come to Iraq with us because of the strain it put on his young wife. The new regs forced him to stay home. Gregory never stopped being my A Team leader. He trained with us. He never left my side. And when our Ramrods were wounded or lost their lives, it was Gregory who handled the families and made sure the guys got everything they needed when they got back to Germany.

A year after we came home, Gregory and the remaining Ramrods with time left on their Army contract, now without the combat strength to maintain our beloved unit, were sliced out to a unit in

Schweinfurt, Germany, as a part of the 26th Infantry Regiment. As a member of Charlie Company, 1-26, they lost thirty-one Soldiers in 2007. Gregory served with many Ramrods who died that year with a unit that got decimated in their sector. Known as the "hardest-hit unit in the Iraq War," their tour was chronicled in a book called *They Fought for Each Other*, by *Army Times* correspondent Kelly Kennedy. John Gregory may be the only living Soldier to serve with two Medal of Honor recipients from the same war. Specialist Ross A. McGinnis was in Charlie Company, First Platoon, 1-26 when he gave his life by throwing himself on a grenade inside a Humvee, saving four of his peers.

Now, deep in the Pentagon, we all stared at the photo of Gregory in Iraq in full battle rattle. The legacy of his service was on display for generations of officers and men to see. We looked on at it in amazed pride. His eyes were focused. Pain and exhaustion were clear in his face. His joking quickly went away after staring at himself. Gregory was back in Iraq now. The photo was a reminder of what we all did for the Army and our nation. One of our own, represented and proudly displayed along one of the Pentagon's nerve pathways. It was a startling and emotional moment.

We moved on, but not a dozen feet later, we saw another giant framed photograph. This one showed First Platoon, Alpha Company and Sergeant (now First Sergeant) John Bandy fighting in Fallujah. We kept on walking, finding more of our time in Iraq and our people represented on these walls. It was like finding Easter eggs in a video game. Turn a corner in this giant labyrinth, and we'd run into another image, another moment. Our Ramrods, our history, carried to the epicenter of American power and might.

It gave all of us goose bumps.

The tour culminated at the area hit on September 11, 2001. The day that changed all our lives forever, sending us on a collision course three years later with the insurgents bunkered down in Anbar Province. The mood among the Ramrods went from awe to reverence. I sensed our morale plummet.

Here was where the War on Terror began. All of us had left part of ourselves on the battlefields that came out of this attack on our homeland. Men like Walter, Meno, Bandy, Gregory, and Fitts devoted their lives for years to this fight. Some of the Ramrods among us went on to fight in Afghanistan as well as Iraq.

We were the shoulders upon which this war was fought.

We studied the names inscribed at the memorial. At first, I thought they included only the 184 who died during the Pentagon attack. But I quickly realized that everyone who had died since then in the Global War on Terror was on this memorial.

The only sounds were the gentle humming of lights and the *whoosh* of the air-conditioning system. The list of names was depressingly long.

John Bandy, overwhelmed by both the moment and the lack of communication, finally asked, "I think we all know someone up there. Is there anyone who doesn't?"

The names evoked moments and memories. Seeing them made it real again. I hadn't thought about this. I hadn't been prepared. My thoughts and effort had been on getting ready for this week. Now I was confronted with the same reality Merrilee Carlson had showed me in Texas all those years ago.

I realized I'd unconsciously slipped back to my old defense mechanism. I'd grieved. I'd accepted. Then unconsciously, I went back to pretending they were serving elsewhere.

Like that cemetery in Texas, that lie could not work here. It could not protect my heart. The wall was a testament to the finality of their fate. There would be no reunion. Not in this life.

This time, though, I faced that harshest of realities surrounded by the Ramrods, and our Gold Star families. Michael Carlson was there. I saw it like a hammer blow. Shrek, all 250 pounds of him, larger than life, still a force of nature in our memories. He was a young man with so much potential. The war cut him down and etched his name into this hallowed place. I looked at the other faces around me. We were all in the same place, thinking about lost friends and how we somehow survived. Every one of us could have ended up on this wall. Yet, in each case, whatever great cosmic tumblers that had to fall into perfect alignment to create a moment like the one that claimed Edward Iwan never happened to us. A gear caught. Something didn't click into place. We moved left and the bullet missed us by an inch to the right. We ducked the instant before a sheet of fire and shrapnel otherwise would have atomized our heads. In battle, the narrowest of margins is the difference between standing and looking at this wall or being names upon it.

Somehow, each of us at the Pentagon that day had jammed the gears, wittingly or unwittingly. We'd counted on our skill to see us through, but the longer we fought the more we realized that was only part of the equation. The enemy always had a say. So did luck. Or God's will. Through it all, we tiptoed on the high wire and somehow stayed on our feet until we reached the safety of the platform on the other side. Home, and a new life, one often colored with the guilt that we survived.

Every Ramrod standing around me that day made a difference in our fight. Every one helped make a difference in the world. They all lived a life that they never expected to have, doing things they couldn't have imagined in situations no one would have believed.

Yet, when their number was called, each man responded without hesitation and never took a step backward. We were the Ramrods, the grandsons of the men who took Omaha Beach over the bodies of their dying friends. Armed with that heritage, and the mettle all average Americans possess, the Ramrods won every battle in Iraq.

Fifteen years later, as we stood in this hallowed sanctuary, staring at the names of our lost family, I realized something else. To a man, we would do it again if asked.

In a heartbeat.

Before we moved on, I saw Merrilee. She'd found Shrek's name and was staring up at it. Seeing her made me wince at the thought of how much I wanted to go back into the fray. How selfish would that be? My kids, my own mom? We live overlapping lives here at home. Dependencies and love—bonds that all us Ramrods would willingly risk again, unconcerned with our own outcomes.

But at what cost to them?

We'd do it again, yes. That is what cleaved us apart from those we loved at home. Our desire to be back in the fray could never mesh with the reality of a mom who only wanted to hold her son again.

20

FULL-COURT PRESS

Lieutenant colonel meno, Colonel Walter, Colin Fitts, Michael Ware, and I were led off to the Pentagon media wing for a last-minute press conference rehearsal. It sure felt like it given what followed—four hours of intensive training and run-throughs, preparing us to meet the press. One would think that in a moment like this one, the American media would be positive and celebratory. The award symbolized so much more than the actions for which it was given. It was a testament to the teamwork, loyalty, and professionalism of the Ramrods. We reflected the fighting tradition going back over a hundred years that made the Big Red One, our 1st Infantry Division, one of the most storied formations in military history. Now our generation had built on that heritage, added to it. That was a moment to celebrate.

Instead we were drilled to expect a hostile press determined to exact another pound of flesh from "Bush's War."

I was already emotional and exhausted, so four hours of pregaming before a press conference had all the appeal of a colonoscopy, but we had to be prepared.

As we entered the practice room, I met Paula Smith for the first time in person. Paula was the Army's senior PR guru and had been preparing me daily in remote learning sessions on how to interact with the media since President Trump's call. The things she had taught me over the past few months would have been spectacularly useful back when I lived my life in the political arena. There were many times I'd stepped in it, or had comments taken out of context and weaponized against me. Paula taught me how to avoid throwing raw meat at the sharks whose job it was to concoct those attacks.

My calls with Paula sometimes lasted for hours. She gave me homework. She assigned me research projects. She was part spin doctor, part psychotherapist, and part Dr. Wayne Dyer on steroids. Above all else, Paula Smith had legendary levels of motivational power, with her straightforward honesty and insight. All that preparation had given me the basic equipment to withstand the scrutiny inherent in the new life the Medal of Honor was forging out of my old one.

Paula looked nothing like I envisioned her. From our many conversations, I conjured a wise, sage-like older woman. Instead she was fashionable and very polished. That part I gleaned over the phone, but she carried herself with a sophistication that didn't trend toward conceit. She spoke with almost a soft whisper, totally understated but every word wise. If something was particularly important, she enunciated each word with precision and clarity to make sure there were no misunderstandings.

The last few weeks had been extremely hectic for Paula. The secretary of defense was forced to resign over a personal issue with his spouse that had been made public, and she had been point on the damage control with the media. When she dropped off my radar in the final lead-in to our arrival in D.C., I felt her loss keenly.*

The media world was her element. She could be a savvy and vicious interviewer, so she would often role-play a reporter when we worked together, firing questions at me with a pace designed to throw me off balance. Those exercises taught me how to think on my feet, stay focused on what we wanted to talk about, and ignore everything else.

---

* Paula's appreciation for the Army originated with her family's long tradition of service. Her husband, a retired lieutenant colonel and Ranger, also reinforced the sacrifices required within Army life during the War on Terror.

"David, they will be swimming toward chum. Some just want a rea-son to pile on you."

Inside the practice room, Ware, Meno, Walter, Fitts, and I all sat down and prepared for round one. Sure enough, as we started the rehearsal press conference, Paula went straight for the jugular and asked me a deeply personal question about my family.

Everyone looked at me. I felt their eyes hollow out my skull.

I made eye contact with Fitts. He just raised his eyebrows as if to say, *Well. Whatcha got there, stud?*

When playing the opposition force in our training scenarios, Paula specialized in exposing flaws, then would teach you how to answer questions about them. She would hover, help me up, then sweep my legs again. This was about learning to overcome adversity, empower-ing by teaching me how to think under pressure and stay focused on telling the stories of those men we lost and loved.

Her words from our phone sessions came back to me in the mo-ment.

"David. Know who you are. Know what your mission is. Why is this happening to you? What do you have to do and how are you going to say it? Do you really love those men? Show the world what they mean to you. Calm down. Breathe. Remember your story. Remember their story. And remember why you fought."

Still, the first pitch she flung at this faux news conference was a ten-megaton bomb.

"Well, ma'am, my family is only a small part of the story. I served with forty other boys who were children to their parents. Some were fathers, too, with kids of their own. My job was to bring them back in one piece. And they returned the favor for my mom and dad and son as well. What is important for people to understand is that this story is about them. We do individual actions that sometimes get at-tention. Without everyone doing their part, we as individuals could have never made it out alive."

For at least a year, the DoD had studied every aspect of my life, uncovered every secret. Every stupid thing I had said publicly or done was duly noted and addressed in our training sessions. Then they threw lies and ridiculous allegations at me so convincingly that Paula and Liz Chamberlain almost made it seem like they had video evidence in their possession. They taught me how to stand in a media firing squad and not give an inch. Through it all, I bought into their method. I came to trust them—something I did not when they first showed up at my house on Army foot locker unboxing day.

I had been drilled. I was confronted. In these training press conferences, I had been accused of everything up to and including genocide. Now the same thing happened to all of us. Paula and the rest of the team flung questions at my fellow Ramrods that were so filled with vitriol that I began to regret dragging them into this.

Fitts looked miserable. Ware looked steady. Meno and Walter had their game faces on. They were in their own zone; officers had long since learned to do this sort of thing.

I closed my mind. I went to a different place. I kept breathing. Paula's voice was guiding me through it all. Finally, composed and of singular purpose, I looked straight ahead. Answers came at tough questions. More absurd questions were parried into easier answers. I could not be bullied. I could not be distracted.

"Impressive, Staff Sergeant Suck-up," Fitts whispered to me.

I felt Doug Walter's empathy. He looked me up and down. I have had him look at me like this before. That always focused me in the past.

Michael Ware was a seasoned expert at everything media. There was nothing you could tell him or instruct him on. He was the consummate pro, since he'd been on both sides of these interviews. Although he more than likely didn't have the blood alcohol level to legally drive a car, in a press conference the man was an incredible PR machine.

Paula ended the session. She and Liz walked up to me, now out of bad-cop mode.

Paula smiled warmly and gave me a final pep talk. "Staff Sergeant Bellavia, you were born for this moment. And you will never, ever let me down."

"Thank you, ma'am."

She continued: "These men love you. America wants to meet you and them. Just tell their story. These men right here with you, and those men who are across the way in Arlington. Your story is about love, and America needs that more today than ever before."

A moment later, we gathered in the greenroom to the main briefing room of the Pentagon. Waiting for us there were a few reporters, talking on conference calls, or video chatting with editors on their laptops. I studied them for a minute. Not too many. It seemed to be manageable. No circus.

"Hey, Bell, can I talk to ya for a sec?" Fitts asked quietly.

We stepped into another room. Just him and me. Fitts didn't say anything at first. Instead he dug deep into that navy blue suit of his and pulled out the secret beer he had managed to get past security. He cracked it open and took a long pull.

I opened a can of Copenhagen, the old Army days habit returned. Fitts found a coffee cup, shredded part of a paper towel and stuffed it in the bottom to absorb dip juice, and handed the cup to me.

"Does it feel like fifteen years to you, Fittsy?"

"Forty or fifty."

"Yeah. Feels like it right now for sure."

"Are you as exhausted as I am, Bell?"

"Yeah."

The door swung open and a couple of the DoD folks stuck their heads inside, checking on us. When they saw our expressions, they gave us space. The door closed and we were alone again.

At length, Fitts began to speak: "Back home we hunt deer different than you boys up north. We use dogs. And we keep those dogs in an old metal box in the back of the truck. And all the while we move around with our trucks, we scream at those dogs. We hit them. We make them really pissed-off. Cuss at 'em. Holler. And then we let them go. They go nuts going after them deer. After we shoot the deer, those dogs go right back in that box. It's the deal. They know the deal. They go back in every single time. They never complain because that's just what they do."

"Fitts, you wanna go in a box or something?"

"Bell, you're missing the point. That's why I loved the Brads so much. They rattled us around inside, got ya all worked up, then let ya go. Then you go after 'em, the enemy, you get the enemy, and then pile back in. Cantrell would cuss at me, hollering like a psychopath. I loved it. I loved him. I am always in the box, Bell. We. You and I . . . are always in that box."

Just like that, all this insanity drained away. The Pentagon, the impending meet-the-press moment. We talked like we were back on a range somewhere, sitting on the ramp of our Brad, a wad of dip under each of our lips. Gone from our minds was the fact that in less than fifteen minutes, we Ramrods were going live on every major media feed in the country and most of the free world.

"Hey, Fitts?"

"Yeah, Bell."

"We were in Grafenwoehr, getting ready for Iraq. And Charlie Company was our opposition force. Their company commander was the OC, what was his name?"

"Reese. Captain Reese," Fitts said, taking another long pull on his beer.

"Yeah, that's right, Captain Reese. So our company was the main effort for all of Task Force 2-2. An assault. Walter laid it out perfectly. Walls was with me. And we were gonna slam Charlie good. You came up to the edge of a berm and you saw they had a gun team. You decided to take the gun team and I was going to flank right and take the objective."

"Bell, I remember that perfectly."

"You took out the gun team. And then you grabbed their 240Bs from Charlie Company and lit up the objective. You took out more Charlie Company guys using their own machine guns than the rest of us."

Fitts started laughing. "They were so pissed-off! One kid whined at me, 'Hey, you can't do that. We only have so much ammo, man. We gotta do this four more times.'"

"A kid came up to you and kicked you off the gun and . . ." I prompted.

"Yeah, oh my god! I remember that, too! Hugh Hall grabbed that kid by the H harness and damn near yanked his head off his shoulders. Do you remember that? Hall wasn't messing around. Reese came up and said, 'Don't touch our guys.' And I was like, 'Hey, Charlie Company starts with us, we are rolling Charlie Company, sir.'"

"Exactly. I took the objective and everything was perfect. Everyone said my guys were flawless. We tried to take them from two sides. The after-action review said I was perfect. My squad was perfect. But that was like two minutes of that AAR. The other thirty-five were spent talking about you taking the guns from Charlie Company."

Fitts smiled at the memory. "True. Your assault was near perfect, though. I remember all the good stuff. And your boys got some awards, right? But yes, that was an incident that needed addressing, most definitely. And I do not blame them one bit. We literally kicked their asses during a night firefight with blanks. You can't have that."

I put the coffee cup to my lips and spat dip juice into the scrap of paper towel at the bottom.

"That's how it went down," I said. "What you don't know is that the assault wasn't perfect."

"What do you mean?" asked Fitts. "You got all the *attaboys* in the AAR."

"Dude. We had a bunch of errors. My Bravo team didn't even get to the objective. When most of Charlie's OPFOR guys ran up to help out their gunners in your near brawl, we just mowed them down as they left the area. So. Really we just shot a bunch of guys who were distracted. Had you not caused such a scene, that would have been mentioned in the AAR. Yet all they talked about was how perfect it was, because you and your squad covered for us."

"So I did good by you."

"You always do good by me, Fittsy. My point is that even when things don't go as planned, there is always a way that it works out. You always have this way of making sure it does. Even when you lose your mind."

"Like a boxed dog."

"Just like a boxed dog."

Fitts was and always has been my best friend. His traveling out to D.C. was very difficult for him. He finished his beer and tossed the can in a nearby wastebasket. I wondered what the janitor who swept this room up would think of finding that in there.

"Hey, Fitts? How's it going downstairs with the guys over at the hotel?"

He sighed and looked at the floor. "Bell, they hate me."

"Come on, man."

"No. Last night I had two guys tell me I ruined their lives. Then Magner threw up everywhere. He's a good kid."

"You didn't ruin anyone's lives, Fitts."

"Bell, you and I both know I was a dick back then. You know I didn't mean to be so rough. I just wanted them to be tough and make it through."

"It worked. They know it did, too," I said.

"Another guy said he hated me and that I was the devil."

I saw real pain in his eyes.

"Come on, Fitts. They were drinking. And we're reliving 2004 again. All of it. The good and the bad. Can't let it bother you."

"Doesn't bother me. They had a few beers. I had more."

He took a deep breath, eyes going to the ceiling now. "Look, Bell. I know they're right. I know they hate me. I don't really care. If Magner would have thrown hands, I would have beat him with his girlfriend's shoes. That is an unavoidable fact. I don't care. My wife was sitting there. I ain't no bitch. Besides, I'd never throw up in front of another grown man. Magner needs to get a grip."

"Magner is one of my favorite Soldiers. Those would be his wife's shoes, not girlfriend. And that kid gave us everything he had. These days he's risking his life for the federal government. What is the deal there?"

"I actually love him, too. I am proud of him. I am. He just hates me. So I gotta be ready in case he jumps off."

A brawl between Ramrods at the hotel? Sergeant First Class Gibson would have ended that before it started.

"This is who I am, Bell. I ain't gonna change."

"Yeah, well, listen, Fitts. You missed the point of the Charlie Company story."

Fitts didn't seem to hear me. Instead he asked, "What's gonna happen tomorrow, Bell?"

"You're gonna come with me to meet the president of the United States. And if things go sideways—if I say something stupid, and I just might—I need you to assault a Secret Service agent. So the story is that I was perfect."

He let out a long, chortling laugh and the pain in his eyes receded. "You got it, bro. You really want me to be there with you to meet President Trump?"

"I can't think of anyone else I would want to be there more."

Fitts just stopped. Conversation over. He squinted into my eyes. He processed what was said and what he was going to say back.

He slowly tapped me on my leg, before he looked down.

"We needed this, Bell."

"Yeah, I think we did."

"No. I mean, the guys. They were downstairs last night having the best time. You know, old friends circled the wagons. Told stories. Introduced their wives and families. We haven't seen each other since Germany. They all needed it and I don't think they even really knew it."

Fitts spoke of the Ramrods as if he were an outsider. It wasn't surprising, I guess. In our daily lives, Fitts and myself, nobody really ever understood us. It left us both feeling disconnected to our families, our communities. This was part of the reason why deployments destroy marriages. We went from sharing the best and worst moments of our lives as a group, only to come home to people who could not relate to our experiences—or didn't even want to hear about them. If we were honest about what happened, people back home would recoil in disgust at what we experienced. Sometimes, just to cope, it felt better to not even be there, in the moment. Just tune out everything around you and go be somewhere else. Usually that somewhere else was back with Alpha Company.

We sat around and realized that if we are honest, most people would run away in horror. If we lied, were so transparently full of shit, our families would pick up on it. Sometimes it was better to just not be there at home.

Here in the depths of the Pentagon, in Fitts's company, I was completely at ease for the first time in years. Being with him, being with Ware and Walter and Meno, seeing the other guys? It brought me peace. I had lacked that. Life went by, day by day, year after year, always feeling slightly off, with me always ending each night feeling like I had taken another barrage of nicks to the heart. You bleed a little every day, wake up to more nicks. More friction. More unsettled unpeace. You think happiness is a fantasy when just getting through the day means absorbing a thousand little wounds.

With Fitts, I could be completely myself. No pretense, no walls. Fitts felt it, too. I could see it. Of course, he never did pretense. Plenty of walls, though. So as we sat there together, the Colin Fitts who had had my back in every firefight reemerged. Gone was the farmer who drank too much. The man I trusted with my life was there again. It was the first time we'd both been truly happy since the war.

Here there were no nicks. Not now. Maybe that was unfair to Fitts and the others. Everyone had leftover axes to grind, grievances long held against other Ramrods. They had buddied up, found their 2004 cohorts, and slipped back in time. Or maybe the 2004 and 2019 divide had grown ambiguous. With us together, things overlapped. Not everyone would be feeling the peace I felt, but maybe through all this, we could all get a little closer to that.

A knock came to the door. It was time.

"Hey, Bell?"

"Yeah, bro?"

"Love ya, man."

"Yeah, yeah. Whatever, dude."

"No really. I do. And I appreciate you."

That was something that had never happened before. It really truly touched my heart. Of course, I had to conceal that with snarky humor.

"Fitts, do you have an erection right now?"

Right then, Liz Chamberlain opened the door and stared sharply at us as we laughed uncontrollably.

"I really hope I misunderstood what I thought I just overheard."

We laughed even harder.

"Quick question, Sergeant Fitts. Your shoes." Liz pointed to Fitts's feet.

"Yes, ma'am. These are mine all right."

"Did you glue your shoes earlier and then smear black shoe polish all over them, about ten minutes ago?"

"They broke apart. They are old shoes. I fixed them. They are good now, ma'am," Fitts explained.

Liz pointed again, this time to a trail of black shoe prints all over the brand-new carpet of the Pentagon's media room.

"Fitts, were you moonwalking?" I asked.

Fitts looked stricken. "Oh my god. That is very unfortunate. I apologize. Me and Kiwi are out of practice. So sorry, ma'am."

Liz explained the damage this caused. "The staff here is pretty livid. Do you think we can limit the trail? In fact, they are threatening to cancel this entire event and bar Army Public Affairs from ever being in here again. That was actually said out loud."

"If you need me to, I can scare the shit out of whoever said that. I am sure they are chubby bitches who sat out the War on Terror," Fitts said defensively.

Liz replied, "Understood, but let's just minimize the damage, okay?"

"Oh, absolutely. I can. Will do. Apologies for that mess."

"Good. We're ready in five minutes," Liz said. "We need you both in the other room. Lieutenant Meno is getting impatient."

"Lieutenant colonel now, ma'am. And yeah, we can't make him wait."

Fitts said to me, "Can you believe Meno is going to run a battalion?"

"I do. And yes, it's terrifying for the Army and NATO. Listen, Meno will do fine. He was born for this moment. I pity whoever faces off against him and his men."

Then I added, "Dude, I can't believe you're tracking shoe prints all over the damn Pentagon."

"They took my beer, man. I mean, we're even."

Liz concealed her annoyance and led the way into a big briefing room with a long table set up at its front, chairs lining one side. The rest of the room was full of reporters, dozens of them. TV cameras on tripods lined the wings and the far back of the room. The moment we entered, still cameras clicked like tiny machine guns. It looked a little like one of those Senate subcommittee hearing rooms I'd seen on C-SPAN.

We settled into our chairs, huge soft-boxed lights angled at our faces. Liz looked us over and saw that we were ready. She took the first question for us from the *Military Times*.

"I wanted to ask, Staff Sergeant Bellavia: when did you first get the idea or start the process, or the campaign, to upgrade your award? What steps did you take? What was that like to upgrade your own award? To upgrade your Silver Star to the Medal of Honor?"

My campaign to upgrade my award? Huh?

I looked over at Liz Chamberlain, feeling a swell of indignation. Like I wanted any of this? My life had been upended. It would never be the same now. The Medal of Honor ensured that the most painful days of my life would forever define me, when I'd spent the last fifteen years trying to run from that legacy.

Liz smiled at me. That calmed me in an instant, and the training kicked in.

"I had absolutely nothing to do with that."

"When did you know that your Silver Star was being upgraded to the Medal of Honor?"

"When I got a call from the president of the United States."

The questions that followed continued along similar trajectories for almost an hour. I fielded them as best I could. I had been asked most of them a dozen times during our practice sessions.

Lieutenant Colonel Meno answered more questions about that night. He spoke of his growth as a leader, a father. Meno was not originally an infantry lieutenant. Most ROTC officers in his position would have seen a slot in a line infantry platoon in Diyala Province as being a setup for career failure. From day one, Meno came to us earnest, willing to listen and learn. He was strong and consistent. We were lucky in Third Platoon to have Lieutenant Chris Walls, a West Point Ranger, followed by Lieutenant Meno, who had been on the adjutant general's staff. I learned that schools and high-speed training are just a piece of what makes men great in battle. Trust. Fidelity. Valor. That didn't come with a certificate anywhere.

Meno took each question, considered them carefully, and answered with deliberation in front of those cameras and all those people watching. He was a rock star. At times he took notes, or made a few corrections to what he said to make sure he spoke the accurate truth. He came across as the seasoned, professional warrior he was.

Walter nailed his questions. He told the reporters that he had interviewed every participant, constructed the map of the house and the surrounding area for the Army. He quickly demonstrated he knew more details about that night than I did. He knew every member of the platoon's vantage point, who carried what weapon system, the symmetry of fire. He made sure to get photographs of every insurgent in the house after I killed them, their location and how they died. The man missed his calling; he should have gone into law.

Fitts did his piece brilliantly. He was not asked many questions, and when he fielded them, he spoke in a down-to-earth, from-the-heart kind of way. The down-to-earth part I'd seen before, but from the heart like that? This was a new side of Fitts. I always figured that even if he had been shot center mass, no bullets would ever hit his heart. Given the things he occasionally said, I sometimes wondered if he had one.

As we faced the media, and the questions turned to Mick Ware, I saw something remarkable happen. Ware was in his element; he spoke with great eloquence. He captivated his reporter brethren with every answer. But there was something more at play in this moment for Mick.

Right there, in the glare of the lights, I realized what it was. Redemption.

The fact that Michael Ware was even there in the Pentagon on the other end of the room was in a way a small miracle. This man had been a thorn in Green Zone Army public relations for years during the Iraq War. Ware would witness what was happening on the ground, come back to the United States, and do enough media to make average Americans question what victory in Iraq would even look like. The Pentagon at large and many generals openly despised Michael Ware because they considered him a cancer on the war effort.

His reporting was never anything but straight-up honest. He never sugarcoated anything; he never allowed himself to be a political tool for any side. His loyalty was only to the truth. The truth was, there was no viable metric for victory in Iraq, not as long as Al Qaeda blew up markets full of Shia civilians and triggered their militias to cleanse neighborhoods of Sunni. The war had become trilateral in the years after the Ramrods went back to Germany. No longer a Coalition versus insurgent fight, à la Fallujah, the war morphed into a burgeoning sectarian civil war, fueled by foreign terrorists, with the Coalition sitting atop this powder keg and getting hammered from both sides.

Mick Ware reported it all with scathing insight. He shared for his viewers and readers what it was like to be in the middle of this war, not from Baghdad's Green Zone, where most reporters loitered, but from the tip of the spear. He brought the experience of the infantry home to American living rooms. He showed our people what we could never talk about when we returned. He did it with an unflinching eye, and it cost him much of his soul. For when he came home, there were no reintegration programs, no VAs to help him. He was on his own, and his spirit suffered even more damage for that fact.

From being reviled in 2004 to being an honored guest in the heart of the Pentagon, Mick's life had transcended the stigma stamped on it by the establishment back in the day, and the perspective of years showed all the value of his work. The generals of 2004 were gone now, and the new generation had come up through the ranks during the War on Terror.

When the announcement came out about the Medal of Honor, I heard secretaries of the Army and Defense make statements like, "Michael Ware is the Ernie Pyle of his generation."

That was what played out for Mick during that press conference. No longer was Ware on the outside, the professional contrarian casting doubt on official press releases from the DoD. Now he was Army and Defense royalty. He was the good guy again.

Mick logged more hours in Iraq than any other journalist covering the war. He logged more time than any Soldier or Marine during the Iraq War. He had the respect of his peers, the media, and millions of readers and viewers who considered him the premier source for all terrorism-related journalism.

But he never had respect from the establishment in the Department of Defense. A decade and a half later, he was honored as one of the best in the very building whose inhabitants once loathed him. This time in D.C. had given Mick a second chance, and this victory lap with the rest of his Ramrod family clearly meant the world to him, as it did to those who loved him. He spoke to his audience, holding court as only Mick could do. I hoped the accolades and this new-found role would finally put to rest some of his demons. Mick deserved peace more than any of us.

21

RAMROD REUNION

I STOOD IN THE SUITE'S bathroom—which was larger than my barracks room back in Vilseck—wrapped in a towel and covered in shaving cream, listening to my phone chime on the counter next to me. Over and over the notification bell fired off. It was evening of day one, the Ramrods were celebrating their second evening of revelry together, and I'd barely had a chance to see any of them. That point kept being driven home to me by the blizzard of photos the guys were texting me.

After the Pentagon and media day, I kept swinging between wanting to spend some time alone or trying to find a way to go join the guys. Colonel Perez had made it clear this was not going to happen.

"There are three rules in this hotel," she mentioned more times than I care to remember. "First: no trouble. Second: SFC Gibson does not leave your side. Three: no trouble."

The Ramrods had already been pregaming for the first major event of the week, a reception for us held by the sergeant major of the Army. The photos depicted events that could most certainly be construed as "trouble" by Colonel Perez, and thus I was kept in this suite, isolated from the very people I most wanted to be with during this week.

I shaved and listened to my phone chiming the arrival of new photos or texts. Gray temples now, yet still a bit of the old me left in the dark hair I'd had cut just before the trip. Some of the guys were going bald, or were already there. We had aged, some more gracefully than others. It was so odd, seeing the people forever captured in my memories of Vilseck and Kosovo and Iraq as wild-haired early twenty-somethings, away from home for the first time in their lives. Those young bucks were on the cusp of middle age now. Some, like me, who were older, had already arrived in that midlife-crisis zone.

I looked haggard. Worn-out. Puffy eyes, dark circles. Six months of minimal sleep and maximum stress will do this, of course. There was a soul heaviness stamped on my face.

I had spent the last twenty-four hours getting an education in what my life would be from here on out. This morning I scrolled my news feed. Apple. Google. *USA Today*. Fox. *New York Times*. *Washington Post*. CNN. CBS News. Doing a radio show, I stayed glued to what was happening around the world and our nation, in search of topics that would be worth discussion on the air. I normally don't go an hour without checking the news updates, but these past few days I'd hardly had the chance.

As I was catching up on the world outside this bubble, a headline that caught my eye read something like, "First Living Iraq Medal of Honor to Be Given . . ."

My interest spiked, and I wondered to myself who could be receiving that. Then it dawned on me.

Oh my god. That's me.

The articles came with plenty of photos and seeing my face out there in the world wasn't a comfort. Fame is an elusive, destructive aspect of modern American life. Maybe earlier in my youth I sought it like so many others, but as I grew up and matured, my privacy became one of the most important aspects of my life. Now I was seeing images from all time periods of my life pop up in news feeds everywhere. Scrolling through them, I felt my privacy torn away, exposing me as awkward in front of the camera, to say the least. Some of the photos were candid ones taken from my civilian life and runs for public office since I left the Army. Those were universally horrible. In them, my mouth was often agape, brows beetled. In a few, I looked like Lee Harvey Oswald the moment Jack Ruby gut-shot him.

These were horrible, and it made me think that maybe there was something to my Amish neighbors and their aversion to photography.

Then there were others from my military days. I looked at them on my phone's little screen, astonished at how young I looked. So naïve. All of us were, I guess.

Looking at all this sent stabs of fear through me. Throughout the rest of the day, I stole glances at the ongoing media coverage, growing ever more alarmed.

I couldn't resist checking the news again before I finished shaving. I put the razor down and picked up my phone. More articles. More interview clips. More talking heads saying my name. The house fight was paraphrased, described, dissected by experts.

I had visions of John Madden with a Telestrator, diagramming a better plan of attack.

Now, you see, what David should have done was hook right and gone into the kitchen first, instead of running that post route into the back bedroom. That's what almost got him killed. The kitchen was the key . . .

I put the phone down on the counter, looked at it. It chimed again. I needed a reprieve, and this was only day one.

The best I could manage was to flip the phone inverted. As if not seeing the screen would have somehow warded off this swelling panic attack.

Reading all those Fallujah retrospectives? It was like reading my own obituary. And I knew that this was the moment of my life that would forever define me.

Chuck Yeager was ninety-six in 2019. He had been a fighter ace in Europe during World War II, a hard-charging, ultra-aggressive crack shot with the elite 357th Fighter Group, flying long-range missions to Germany in P-51 Mustangs. He served our country for thirty-four years and earned a promotion to brigadier general despite having only a high school education. He wore a chest full of valor awards—two Silver Stars, three Distinguished Flying Crosses—and was wounded in action.

He had an amazing life and career. Yet he would always be remembered as the "Fastest Man Alive"—the first human to break the sound barrier. He did that at twenty-four, and lived in that accomplishment's shadow for the rest of his life.

I picked up the razor and went back to shaving, thinking about guys who peaked in high school. The state champion quarterback who gets hurt in college and never gets a shot at the NFL. The power forward who never could quite compete with the country's elite in college. Springsteen's "Glory Days" syndrome.

This week felt like I was about to be cryogenically frozen in 2004 for the rest of my life. The Medal of Honor defined me. No matter what I accomplish in my life from here on out, it will never be equated with November 10, 2004. The medal meant I peaked on my twenty-ninth birthday.

Every article mentioned that I was the sole living recipient of the Medal of Honor for actions during the Iraq War. I would become a symbol of the war. The cynical part of me thought, *mascot*. The face of the most unpopular war since Vietnam.

More text notifications rang in. I couldn't resist a look. Picking up my phone, I saw more photos of the Ramrods. Selfies. Shots of everyone together, drinking together, circles of cliques from 2004 intermingled. There was Mick Ware, right in the middle of the shenanigans. Was everyone really getting along? How was Fitts doing? I scrolled through them, thinking I could as easily have stayed at home and watched all this through the keyhole of social media. What a weird and unexpected aspect of all this, being isolated from the very people I needed the most.

I finished shaving, dressed in the gray suit again. White shirt. Canary yellow tie. Then I checked on the boys and Vivi to see how they were progressing. I tied their ties for them and told them they looked beyond fantastic. I had never seen them this dressed up, and the mood that matched my suit color brightened with pride at the sight of them.

Sergeant First Class Gibson walked into the master bedroom, wearing dress blues and beret, holding a professional laundromat steamer in one hand. In the other he held my uniform for tomorrow's White House ceremony.

I looked at it with a mix of awe, love, and regret. Dress blues. My stripes. Ribbons. The rich gold highlights, the Infantry Blue fourragère—the braided cord denoting our brotherhood that we wore on the right shoulder at formal events. The uniform was immaculate.

How far could I have gone? Would I still be in? Would I have made sergeant major? What would CSM Faulkenburg have said to that?

"I ripped the guts out of that uniform," Gibson said. "Cardboard is out of the beret. Carboard is inserted into each inside of the jacket. You will move like the Tin Man, but you won't wrinkle. This isn't about comfort; this is about perception. Shaved the fuzz out of everything, too, then used hundred-mile-an-hour tape to get the fuzz pills off the jacket."

"I don't even know what to say." The uniform was a work of art, something only a lifetime professional would have known how to prepare.

He pulled out a can of dip, cracked it, and put some under his lip. "Want some?" he asked.

"Probably should. Won't be legit without it."

"Ha! That's what I was thinking, too."

I pinched a wad and stuck it under my lower lip.

He racked my uniform in the closet, turned, and announced, "Showtime for tonight. You ready?"

"For what?"

"Everything to blow up," Gibson said flatly.

"What do you mean?"

"Dude, your guys are shit-faced. They need blood transfusions and liver transplants. The hotel has never seen anything like it. They've had to make three extra liquor runs to restock their bar. In the last twenty-four hours."

I just stared at him. I hardly drank myself, even these many years later. A big part of me wanted to just bolt downstairs and pile into the fun.

"David, you don't understand," Gibson said. "Imagine a tailgate party before the Michigan–Ohio State game, in ancient Rome under Caligula, at Woodstock."

"Um. That's a lot to imagine."

"Colonel Perez and I will handle any . . . what does she call it? 'Potentials for disruption.'"

"Thank you, Sergeant."

"Let's go get your family," he answered.

"I can't wait to see them again," I replied automatically, thinking of the Ramrods streaming upstairs into the ballroom being used for the reception hall.

"Other family, dude."

"Oh yeah, right."

We rounded up the kids and my mother and headed out the door into the hallway, where Gibson led us to an elevator.

"Entire floor is sealed off, so there's no possibility of unwanted guests crashing the party," Gibson told us as the elevator doors closed behind us.

Instead of going to the reception floor, the elevator descended to the lobby. The doors parted and suddenly Staff Sergeant Gary Frey burst between them and bear-hugged me like we'd just won the Super Bowl.

No time for introductions. Frey just squeezed the air out of my lungs right there in the elevator.

Gary Frey and I had reported to the Ramrods ten days apart when we first went to Europe. We were much older than our peers. Gary had a master's degree and had prior service with the National Guard. A superb athlete and our platoon's best basketball player, he had re-joined the Army because of 9/11. There was a lot of competition between us as we rose through the ranks, but we had always main-tained a steadfast friendship. The competition sharpened us, made us better. Eventually he went mounted and became part of one of our Bradley crews. I stayed as a dismount. After Kosovo, both of us had been promoted to staff sergeant and ended up serving in different platoons during our time in Iraq.

The elevator went up to the reception floor, Frey telling me quick tales of the Ramrods in D.C. that surely would morph into urban 1st ID legends in the years to come.

We reached our floor. The elevator doors opened again and we stepped into a long hallway leading to the reception hall. That dis-tended, blurred sense of unreality returned. People were flowing toward the room, finely attired in suits and beautiful dresses. Old. Young. Kids. All people who meant something to me. Smiles and greetings as we walked, faces long missed swimming in front of me. It was reunion overload, just like the lobby earlier.

Suddenly a barrel-chested man with broad shoulders blocked my path. My family crashed to a halt, staring at this giant with hands the size of first baseman's mitts. He put those mitts on my shoulders and gave me a dead-eye stare, not saying a word. Then a half smile formed on his face. He nodded once.

It was a sign of approval from Command Sergeant Major Darrin Bohn, one of our generation's greatest NCOs. Rumor was he'd been in the running to be the next sergeant major of the Army, making him our service's senior noncommissioned officer. No matter how high he went, though, his heart was all Ramrod. He had taken over for CSM Faulkenburg after he was killed during the first hours of the Fallujah offensive, and kept 2-2 going even as other leaders died in the days to come. He steadied us, kept us in the fight with his example and skill. We'd known him well already, as he'd helped train us in Germany. His many lessons ensured more than once that I got home to Evan.

One nod, then he released his grip on my shoulders and stepped aside. It was an homage, a sign of silent respect. Such moments made me ache for the Army anew. Those moments—they are priceless. To have a man whom others consider a legend make such a gesture—well, I know of nothing else that can evoke a more powerful sense of affirmation and pride.

I took a couple more steps toward the reception room when Omarr Hardaway swooped in and lifted me off my feet. My giant friend, our Alpha Section's Bradley commander and gunner, swung me around like I was a little kid.

"Love you, Docta. All my family is proud of you. Know that."

"Big Smooth . . . love you . . ."

Then Cory Brown barreled over. Almost as big as Hardaway, he looked like an onrushing NFL defensive end. Brawn and brute force. Cory was another one of our Bradley commanders, a man who utterly dominated fear time after time in Fallujah. He leaned heavily on a violence-of-action, *shoot first, then worry and ask questions later* approach to combat in Iraq, and did so for one reason: he'd have done anything to make sure all of us dismounts got home safely. In Fallujah, when things got really bad, Cory's Brad came charging, a wake of death behind his tracks. He and his gunner, quiet and shy Shane Gossard, killed more terrorists than COVID-19.

Now Shane blindsided me with a hug, and I found myself between two of the most dependable men I've ever known. These two used their Bradley like virtuosos, saving us countless times after the enemy pinned us down and dominated us with superior firepower. The sight and sound of Brown's Bradley churning to our rescue, Gossard snapping out deadly accurate bursts of 25mm auto-cannon fire: those memories still bring a flood of gratitude to me. When our backs were to the wall, in our worst moments in Iraq, these guys always fought their way through to us. Together they saved scores of lives, Iraqi and American.

Now I was crushed between them in a full ménage-a-man hug, ribs bent into my lungs. All I could smell was cigarettes and alcohol. The cologne of the Ramrods.

"I wish Gonzo was here," Brown said with tears in his eyes.

Their Bradley driver, Luis "Gonzo" Gonzales, was a stalwart member of our team. He was killed in action five years after Fallujah, when his vehicle was gutted by an IED in Afghanistan.

More Ramrods streamed over to me, and I hadn't even made it to the reception room. Photos. Hugs. More secondhand alcohol exposure. Faces came and went. My emotion meter pegged out. I saw Patrick Magner in front of me, now a federal law enforcement officer, looking like Serpico with a cool-guy beard and leather jacket. Next came Tristan Maxfield, the most handsome Soldier I have ever seen. If Maxfield could carry a tune he would be on the cover of every teen magazine in America. Luckily for us, his main talent was shooting SAW rounds into bad guys. He was a rock star in Fallujah.

I moved on through the crowd, only to be ambushed by our platoon's Filipino supersoldier, Warren Misa. He was the one man who never got tired, no matter how many days in the field, how sick we all got, how many firefights we had waded through. He had a never-quit attitude and never bitched. Now, fifteen years removed from our hardest battles, Misa looked exactly the same—like time couldn't work its evils on a man with so many reserves of energy and resolve. He looked like he'd just stepped out of 2004.

I last saw Misa at Staff Sergeant Scott Lawson's funeral a few years before. We were the only two Ramrods that made it, something that deeply hurt both of us. It wasn't personal. Life and the world take over. But I wanted the whole crew to say goodbye to that stud. He was huge for us then. Seeing Misa again brought me back to that moment. Saying goodbye to Scott by laying my Silver Star in his coffin with him.

This had become almost an out-of-body experience by the time we finally reached the reception hall. All around me I saw friends. Family. Comrades. My brothers Dan and Rand, my uncles and aunts. Cousins. High school pals. Work friends. Coaches. My mother was holding court with my literary agent, Jim Hornfischer, and his family. Shrek's mom, Merrilee Carlson, was talking to John Bruning, my coauthor on *House to House*. Teachers. Friends. Almost everyone still living and important in my life before 2018 was standing in this room like an episode of *This Is Your Life*.

By himself in one corner of the room, against the windows overlooking the Pentagon and the Flight 77 Memorial, stood Fitts. Holding a beer in a koozie, a blue cooler behind him, he scowled miserably. He wasn't just uncomfortable; he was aggressively dissuading anyone from approaching him, like the conversational equivalent of a Claymore mine. Dare to approach and he'd clack off and turn anyone wanting to confront him on his past to pink mist.

I felt a stab of guilt for practically coercing him to come. He was clearly hurting, balled up, defensive, ready to strike anyone about to maim him further. I had hoped the guys would see Fitts for who he really was, and why he was such a relentless hard-ass back in 2004. Underneath the fierceness, the brutal honesty—he has always been all heart. A man like that does whatever it takes to keep the people he loves alive. Fitts was brutal on the Ramrods because he knew combat would be brutal on them. If they could survive him, they could survive Iraq.

But the old wounds, the grudges and the memories of some of Fitts's toughest acts, died hard in some of the Ramrods, and the guys weren't willing to accept him. So Fitts posted up in that corner and preemptively rejected the world.

It was easier that way for him.

Lieutenant Colonel Joaquin Meno saw Fitts, too. I watched him flank his defenses, slip behind him, and give him a huge hug from behind. Fitts looked up at me, genuine astonishment in his eyes. Unconsciously, Fitts's hands went to Meno's arms to hold them against his chest.

The first step toward our badass black sheep had been taken.

I mouthed the words, "Told you."

He nodded and mouthed back, "I know."

Sergeant First Class Gibson, totally unaware of the moment and its subtext, checked in on me. "Hey. Why are you wearing a yellow tie?" he asked. "I steamed the red one for you."

I had worn it earlier today to the press conference and hadn't thought anything of it.

"You have blood on it, you know," Gibson added, pointing to a splotch. I peered down and realized somebody must have cut themselves shaving and left a trail of blood drops across both suit and tie.

"You good?" he asked.

I looked back over to Fitts. He and Meno were deep in a conversation now. Meno was smiling and laughing at whatever they were remembering. And damn if Fitts didn't look happy. Salt-and-pepper beard, his dark and wary eyes now shined with comradeship. Friendship. The bond. We all missed it. We all felt its loss when we moved on in life, a void that nothing else could ever replace. Fitts, isolated as he was already, shared it with only a select few. He liked to appear soulless, unfeeling, tougher than tough, but I had seen how he loved his two little girls. Beneath the armor of indifference, he was a man at war with his own reality: that he did love the Ramrods, just as he did his family. Rejection by them was like a crucifixion to him.

Out of nowhere, someone kissed my face. Sandpaper stubble on my clean-shaven cheek. I felt something wet on my neck. Tears. I couldn't see his face, jammed together with Ramrods everywhere, his cheek against mine.

Who is crying?

He pulled away and I saw Sammy's face. Our interpreter, who looked like actor Andy Garcia's clone. Handsome as he was tough, he had always been an emotional man, but one whose rock-solid loyalty led me to trust him so thoroughly I once gave him my own M4 to clear a building. He looked at me, astonished. He'd patrolled with the 4th Infantry Division for eight months without a rifle. 'Terps were rarely trusted enough for that, for fear of a green-on-blue shooting incident.

Sammy took the weapon. He inspected it, removed the magazine, and cleared it, sending an unused bullet flying from the chamber into the ground at our feet. Then he slapped the mag back in place, racked a round, and set the M4 on safe. He bent down and picked up the bullet and handed it over to me.

With the weapon at low ready, he slowly raised his eyes to me and said, "I am ready, my staff sergeant."

From that day, Sammy was no longer just an interpreter; he was a Soldier. He wasn't just a Soldier; he was a Ramrod.

There in the middle of the reception hall, his fellow Ramrods mobbed him in a massive group hug. All on Sammy. Our adopted Ramrod.

Gibson made his way through the throng and said we were all needed in a conference room off the main ballroom for group photographs. The Ramrods moved as a gaggle over there and lined up together in front of a backdrop replete with the Medal of Honor and an enormous photo of my face from 2004. Between professional shots, everyone pulled out their phones and we started taking pictures of each other.

The foreground where the professional media managers stood with Sergeant First Class Gibson was drowned out by so many familiar, long-unheard voices around me. Between camera clicks, they told stories, busting each other's balls like they did years ago. The laughter. The tale-topping. It was just like being back at Normandy after patrols. Nothing had changed. I felt a surge of happiness, the kind that had eluded me for years. Why hadn't we done this sooner?

As the night wore on, I realized something. Nothing had changed, except me. I had changed. I listened to everything as memories poured forth from the guys. Some of these stories started to make me feel like a father hearing their sons describe in graphic detail a night involving multiple prostitutes in Sofia, Bulgaria. Mainly because I was literally hearing someone tell aloud a story in graphic detail about a night involving multiple prostitutes in Sofia, Bulgaria.

I felt like a seventy-year-old prude, looking around to see where my mother and Merrilee Carlson were. They couldn't be exposed to this sort of stuff.

One Ramrod shouted out that he had met up with one of my Soldiers a few years back. They headed out in two cars, each with their girlfriend with them. They had both been drinking. A cop pulled over the lead car. Out of blind loyalty and to avoid a license-seizing DUI offense, Ramrod A drove a block away and discharged his concealed-carry pistol twice into the ground. The cop heard the blasts and took off, and that allowed A's battle buddy, Ramrod B, to leave with a warning.

I started to hyperventilate. I didn't want to hear that.

"What is wrong with you maniacs? You can't drink and drive. Why the hell are you telling me this? You discharged a gun in a neighborhood at night? What were you thinking?"

"Sarge, I did it for my guy. You taught us that."

Indeed, I had. The loyalty extended well beyond the sphere of combat, well beyond garrison duty in Germany. That part I could get on board with, but the rest? I loved these men. I didn't want to know this stuff. It was information overload. I was in my mid-forties now, more and more like my father every day. Maybe back in Vilseck I would have thought that was a descent into prudery. Now I saw it as growing up.

I stepped away feeling polar opposites with conflicting emotions and grabbed a glass of water. I drained most of it in one long pull, then reached in and splashed the dregs on my face like a cornerman during a prizefight.

Behind me, the men were getting louder, happier. Having the best time together. I looked back and watched them, smiling at how we all were probably experiencing the same range of emotions. This was so badly needed. For all of us. It happened thanks to the incredible kindness of western New Yorkers and my radio station, who donated tens of thousands of dollars so their travel would be covered. What a blessing.

I waded back in and was soon engulfed again. The stories tumbled out. Fitts cracked another beer from his cooler. Knapp and Ruiz took turns spinning yarns. We grew even louder and more rambunctious. Laughter and liquor fueled the moment as we all felt the bond we had so dearly missed.

All of a sudden, it ended. From uproarious hilarity to stark silence, like a record needle being scratched to the side of a piece of vinyl. Faces froze, mouths in midsentence, everyone paralyzed, eyes fixed at the entrance to the room.

I turned around, as if in dreamlike slow motion, the revolution seemingly taking forever. There, standing quietly in the doorway, was Captain Sean Sims, staring right at me.

22

WHERE COMPASSION
GOT YOU KILLED

My GUYS WERE DONE. The whole platoon was done. Days and nights of constant fighting left us violently ill, covered in cuts, abrasions, and bruises. We were coated in grime, grease, and sweat and peppered with powdered concrete that gave our skin a grayish-brown tint. For most of the day, we'd been trapped atop that half-constructed building, taking heavy fire. Maxfield, our virtuoso on an M249 SAW light machine gun, had been medevaced only a short time before we'd found this place among the rubble to rest.

He wasn't here. I couldn't see him and know he was okay among the guys in this courtyard of a compound we had paused in for this break. The men looked as bad as I felt. A few had taken their boots off to reveal bloody socks and feet. Others were eating MREs, or just trying to catch a few minutes of sleep. Fitts stood next to me, smoking quietly, regarding the men, unspoken between us the same question: *how much more of this can we take?*

Overlaying the anxiety about Maxfield came the grief for Edward Iwan. In the parasympathetic backlash of the daylong firefight we'd been in, the dark, breaking pain of his death crept in. Gone was the fury, the mindless rage I had felt after Fitts broke the news to me.

Now all I felt was pain. Pain for Iwan. Pain for J.C. Matteson, who was the only other Ramrod from my hometown. He had been killed just before Iwan, and we'd learned the news while moving back from that half-constructed building after the firefight finally ended.

Pain for Sergeant Major Faulkenburg, our battalion's father figure.

I lit a cigarette and took a long drag, feeling something akin to broken glass tumbling around inside me, churning and cutting like a hurricane-shattered window scything all in its path with wicked fragments.

I think I realized then that there would be no coming back to normal after this. November 10. The house fight, two nights before, the friends lost. The sight of Tristan Maxfield's RPG-wounded leg. The dead and dying all around us.

The look in the man's eyes as I snuffed his life out with my Gerber.

We were as broken as the city around us. Debris-strewn streets. Collapsed and demolished buildings in sight. Those still standing had few windows left, their facades pocked with bullet scars. We were in a hellscape, and there seemed to be no end in sight. Block after block remained to be cleared. Hell, we hadn't even driven into the southern half of the city yet.

There was no way through this, except to finish the job or get carted out like our wounded and fallen. I had never felt more trapped, especially after the discoveries we'd made in this neighborhood.

The night before, when we first entered this block, we found this thick-walled compound, and Lieutenant Meno had selected this place for us to bunk down because we thought it was the tallest, safest building in the neighborhood. Inside we found scores of boxes of 7.62 ammunition, loose rounds waiting to be stuffed into AK-47 magazines. We set security before dawn and cleared the houses around us.

In the darkness, Private First Class Stuckert discovered a fighting position—a large bunker cut into the side of the house across from our compound and partially dug out at its foundation. I told him to grab a 9mm pistol and go look inside. He peered in and discovered it was more than ten feet deep, with a small table at the bottom. He waved me over. I took a look and realized this was not an ordinary bunker. Taking his pistol and a flashlight, I crawled partially through the bunker's firing slit. The ground was slick with mud, and the opening was so narrow I could barely use my hands. I slipped and nearly fell into the bottom of the bunker. Knapp grabbed my legs and caught me.

It wasn't really a bunker at all, but more of a junction between two long, crudely built tunnels. One went under the road, across the street toward our compound. The other one veered left and down toward another house with a walled courtyard down the street. The tunnels were shored up with cinder blocks and corrugated plastic roofing, but in the soft, wet earth they looked very dangerous, ready to cave in.

Knapp went halfway into the opening in an effort to pull me out. Somehow he managed it alone. We went across the street, following the trajectory of the one tunnel to our compound, and discovered an entry point concealed under some debris and a large white bathtub in the front yard.

We reported this discovery to Captain Sims, who decided we would check it out in the morning after first light. In the meantime, we put three Soldiers—Private First Class Pulley, Stuckert, and Staff Sergeant Lawson—on the roof of our compound as apex security. One would stare right down on the tunnel entrance. Should someone crawl out from under the tub, they would be hit immediately by a burst from a 240B. The others kept watch on the bunker across the street, and the house we suspected was the other entry point for the second tunnel. For good measure, one of our guys took a giant, steaming dump directly into the tub. A gift for any tunnel-crawling insurgents who decided to prairie-dog out that hole underneath it.

Okay. That somebody was me.

Meanwhile, the rest of the platoon settled down inside the compound to grab an hour or two of sleep. Right before dawn, Pulley and Stuckert saw a group of five Soldiers dressed in full American kits, wearing night vision, Kevlar helmets, and carrying black M4 rifles, running down the street in front of our compound. They seemed to be coming for American-held lines where our sister element, Team Tank, was covering our flank. As they studied these men, they saw that one of the five wore dark pants. They sprinted along the street, moving with no tactical purpose or discipline.

Who were they? Could they be Iraqi National Guard? American special forces? Wayward, confused 'terps? Insurgents in our gear?

Stuckert, Pulley, and Lawson had a split-second decision to make. Lawson was the NCOIC—the noncommissioned officer in charge. He reported that they decided to open fire in an effort to scatter them back toward Team Tank's sector. They shot high on purpose to deliver a warning, not a killing blow. After all, they could very well have been friendly forces and Lawson was rightfully not about to risk a blue-on-blue incident.

The sudden burst of incoming fire scattered the five immediately. They reversed course and bolted back the way they came, then dove into some buildings between us and Team Tank's positions.

Lawson reported it up, and Meno passed it to Company to be on the lookout for these five men.

As the sun came up that morning, the tub moved. This could have been for a number of reasons. The ground was soft and wet, the tub heavy. It could have just settled a bit in the mushy ground. The guys all thought it was funny, cracking jokes about how the enormous turd had broken it loose from its moorings. It was probably nothing, but we wished it had been a terrorist, since it would have been the dumbest thing they could have done. Had a head appeared from under the tub, Lawson's machine gun would have voided the brain inside with a single, point-blank burst.

We logged the movement and reported it to Company.

Sims reported back that he would come take a look at the tub and the tunnel system as soon as he got the chance.

The sun was higher now, casting the neighborhood in golden-hour light. It was still cold, the ground damp, and by now we had three machine guns triangulated on the bathtub tunnel entrance. We felt pretty secure as a result.

I looked over at Fitts. He was watching the bathtub, smoking a Black & Mild cigar thoughtfully. Our shop talk continued. "We're gonna have to put Ruiz back on a SAW," I said. He nodded but said nothing. Without Maxfield, Ruiz would have to bring the heat with our light machine gun, though he hadn't touched one in months. He would step up. He always did.

We managed to get SAWs for our entire squad. After today? Losing control of that fight and being totally dominated by superior firepower? We made deals to make sure that never happened again. Total nightmare.

We were talking this over when Specialist Joey Seyford and Sergeant Travis Barreto, both from our company headquarters element, came over to greet us. Both had lit smokes dangling from their mouths. That's about where the similarities ended with these two. Barreto looked focused, driven, borderline angry. His Soldier face. His expression rarely deviated. Seyford looked more laid-back, which for Fallujah was quite an achievement. Seyford had a way of lightening the mood, to make everyone laugh and make the suck tolerable for just a little bit longer.

Barreto rarely laughed. Serious and intense, he made no effort to conceal how much he hated the war. At times we got the sense that he hated the Army, too. Confident cardplayers will show you their hand before they ask you to see yours. Beat this. Can you do it? Barreto was the person who never asked you to see your hand, nor ever showed you his.

It took time to see the depth and decency of the man. He lived by a simple code of loyalty. You were either loyal to him or not. There was no gray area there. And if you were, Barreto's fidelity to you was so intense that you'd have no better friend or ally. Cross him once— break that code of loyalty—and you were dead to him. There was no redemption or second chances with him. Barreto didn't have a wife and kids he was fighting to get home to. He was fighting for the day he could have a wife and kids.

In combat, he was a machine. Cool, calm, the master of his fears, he would drop to a knee, and fire his M4 with controlled accuracy that dropped bad guys and saved the lives of the men around him. He never smiled at the end of a fight. There were no fist bumps or high-fiving him, either. Instead he was all deep sighs, head shakes, and long drags on a good smoke.

He was in that mood now as he approached us. Long day, for sure. Both he and Seyford looked as exhausted as we were. Stubble, that squeezed expression seen in men under tremendous pressure with no letup in sight.

Seeing Seyford affected like this alarmed me. He was one of the toughest human beings I'd ever known. During a range day in Kuwait, a member of First Platoon accidentally triggered his SAW and sent a 5.56 round right into Joey's ass. As the thunderstruck company looked on, Joey laughed about it. He returned to duty a short time later.

A few months later at FOB Normandy, Seyford accidentally broke a glass partition in a door, cutting his wrist and severing several tendons. He could have probably gone home. Instead, he half healed up and returned to duty.

On November 8, 2004, during the assault into Fallujah, he was riding with Lieutenant Iwan in a Humvee. Yes, they actually went through the breach in a Humvee after their Brad broke down. Such a soft target attracted the attention of an RPG team. They sent a rocket right into the rig, spraying the interior with shrapnel and almost severing the foot of an Air Force combat controller who was driving. Joey, in the turret, caught a sliver of shrapnel in one eye. Yet he wiped away the blood and rolled into the city anyway, ignoring the pain to stick with the men he loved.

Nobody would have blamed Joey a bit for going home after any one of these incidents. But this Ohio native refused to leave us. Now, as he hobbled to a standing stop a few meters away, I wondered if Seyford was running out of pluck, wondered how Alpha Company was going to push through to the end of this.

"How are you, Sergeant Bellavia?" he said as an unexpectedly wide grin crossed his face. There it was. The light and *the suck ain't got me yet* look that always lifted us in our worst moments.

"Fine, Seyford," I lied. "How are you?"

He looked us over, eyes traversing across Third Platoon.

"Rough one out here, huh?"

"Nothing you can't handle."

He burst out laughing, and for a split second, I felt a surge of energy return.

Barreto frowned. He was struggling with Iwan's death, and his usual seriousness had trended toward something more grim now. Resolute fatalism, maybe?

We chatted back and forth for a few minutes, avoiding anything serious. We didn't talk about Iwan or J.C., or our sergeant major. We kept to safer subjects.

Down the street, I saw Captain Sims walking toward us. I hadn't seen our company commander in days—not since before the house fight on my birthday two days before. Even then, it was from a distance, and we hadn't spoken.

Sims walked like a man who had a boulder on his back but was too proud and stubborn to admit the weight was crushing him. Upright, shoulders square, he made his way to us. In some ways, I suppose, taking Alpha Company into Fallujah was his destiny all along. He was the son of an Army officer who survived two tours in Vietnam. His uncle also fought in Vietnam, completed two tours, and was disabled by wounds received there. His grandfather was a thirty-six-year, two-war veteran of our beloved service. Sean had been born in Taiwan, went to high school in Korea, and came home for college to the country his family had given their lives to defend.

Sims had been a high achiever, never a type A, but rather a devoted, studious, and introspective officer with plenty of grit. He checked all the boxes before coming to Vilseck: Pathfinder and Airborne School, Ranger School, Armor Officer's School. At Infantry Officer's Basic, he had been his platoon's top graduate.

Along with the weight of leading a company into the worst urban hellscape U.S. forces had experienced since Hue City, Vietnam, in 1968, Captain Sean Sims carried the legacy of his family's heritage on his shoulders as well. Watching him come our way, I decided to offer him a little Soldier humor.

I grabbed some wires, walked over to the tub, and stuck them into the shit. A moment later, when Captain Sims reached us, I said, "Sir, check out this IED we found!"

Wearily, he glanced over and down. I'm not sure he thought it was funny, though he was a good sport and riffed on it: "Dear Lord! Does he need a dust-off or a chaplain?"

While we were laughing, I noticed his eyes were red-rimmed and bloodshot. Total exhaustion. He had been up for five days with virtually no sleep. Then I remembered Edward Iwan, and I knew he'd been crying over the loss of his dear friend.

He crouched and peered under the tub at the tunnel entry point. Then he rose, our laughter drained away by then. I found myself standing beside a man transformed by the experience of the past week. The Captain Sims I'd locked horns with was gone. Sparing the Iraqi people the ravages of war so we could rebuild the country and go home had always been his priority. He had seen the complexities of trying to impose rule on a nation still deeply divided on tribal and sectarian fault lines, but had thrown himself into that effort with every bit of skill and professionalism he possessed.

None of that mattered here in this killing ground of booby-trapped buildings and kill zones. Fallujah was the closest we would ever get to a conventional fight in the entire two-decade-long Global War on Terror. A pure kinetic spasm of violence devoid of civilians on the battlefield—they had been evacuated before the battle began—so the only thing that mattered was keeping our men alive and killing the enemy, one room, one house at a time. It was grueling, methodical, mind-numbing work punctuated with some of the most vicious fighting any of us would ever see.

Sims recognized all that, and had grown into the new role. The losses we had sustained were eating at him, though, just like they were the rest of us.

"Sir," I said, turning serious, "Lieutenant Iwan . . . I'm . . . sorry for your loss. We all loved him."

Captain Sims nodded a thanks but told me that we would deal with that later. He asked how the men of Third Platoon were doing.

I lied. "Good, sir."

He could see them through the gate of the compound, beaten down, worn-out. Fried from the hours-long pitched battle we had just fought.

He regarded the men for a long moment, seeming to come to some conclusion he didn't share as he watched them. Then he turned to me, squared up, and said softly, "I heard about what happened the other day. That is some Audie Murphy stuff."

I didn't know what to say. He sounded alarmed. So I said nothing.

He took a step toward me and continued: "Listen to me. What you did was hooah, but it was stupid."

He drilled me with despair-filled eyes and admonished, "We can't take crazy chances like that, you understand me?"

"Sir?"

"We can't risk any more loss. You have to use your head. You and Fitts—you're important to these men and you need to stay in the fight."

"Yes, sir," I managed. I was numb, so utterly spent, but I understood there was more to it than the value I possessed to the squad. He was worried about me. Genuinely. Sean Sims was a devout Catholic. He read his Bible frequently. He ordered his life around his Christian beliefs. By that gate, he showed how much he cared about his rebellious, wrecking ball of an NCO who had caused him so many headaches. The hatchet-burying discussion we'd had just before we went into the city had been genuine. It wasn't pretense. He meant it.

There was a crew from CNN that Lieutenant Colonel Newell had attached to Captain Sims's element. They wanted to film the inside of a building for some B-roll footage for their nightly Fallujah coverage. Fitts, Lieutenant Meno, and I still had to get through another couple of blocks on this street before dark, so we would have to get moving again in a few minutes.

Sims told us to stand down, get some rest, and get some more chow. He and his command element would go clear the house that the second tunnel apparently led to, then let the CNN crew come and join them to shoot some B-roll. That particular house had already been cleared twice, once by our platoon before dawn, and then by First Platoon a few hours later. We had been planning to go through it more thoroughly and see if the tunnel actually did run over to it, as soon as the men finished eating.

"Sir, are you sure?" Fitts asked from the gate when he heard Sims's order. Sims nodded. He saw how sick the men were. He was in the same boat, just as tapped out as the rest of us. But he was thinking only of their well-being.

I looked down the block. Sergeant Major Bohn's words came back to me in that moment.

Nothing is cleared unless you are standing in the room. Don't forget that.

This seemed routine. Still, it didn't seem right for our company commander to be doing our job.

"Please, sir, let us go do this," I protested.

He waved me off. "Stand down. Air out your feet. Get some chow. We'll take care of it."

My expression clearly conveyed I wasn't swayed. This was our job, not his.

Gently, he underscored his order. "Staff Sergeant Bell, we can clear that house over there on our own. That's what our guys do."

I should have said or done something totally insubordinate. Punched him. Yelled at him. Anything to let us do our job.

I said nothing. A sense of gratitude pierced the numbness I'd been feeling since he chided me for the house fight.

He said goodbye to us and walked off to assemble his security detail. Barreto watched him for a beat, then turned to me. "You guys get some more rest. You all look like shit."

Joey Seyford nodded agreement.

"Be safe in there, guys," I told them both.

Looking back, if I really had a feeling that something was off, I would have grabbed Fitts and Lawson, or anyone near from First Platoon, and just cleared the house before Sims could have done it.

Instead, I stood with Fitts and watched him walk away. The CNN crew went back to the Bradleys and waited for the buildings to be cleared. They planned to link up with Sims once the immediate street was cleared.

Fitts and I went and checked on our guys, then sat down on a giant, threadbare couch inside the compound's main house with the rest of the platoon racked out around us. Some of us smoked, or ate. Others cleaned their weapons. I was too beat up to do anything but zone out. I couldn't catnap, but my brain checked out, for sure. I sat like a zombie on the couch, a million thoughts struggling to burst through the numbness, but none succeeded.

A commotion above us caused me to jerk back to the moment. I opened my eyes in time to see Specialists Jesse Flannery and Chris Ohle running downstairs from the roof of our house.

A swell of gunfire erupted down the street, a mix of AK-47s and M4s. All of us snapped to it, dropping MREs, grabbing boots, and loading mags into weapons.

Flannery hit the bottom step and shouted, "There is a shit-ton of fire coming from outside. They're saying on the radio that Six is down. They can't find him!"

A wild firefight raged down the block. Sustained fire, followed by a short silence, then a swell of firing again. Some of the shooting seemed to be moving away. We tossed on our gear and ran for the streets, Brads behind us, getting ready to assist on what would be the opposite side of First Platoon. Confusion reigned. Nobody knew where Captain Sims was.

Our commander's security element included Seyford, Barreto, an Air Force combat controller whose job was to call in airstrikes, and Sammy, our 'terp and a former member of the Iraqi Republican Guard.

First Platoon sprinted from building to building. There was no sign of American forces around the house with the suspected second tunnel entrance. We heard on the radio that Sims's Air Force controller was down, shot at close range. Joey Seyford was also wounded. Where were they?

The echo of gunfire reverberated throughout the neighborhood. This would be confusing enough in any abandoned city. The acoustics play hell with perfect senses as sounds bounce around the streets and empty buildings. Here in Fallujah, we had thousands of combatants exchanging fire all around us for miles. It was an impossible task to home in on precise fire, especially when all our senses were dulled after so many firefights. Some of us even had ruptured eardrums.

Pieces of what happened began to emerge from fragments of conversations and radio chatter. Exactly what happened took years to unravel.

Captain Sims had led the way into the house with his security element. They'd taken fire. Sims went down, the Air Force controller got shot in the doorway. Seyford was hit next, a bullet pierced his deltoid.

While Sims and the Air Force controller fell to the ground, Seyford pushed forward, firing his rifle with his one good arm. A round ricocheted off the wall and snapped into his leg, wounding him a second time.

He staggered and caught sight of Sims on the floor. He screamed out for Travis Barreto, who was pulling security on the roof at the lip of an old artillery-shell impact. The blast had torn part of the roof away, giving Travis an overhead view of part of the house's innards. Even so, Barreto did not witness any of the Americans engaged by the insurgents and only heard the gunshots. When Seyford called for him, he jumped down to get into the fight.

Seyford, bleeding profusely from his leg and arm, noticed a larger blood trail in front of him. He could hear moaning from wounded insurgents in the room just beyond.

Barreto banged through a door, firing as he entered the house in a nearby room. Sammy joined Seyford and began shooting into the room with the moaning insurgents. Barreto ended up carrying both wounded Americans out of the house to safety. Of Sims, there was no word. They'd last seen him, down and still, lying on the kitchen floor.

After everyone pulled out of the house, Barreto and Sammy searched for whatever they could to get the wounded men over the tall compound wall. They found some oil barrels, which they dragged over and used like step stools to pull Seyford and the Air Force controller up and over the wall to a waiting Bradley from First Platoon. After they were put aboard, Barreto climbed inside, too, and went to work giving them medical aid.

The controller was bleeding out and needed immediate medevac. Seyford was losing more blood, too. Between the chaos of the firefight and the dire state of our wounded, the Bradley sped off with all of the Soldiers who could tell us where to look for Sims. Sammy, meanwhile, had taken fire down the street and was totally engaged in a life-and-death gun battle. What was already chaotic had become a frantic search to figure out which house Sims was in and how badly he was wounded.

As this scene unfolded, my visibility on the situation remained confined to the disjointed radio chatter. I kept thinking about those tunnels. How many were there? Did they get behind us? Could those men we'd seen in the night been insurgents dressed in our gear?

Not until Sammy linked up with First Platoon did they finally find the house. Until then they just chased gunshots and echoes in the frantic building-by-building search.

With Sims gone and Iwan dead, we had two lieutenants left: First Lieutenant Jeff Emery of First Platoon, and Lieutenant Meno. One man had to keep Battalion in the loop of what was happening. The other had to assume command of Alpha Company, which Emery did. It was the absolute worst moment to take charge.

First Sergeant Peter Smith listened to all this on the radio and knew what had to be done. He began barking orders of his own. He told Meno to take Third Platoon and swing to the backside of the house with the suspected second tunnel entrance. We moved at once but found nothing—no sign of our guys, no sign of the enemy.

The firing tapered off. We saw nothing from our positions, no sign of the enemy. We waited for word from First Platoon, holding a blocking position on their flank. They found the right house and radioed an entry team was going in.

They found Sims without a pulse. When the news broke over the radio, it seemed like the entire war—the world—came to a crashing halt. Our commander was dead.

Somehow, in all the chaos, a photojournalist crept into the house and took a photo of Captain Sims's body. The photographer was caught, and later thoroughly roughed up for what he was doing, yet he managed to hide his compact flash card with the photos he had taken on it. The photo ran in countless overseas newspapers, and remains one of the first to pop up on Google when a search is done. The image caused incalculable damage to the Sims family, and despite many efforts to get it removed from various websites by myself and others, it is still out there today.

That day has haunted me and many other Ramrods ever since. Being at the pointy end of the spear was not Captain Sims's job, that was what his wrecking crew was for. His compassion for us, wanting to give us a break, led directly to his death.

The wounds of that day lingered. They still do. Everyone involved in the fight had different angles, different perspectives, and the scene was so chaotic and violent, more questions than answers remained. I never was able to piece together exactly what happened.

In 2008, on my final civilian embedded journalist tour in Iraq, I ran into Sammy at our old stomping grounds in Diyala Province. He just happened to walk by me one night at FOB Normandy while I was looking up at the stars, lost in thought. He recognized me at once, rushed to me without so much as a "hello," and embraced me.

"Oh, Staff Sergeant Bellavia. I love you so much," he said. "I miss you, my Ramrod brother. I miss Captain Walter. And Captain Sims."

Sammy grew very emotional when he mentioned our commander. Theirs was a very close bond. Perhaps more than any other Ramrod, Sammy felt his loss the hardest.

"I did everything I could," he said. "Believe me when I tell you. I would have died for him, you, all of them. Walter. I would have died for all of you. Ramrods are my family, too. I am one of you. You loved me more than any other unit in the Army. Some of these men treat me like a spy. Like a terrorist. They took my rifle. They don't let me travel. They don't respect me like you did."

That night, Sammy told me what he had seen happen that day. We sat for hours that night talking about Sims's last moments and the rest of what we'd seen in Fallujah. I realized that Sammy had no one else to share this with and that this was the first time he was addressing that day.

Joey was ahead of him in the stack when they entered the house. Seyford took a round in the arm and shoulder but didn't stop moving. He spun and ran into a side room, where a pile of U.S. Army uniform tops lay beside a couple of blankets. Two insurgents were concealed under those covers, and Seyford found himself in a gunfight only a few feet from the enemy, totally exposed. He hit one before they shot him a second time. Unable to use his arm, he literally flung his M4 at the remaining insurgent.

Sammy came into the room behind him right then.

"I couldn't get a target. I didn't want to hit Seyford. I got two of them. One Seyford shot, too. I don't know, maybe Barreto hit him. He was bleeding when I hit him center. In the chest."

Sammy started to weep. "Sergeant Bell, I could see my commander on the floor in the kitchen . . ."

He broke down completely. Nothing I could say made it better for Sammy. Nothing he could say would make it any better for me.

We both knew the truth. Captain Sims's death led to a series of decisions that probably saved half our platoon.

Ordered to advance less than an hour after Sims's death by our task force commander, Lieutenant Colonel Newell, our first sergeant went to see him to discuss getting additional firepower assigned to us. Newell agreed. He asked for artillery, and was given all available batteries.

We put our Brads out in front, our dismounts in wedges behind them, and at the appointed hour, pushed south from Sims's final firefight.

Rapid machine-gun fire strafed from upper-story buildings. Bradleys and tanks reported back. During those exchanges Soldiers couldn't hear the commands given to them across the squad wedge.

Then all vehicles stopped. All firing ceased. Over the radios we heard, "Dismounts take cover."

The skies opened up and 155mm high explosives destroyed everything in front of us. We crept behind our Bradleys. They barked their own 25mm in front of us. Soon in their wake, we would double tap scores of wounded and dead insurgents.

First Sergeant Smith directed the artillery barrage via radio, walking the curtain of steel forward as we crawled along behind it.

I couldn't hear anything but the thunder of the impacting shells. The ground quaked. Dust and blood flew through the air. The Bradleys spit cannon and machine-gun fire, adding to the carnage.

The entire area was destroyed. Dead and dying insurgents lay everywhere in the rubble and rebar, some blown clear out of buildings, others shredded by direct impacts. The Brads churned on, running over some of the body parts, their treads growing gory and crimson and caked with concrete dust.

One thing was clear: no more Ramrods would die that day. Sims's death was the final straw for our battalion command.

First Sergeant Peter Smith walked those artillery rounds down the street in front of our advance, and the 1st Infantry Division killed more enemy that day than any other day in the Second Battle of Fallujah. In the aftermath of the carnage, we guessed there'd been a hundred and fifty, maybe more, insurgents waiting in those buildings for us to enter and clear them. If we had done that, we'd have lost a lot more men.

Sammy and I and everyone else in Alpha Company got a second chance at life with Captains Sims's death. It was his last gift to us, an act we'd never be able to repay. We all struggled with that debt, no one more than Sammy. That night in 2008, I saw we were both bound by survivor guilt. He was dreadfully lonely, treated like a second-class citizen by the new unit he supported. In that moment in Diyala Province, I think we were the only two people who understood each other.

We both broke down, hugging each other as we talked about the war until the sun came up to reveal a frigid dawn.

23

THE SONS OF FALLUJAH

BLUE GINGHAM DRESS SHIRT. Khaki slacks. Rust-brown belt. Dark hair, longer than I'd ever seen in Iraq, from his right temple. Same dark and introspective eyes. The room remained dead silent, frozen by the vision in the doorway.

A younger, more wiry Sean Sims stood self-consciously and stared back at us. I nearly gasped. My face went blank with shock.

He smiled shyly to this room full of drunken Ramrods, revealing a set of silver-gray braces.

Not Captain Sean Sims.

"David, I want to introduce you to my son, Colin," Heidi Sims said as she entered the room and broke its stillness.

Colin stepped toward me and the rest of the Ramrods. I was the only sober one in this zip code, and I was seeing a ghost. No, not a ghost. Our commander's legacy.

Colin, straight-backed, straight-shouldered—no slouching, rounded posture here, as seen in so many his age—offered his hand. I shook it warmly. His grip was firm. We hadn't even spoken and I could tell already that Heidi had raised a strong, respectful, and dignified young man. She did that on her own, her own love letter to Sean. *I raised your boy in your image. To be the measure of his father.*

Heidi never remarried. She had the love of her life in Sean. What's the point of second best after that? Besides, no other man would raise our captain's son. Widowed young, while her peers were still out partying, having fun at clubs and blowing through their roaring twenties, Heidi was guiding Colin to manhood. The pain, the loneliness of that life, counterbalanced by seeing Colin flourish and grow, had to have been an exceptionally difficult path.

I shook his hand, searching for words. Finally, I said, "Your dad . . . would have been so proud of you."

"Thank you," he replied. Even his voice sounded like our fallen captain's. Younger, a quarter octave higher. In time, when he traversed his teens, I could see it being nearly identical.

"He loved you so much. He talked about you constantly . . . so proud of you."

Colin's eyes filled with tears. Yet he kept his poise and composure, unafraid to show emotion in front of this room full of strangers who loved him as their own.

"He's here, Colin. He's here with us, and I know he's so proud of you."

The paralysis was broken. The men began to inch toward us, unconsciously forming a horseshoe.

"Can I introduce you to the guys who loved your father, too?" I asked him.

"I would really like that," he answered softly.

I turned to the Ramrods, seeing Travis Barreto, stock-still, face like granite.

"Do you know who Sergeant Travis Barreto is? Do you remember that name?"

"Hey, Colin. I am sorry for your loss. Your father meant a lot to us all." Barreto almost edited his own sentence. Not wanting to get too into the weeds. Careful not to upset Heidi or Colin. Guarded, careful.

"Colin," I said, "these men are really special. And they really loved your dad. This is Seyford. This guy was wounded multiple times and helped get the bad guys who hurt your father. Barreto, Seyford, First Platoon guys are over there. Have you met Sammy?"

Sammy hugged Colin. "You look just like your father. You are your father. And everyone here loved your father. And we love you. You are protected here. And will be for the rest of your life."

My heart just stopped beating. I was so excited to bring Colin into the Ramrod fold that I hadn't considered how this would affect those of us there that day. Now I saw the pain again. Sammy started to cry. Barreto and Seyford looked like they were reliving that terrible day in November all over again. It had been the fight of their lives, but they glossed over it like it was a religious tract left at a bus station.

Maybe there had been a reason we'd not honored our promise to Captain Sims after all. Besides the geography, besides the fact that we all tried to put our heads out of our combat memories and focus on being in the moment as we built new lives—there was the guilt, and the pain. Maybe the truth was Seyford, Sammy, and Barreto didn't want to be in this moment at all, ever. I could see in their eyes they were long gone, far away from this safe conference room, rooted in the memory of those terrible hours.

I had forced it to happen, thinking we all wanted the same thing. Shaken now, I wondered if I had just torn open the old wound, and I could see its effects. I had no right to throw this at the guys with Colin Sims standing there in front of them. They didn't deserve this. I felt horrible and selfish forcing them to face the consequence of these memories.

Perhaps some promises are just too difficult to fulfill.

Then I heard Colin say, "Thank you, guys."

Something switched after that. Sean Sims's son had *accepted us*. We had tried. We'd done everything we could do to try to save his father. Not a man there that day wouldn't have given his life for our captain, to ensure this moment would never need to come. It was clear Colin knew that, or at least sensed it. And that took the edge off the anguish.

The men began to talk. As they clustered around him, Colin became the center of attention as each man took a turn telling stories about his father. Handshakes weren't enough for this moment. The men bear-hugged Colin like he was their own boy. In the end, we finally did begin to honor the promise we had made to Captain Sims that sunset as we sat on the Bradley ramp. The funny stories, the noncombat ones—they tumbled out of the Ramrods like long-lost secrets waiting to be shared with the only person who would value them as much as we did.

It was a start. There was more to share with him, much more. The reception wasn't the place for those stories, but the foundation had been established. The men in the room were no longer strangers, no longer mere names his mom may have mentioned in the past. Colin became one of us, and we a part of him.

I listened and watched this beautiful, agonizing, soul-cleansing process unfold. The room grew louder, Colin's voice more muffled. I heard his father talking to me. *This isn't how we do things, Sergeant Bellavia. No more Audie Murphy stuff.* A voice whose sound I'd long forgotten, the timbre in it. The earnestness. The steady confidence of a man convinced he was on the righteous path in the most hellish playground of moral gray areas imaginable.

My eyes burned. The emotional toll was not inconsequential. I began to envy the guys for their alcohol consumption. Just something to take the edge off, numb this even a little. I could have used that, but Sergeant First Class Gibson would have swooped in and swept away any glass stronger than punch.

The memories zipped in and out, flashing me between that room and moments of my life I'd all but forgotten. I was the precog in the film *Minority Report*, floating in an enclosed tank as images fired everywhere. Each voice triggered another good day. A bad day. The worst day. The best day. The mother of all catharses.

Around me played out every clichéd movie ending. Hugs and professions of love. The pent-up emotions of it all breaking loose, perhaps for the first time for all of us. I bounced from feeling horrible and selfish to wondering if this was the ending we all should have had when we came home in 2005. Why had we waited? Why had we wasted so much time? Everyone clearly needed it.

I needed it. Difficult, draining, full of love and pain, everything began flowing out of me. Vilseck. That night of my cold, dark homecoming. Searching for Evan. Now, a young man, I could see him watching this scene unfold in a way he never would have understood in the darkness. A demon exorcised; a *never-had* moment restored. We had all come home together at last.

. . .

The night was over. I was back in my room, sitting in a deep chair and looking out the window at the new annex the Department of Veterans Affairs just purchased for Arlington National Cemetery. The next generation of those laid to rest would soon fill that space. What after that? As long as there is a United States, our sons and daughters will be laid to rest in Arlington. We will run out of space again long before we run out of wars.

I thought about that as I wondered where the Ramrods were and how the after-reception party was going. Being separated from them, stuck in this hotel room with orders not to participate, was both a blessing and a curse. Being around each other, a full gamut of emotions whipsawed me. I felt the exhaustion of all those conflicting feelings now. Still, there was nowhere else I would rather have been than with them that night, no matter what memories came zinging back around at us. At least we'd be together.

It was time to get some sleep. The ceremony was tomorrow, and we'd been promised a quick tour in the morning of the memorials in D.C. Before I could get up, knuckles rapped on the suite's front door. A pause, and I heard a key card click the lock open. I peered over from the chair to see Gibson in the doorway. He smiled and said, "Hey, don't tell Colonel Perez about this. Okay? Figured you needed this. All right. Don't jam me up?"

Having zero idea what he was referring to, I agreed.

The door swung open and four Ramrods stormed into the room. The scene went from dead quiet to riotous laughter in an instant. The commotion attracted Evan and Aiden, who wandered in from the next room over to see what was happening.

Omarr Hardaway, Colin Fitts, Chris Walls, and Cory Brown sat down around a large conference-style table with me. We were all laughing, telling *do you remember* stories of Army life—the funny things, the outrageous ones. I went from dead tired to happier than I'd been in forever, surrounded by men I loved and who loved me back.

Lieutenant Walls shouted over the others, who were all telling stories simultaneously, "Boys, did you know your dad thought he was a medical doctor because your grandfather was a dentist?"

Omarr Hardaway burst into hysterics. "Docta . . ."

I rolled my eyes and started laughing, too.

"Am I wrong?"

"You ain't wrong, LT," said Big Smooth.

Walls looked over at my boys, both smiling with anticipation of the story behind this.

"We went to Kuwait before Iraq. And Fitts, Brown, and Hardaway were sent early in what we call an ADVON, or advanced party. The rest of us, your dad and all the guys downstairs—they all showed up a little later, waiting for our ADVON to bring our vehicles and re-unite our platoons. Hundred-and-twenty heat. Like a furnace. Wind blasting sand in our faces."

"Aiden and Evan—it was so hot. So damn hot. You don't know hot," Cory Brown interjected.

"Boys," Hardaway added, "the chow lines took hours to get through. An entire division in one camp city. You would wait in line for breakfast and you would just miss the tail end of lunch."

The boys nodded their heads, lit up and happy, soaking it all in.

"That food tasted like boiled dicks. Let the POG eat a steamed hot dog. MREs and water were just fine," Fitts added.

"And by the way," I said, "your uncle Colin here knows of what he speaks. Long regarded to be a connoisseur of all dicks. Fried, roasted, and boiled."

The table burst out into laugher. Fitts realized that he had walked into that one. He was overjoyed that he had a connection with my children. He seemed touched in the moment that he was Uncle Colin. My children agreed. The guys looked around at each other. My boys to Fitts, who quickly tried to change the topic back to the humor.

"Got me, Sarge. Allow me to correct myself. They tasted horrible. There."

"So your dad decided to start training with his Soldiers and our new CO, Captain Sims, comes over and his eyes are all puffy and red," Walls continued.

"'Hey, sir, you have pink eye. And it's superbad,' your dad told him."

"Oh man. Ohhhhh man." Fitts laughed in anticipation.

Walls looked over at Fitts, then back at my boys. "So Captain Sims says, 'We have a problem, SSG Bellavia. We only have six vials of this goop, medicine you put on it. And it's going around First Platoon really bad.' Your dad is like, 'Six vials for the company?' Captain Sims says, 'No. Six for the entire battalion. We will need a week for resupply.'"

I listened quietly, watching my sons as this story slowly spooled out. It was one of the legendary screwups of my career, and the boys were hearing about it for the first time—not from me, but from my guys.

Walls said, "So your father decides to make an NCO decision, based on his vast medical knowledge."

"What the hell were you thinking, Bell?" Brown erupted amid peals of laughter.

Before the punch line arrived, I decided I needed to explain things a bit to my sons. "Boys, everyone knew my father was a dentist. I grew up in a dental office. I could pull a tooth right now. I knew it was either pink eye or ocular herpes. There is a viral pink eye and a bacterial pink eye. It looked more severe than the bacterial conjunctivitis. So, I thought it was viral. . . ."

"Which is total horseshit," Walls said and recaptured the narrative. "Your dad can say whatever he wants. It was obvious it was pink eye and by the way, kids, this was bacterial pink eye. Everyone with the medicine got better." Walls laughed.

"What did you do, Dad?" asked Aiden.

"So an hour later—" I started. But Walls interrupted.

"Bell, I am taking this over. What did your dad do? Well, an hour later *your* dad put *my* platoon in a formation with First Platoon. I wasn't there. Neither were Cantrell and the others, like Hardaway, Brown, or Fitts. They were still with the vehicles. So, your dad has no adult supervision."

That cut my boys up. They looked so happy, surrounded by my Ramrods, listening to this story, that the emotional content of the day was forgotten.

"Your dad decides with zero semesters of medicine to pass known pink eye to everyone in both platoons. He went from man to man and rubbed everyone's eyes with it."

Brown chimed in: "And he tells the men to put on their NBC pro gas masks for the next four days."

"Four damn days!" Fitts echoed.

I tried to save face by showing I suffered right along with everyone else. "Honestly, Evan and Aiden, those were the most miserable four days of all of our lives. The sandstorms. The heat baking our tents. And we have our masks on with infected, itchy eyes. We all wanted to die."

"I am the officer in charge of this platoon, I find out," Walls said, "I scream, 'Stop diagnosing people! This isn't a virus. It's a bacterial infection. You will literally get it again in like two weeks. Most of pink eye is shit-to-eye contact. You literally rubbed shit in everyone's eyes for no apparent reason.'"

Brown pointed out, "Bell says through his gas mask, 'Betcha it's gone tomorrow, sir!'"

I tried to rally: "I became the Dr. Jonas Salk of the 1st Infantry Division and I helped eradicate pink eye in 2-2 Infantry."

The guys refused to let me off the hook. Walls demolished that fiction. "Bullshit. A week later, Captain Sims and I were talking in the command tent when this story came up. And he starts rubbing his eyes again. I could see the crimson back in them. Sims had pink eye. Again. So I called your dad over, explained that this experiment was absurd and now was coming back to haunt us."

"The mounted guys, we all come back to the platoons and these dirty bitches give that shit to us," Hardaway explained.

Fitts looked over at my boys and loudly asked, "You know how we beat that pink eye shit, boys?"

"How?" Evan asked.

"We sent your dad into another tent."

My sons howled with laughter right along with us. I think they realized right then that the room was full of unconditional love, and that drove the humor and the great memories. Not since I was a little boy with my family had I been around a table with this many people and known that with such certainty. My Ramrods were gasping for air. My boys were respectful, curious, and laughing right along with us.

After fifteen years, my two families were finally blending. Seeing this play out in real time filled my heart with appreciation and love for the men around the table.

I caught Sergeant First Class Blake Gibson's eye. Silently I bowed my head in appreciation for this gift he had given me. As an infantryman himself, he understood how important this was, and with his lip full of a golf ball–size clump of Copenhagen, he nodded his head in confirmation. Silently giving his version of, "No problem. I got you."

I needed this moment desperately.

Yet, the smiles and laughter that surrounded this table gradually gave way to a new sense of awkwardness. It felt almost like a sickness coming onto me.

Then all at once, the sickness took over. Like air brakes blowing out on a runaway semi, all the goodness vanished. I slammed into deep guilt. Then pain. Then crippling sorrow. I was doing what Sims and Faulkenburg would never be able to do. I was with my family again, my family hearing these stories for the first time. They were meeting their new uncles. Brown was happy. Hardaway was laughing. Fitts was drinking beers and laughing—well past his angst that everyone hated him. Walls was smiling his perfect giant smile. And I was on the verge of a nervous breakdown.

That night, my Ramrods fulfilled the promise for me. I had had the luxury of telling my boys everything. Sean Sims never had that chance with Colin. My boys? They were old enough now, and I had never even tried. It felt like a luxury squandered, especially given how much my experience as a Ramrod shaped their own lives.

How can any son or daughter of our battalion truly understand their father without understanding this bond? The hardships and the trauma? Colin, Aiden, Evan, Vivi—they were the sons and daughters of Fallujah. To know us without knowing that part of our journey was to not really know us at all. It took this moment, and my men sharing these tales, for me to realize I would need to rectify this someday, sooner rather than later. Boys want to see their dad as larger than life, bulletproof. Beyond reproach. As young men, they also want to see their fathers for who they are. The real man, the steward of their lives, flawed however he is, and to understand him. When I got to that point in my own relationship with my dad, that was the turning point where our love for each other grew into something more mature and far more bonding.

All I ever wanted to be was a father. I dreamed for the day my children would look up at me the way I always looked up to my dad. Around this table, this was the first time in my life I felt it.

Memories of my father peppered me when I looked at my sons' eyes dancing with laughter. When I was seventeen, in the summer of my junior year, my dad started a group for teens whose mission was to wait until marriage to have sex. The Fourth of July was the biggest event in our small town of Lyndonville, New York. Our population of seven hundred and fifty would balloon to three thousand in one afternoon. The fireworks, the parades, the chicken barbecue, and the macramé plant hangers made this the go-to location in Orleans County. Inevitably, there was going to be a float for his new organization.

My father came to me and explained how difficult it was to get older kids to join his group. I was stunned. How richly bizarre it was that teenagers didn't want to ride downtown declaring to all their peers they were virgins and not open for business. With a sober face and piercing eyes, he asked me, "David, I would like you to be the King of our Virgin float."

Not having read the bylaws of the group to see if this sort of nepotism was allowed, it was quickly revealed that this was an acceptable policy. There was no disqualification in being related to an officer of the group in naming me King of all the Virgins, without a proper vote or at least a board meeting. I was a good kid. Shy, not exactly a ladies' man, and, in fact, a real, bona fide virgin at seventeen.

I just really didn't want to be on a float, being pulled by a John Deere tractor in my hometown, declaring to my entire community that my prom night didn't end like I had told all my friends.

I was introduced to my Queen. She was twelve years old. Every other kid on the float ranged from the ages of nine to a very mature thirteen. But I loved my father. I could not let him down.

"People like you and if they see that you are waiting, maybe they will wait, too," he said to me.

"Dad, you are far overestimating my ability to influence my peer group. No one cares. This is humiliating."

I rode on that float on a throne of chastity while girls who hadn't even reached puberty tossed Tootsie Rolls to my laughing peers.

I wore that crown. I wore that sash that read I DON'T UNTIL I DO.

That was the most emasculating twenty-five-minute tractor ride of my life. When the parade ended my dad came up to me and said something I have never forgotten.

"David, that was a very difficult thing I asked you to do. Remember this: if you live your life doing things that are difficult, but are right, you will find the strength to do tougher things when they count the most."

My hero asked me to do it. And I wouldn't have changed a thing, because it made my father proud of me. Now I saw my boys looking at me like I looked at my father that day, for what felt like the first time. It was a fleeting moment of complete fulfillment.

I just wish my dad had been able to see my boys with me that night in the suite as the stories flowed and more Ramrods evaded Colonel Perez to join us at the table. First Sergeant Smith, Hugh Hall. The laughter continued unabated, and I rose to the occasion several times, but beneath the revelry, I could not help looking back out the window at Arlington's headstones, stretching into the darkness.

My dad missed this moment. He would have loved every second of it.

Shrek would never have a moment like this. He never even had the chance to have kids.

J.C. and all the others. So much potential lost to family and community.

Just like that, I lost the ability to enjoy this night. It felt like a stolen moment that others far more worthy should have had but were denied by fate and circumstance.

Ten minutes ago, I was dancing on a cloud. Now I was in free fall from it, no parachute in sight.

Sergeant First Class Gibson entered our clubhouse and announced it was time to wrap things up. "Hate to break it up, boys. We have a long day tomorrow and a lot to go over."

I stood up and Peter Smith, wearing a leather sport coat like a typical German fashionista, bear-hugged me first. "Hey, homie," he said in his Teutonic-accented English, "I am so proud of you, buddy."

The others manhandled me on the way to the door. My boys retreated to their room for the night. Alone again, I walked over to the window and its panoramic view. That sliver of Arlington drew my eyes anew, and as I stared into the night, wondering what the future would bring and if I could handle all that would be thrown at me in the months ahead, I said a silent prayer for Edward Iwan, Sean Sims, and Steven Faulkenburg.

24

THE COMMANDER IN CHIEF

**WASHINGTON, D.C. — THE WHITE HOUSE
DAY 2 — JUNE 25, 2019**

THE BUSES WAITED FOR us outside the hotel lobby, stewing in a cloud of diesel fumes as our guests went through a security line complete with a pair of metal detectors in the hallway. Bags were being searched, and any hit on the metal detectors prompted a very thorough run-over with a wand. Belt buckles, loose change, a forgotten key or two on a small ring—all of these things triggered the understated digital beep of the detectors.

While our friends and Ramrods stood their turn in line, I was sequestered in a room with my children, my oldest brother, Dan, my mom, and Colin Fitts. We all held hands as Brigadier General Chaplain Thomas Solhjem led us in one of the kindest and most sincere exchanges and prayer I've ever had. When I first saw him, I wondered what type of chaplain becomes a general. Well, one of the best in the Army, it turns out. He somehow verbalized every worry and concern I'd been feeling and eased the tension with his words. He learned everyone's names, talked to us individually to learn a bit about ourselves, and personalized his message to each one of us. It was simply remarkable.

"There are times when we think light and attention is on us and we don't somehow deserve the attention. The pressure is that people will find out something that reveals that we are unworthy of that attention. Today is the opposite of that. And your Soldiers all here, they are in that light, too. The men we lost. They are here. Breathe and realize the mission before you is the same one that brought you here. God had you then. God has us now."

When he finished, we went downstairs and went through security just like everyone else, then climbed into a limo bus at the head of a column. In front and rear, D.C. motorcycle cops waited to escort us to the White House.

With all the guests aboard the other two buses, the D.C. police fired off their lights and sirens as they rolled out, leading the way into the heart of the capital. They stopped all traffic and we barreled through intersections without concern for red lights. The deeper we drove into the city, the more pedestrians and summer tourists stopped to watch us. Soon they lined both sides of our route, standing and waving as we passed. I wondered if any of them had any idea who we were, or if they just reacted to the police escort signaling something important was going down.

There weren't any sounds coming from our lead bus. Everyone was in awe of the motorcade. This fantastic escort through the capital of our nation was an experience no one would ever have again. The D.C. police acted like Moses splitting commuters to the side.

My children were in awe. Everyone was gobsmacked by the motorcade escort. Even Fitts was impressed by it.

We reached the White House and the buses parked in front of another layer of security. A second round of metal detectors, bag searches, and waving wands awaited everyone, along with ID checks and names cross-referenced to the master guest list. There were no exceptions, and even the Medal of Honor nominee received a thorough scrubbing.

While we were led to the Red Room, the White House staff treated the guests to a tour of part of this sacred American landmark. Downstairs, my family saw the chinaware from each presidential administration. Portraits lined the hallways, the history of those who lived in residence here during their tenure in office on full display. Upstairs, the Army band played as immaculately attired staff handed out champagne and hors d'oeuvres.

My phone vibrated. I plucked it out of my dress blues pocket and saw Travis Barreto's name floating on my screen.

"Travis?" I said, answering it.

"Sarge . . . Bell . . . it's Barreto. They won't let me in, man. They said my name is wrong and they are saying I can't go."

"Wait, what?"

"Something is wrong. And the Social is wrong. Can you get me in? I am so sorry to bother you."

"I got you, man. No worries."

Standing in the Red Room, Fitts beside me, I had no idea how to fix this. I thought of Colonel Perez, but she was nowhere to be seen and was probably in full orchestration mode to make sure this event came off without a hitch. I sent her a text anyway.

After a brief whirlwind tour of the White House, my family, my brother, and Fitts were locked into the Red Room, away from all the other guests.

I looked over at Fitts. He was clearly lost in the moment, wondering how on earth two door-kickers like us had ended up in a room that Dolley Madison used as a parlor to entertain her guests. Abraham Lincoln sat in this room. Rutherford B. Hayes secretly took the oath of office here after the contested election of 1876. There were the red walls, covered with paintings full of our heritage and the traditions here at the White House, the furniture, beautiful antiques that matched the décor, meticulously cared for, so well as to look brand-new.

A butler arrived with a silver tray full of bottled Diet Coke, President Trump's favorite drink. It telegraphed that the president would soon join us.

The butler laid the tray down on a tabletop and asked, "Sir, is there anything you need from us or the president of the United States?"

I almost said no. But how many times in your life does anyone ask that question of you? So, I threw a Hail Mary.

"My buddy Travis Barreto is having some issues getting in at the front gate. He is a really good Soldier. A great man. He has to be here. There must be a mistake with his Social or something."

The butler stared at me.

His gaze said it had either been a rhetorical question or was an offer for food and beverage only. I would have been better off asking if the Buffalo Bills could get a better pick in this next upcoming college football draft.

A Secret Service officer came into the room. He had overheard what I'd said. He asked, "What's his name?"

"Barreto, Travis."

He looked at a list on his clipboard.

"I see a similar name here. Must have been a typo. Sorry about that. On it."

The butler retreated and the Secret Service officer went out in the hall to contact the front gate. Fitts had moved to the windows, and when I looked over at him, he was studying them.

"Hey, Bell?"

"Yeah?"

"Get a look at this."

I walked over and joined him. He pointed at the glass and said, "You realize this is bulletproof for a fifty-caliber and you can see straight through this? Like crystal clear?"

This was the last thing I had expected, my battle buddy checking out the force protection here. Old habits die hard, I guess.

"You have any idea how hard that is to get, let alone make? This place is amazing."

"Hey, Fitts, can you focus on not shooting anything or anyone for one day?"

"Roger that," he said sheepishly. I wondered if he had hidden a beer somewhere in that suit of his again.

"Hey, about Barreto," he said. "Don't worry, Bell. Those Secret Service boys'll get him in."

Through a crack in the Red Room's door, I could see a sliver of what was happening in the reception area. An Army band played classic Americana tunes while more guests spooled their way upstairs to retrieve a glass of champagne. Generals. Senior Army NCOs. The acting secretary of the Army. Congressman Dan Crenshaw. Medal of Honor recipients—seven others whose valor stretched from Vietnam to Afghanistan. They mingled among my family members and my Ramrod family.

I wished I could be out there with them.

Colonel Perez zoomed into the Red Room at warp speed. She was busier than the deck crew of the *Carl Vinson* during air ops as she co-ordinated and oversaw everything here. She handled it with absolute confidence, with zero sign of stress on her face. She was incredibly impressive.

She waved over a young lieutenant who said, "Staff Sergeant Bellavia, the Army has a surprise for you. Are you ready?"

This surprise had been mentioned many times for months by Colonel Perez and others. There was an inordinate amount of intrigue involved here, along with ironclad secrecy. They had teased me with it, but never let on what it might be.

Okay, I admit, I had been hooked. My imagination started to run riot, and I had visions of some promotion with the good folks at Dodge or something; maybe they'd present me with a factory-fresh Ram pickup. Maybe it was a lifetime pass to all the national parks, or tickets to SeaWorld. I had no idea, but this was unusual enough that I genuinely grew excited about it.

The moment of its unveiling had come. In the White House? That made it even more special. I feigned like I didn't care but inside was like a kid whose parents tease them that the biggest thing in the world is coming.

When I was eight, my father told me while on a fishing trip that he was coming home from Canada and that he had a big surprise for me. I was hoping for Hot Wheels or wrestling action figures. He came home with a full beard. I was supposed to be happy that my father had enough facial hair to consume his entire face over six days of him fishing on Lake Ontario.

Let me tell you . . . major disappointment.

"Staff Sergeant Bellavia, do you remember me?"

I turned to one side and there standing with a big grin on his face was Staff Sergeant Gustavo Reina.

The man who recruited me into the Army.

I hadn't seen my recruiter since before I left for Basic in 1999.

"Holy cow. SSG Reina."

I loved Staff Sergeant Reina back in the day. He was my first introduction to the Army. He exemplified leadership and comported himself exactly as an NCO should. He mentored me and sent me on my way. I'll always be grateful for my path, and he was the starting point of the most important part of that journey through life.

We hugged it out. The Army had spent considerable time and effort tracking him down, and getting him to D.C. to reunite us. Army Recruiting Command did stories on him as well—Staff Sergeant Reina, the man who recruited the Iraq War's first living Medal of Honor recipient. It was a total surprise, and amazing to see him after all these years, especially in this venue.

Still, after the buildup, I felt a little like the day my dad showed up in our kitchen with more facial hair than Grizzly Adams. I was at least hoping for an action figure.

The lieutenant, Colonel Perez, and Staff Sergeant Reina excused themselves, leaving Fitts and me alone again. I peered through a crack in the door, watching the crowd milling in the reception area. I saw old college buddies, friends from church, my work colleagues— even high school friends. It was a *This Is Your Life* kind of moment, or maybe like a wedding with all your many circles of friends and connections concentrated in one place. Or maybe it was like a funeral, the passing of a life, and the celebratory wake after with everyone saying, *he's in a better place now.*

Through the crack in the Red Room door, I saw John Bruning, standing alone next to the Army band, camera in hand. He was looking around, hopelessly out of place, but absorbing all the treasures of history in this hallowed house around him. I would have loved to have known what he was thinking right then.

John was a writer by profession, an historian in title. He always saw life through the lens of the annals of American history. I wondered if he was thinking about Teddy Roosevelt, or maybe the burning of the White House in the War of 1812.

He moved away from the band and stood beside one of the White House staff. In a room full of potential clients for his writing career, Bruning was getting to know a waiter.

Bruning has written four *New York Times* bestsellers. Old and out of shape, he embedded with an infantry company in New Orleans during Hurricane Katrina in 2005. He embedded again in 2010 during the Afghan troop surge.

Our story started back in early 2006, when a veteran who had a crazy idea to write a book about his Iraq War experience was introduced via email to him through our mutual agent, Jim Hornfischer. One email turned into a three-hour call. That call became one every day. Some nights, we stayed on the phone well after midnight, talking for hours about things that had nothing to do with the book we were working on.

That's how *House to House* went from a writer partnership into a deep and meaningful bond that has traversed every up and down in my life since then. The Army gave me the Ramrods. Postwar, I had civilian John Bruning for my intro to the real world.

Until the sergeant major's reception, we had never met face-to-face. Our friendship stretched over thirteen years of remote conversations via text, phone, and email. I have met few men outside of combat fatigues who were more loyal or decent. He lived in Oregon. I was based in Buffalo. Life went on. Bruning by phone, almost weekly for years. When I told John about the call from President Trump, my news was his news. His selflessness and empathy was something that changed my perception about the human condition. That was John R. Bruning.

We first met at last night's reception—just a brief hug. Later, I ran into him in the hotel hospitality room. He had forgotten to have dinner and had gone in looking for something to eat, running right into my family. There, looking tired, tie undone, I found him talking to my nephews John, James, and Chris.

Over our time in D.C., I marveled at the reaction of watching my Ramrods engage with an unassuming civilian who never advertised that he'd written *House to House* with me. When the Ramrods realized they were talking to the man who helped craft the very book that defined our war experience, watching John's reaction to their kind words—well, it was the first moment since the book was released in 2007 that Bruning sensed the gift he gave to all of us.

What Michael Ware did for the Ramrods in 2004 put us on the map, gave us national attention via *Time* magazine. What Bruning did for us in *House to House* allowed our families and friends to process what all those experiences in Iraq meant. This was an incredible gift. And he had zero idea he was beloved and admired by so many tough, rarely sober, fighting men of the Big Red One.

Seeing Bruning smile was something that warmed my heart. Knowing he was respected and around people who admired him made it even better.

Writing is a lonely, thankless life. Most professional writers who collaborate do so helping tone, shape, and filter other people's stories. Rare is the day they get to meet the participants. Rarer is the time they get the thanks and appreciation for impacting lives in the way Bruning did for our Ramrods. For John, his career choice and experiences in Katrina and combat turned him from an outgoing, life-of-the-party type to a late-in-life extreme introvert. There in the White House, I could see he was not the cocktail-set type.

So could Merrilee Carlson, Shrek's mom. She descended on my writer friend and took him under her wing. Before long, I saw my own mother head straight for him like a guided missile. They had met the night before at the reception, too. Now my mother gave him the kind of hug normally reserved for family. He looked stricken with emotion. Bruning, underneath everything, tends to be over-emotive.

Seeing two moms dig Bruning out of his shell was an amazing thing. Unfortunately, an Army master sergeant appeared and forced me to refocus. "Staff Sergeant Bellavia, we need to rehearse the ceremony now."

Fitts, my family, and I followed him into the East Room, which was set up with rows of folding chairs and risers in back for the press to stand on. On television, this room looks enormous. In reality, it feels small and cramped. The three hundred seats crammed into the space left little elbow room. My friends would have to get cozy.

The rehearsal began almost before I finished absorbing the scene.

"Okay, so you and the president walk in," said the Army master sergeant. "I need someone to stand as the president."

He looked around at my family. His eyes settled on Vivienne.

"Ma'am, how old are you?"

"Nine," Vivienne responded.

"Madam President, will you walk with your dad for this rehearsal?"

Vivienne beamed from ear to ear, and the tension and waves of emotion I'd been feeling were swept away with joy as I saw her embrace this role. We walked together down the narrow main aisle, then stepped on the stage together. The master sergeant walked us through all the cues. I turned as ordered, and Vivienne simulated putting the award around my neck.

When we finished, I turned to look at her, a rush of love for my not-so-little girl. She stared up at me with guileless eyes. Transparent, a pure soul devoid of pretense.

She was standing beside the podium with the presidential seal on it. Spontaneously, I asked, "Viv, you ever think that one day you could be president?"

She looked around, considering the question, then said, "I don't think that interests me, Dad. Besides, this room has too much yellow."

Rehearsal over, we were led as a group back to a private room nearby.

"Open bar, bro," Fitts noted as he took up position next to the crack in the door. "I mean, what were they thinking? Those are Ramrods out there!"

I looked over at my brother Dan, ten years my senior, and said, "Hey, remember when Andrew Jackson was sworn in and those hillbillies he invited trashed the White House?"

Dan started to laugh. I added, "They roll any more liquor in here, we're gonna get a redux."

Ever since our dad passed, Dan became my go-to counsel in almost every decision I had to make. He had always been a rock of support, and our age gap always made him larger than life to me. In the past eighteen months, he'd grown into a mentor, and he unerringly offered wisdom that provided the right answer to every issue. What our dad couldn't be anymore, Dan grew into. He was the head of the Bellavia tribe now.

"Staff Sergeant? Do you want to sit at the president's desk for a quick picture?" asked the official Army photographer, Specialist Kevin Roy. This young specialist had taken hundreds of photos in two short days. He was working his tail off and just sat there documenting every aspect of my movement. Far exceeding his rank, he impressed everyone from my unit with his professionalism.

"Not especially. Is that a problem?"

"Whatever you want to do, Staff Sergeant." Specialist Roy was an earnest and decent Soldier. Just doing his part. I instantly felt bad for saying that.

"Bellavia, sit at the desk and take a photo," yelled an officer from the back of the room.

"Yes, sir."

I sat and took an awkward photo. This felt like *bring your infantry-man to work day* at the White House. I did what I was told.

Fitts could see the momentary peace I'd felt was shot through. Nerves. Stress. A sense of unreality about this all just crashed into me like waves on a beach again.

"Bell, you need to breathe. Can you relax, bro? It's not like we are gonna die at the end of this. You know what you need?"

"What, Fittsy? What do I need?" I couldn't even fathom what he was going to say.

He didn't say anything. He just handed me a can of dip.

"Knapp made sure you got some of this. Your boys are always looking out for you. Take some. It'll take the edge off. Just toss it out when you are about to go in front of the world."

"Thanks, man."

I tucked a modest amount of dip into the pocket of my lower lip. The old pit, chiseled into my mouth from the old days, had been reestablished and I felt the old rush of nicotine surge into me. It took me back to Iraq, a habit that always calmed me in a crisis.

"Ladies and gentlemen, the president of the United States . . ."

I turned to see Ivanka Trump enter the room first, Donald Trump right behind her. Cameras snapped in bursts as flashes strobed the room.

President Trump walked right up to me. He always seemed larger than life on television, but so can Tom Cruise and he's what, five seven? President Trump in person is a large, dominating presence. As he offered his hand, and when I took it, mine was swallowed in his grip. He squeezed so hard I had to squeeze back just to assert myself. It was clearly a test. *Are you alpha?*

I forgot to make eye contact. Instead, I focused on his teeth. Very white and clean. A stray thought ran through my head that maybe I should take better care of mine.

That's when I realized I still had a golf ball–size wad of dip in my mouth.

Holy shit. I have to get rid of this. But how?

He congratulated me as my family fell into a small line. Slowly, the president greeted every member of my little group. He laughed, bantered with my family, talked to each person for longer than he needed to. He left everyone—even Vivienne—smiling.

When he came to Fitts, the old warhorse grabbed President Trump's hand like they were Lee and Grant at Appomattox. Not even the president could intimidate Fitts. Fitts shook his hand like an equal, man-to-man. Looking back, I think President Trump appreciated that kind of soul.

When he finished talking with everyone, he led me over to a desk where the citation and orders for the Medal of Honor rested.

"You know it's not official until I sign this, David. You can't say no."

"Yes, Mr. President."

"Do you want to say no?"

"I really do, sir."

He stopped and stared at me for a beat, thinking about that.

"Your life is already changed. I can see it in your face. But this is happening for a reason. And you will make me and our great country proud."

"Thank you, sir. I will do my best."

"I have been looking forward to this all day. All day. These are the only days I look forward to."

"Me, too, sir," I said, my foot-in-mouth disease on full display. How could I be looking forward to something I wanted to say no to?

The truth was, this was an opportunity for me to meet the man who was so polarizing our country. I wanted to see who he was without the filter of the media's lenses.

I wasn't about to explain that. So, the president just looked at me strangely, then laughed at my awkwardness.

He produced the largest Sharpie I'd ever seen. All black, with his name inscribed on the end of it.

"You know, David, this award has been sitting around awhile. I guess Obama didn't want to sign it. I guess no one wanted to give the Medal of Honor to a living Soldier from Iraq."

He pointed with the Sharpie, adding, "You can see someone tried, at least started to sign these orders here. You see that?" He pointed to the Medal of Honor orders next to the citation.

There was a small line that appeared to resemble a signature of someone, unfinished.

"Well, guess what?"

"Sir?"

"I am signing it. And I am signing the actual citation, too."

President Trump wrote over the previous signature start, then added one on the actual citation, something that is never done, since a signature isn't required on it.

"There. Thanks, Obama. What a disaster he was for our military. Just a disaster," he said, shaking his head.

The choreographers of the event ushered my group to their seats in the East Room, leaving me alone for the moment with the president, some Secret Service officers, and two military escorts.

We stared at each other, unsure what to say. I had met President George W. Bush four times back in 2006 and 2007. Each time I was impressed with the entire White House experience, but also how different the president was from the way he was portrayed by popular culture and the media. Bush always seemed awkward, almost ashamed of the power he held. Talking with President Trump that afternoon, I could see he embraced it. Embodied it.

"What do you think about Iran?" he asked. The Iranians earlier in the day had shot down one of our drones over the Persian Gulf, and the United States was mulling over a measured response.

"Sir, I don't think about Iran. But I promise you they think about us."

"You are right about that," he said, laughing.

He adjusted his suit and changed his entire focus. The small talk ended. He prepared to address the country, and the world.

Wordlessly, he pointed to the ground to his left. Implicitly, I understood that was where I was to stand. I moved into position. No words. No eye contact. A moment later, we moved into a hallway, pausing to wait for the cue to walk down a red carpet into the East Room. Staff swung open the two massive doors and I saw the place was filled to capacity. My people. Distinguished guests. The Ramrods, and more media than I could have imagined. They clung to the risers in thick layers along every wall in the room, all armed with TV and still cameras.

Music called the audience to attention. Everyone in the room rose to greet the president.

He looked me over. His eyes went from my polished shoes on up over my dress blues, and I gave a momentary prayer of thanks for Sergeant First Class Gibson's next-level attention to it. Then the president's eyes stopped at my face. His brow furled.

"Are you really going to keep that in?" he asked.

I totally forgot I had a dip in my lip.

"I am so sorry, sir. I was just nervous."

I couldn't go into the room like this. I couldn't swallow the juice, or swallow the dip. I was way out of practice. I would end up throwing up. And there can be no vomiting in the White House. Ever. I was completely screwed.

"You have tobacco. You have tobacco in your mouth?" he asked incredulously.

"I am so sorry, Mr. President. I don't mean any disrespect."

"Ladies and gentlemen, the president of the United States accompanied by Medal of Honor recipient, Staff Sergeant David G. Bellavia, United States Army."

He smiled in amazement, laughing. Instead of being angry he said, "David, you're a wild man. You know that?"

The tension broke for just a minute.

"Never seen that before. You're a wild man. A wild man. Well, it's in. Just don't spit on my carpet."

Dip juice trickled down my throat, turning my stomach to a churning mess. I realized as the Army orchestra broke out with "Hail to the Chief" that I was surely going to honk.

Somewhere in that room, I knew, Fitts was laughing.

25

EAST ROOM TO FALLUJAH

PRESIDENT TRUMP LED THE way to the stage where a podium waited for him. I took station on his right, eyes locked on the back of the wall. I barely saw the reporters and camera crews, though. I was focused on not screwing up any further. The dip juice trickled down my throat, and I silently cursed myself for accepting it from Fitts.

The president stepped behind the podium, looking stern, brow furled and jaw set. In his unusual, staccato style, he began the ceremony. Around us were not only my guests, the Ramrods and our Gold Star families, but seven living Medal of Honor recipients sitting together in the front row off to the president's left. Army brass, civilian Department of Defense officials, congressmen and congresswomen. The president welcomed Liz Cheney in his opening remarks.

The room went quiet and respectful as the president spoke. "Today it's my privilege to award the highest military honor to an American Soldier who demonstrated exceptional courage to protect his men and protect our nation. Will you please join me in welcoming Staff Sergeant David Bellavia?" He turned to me and added, "David, thank you."

Polite, White House–appropriate applause lasted only a few seconds. A catcall rang out. Then a second. Encouraged, a swell of cheers and shouts filled the room.

"RAAAAMRODDDS!!!"

"DEUCE-DEUCE!"

"DUUUUUKES!"

For nearly thirty seconds, the Ramrods cheered like this was a promotion ceremony outside the barracks in Vilseck, not a solemn White House event with our commander in chief as our host.

President Trump was startled by this. Normally the Medal of Honor ceremonies are subdued and full of reverent applause. The Ramrods of the Big Red One made it clear that afternoon that we were not that type of audience.

Trump loved this—he was always at his best with an animated and engaged crowd—and he went from stern commander in chief to the charismatic and jovial man the nation had seen at his many rallies. The crowd lit him up and his happiness at that radiated with every word after.

I stood at attention, anything but lit up. I thought of the members of Congress, the row of generals sitting with General Mark Milley, chairman of the Joint Chiefs, and a bolt of panic shot through me. I tore my eyes away from the back wall and looked down at the guys. Some stood up, were standing now, arms raised and shouting. A few others in the room stood as well. But not the front row of Medal of Honor recipients. Not the generals. And not our political leaders.

I tried to subtly shake my head to wave them off and get them to comport themselves. Clearly, I'd been a civilian too long and I'd lost my NCO mojo, because they totally ignored me. I gave up and switched course. Forget convention. Forget the setting. There is never a bad time to express love, and that's exactly what the Ramrods were doing. These were men without pretense who were always all heart. The best warriors always are.

Chairman of the Joint Chiefs of Staff General Mark Milley seemed to take the cheering as a personal affront to the Army. He shot daggers at the Ramrods at first. Then, I think what was really happening here struck him. This wasn't about being rowdy at the White House; it was about esprit de corps. Men who bonded in his Army and who had rediscovered that bond, stronger than ever, here in our capital.

He broke into a smile, and finally nodded his head at the Deuce-Deuce vets.

"David is the first living recipient of the Congressional Medal of Honor for his bravery in the Iraq War," President Trump stated.

The Ramrods didn't wait for him to finish before unleashing a second round of hoots and cheers that carried over the applause from the respectables in the audience. This time it died down relatively quickly. Trump clearly enjoyed the additional shot of energy their enthusiasm delivered. He waited for quiet, then introduced some of the distinguished guests, even leaving the podium to shake hands with the new acting secretary of the Army, Ryan McCarthy, before continuing with his speech.

I tried to stare straight ahead and not think about anything but what I was supposed to do next, and when to do it. I could feel the eyes of my friends and family, the Ramrods, the dozens of television cameras piping this scene into homes around the country. I could feel my grandfather on the other side of a screen in western New York, the man whose stories of Normandy and the drive across France led me to this life in the first place.

President Trump mentioned my dad at that moment, how we'd lost him in 2017. I missed him more right at that moment than just about any other time before. If I had just been able to look out into the audience, see him and his steadying presence, I would have been okay. In the moment without him, I was whipsawed with emotions. Regret. Awkwardness. Fear. Was I worthy of this? What was this going to do to my life?

The dread set in. I knew what was coming: the story of what happened on November 10, 2004.

President Trump narrated a biography of my life. From my grandfather's service, to my desire to be part of "the noble adventure" of life in the infantry and service to my country, to my time in Germany and Kosovo, then finally to Iraq.

"After nearly a year of combat in Iraq, David led his squad into battle to liberate the city of Fallujah. . . . That was a tough place."

He emphasized the name Fallujah in such an odd way, it jarred memories loose. They whirled forward into the present like shrapnel from the past, fragments of things once whole, blasted to shards by the impact of fifteen years of wanting to forget.

What makes the mind remember some things and forget others? As distance grows from the event, it fades, slivers peel away and are lost. An image remains. A motion. Words spoken or prayers given. But the feel of the moment? The intensity drains like an old Polaroid photograph, the years pulling away the details until something brings them back from that bin of the forgotten. The trigger can be anything, a sound, the voice of someone there in that moment, a smell. A song. In a rush, our minds reassemble the fragments, the color is restored. The Polaroid looks like it is fresh from the camera. You're right there again, seeing everything, feeling all the same emotions.

It is one of the most jarring aspects of the human condition.

"This operation was the bloodiest of the Iraq War. For three days David and his men kicked down doors, searched houses, and destroyed enemy weapons never knowing where they would find a terrorist lurking next. . . ."

Those words—God, hearing our president say them in front of my family created seismic vulnerability in me. The darkest secrets I'd kept hidden away in those locker boxes in the barn since coming home, first opened to the team that came to my house, turned out to be a preseason game compared to this. While I stood in the East Room, all was being revealed to those I loved most—and to millions of total strangers beyond the walls.

How do you even deal with this?

Trump continued: "The third day of battle was November tenth, David's twenty-ninth birthday. . . ."

It was all going to be opened right here; the contents of my heart and those memories, spilled out in the East Room, never to be restored to their rightful and purposeful place deep in the shadow of my life.

I thought I'd be okay with this. I had been trying to prepare myself. I'd been reminding myself that I'd written my memoir; the stories were out there. The book was like writing those memories into a message in a bottle, then setting them adrift at sea to be found somewhere, someday by strangers on a distant shore. There was comfort in that anonymity, and the barrier of geography and time made it safe.

This was live, in real time, totally different. Unknowingly, President Trump flayed away the layers of defenses the years had built up, one sentence at a time.

"That night, his squad was tasked with clearing twelve houses occupied by insurgents. . . ."

The room was dead silent now. Gone was the rowdy mood, the joy and celebratory cheers. My eyes glanced down at Fitts. In that blue suit, meticulously clean and worn with the same pride our drill sergeants taught us to wear the uniform in Basic. Older, now, of course. His face fuller, the gray in his beard jarring tells of middle age. His eyes—the years left them unchanged.

"Dude! You almost killed my entire squad!"

His eyes shined with fury at me that day. November 10. Those houses we cleared were full of weapons and ammunition. We used C-4 for the job, but we ran out of blasting caps, so I had Cory Brown and Shane Gossard shoot a pile of rockets with their Bradley's 25mm gun. The pile exploded. Several of the rockets touched off and went sizzling in all directions, my squad hitting the deck as they went past. Several went straight into a nearby house Fitts and his squad were clearing. When he emerged, those eyes pinned me with pure rage.

Now they looked up with a mixture of emotions. Pride, maybe? A sense that we'd reached a summit that had redefined all of us? I couldn't read him, and that never happened.

". . . a very dangerous operation . . ." Trump continued.

Dangerous.

The street was a charnel house. Insurgent bodies, bloated and blackened, some already covered with a sheen of green moss, lay strewn in the rubble. The stench of death settled heavily on all of us. It permeated our uniforms and became part of our funk. Behind our platoon, a row of feral dogs trailed us at a distance. Starving, they had learned quickly that we provided them with fresh meat— the insurgents we killed. Their tails wagged like puppies, but their jaws were stippled red with human blood. They waited for us to deliver another meal.

We kept clearing block after block, dragging weapons, ammo out and destroying them, finding no insurgents. The work was back-breaking and unbearably stressful. Each room could mean a booby trap—we found them everywhere. Or it could mean we would walk into an ambush. The insurgents weren't stupid. They had studied our tactics. They flexed to find ways to inflict maximum damage on us. They set up room-to-room kill zones inside buildings, ambushes out of the sight of our drones, our aircraft, and our armor support. They pulled squads into point-blank firefights where the contest was man-to-man, within rock-throwing range.

Three of our scouts went through the front door of a house, only to be met with a hail of gunfire from a crew-served machine gun, set up in a house, covering its entrance from mere feet away. Staff Sergeant Jason Laser took a round in the chest. Staff Sergeant Andy Karnes grabbed him and tried to get him to safety. The fight only ended when Staff Sergeant J.C. Matteson killed the machine gunner with his automatic grenade launcher.

Very dangerous. To say the least. Imagine doing a hundred home invasions a day in Gun Barrel City, Texas, but with everyone armed with automatic weapons and RPGs.

Trump's hands gripped both sides of the podium as he said, "They entered house after house and secured nine of the buildings. . . ."

It was after midnight by then. We were sore, scraped, and desperately tired. There was still another house left to clear, a big one. This neighborhood had once been home to Fallujah's wealthiest residents, with well-manicured palm groves and thick-walled compounds. Now war had torn it apart.

Mick Ware, always near with his video camera and Aussie snark, looked totally smoked. The constant threats and sleepless nights had left his eyes hollowed out, beyond caring if he lived or died after three days of nonstop fighting. In the East Room, my eyes flicked to him now. He was staring at me with deep sadness in those eyes. We had all lost something in this moment our president was sharing with the world, Mick probably more than anyone else. He came home without the brotherhood. Without the VA system to help him find his new normal. He had wandered through the fifteen years since, forced to figure out how to make peace with the war that left him so profoundly scarred. It was a struggle he battled alone. Nobody ever thinks about how war affects the journalists who cover it. They are a special lot, courageous and resourceful, daring in the moment. The memories plague them, too. For Mick, his journey from Fallujah to this White House moment had been a bruising one for my dear friend.

Trump looked over to the right, set his weight on his left leg, and dropped his shoulder. He looked up into the cameras, almost as if he was at one of his rallies where he would frequently do this, speaking to the rafters. "Then came the tenth one. That was a tough one."

The tenth house.

The memory of its front door flung into my here and now. Untouched, undamaged. Heavy and ornate, made of steel and sheet metal, with a beautiful glass window in its middle. This was a door that was meant to convey power and position—a person of importance once lived here. And yet, as we stacked up in the darkness to go inside and clear it, my Spidey sense that had saved me several times already did not tingle. There's some extra instinct buried in our kernel code that telegraphs danger in critical life moments. I had long since learned to trust it. But at that door, there was only stillness in that part of me.

Trump's words triggered memory after memory. I tried to stay in the East Room, focused on not swallowing my dip. The president's words became a bridge between past and present that sent images tumbling back into my head.

The room remained silent. The mood changed and grew more tense as the president spoke. I realized that the same thing happening to me was happening to all of us there that night. Stolen glances at the twelve of us who were there that night at that house and now in the audience confirmed that. We were all reliving it, with Donald Trump as our narrator.

"I don't care whose squad you're in, get in the stack ASAP!"

The words echoed in my ear. Fitts, weary and angry, at his boiling point in part because of sheer exhaustion and my snafu that nearly clocked his squad, but also because his half-healed wounds left him in constant, throbbing pain.

The ornate front door was unlocked.

We should have seen that as a bad sign. No need to kick it in. In Fallujah, this was an invitation. After all, who flees their Iraqi McMansion without locking it up first?

Trump's voice fueled the memories, filling the room. Those of us there listened as if in a trance, the scenes playing out in our heads.

"As they entered the house and moved into the living room, two men were behind concrete barricades. They opened fire on David and everybody. . . ."

The chandelier exploded.

I had forgotten that part. It sent slivers of glass spinning through the living room.

Then I saw Chris Ohle in a doorway, as a hurricane of flaming red tracer bullets striped the air around and over him. The bullets missed him, but only because Warren Misa yanked him out of the kill zone.

Those tracers. They lit the room like hellish little flares in our night-vision goggles. They sizzled in the back wall and fires bloomed in the trash that littered the floor.

Trump's voice was surprisingly soft and even, bordering on empathetic. His delivery was smooth as he read from the teleprompters, turning right, then left, then looking at the audience while he intoned, "In the dark of night, shards of glass, brick, and plaster flew into the air, wounding multiple Soldiers. The rounds of fire ripped holes into the wall separating the Americans from the terrorists."

Private First Class Jim Metcalf's voice, surprised, scared.

"I'm hit! Oh hell I'm hit!" He buckled and fell to the floor, hands on his stomach.

"OOOOOH! I'm heete!" cackled one of the insurgents on the other side of the living room wall. Then they loosed another long burst at us, sawing away bricks and filling the doorway between us with more red streaking tracers.

They mocked us. We were trapped in their kill zone, and they laughed and sawed away at the wall, making fun of our predicament. It was surreal, unnerving. Around me, the Ramrods looked beyond spooked. We had heard the enemy shouting and screaming before, but never like this. Never this close, and never directed at us personally.

Outside, our security element with our 240 Bravo machine guns took fire from other rooms in the house. A bullet impacted in front of Joey Swanson, whose eyes were hit by fragments. Sergeant Jose Rodriguez, Meno's radioman, was hit. Meno grabbed him, pulled him out of the line of fire in the courtyard, and flung him into an outhouse.

"I need a 240!" I screamed from the house. Swanny, Hall, Mc-Daniel, and Lawson were all out there, enduring a barrage of gunfire from the kitchen, and probably from the other story of the house as well. Swanny answered the call as best he could. Nearly blind, Swanson and McDaniel rose up from the ground, got on a knee, and shouldered their machine guns as if they were rifles. Together they poured fire into the kitchen as Lawson coached Swanny onto the target area before unleashing his own barrage with an M14.

Wild laughing erupted on the other side of the wall. Untethered, disjointed catcalls and insults fumbled out of their mouths. They sounded drunk, or high. More bullets. More damage. The situation reached critical mass.

Enemy fire laced through the door nearest to me. They made Z patterns with slower and more controlled bursts now, a sign they had some skill and training. It was a weird dynamic that counterweighted the insane sound of their voices calling through the firelit darkness. High, but well trained and professional. They carved another Z into our wall, bricks shattering or tumbling to the floor.

Three of those bricks shattered right above Fitts's head. His back was to the wall separating us from the two insurgents shooting at us. Every volley took a bit more of that wall down, gradually chewing away at our only protection from their machine gun and automatic weapons. The men inside the living room were trapped. They couldn't get back to the foyer and the front door without running across the kill zone of Ohle's doorway.

"Brother, I need you, man," he said wearily right then as our eyes met, "I need you in a bad way."

In the East Room, my chin dropped; my lower lip tightened around the dip. I caught a fleeting glance of Swanson in the audience, gray flecking his temples. His wide eyes and face were frozen, like a window sign at a store saying, "Be right back." Swanson's gaze stared off, present in form, but his mind had defaulted back to that courtyard.

Steven Mathieu slid his SAW light machine gun over to me. I grabbed it and pulled it to my shoulder.

"Nutsack has two hundred, Sergeant Bell!" Mathieu screamed over one of the breaks in firing. Momentarily confused, he said "nutsack," a soft cloth magazine, but in the dark I clearly felt there was a plastic drum underneath it. Two hundred rounds. Much better than my M4's thirty.

"Screw these dudes," Hugh Hall yelled out in frustration.

"My eyes. I can't see shit!" Swanson screamed out.

Over the staccato memories of chaos and desperation, I heard Trump's weirdly tranquil voice intone, "David knew they had to get out. David thought that they had had it. He leapt into the torrent of bullets."

26

AMERICAN PRAYER

PRESIDENT TRUMP'S WORDS FILLED the room like an incantation that conjured our 2004 reality. It cast a spell across all of us who were there in the East Room and that Fallujah house.

"David took over—he just took over. He provided suppressive fire while his men evacuated, rescuing his entire squad at the risk of his life."

I swore. Yelled. Screamed. Vile words. The president doesn't mention that. Words never spoken at a public event in the White House remained in the past, the moment sanitized for the global audience. But we knew. We all knew that no matter how hard historians and politicians try to get it right, such speeches and written histories can only be an approximation of the truth.

In the darkness, I stepped in the kill zone doorway, SAW readied. Two men, perhaps a dozen steps in front of me, crouched behind a concrete Texas barrier—the kind you see on highways in America—that they had somehow dragged into the house and shoved beneath a stairwell. They had created a perfect mini-bunker, with an open door to the rear yard at their backs in case they needed to make a hasty escape.

One leveled two AK-47s on the barrier, stock in each shoulder like something out of a video game. The other manned a belt-fed machine gun. Through my night vision, I saw their faces in total clarity.

My finger hooked the trigger and my SAW spewed bullets. Eight hundred and fifty a minute, chewing through the two hundred slung under the weapon in its hard ammunition box. The two men ducked as chunks of concrete spun crazily around them, kicked up as rounds struck home.

I sidestepped left, shrinking my elbows tightly down to my sides. Form as perfect as I could manage. Moving low and steady. Forcing a kill shot to hit me in my face, really hoping that I made such a small target picture that that never happened.

Form good, yes. But I fired no short bursts, no controlled fire. I went cyclic, transmitting the urgency and the panic welling inside me. I swore and screamed at the enemy as behind me, Fitts and the rest of the men used my diversion to escape the living room and get back outside.

The SAW ran away from me. I relaxed my finger, but it kept firing—which was why we trained never to go cyclic. I knew I would be out of ammo soon. I'd lost control.

A burst tore right over my head. Like miniature F-16s they flew in a cluster, and I felt their wake.

"YOU MOTHER . . . PIECE OF . . ."

Jingoistic pro-American, ugly, derogatory words flew out of my mouth. Anything to carry me toward this enemy. I was on a knife-edge of panic and fury, forcing myself forward toward them. They were mine.

Get out. Run.

I was going to break them into pieces.

You're going to die. RUN!

The SAW clicked. Bolt back. Weapon empty.

I was alone with an empty weapon. I could feel the heat radiating from the barrel and the smell of gunpowder smoke filled the room. Now the silence made my ears ring. I grabbed an M4 magazine and hoped the good people at FN Herstal had corrected the thirty-round-magazine alternative feed-jam issues since Basic Training, which was the last time I'd attempted this.

First attempt, I couldn't line it up in the dark. Second attempt,

I missed. Third, it slid in. Then I charged the bolt. Pulled the trigger; nothing. I tossed the mag and ran just as the two insurgents opened fire again.

I felt like a coward for not finishing the job.

In the East Room, President Trump made no mention of that fact. The raw truth was that I felt humiliated, unmanned by the taunting jibes of our enemy who surprised us, who had gained the upper hand and forced us to run for the first time in our entire Iraq deployment.

Instead, the safe-for-East-Room narrative continued without mentioning those things. "Only when his men were all out did David exit the building, but the fighting was far from over. Militants on the roof fired down at them with round after deadly round. A Bradley Fighting Vehicle came to the scene to suppress the enemy and drove them further into the building. Knowing he would face almost certain death, David decided to go back inside the house and make sure not a single terrorist escaped alive."

Why did you go back in?

People have asked me that many times over the years.

Why? If I hadn't, I would have had to live with the humiliation the rest of my life. You only get so many chances to prove who you are, if only to yourself.

I remembered my voice, almost pleading. "Everything is fucking crazy. We just got shot at from point-blank range."

Another fragment came back to me. "Yeah—I wanna go back in after them. I wanna go. I wanna go."

This was the tough part. The part that seared the Ramrods in the years since. I could see them now in the East Room, swallowing hard, their Adam's apples slowly bobbing. Eyes averted, most looking down now. Even Fitts. They knew. But nobody else in the audience did. Friends I knew before the war, out in the audience now, were quiet and clueless. The ones who befriended me after I came home? They had no frame of reference beyond Trump's words.

The Ramrods knew. The chaos. The exhaustion. The many wounds we suffered. Blood splatters littered almost everyone's uniforms now. We were strung out, on our last legs after three straight days of this bloody and gruesome insanity. We were going to tip into non-battle-capable if pushed any further without some rest and respite from the horrors and trauma unspooling around us.

The sounds of battle raged through the street. I paced, and swore, psyching myself up.

I had to do this. Otherwise I would have considered myself a coward for the rest of my life. And I couldn't deal with that.

"Fuck it," I said, almost as a last goodbye to myself. Or hope.

Michael Ware stood in front of me. Forcing me to stop my pace. Forcing me to make a decision. He stared at me with dead eyes, his face slick with sweat. No emotion, no fear. He had thrown his lot in with the chaos and had abandoned hope to do it. Whatever road brought him to me was as unfulfilled and incomplete as mine. Whatever we were looking for in Iraq, in war, or in Fallujah, we found it together in that moment.

I could read his inner thoughts, as I felt he could read mine.

"Fuck it," he echoed back, a half smile forming on his lips.

Had he not forced a decision, I would not have made one in that moment. This was happening and Ware gave me the confidence I didn't have in myself to do what I knew I needed to do.

He was coming with me. Scott Lawson was, too. He had spent much of the deployment as a rear-echelon NCO. He wasn't going to miss this. The three of us made a weird fire team, one man armed with a camera, me with Santos's M16A4 with a grenade launcher, and Lawson only with a 9mm pistol.

What we did transcended doctrine and training, and probably logic. Here was a tear point in the Ramrods' hearts, for those who didn't come with us have wrestled with the guilt of that decision ever since. Some thought they didn't measure up, and have told me so in conversations long after the fighting ended. That was ridiculous, of course. Hearing that crushed me. These men, my men, fought with ferociousness through the entire battle, before this tear line and after. They had risked their lives for each other, saved each other countless times. Stood in harm's way with rockets flying and bullets impacting all around them. They never broke. They never showed any sign that the mayhem and chaos of combat got the better of their warrior hearts.

What we three did that night was pure crazy. Something in each of us was missing, and we thought we could find that part of us inside the house.

We set up the SAW gunners around the building. I would grab the foothold in the house again. I would do my best to kill or drive out whoever was still alive inside. If they ran, they would run right into the guns of my crew of hardened, steely-eyed Ramrods armed with automatic weapons.

At the front door, it sounded as if Mick put something down in the doorway. I thought it was his video camera, but it turned out to be just a bag. He paused for only a moment, then continued into the house directly behind Lawson and me.

The floor was wet and slick from the Bradley barrage of 25mm shells, which blew apart the plumbing while setting little fires in nearly every room. The carnage redrew the interior of the house, and I noticed things I hadn't before. Blocks of explosives were wedged like bricks of cheese into areas, or smushed flat into sludges of mush. One Soviet-era explosive lay on the ground, a thin wire trailing out of it with a blasting cap embedded in the plastique.

Those bricks were everywhere. They had turned the house into a gigantic IED. Perhaps the only reason they didn't detonate it when we came inside was self-preservation. These insurgents didn't want to die as suicide bombers. They wanted to stay alive and keep fighting. That made them exceptionally more dangerous than those with a death wish.

My eyes were burning. My ears were ringing. I couldn't feel anything inside my body. I wanted to vomit. That smell was the worst. Rotting fish from the stagnant water. Sewage. Spoiled food.

In the moment, our personal motivations for what we did in Fallujah may have been different for all of us. Five years later, it morphed into something else with introspection. Fifteen years later, wisdom from experience lent another view. In 2004, I thought I hated our enemy. I went in that house with singular focus: kill the enemy. I always thought that fired my furnace of rage.

In middle age, wearing a perfectly constructed ceremonial dress uniform I never wore as a Soldier, with millions of strangers looking on at me at the president's side, I realized it hadn't been hate after all.

It had been fear. Fear that those insurgents inside the house would take from me the only things that mattered: the men I loved as family and seeing my little Evan again.

The rage came from fear. The fear came from love.

I loved what the Ramrods allowed me to be. I loved the purpose they gave me. I loved the way they allowed the world to become black and white, no gray areas like officers seemingly always pointed out.

Our skin colors were different, we canceled each other's votes on election day, but Ramrods always stood with me in the cold, under fire, and put down the enemy whose sole devotion was ensuring we'd never get a chance at a life back home.

The Ramrods taught me that combat required something more soul-depleting than simply dying for a cause. Killing to protect someone you love was the hardest thing a rational person could ever do. The Ramrods displayed that love in every firefight.

The East Room remained absolutely still. We relived this nightmare together in silence. We didn't need words. We all knew what this felt like.

". . . He quickly encountered an insurgent who was about to fire a rocket-propelled grenade at his squad. David once again jumped into danger before he had a chance to launch that grenade."

Perfect teeth.

The image of the man I killed hit me with almost physical force. Those teeth. I was a dentist's son. I knew good work. The guy had worn braces as a kid.

His eyes stared wildly at me, mouth open, shocked at my reappearance in the doorway. He knew I had him, and that emboldened me.

"JEW!" it sounded like he spat at me, his last uttered word, an instant before my first bullet hit him.

This time, I didn't stop; I didn't run. I sidestepped out of the doorway's fatal funnel and fired again, catching him in the pelvis and spinning him around while his comrade on the machine gun bolted and ran. I pivoted and fired at the comrade as he dove through the kitchen door. I thought I might have hit him in the back of the shoulder before he disappeared.

I slid sideways, then backward until I reached the bottom of the stairs while covering the kitchen door. I knelt and waited for somebody to come out of the kitchen as Mick Ware's voice dimly reached me. He was in the living room, calling to see if I was okay, and for a moment, I was so far up my adrenaline frenzy that I didn't even recognize his voice.

Then somebody moved upstairs above me. A boot scrape. A footfall. Approaching the steps. There was a landing halfway between the floors, so I couldn't cover down on the top floor from where I was.

I could be rushed by two men from two locations. I had put myself in a trap. I started to lose control. My pulse spiked. I tried not to hyperventilate, but my breaths were shallow, each one sucking in that putrid stench filling the house.

Lawson appeared in the living room doorway. I saw him for just an instant before the insurgent in the kitchen burst through the door roaring, "Fucking Jewish dog!"

The insurgent spree-fired his weapon, hitting the ceiling above me. I fired back and he ducked into the kitchen again.

Lawson was down to one clip for his 9mm pistol. He recoiled from a hit near the wall he used for cover. His shoulder looked slick and wet. I wondered if he'd been wounded in that last exchange.

"Lawson, you okay?"

"I think I've been hit."

I told him to get out, as he moved his fingers to check mobility, his other hand on his neck. He refused. Finally, after I said I needed a SAW and a shotgun, he backed out of the doorway.

The man upstairs moved again. His boot thudded on one of the steps. I swung my rifle, not sure what to do next. The guy in the kitchen could come out again at any moment.

I glanced behind me and froze. There was a doorway just off my left shoulder. I had had my back to an uncleared room this whole time.

Carefully, I slid into the room beyond the doorway.

President Trump took a breath, shifted his weight again, and looked directly into the assembled crowd. "Next, two more insurgents came out of hiding and fired at David. He returned fire, killing them both."

"I will cut your head off," said the one who moved down the stairs.

I was in a bedroom, tucked into an alcove across the doorway. One of the guys under the stairs charged back out from the kitchen, snub-nosed AK in one hand. He swung into the doorway, weapon blazing. Had I not been in the alcove, he would have killed me. I pulled the trigger. Saw a fan of blood. He vanished out of the room, back toward the kitchen. I caught him in the knees, stomach, and pelvis. Down the stairs I heard another. Slowly creeping. Using a gap in the side of the frame, I put him down. He fell away from the doorway and collapsed without entering the room.

"Then a third assailant burst out of a wardrobe . . ." Trump said slowly, to emphasize the insanity of that moment. Then he vamped, ". . . wearing a wardrobe."

Hardaway laughed at that. I glanced down and saw him looking at me. The memory of how I told him what happened afterward struck me.

The assailant burst out of the armoire, short AK tucked under his arm, firing wildly. He was so close I smelled his funk, and he would have killed me with one of those random shots had he not tripped on a dress that spilled out of the wardrobe with him. He stumbled, bullets flaying the wall, floor, and ceiling, and fell. The armoire came down right on top of him, miraculously giving me a piece of cover at the same time. It was an incredible stroke of luck. He regained his feet, after falling over the mattress of the bed, fired from the doorway, then ran upstairs. I wounded him in the back and leg as he ran.

"Racing after him, David engaged in hand-to-hand combat and killed him, too."

Strictly PG-13 for this venue.

Flashes of him, screaming, kicking, spitting, and swearing at me as we locked in a death wrestle, fighting like feral animals, eyes crazed with adrenaline and fear. I bludgeoned him with my helmet. He bit and tore at me until I struck him again and knocked him on his back. I drove my Gerber knife into his collarbone, severed his carotid artery. His blood sprayed me as his hand came up and touched my cheek in a terrifying last caress. Then his eyes went flat and his arm fell to the floor.

I was bone-weary and spent. Catching my breath was labor and my eyes were burning. My helmet was somewhere on the floor in the smoke. I had done my best to put that through his face in the melee. My IBA vest was open when I used the front plate like a bird's wing to smash his head in as I held him close to me. I looked down at him, sprawled beneath me, and felt more weary and pain-racked than any other time in my life. I stood up and collected my gear. I needed a smoke in the worst way, so I stepped out onto a patio that overlooked the palm grove, cupped my hand, and lit a Marlboro. Fitts and the others would find me, and then I knew I'd be okay.

"Bleeding and badly wounded, David had single-handedly defeated the forces who had attacked his unit and would have killed them all had it not been for the bravery of David."

Trump paused a beat, then added, "Just then yet another combatant jumped down from the third-story roof and attacked. David shot him and the assailant fell off the balcony. Alone in the dark, David defeated four insurgents and seriously wounded the fifth, saving his Soldiers and facing down the enemies of civilization."

Captain Sims wanted us to fight a dirty war cleanly. Avoid the dark side. In that house, I became the darkness. Just as Captain Sims had warned, I had lived with the consequences for fifteen years. The darkness never quite went away. It shaded parts of my heart that once shined in light. The president asked all the Ramrods to stand, and their movement to their feet snapped me back in the moment. I had been filled with despair and emotion during this speech, reliving the experience. As I looked out on my fellow Ramrods, though, I knew once again that I hadn't gone through this alone. We had relived it together in front of countless people.

As the Ramrods stood to be acknowledged, East Room–appropriate applause rippled through the crowd. No catcalls, no shouts. This time my Ramrods were being acknowledged and they stood in silence as the rest of the crowd honored them. The applause grew, swelling louder and louder. A few people rose to their feet. More followed. Soon the entire room was standing, facing the Ramrods and clapping with profound respect. It was an homage that touched us all, especially when the men saw the seven other Medal of Honor recipients in the front row stand and face them, clapping loudest of all—a gift from two generations of American warriors who knew the cost all of this inflicted on them.

Next, President Trump asked our five Gold Star families to rise. I saw Heidi Sims and Colin stand awkwardly. Shy. Used to being the forgotten victims of this war, they looked on the verge of tears as the room's solemn and respectful applause turned into another standing ovation. I saw Merrilee Carlson off to Trump's left, my postwar friends beside her clapping with tears in their eyes. She had come alone, but had found family among them. John Bruning; my agent, Jim Hornfischer, and his wife, Sharon; and Michelle Lawson, Scott's sister-in-law.

The generals and the congressmen stood, too. And there was the chairman of the Joint Chiefs of Staff, honoring Sean Sims's son and widow, moving his eyes from one family to the next. This was the ultimate cost to the nation. Families devastated, communities and their countless threads of connection torn asunder by each loss. Perhaps, this week and this afternoon would help build new ones.

The Ramrods were ready.

It came time for the award to be placed around my neck. Vivienne and I had rehearsed this well, but in the moment I blew it. I was supposed to execute a facing movement to the right so that the president could step behind me and put the award on. Emotionally spent and nervous, I turned too soon and put my back to the president too early.

He tapped me on the shoulder and said, "What are you doing? Not yet."

President Trump glanced down at the Ramrods, pointed at me, and started to laugh. The guys broke up laughing, too. Like a hitchhiker he gave me a sideways thumb-out and quipped, "This guy. You see this guy? What's wrong with your buddy?"

The audience burst out laughing. The Ramrods laughed harder. Medal of Honor be damned; nothing prevented them busting anyone's chops. I knew I'd be in for years of ribbing over this gaff.

The ceremony continued and grew solemn again. An Army official read the official citation, then the president put the Medal of Honor around my neck. He straightened the medal at my tie, then stepped back as the Ramrods erupted in cheers again. I stood awkwardly, shifting weight from foot to foot, lower lip tucking under upper one, feeling every emotion at once. It was totally overwhelming me.

I caught my face in the reflection of the nearest teleprompter. Serious, dark eyes were opaque. I looked like I was in shock.

"Your country is proud of you, David. This is the greatest honor any American can receive. You are now forever a part of this great nation. You are a part of history," Trump said.

The president asked my family to join us onstage. This has become a traditional gesture to acknowledge the family.

My mother walked up to meet the president along with my brothers, Dan and Rand, and my three beloved children. Their mother stepped up, too. Sharing the stage with them was unforgettable. My family, together, in front of countless people across the world. The effects of November 10 have rippled through their lives ever since, even if the kids had not known it. They earned this, a gesture that was at once an homage to them by our president and atonement for all the hardships we'd experienced as a family since my return.

As I stood there, though, my heart and head told me this needed to be, first and foremost, the Ramrods' spotlight. Their moment. I needed to give this honor there on the stage with the president to the men. To Merrilee and Colin Sims, where it rightfully belonged. I moved to President Trump and asked him, "Sir, can I bring my Ramrods up here?" I pointed to the audience.

Trump was surprised. This wasn't just a break in protocol; this was taking a wrecking ball to it. But this president was never one to adhere rigidly to past traditions.

He asked, "How many are we talking?"

"All of them, sir."

He looked them over and said, "Let's do it. Bring them up. Come on up here, guys." President Trump rolled his hands over to welcome them up. "Get up here."

The men rose and made their way forward, the audience spellbound by the sudden display. President Trump shook each man's hand. When Sammy met the president, I choked up. A man whose path from Iraq to his new life in America was inextricably linked to our time together was thanked for all he'd done for us by our commander in chief.

The Ramrods flowed onto the tiny stage. This felt right. This wasn't my award; this was our award. *Our* moment, not mine. We fought the Battle of Fallujah as one family. We would share this stage as one family. It reminded me I was never alone. I always had them.

These men never betrayed me. Never let me down. They did

everything I asked of them and more. They are the reason I am alive and did have my reunion with Evan after all. Of course, they were also the reason I was wearing this award.

More men packed onto the stage. Merrilee Carlson stepped up next to the president, but lost her balance. She slipped, nearly fell, and President Trump caught her by the arm, pulled her safely to him, and whispered in her ear, "I'm sorry for your loss."

There we were, shoulder to shoulder one more time—the men I had slept beside in body bags during those freezing Fallujah nights. Now we were in dress uniforms and suits instead of full battle rattle.

Captain Sims led the way for this moment. He showed us that true leadership didn't end with our time in combat. It took me fourteen years to figure that out. He wanted us to fight scrupulously not because he saw it as a path to victory, but because he knew it was the only way we would survive the aftermath of war.

I had never known an officer who looked that far ahead. He wasn't trying to be just our commander in Iraq; he felt that responsibility would be his forever.

It was fear and selfishness that drove me to make those calls in the days after the Medal of Honor team opened my locker boxes. As this event unfolded, I understood the vision of our forever commander. The Medal of Honor brought us back together; it was our unifying force.

I moved off the stage to make room for all these guys. Barreto and Seyford, having had issues getting into the White House, had gotten seated in the back. I could see them looking up, realizing they missed this opportunity. They turned to sit down, but I moved to them and said, "Get up here, guys."

They ran up and got onto the stage, hugging me after they joined the team.

Doug Walter. Joaquin Meno. Peter Smith. Ric Brown, our chaplain. Michael Gross. Piotr Sucholas. Shane Gossard. Hugh Hall. Warren Misa. Chad Ellis. John Gregory. Chuck Knapp. Colin Fitts. Tristan Maxfield. Mr. Matteson. Mrs. Carlson. Michelle Lawson. Heidi and Colin Sims. Patrick Magner. John Ruiz. Alex Stuckert. Gary Frey. Omarr Hardaway. Chris Walls. Darrin Bohn. Sammy. Bryan Lockwald.

Right then, I knew Captain Sims's legacy would be more than this moment. He gave me purpose. Instead of drifting away from the Ramrods after we went home, I made a silent vow to be there for my men, to be responsible for them and share with them the honor and attention this award would bring. The limelight would never be mine. It was ours.

The fear, the nervousness, the dread of the past vanished, replaced by a profound sense of love for the men and families around me. The waves of emotions since all of this began grew still. I felt like I'd finally come home.

The audience clapped long and hard. Trump leaned over to one of his aides and whispered something. The chaplain who gave the invocation at the start of the ceremony stepped up to the podium.

"Say a few words," Trump whispered to him.

It was impromptu, a spur-of-the-moment ask in front of the nation. The chaplain was pure clutch. He nodded and winged it.

"Please join me," he started. Heads bowed, eyes closed. The Ramrods crossed their arms in front of their bodies. Irreverent bastards all, but reverent to their core, the great duality of the American infantryman on display to our nation.

"Most holy God, as we go from this place, let this ceremony be a reminder of your faithfulness and a challenge to us all to live a life of courage and honor, placing the needs of others first."

In that house on November 10, I uttered a silent Soldier's prayer before I stepped into the doorway. The enemy chanted mantras. I had my own. I had my faith. God saw me through the darkness until Fitts and the others could find me on that patio, traumatized, my wounds bleeding into the smears of my enemy's blood on my uniform.

Shoulder to shoulder, we listened to an American prayer. No other nation will ever match our ability to empathize and seek the elevation of humanity. The hope we represent shines across our planet, inspiring those on distant shores that life can be better, can be redeeming, and that freedom is the only righteous path.

The chaplain continued: "Bless our nation and keep the lamp of liberty burning bright. In your most gracious and holy name I pray. Amen."

The crowd echoed, "Amen." Heads rose. I saw pride in the eyes of my brothers onstage. I knew now that the void I had felt for all these years was the loss of them in my life. After the bonds we forged together, we tried to go on apart. But we cannot heal alone; fifteen years proved that. Here, I saw hope that we would somehow find the way to shine light into those damaged, aching shadows in our souls. More time would be needed, of that I had no doubt. But with the past revealed, one thing was for sure: the Ramrods will never live in darkness again.

APPENDIX

LEGACY

THE DAY AFTER THE White House ceremony, I was formally inducted into the Pentagon's Hall of Heroes. This event was my opportunity to speak about the award and my time in the Army. As I worked on the speech, I wanted it to be something more than just about me, or the award. I wanted to talk about the legacy of Task Force 2-2 and how the Ramrods fit into the American tradition of service.

To my astonishment, the speech went viral on social media and YouTube, tallying millions of views. Every time American servicemen and -women have faced a challenge overseas since that day at the Pentagon, the video gets posted and reposted anew. It has been a humbling sight to see this, and a comfort to know the speech speaks to greater truths than just one task force's experience in a war most just want to forget. Maybe, after all, that will be our greatest legacy—a reminder of what makes the American warrior so unique in history.

Here is the full text.

Thank you for your support. Your presence, and my good fortune to be able to share this occasion with my men, my family, my friends, has eased the awkwardness that I'm feeling right now.

What's more, I am especially proud of the recognition that this award brings to my unit, my leaders, and my peers of the mighty Ramrods of 2-2 Infantry, 3rd Brigade, 1st Infantry Division. Combatants bear witness to all aspects of the human condition. It reveals the darkest parts of the human soul, while residing side by side with the most exalted characteristics: nobility, honor, valor, and God's grace.

Why do American warriors under fire do what men have done since this nation's inception? This is a common thread that connects the militias of Lexington and Concord with the warriors of Fallujah: it is our love of nation, our way of life, and our love by those who we serve with side by side.

We defend. We avenge. We sacrifice. We bleed. And we are willing to die for this unique creation, the United States of America.

I am complete for having experienced that kind of sacrifice with my fellow men-at-arms, and those who died. They gave their lives for me. They gave their lives for you, and countless citizens who will never know them. I'm talking about Sims, Faulkenburg, Iwan, Gonzalez, Vandeyburg, Matteson, Garyantes, Shrek, Sizemore, Mock, Rosales, Cardenas, Sprayberry, and Pruitt.

Those were our countrymen. Those were our friends. And these men will never get the chance to experience the cycle of life, the birth and growth of their children. They shall not grow old, because they chose to stand in our place and face the enemy for us.

It's not enough to acknowledge the fallen by name, or just inscribe their names in marble as proof that they lived and died. To truly honor the fallen, we must acknowledge how and why they gave their lives. Their death wasn't a random act or a splash of misfortune. These men and women voluntarily put themselves in harm's way, prepared to die, so that we may rest secured at home. They are the insurance policy that guarantees that our founding documents, our God-given rights, are more worthy than their own tomorrows.

When the news that Faulkenburg, Sims, Matteson, and Iwan had fallen, the reaction, the shock, the disbelief, the grief—it was transformed into resolve and rage to complete the mission assigned to us and give us even greater tenacity under fire. Their sacrifice gave us clear focus to fight using a reserve that we never knew we had. We broke the will of our adversaries, the enemy was defeated, and because of that, we came home.

For the infantrymen in combat, there is nobility and purpose in our lives, and that is unique. But we don't see ourselves as a people apart. We are America's warrior class. We are citizens of the United States, and treasure this land more than any overseas posting.

The Army provided me with purpose and appreciation for the blessing America has bestowed upon us all. I am forever grateful to the United States Army for making me able to count and cherish those blessings in a way that is unique to most, and to those who . . . wear the uniform. I think the uniform, I think my Army, has made us all better men, fathers, employees, husbands, and citizens.

The controversy that swirled over the Iraq War was not a departure from other wars that America has fought. Just a short distance from where I grew up in Orleans County, on the Canadian side of the Niagara River, it was settled by a loyalist who supported King George. With the exception of the surprise attack on Pearl Harbor, open dissent has been at the core of our very being, and war has never been particularly a popular undertaking.

American Soldiers have never confused the United States with Sparta. The best leaders in battle become that way by being loyal and dutiful subordinates. We don't get a vote. We execute the lawful intent of our government. There is no political affiliation on our dog tags. We continue the warrior legacy of the United States without regard for adulation or unanimous approval, either.

The Iraqi veteran has maintained and, in many circumstances, far exceeded the highest traditions of military service to this great nation. Of the 1.5 million men and women who have served in Iraq, the valor they displayed was often subsumed by political rhetoric at home. That in no way diminishes the accomplishment of our troops, or the accomplishments of my generation at war. The award is recognition of that, and it should be seen as a validation of our efforts, not as a reward for the action of one individual in one house in Fallujah.

When I think of Iraq, I think of Colin Fitts, a man shot by three separate weapons systems. Nobody would have raised an eyebrow if Fittsy retired. Instead, Colin Fitts returns to combat duty for two more years, to shed more blood for this nation that he loves.

When I think of Iraq, I think of Chris Ohle, the young SAW gunner whose job it is to open doors and put down reflexive fire to people who happen to be shooting back at him. And he was able to do that, because behind him was Sergeant Warren Misa, ready to pull him out of that doorway and undoubtedly save his life.

I have Chuck Knapp, my team leader. Chuck Knapp saved our entire 3rd Platoon, Alpha Company 2-2, when he stopped us from entering a building-contained IED that would have killed all of us.

I think about Maxfield, my SAW gunner, who asked our doc, Abernathy, to fix his injured foot in the prone position so he could continue to knock down targets under fire while he was getting fixed up.

My guy John Ruiz, who shielded the body of his buddy from incoming fire without fear of risk to himself.

When I think of the Iraq War, I think of Piotr Sucholas—brave, strong, and steady.

Our engineers, who devised and deployed remarkable weapons systems that saved countless lives.

Our tankers, 2-7 Cav, on the other side of Fallujah, that hardly gets any notice for what they did. There were indispensable Bradley crews who busted through walls.

Omarr Hardaway, James Cantrell, Chad Ellis, who, without a functioning 25mm Bushmaster cannon or tow or coax—and let's not discuss how that happened—he used his rifle to suppress the enemy.

Cory Brown, the grizzly bear from Montana.

Shane Gossard, humble, beautiful, kind.

Brad Unterseher, Dilalu, the Bradley teams, and those crews are the reason why children have fathers today, and those teams shielded our dismounts from rocket fire that was meant to take our lives.

Cory McFadden, John Bandy, Wilson, Gary Frey, Kane, Sherwood. They never took a step backwards under fire.

Sergeant John Gregory is one of the toughest, most decent men I've ever served with. He had a tour from hell a year after we came home.

Our drivers, Marcoot, Gonzo, Woodberry, Hunter, Perez. They got us there, where we needed to go, and they did it with bravery and valor.

Iraq makes me think of Victor Santos, a fiery, brave Soldier who cut his combat teeth at Iraq and went on for more in a Ranger regiment.

McDaniel and Swanson, young kids shouldering 240 Bravos on their shoulder, suppressing enemy fire from feet away.

I had Stuckert. I had Metcalf. I had Flannery and Gross. And I had our door-crushing "He-Man," Hugh Hall.

That is my Iraq War, and it makes me proud to have told my dad no to dental school. I learned much more from living and fighting with these men than I ever could have from a lifetime of doing root canals.

My unit's leaders died leading men from the front. When our company commander, Sean Sims, died, he was killed in a house fight.

Joey Seyford and my interpreter Sammy, who just became a U.S. citizen a week ago, were there to engage the enemy in efforts to save my company commander's life. Seyford engaged the enemy, and threw his weapon at them, engaging him with the buttstock of his rifle after being shot in the shoulder.

Travis Barreto and my First Platoon fought their way to extract wounded and fallen Ramrods under intense enemy fire.

My Iraq War. I had Captain, now Colonel Doug Walter. I had First Sergeant, retired Command Sergeant Major Peter Smith. These were company leaders who put aside loss, put aside trauma, to direct young warriors during the most stressful times of our lives—young lieutenants like Chris Walls, Jeff Emery, Lieutenant Meno. They learned how to lead and cover down when their peers had fallen.

And finally, there's Scott Lawson, a true friend. We lost him in 2013. He entered the house with me that night in Fallujah. He gave me strength; he gave me confidence that allowed me to survive that night, and many other nights since then.

And I have to mention this guy, Michael Ware, a combat journalist that would cover a story, and becomes part of the story. You know, before I got to know him, before I got to see him in action, I would have told you he was 100 percent worthless and a nuisance. Now, that number is 65 percent. I was wrong. Michael Ware is now the Ernie Pyle of his generation. His reporting is a testament to what we all did, and if it's not for men and women like Michael Ware, our story would have gone unremarked.

Most of the men I just described got little or no recognition for their valor. In subsequent deployments, some would lose their lives years later. It is our duty to tell the story of our brave men and women who sacrificed so much for our fellow citizens.

As I've tried to communicate to you today, this is not a celebration about me. I'm not mouthing a cliché. We have much more work to do when it comes to the Iraq War veteran. We are not there yet, and we're not even close when it comes to educating our fellow Americans about what was accomplished, what was sacrificed, and what we all went through.

Our survival as a nation depends on it.

We honor our brothers and sisters in the United States

Marine Corps. Anbar Province was their fight. Men like Brad Kasal, Rafael Peralta, Christopher Adlesperger, Brian Chontosh, Jeremiah Workman, Sergeant Craft—they gave the enemy everything they could handle. The Navy and Air Force completed the remarkable display of American valor and might and fought shoulder to shoulder with the United States Army in Fallujah and all over Iraq.

This entire military is one cohesive, dedicated force, and the threats to our nations, they don't sleep. They're watching our every move—Iran, Russia, China, North Korea, ISIS, Al Qaeda. They may be watching this right now.

Our military should not be mistaken for a cable news gabfest show. We don't care what you look like. We don't care who you voted for, who you worship, what you worship, who you love. It doesn't matter if your dad left you millions when he died, or if you knew who your father was. We have been honed into a machine of lethal moving parts that you would be wise to avoid if you know what's good for you.

We will not be intimidated.

We will not back down.

We've seen war. We don't want war. But if you want war with the United States of America, there's one thing I can promise you, so help me God: someone else will raise your sons and daughters. We fight so our children never have to.

We fight for one day when our children and our enemy's children can discuss their differences without fear or loathing.

We fight so that anyone out there thinking about raising arms against our citizens or allies realizes the futility of attrition against a disciplined, professional, and lethal force built to withstand anything you can dream of throwing at us.

Americans want this kind of country.

Americans want this kind of world.

And we stand ready to defend it, to protect us, so help us God.

May God bless this beautiful Army.

May God bless our Marine Corps, our Navy, our Air Force, and Coast Guard.

May God bless our allies.

And we already know that God blessed America, because He gave us the greatest fighting force this world has ever seen, 2-2 Infantry and the 1st Infantry Division.

Thank you, Ramrods—duty first, Dukes.

Remember the Ramrods, their love for each other, and the valor they performed for one another under the worst imaginable circumstances.

———

ACKNOWLEDGMENTS

THIS BOOK WOULD NOT have been possible without the immense talent and mentorship of John R. Bruning. I am better in every possible way for his friendship, as are so many countless veterans, families of those who served, and even more grateful citizens that he has given voice to for over twenty years. Writers are lauded for their bestsellers, and Bruning has a stack, but his generational-impacting works of military nonfiction stand apart from his peers, as does his deft understanding of the reality of war. Bruning's unique voice is one of the most important in the GWOT era. And he is an even better friend.

I would have paid for a Peter Hubbard blurb on a book carrying my name. Having this man, with his incredible body of work and domination of his craft, edit this book has been one of the most incredible experiences of my career. His sense of humanity and decency made this book complete. I am humbled by his talent. Incredible thanks to him and his team at Mariner and HarperCollins for this unbelievable experience, and for giving our Ramrod story the home their many sacrifices warranted. I am blessed to have you behind this project. Deep appreciation to the art department, the sales division, and the media associates that worked so tirelessly for this book to be in the marketplace.

Jim Hornfischer was a dear friend and an incredible agent. We truly miss this giant that lived amongst us. This book was his idea and the last project I had the privilege to partner on with Hornfischer Literary Management. On behalf of his friends, his clients, John Bruning and I would like to acknowledge his profound impact on our lives, his ability to organize ideas into bestselling books, as well as his individual greatness as one of our nation's leading naval historians. We send our love and gratitude to his family and his beautiful wife, Sharon.

A big thank-you goes out to the brilliant Will Murphy and the fantastic team at Folio. Steve Younger, for his sage leadership and wisdom at Myman, Greenspan, Fox, Rosenberg, Mobasser, Younger and Light. Thanks to the legendary Howie Sanders at Anonymous Content. Thank you to Ross Howarth at Duty 1st and Tom Fireoved at Franchise Sports and Entertainment, along with Spencer Bass at XSM Global for all your support of this book.

My deepest appreciation to my Army brotherhood: the Ramrods. To our fallen and the Gold Star families whose pain we share every day: we live for those we lost and make the best of every moment with which we are blessed.

For all their help, support, and encouragement, I also want to thank Paula Smith, Elizabeth Chamberlain, MSG (Ret.) Rob Couture, Colonel Carrie Perez, Fort Hamilton, Colonel (Ret.) Doug Walter, CSM (Ret.) Peter Smith, SFC (Ret.) Blake Gibson, Colonel (Ret.) Peter Newell, CSM (Ret.) Darrin Bohn, General (Ret.) Paul E. Funk II, and Michael Ware.

A special thanks to Dr. Marc Epstein, who helped edit my Pentagon speech.

To my wonderful family, you have all my love: William, Marilyn, Dan, Rand, Timmy, Betsy, Erin, Dino, Lucy, Bill, Uncle Paul, Sue, Papa Joe, Larry, Aunt Sandy, Uncle Sal, Aunt Jane, Rhonda, Katie, Evan, Aiden, and Vivienne.

Special thanks to Tim Wenger and Tim Holly at Audacy.com.

ABOUT THE AUTHOR

STAFF SERGEANT DAVID BELLAVIA spent six years in the U.S. Army. He served with his unit in Operation Iraqi Freedom during the battles for Najaf, Mosul, Baqubah, Muqdadiyah, and Fallujah. Bellavia was awarded the Medal of Honor for his actions on November 10, 2004, in Fallujah during Operation Phantom Fury, "for conspicuous gallantry and intrepidity at the risk of his life above and beyond the call of duty." After leaving the Army, Bellavia returned to Iraq as an embedded reporter in 2006 and 2008, where he covered the heavy fighting in Ramadi, Fallujah, and Diyala Province. He is the author of *House to House* and hosts the syndicated radio program the *David Bellavia Show*, heard daily on Audacy.com. Born in Buffalo, New York, and inducted into the New York State Veterans' Hall of Fame in 2005, Bellavia lives in western New York.